ALPHA 90

Edited by
Jean-Paul Hautecoeur

ALPHA 90
Prepared by the
Direction générale de l'éducation des adultes
of the ministère de l'Éducation du Québec

with the assistance of the
National Literacy Secretariat of the
Department of the Secretary of State of Canada

Cover photograph by André Mathieu
"Hymen de lecture," 1989

Legal Deposit: Third quarter 1990
Bibliothèque nationale du Québec
ISBN: 2-550-15298-0

CONTENTS

INTRODUCTION

In December 1986 a workshop on the prevention of functional illiteracy and the integration of youth into the work force was held at the UNESCO Institute for Education (Hamburg, F.R.G.) by European specialists in this field. The chief objective of the workshop was to develop international cooperation in the area of research on both professional practices and the players involved (cf. Final Report: Introduction).

This workshop offered an ideal opportunity to learn about the research, experiments and activities being carried out in "Europe" (which, for UNESCO, includes Eastern Europe, the U.S.S.R., Canada and Israel), to meet with European researchers and to develop joint research and publication projects with new partners. The Canadian Commission for UNESCO and the UNESCO Institute in Hamburg kindly made it possible for me to attend the workshop as an observer. *ALPHA 90* is the result of that experience.

The research recommendations formulated at the 1986 workshop targeted specific fields, including illiteracy, successful literacy projects "involving a solid commitment from the illiterate adults concerned," evaluation and a comparative study of various projects. Participants also emphasized the importance of disseminating research results among "the institutions and individuals most likely to use them." To promote international cooperation it was felt that, in addition to establishing a coherent action-research program, it was essential to set up a literacy network in Europe to facilitate the exchange of expertise, information, references and documentation.

Priority action-research themes, a strategy for disseminating research results and the creation of an exchange network (of readers, producers and disseminators) on illiteracy and literacy activities...Québec's *ALPHA* publications had been striving towards these same goals, although its field of action up to this point had been limited, even isolated (contact with English Canada on strategic linguistic and cultural questions is distant at best, while with the United States it is practically nonexistent). The 1986 workshop offered *ALPHA* the chance to broaden its scope by enlisting European authors, to introduce other literacy strategies and approaches in Québec, to participate in joint comparative studies or evaluation projects, and to place its modest publication and dissemination methods at the disposal of the vast network that was to be created through the UNESCO Institute in Hamburg.

Ways had to be found, however, to ensure that the recommendations and projects of the Hamburg workshop would be implemented, at least partially and in a very real context (there is something very unreal about the diplomatic atmosphere of an international conference). Two working conferences provided the chance to do just that. These conferences were organized by the Centre universitaire de formation continue of the Université d'Angers (CUFCO) in France, and focussed on the theme of applied research within the European community.

Practitioners and researchers alike met in workshops where they shared their experiences and established a literacy network. As a result papers were written and various joint projects undertaken, including the group's contribution to *ALPHA 90*, which in turn led to *ALPHA*'s participation in developing the network which would become part of the larger one being created at the UNESCO Institute (see Pierre Freynet's text).

All the participants at the first conference, held in Angers in April 1988, agreed to contribute to *ALPHA 90*. At the second conference, held in London in December 1988, the conditions of this participation were finalized. A seminar on the theme "Writing and results in adult basic education," held in Angers in April 1989, included additional participants, namely, a group of Irish literacy students who led a workshop. As I was unable to attend this seminar all communications concerning publication had to be carried out by mail, telephone and fax. A number of planned contributions had to be omitted, while others which had no direct link with the "network" were added. These then are the events which led to the publication of *ALPHA 90*.

It is worth mentioning the conditions under which *ALPHA 90* was produced. Because *ALPHA* is distributed free of charge most people picture a comfortable editorial office, numerous staff and considerable resources. This could not be further from the truth! Literacy research has neither the status nor the funding enjoyed by educational computer applications or by certain major educational publications.

However, let's backtrack...For *ALPHA 90*, International Literacy Year essentially means achieving two important objectives, or rather laying the foundations for their achievement. The first is **to globalize literacy research**, thereby developing contacts (with Europe to the east, Canada to the west, the United States and Third World to the south, and the First Nations to the north) and creating links, opportunities for joint projects. The second is **to disseminate the results of this research** in such a way as to reach "the institutions and individuals most likely to use them" (as recommended by the 1986 Hamburg workshop).

For *ALPHA*, the globalization of literacy research will be considered within the Québec context. I have already alluded to Québec's cultural insularity within the North American continent (in this issue Serge Wagner sensitively describes the minority situation of Canada's francophones) and to the importance of linking up with the European francophone network. *ALPHA 88* discussed these two points in depth (that issue included a contribution from Haiti, thus stepping outside the network of European countries and other industrialized francophone nations). The second reason for globalizing research is pragmatic, methodological, and not related uniquely to the francophone community. Many benefits can be derived from observing, analyzing and interpreting what is occurring on a local level in light of the knowledge and experience acquired elsewhere (thus transposing a single local context to a multiple local context). This exchange makes it possible not only to confirm local initiatives by comparisons, but also to improve and modify them. Programs can be enhanced by trading expertise, models, materials, and so forth.

This issue of *ALPHA* provides several examples of the advantages of broadening one's field of expertise. In microcomputers, the achievements of France's Centre université — économie d'éducation permanente (CUEEP) and Laboratoire d'apprentissage de base par ordinateur (LABO) are sufficiently advanced and productive for us to consider applying them here, as part of a new strategy. This could be described as "taking the school out of literacy training" and ensuring the occupational reintegration of literacy students. Researchers at the University of Amsterdam demonstrate how the theories of Paolo Freire and Célestin Freinet can be adapted to modern theoretical perspectives (socio-rhetoric) applied to a participatory action-research process. This process could prove to be a source of inspiration for Québec's community-based literacy movement, which continually searches for teaching methods which address social requirements of autonomy. The experience of the University of Amsterdam, along with that of the University of Lancaster, Great Britain (both known for their research in applied linguistics and their commitment to the field of everyday literacy practices) could have a positive influence on the linguistics department of a certain Québec university, where the training program for literacy instructors has failed to stimulate either research or projects carried out with people in the field, just as it has failed to halt the plummeting of literacy enrolment figures (see the introduction to *ALPHA 88*). An area for comparative research, and one in which Québec has substantial experience, is the incorporation of literacy training into the school system and the consequences of such a measure.

There are similar or comparable problems which are experienced by all local organizations or nations. Certain issues common to all industrialized countries warrant our joint attention. Significant transnational trends impact on local problems and influence how they are assessed and resolved. These trends include the globalization of the economy and the change in the relationship between education and employment in industrialized countries, the crisis of school systems and cultures caused by growing illiteracy among young people, communication between governments and large segments of the population now said to be "functionally illiterate" and the emergence of a new aspect to the duality of society, i.e., duality in communication and human rights. Jean-Pierre Vélis' paper, the only comparative one in *ALPHA 90*, illustrates this reality as it exists on both sides of the Atlantic despite differing perceptions, languages and policies. It is obvious that, to deal with common issues, we must develop truly international working strategies — which are not the exclusive domain of specialized research centres and institutions. Our action-research and participatory research practices also imply the broadening of local, provincial and national fields of expertise, which has become a common phenomenon within the European Community and between English Canada and the United States. (For a detailed definition of action-research, see the introduction of *ALPHA 88*).

The technical, terminological and methodological aspects of international cooperation in research also merit attention. Take for example the evaluation of functional illiteracy in industrialized countries with comparable levels of development...We would have to determine standard evaluation criteria if we decided to do a comparative study not only of the scope and degree of illiteracy, but also of government measures, legislation, training costs, etc. Currently it would be difficult to imagine a comparative study on the results of different training measures, as there would be no clear indication as to the nature of the input and the context in which it was obtained.

The objective of globalizing research obviously implies that research in basic education and literacy training must be adequately developed on a local level and must have functional objectives. In Québec this means that research in this field must be expanded to include the university community, still conspicuously absent from local-level experimentation and action-research. Over the last five years all efforts and funding (the latter substantial: see the article on Québec policies) have been channelled into setting up a literacy program under the aegis of the adult education network, but coordinated with the entire school system (elementary-secondary, and general education). Only the development of a federal subsidy program and the timely arrival of International Literacy Year made it possible to carry out some of the planned research projects. A comparative research topic that could be explored in a number of national and international contexts would be the role, resources, status and impact of research activities in national literacy programs (see the articles by Gertrud Kamper and Helga Rübsamen from Germany, David Barton and Sally Murphy from Great Britain, the National Adult Literacy Agency from Ireland, etc.).

To attain the second objective for International Literacy Year, i.e., to fine-tune *ALPHA*'s dissemination strategy, several initiatives have been taken this year. These include the publication of both an English and a French version of *ALPHA* (made possible through the participation of anglophone authors and the assistance of the translation service of the ministère de l'Éducation du Québec and of the federal government's Secretary of State), the request for cooperation from Canadian agencies in informing their networks of *ALPHA's* publication in both languages and ensuring its distribution, the request for the same type of cooperation from authors working with agencies already involved in network communication, and the participation of the UNESCO Institute for Education in the publication and distribution of both versions of *ALPHA* in Europe. The cooperation of central literacy agencies should markedly step up *ALPHA 90*'s dissemination outside Québec and should also create links with previously unknown individuals and institutions who are involved in research and are interested in participating in one way or another in future projects.

We now know the origins of *ALPHA 90*, as well as the circumstances under which it was produced. The authors of the articles were free to choose their own topics, which in almost every case reflect a local, provincial or national history of literacy provision involving a research procedure. The theme most common to all these papers was that proposed by the original group at the Angers conference: "The links between research and practice," which is in fact the title of one of the articles and of a British publication (see D. Barton and S. Murphy). An article which did not make the deadline — the subject proved to be too complex — was to have analyzed the relationship between these two approaches, which can merge or be mutually exclusive.

This publication was initially intended to explore and document the field of literacy, and to answer questions such as: What is being done in the countries of the European Community and in North America, or rather, what is being accomplished by a given person, group, or organization in a particular context? Which questions are being asked in practical situations? How does research fit into planning, production and education activities? What solutions are being proposed?

A future objective could be to determine priority questions or research themes and to attempt to deal with them as a group, based on local or national patterns. We could also decide to develop comparative research in specific areas, such as literacy ideologies and their political ramifications, government investments in literacy, illiteracy discussions and measures, or a comprehensive evaluation of literacy activities. Working in such close collaboration calls for the creation of favourable conditions, and this will require more effort than simply relying on long-distance communication at irregular intervals. It will also require a relatively stable location from which to coordinate these projects, along with political or institutional support, and a minimum of resources. As we have seen such is not currently the case.

The order in which the texts appear was inspired by Jean-Pierre Vélis' book, *Lettre d'illettrie*, a personalized report presented at UNESCO and dealing with literacy in industrialized countries (the article appearing in *ALPHA 90* is one chapter). Vélis notes that literacy enjoys a different status on each side of the Atlantic. From his perspective, i.e., in France, the problem of illiteracy in North America is by and large a public affair. Politicians use it as a strategic national issue, both in the United States and Canada. Public and private mobilization and action have been impressive and have swept the question of literacy right into the strongholds of the media, industry and national policy-makers. In Europe, where the social realities are similar but less publicized, the "ostrich policy" prevails: illiteracy is downplayed and both the problems and their solutions are envisaged in relation to the school, i.e., from a purely academic perspective.

America vs. Europe, "new literacy" vs. low-key volunteer action... For *ALPHA 90* the advantage of this dichotomy was that the articles could be ordered according to continental rather than national geopolitics, thus making it possible to continue the study begun by Jean-Pierre Vélis, but from a more specialized point of view. However, this dichotomy has also been a source of dispute. In the United States, French Canada and Québec, and among the First Nations, the issue of literacy cannot be reduced to mere slogans or media hype on "new literacy." A number of national situations, contexts and research developments in Europe are equally as valid as the corresponding situations on the other side of the Atlantic. Some situations are incredibly similar: the same problems must be dealt with, solutions derive from the same sources, etc.

The first North American part of *ALPHA 90* reveals another reality hidden behind the prevailing literacy practices and discussions. The first article recalls the history of literacy provision in Québec and illustrates that, in 25 years of policies, we have not succeeded in separating literacy from academic contexts and objectives. Serge Wagner writes that, although literacy education for francophones is a political issue in Canada, it is so in opposition to the policies of the anglophone majority and is thus identified with the struggle for survival and the defense of basic rights. Mike Fox and Catherine Baker tackle alarmist statements on illiteracy, simplistic reductions of the problem, and flaws in the one-dimensional training measures that exist in the United States. They propose diversified action, other types of services and large-scale campaigns of the nature they are currently attempting. A second article on Québec analyzes the potential attraction of school-based literacy programs, only to conclude that a shift is in order: we must stop offering standardized services and begin assessing the real demand, and work to meet the needs of the system's underprivileged, rather than its professionals. The last text, a Montagnais testimony, is in complete contrast to virtuous treatises extolling the virtues of literacy education. Rather, it presents literacy as a process of forced acculturation and linguistic, cultural, territorial and political subjugation. And there is still more to come...

The second part of *ALPHA 90*, which deals with Europe, is opened by Pierre Freynet of CUFCO in Angers, France, who took the initiative of creating and coordinating the informal exchange network between the numerous local contexts and a continually expanding global European space. The article by David Barton and Sally Murphy looks briefly at 10 experiments related to literacy practices. In a second text David Barton uses a conceptual point of view to explain one of these case studies on the uses and meanings of literacy in everyday life: a look at literacy in the plural, which should be applied to the search for alternatives to the forced literacy described by Mike Fox and to my analysis of "school-based" literacy programming in Québec.

A similar, more anthropological, approach used by the CUFCO group consisted in incorporating sociological considerations and observation into a training program for literacy instructors — a program which was combined with participatory research on "illiterate culture." Though the research came to a dead end, the report is nonetheless eloquent. While the researchers indulged in epistemological harakiri, the participants or observers in this experiment seem to have vanished along with the original hypothesis. In this particular case "action-research" became action with a capital A, leaving little to mark its passing...

A paper on illiteracy, its distribution and social transmission was contributed by Fie van Dijk. This article briefly discusses illiteracy among women, and should be read in conjunction with the article by Franca van Alebeek and Tineke Krol, also from the University of Amsterdam. These two authors base their article on a situation comparable to that of CUFCO: using a "socio-rhetorical," participatory research approach to provide in-depth, adequate training to literacy instructors. The Alebeek-Krol project resulted in the development of a training manual prepared by the instructors and learners, but which is not used extensively by the instructors — classical teacher training is in direct opposition to both the dynamic (Freinet) and critical (Freire) view of the world upheld by researchers and of the objectives for changing communication methods which the authors attribute to basic education.

Ireland's National Adult Literacy Agency (NALA) presents an overview of the development of that country's mostly volunteer literacy movement, vigorously defending the advantages of this independent action and also pointing out its weaknesses. NALA's article illustrates the effects of an action-research process on the everyday activities of one group, referring in particular to learner participation in the overall dynamics of the agency.

Gertrud Kamper and Helga Rübsamen advance the hypothesis that learners' cognitive and perceptive faculties are unequally developed, and that the learning difficulties they experience in reading and writing can be partly attributed to inappropriate teaching methods. Based on the Soviet theory of activity these authors propose a gradual, technical modification of teaching methods to prevent the development of learning difficulties. They are of the same opinion as Franca van Alebeek and Tineke Krol: teachers who have transferred to literacy training are not adequately prepared to use experimental teaching approaches. The instances of failure (a taboo subject which is swept under the rug) among those using a school-based approach are the result of the unfavourable conditions that prevail throughout the educational structure.

The next three contributions deal with teaching children to read and write, or the enculturation of children. Jacques Fijalkow, working from an interactive theoretical perspective, presents a report on an action-research experiment that he is conducting in a school system with the aim of modifying the social relationships that determine the success or failure of children's integration into the school system. Véronique Marissal, whose methodology has much in common with that of Fijalkow, describes the experience of Belgium's "homework" schools, where recent developments are affecting relationships with the regular school, parents, social partners, and particularly literacy groups, in which the parents of homework school students apparently do not become involved. The door is open for "intergenerational" action and interaction among the various groups of players, but their positions remain unchanged. Anna Lorenzetto also presents an original methodological model based on a local cultural and intergenerational action, targeting the participation of young children and adults — including grandparents — in a single cultural development project involving other community representatives. (Unfortunately Lorenzetto's article arrived too late to be included as more than a brief summary).

The article by Thomas Gonzalez and Florentino Fernandez also deals with methodology, in this case, in relation to sociocultural animation in Spain's underprivileged rural areas. The authors feel that this type of approach is essential in this context, given the massive depopulation of certain rural areas and the urgent need for action. Raising the consciousness of the local inhabitants through action aimed at attaining the "possible dream" (Friere) is the only potential weapon against exile, itself a synonym of cultural death. This is the only text on this subject; a contribution from Portugal would undoubtedly have shown the strong influence still exercised by Paolo Freire in these two countries of southern Europe, only recently freed from political dictatorships and since then undergoing drastic social changes.

The last authors appearing in this issue of *ALPHA*, unlike the other European authors, are not members of the action-research network. Their link with the *ALPHA* collection is the experimental use of microprocessing in basic education, the subject of an earlier publication.* Jean-Louis Berterreix has contributed a monograph on LABO, in southern France. This organization has systematically incorporated the use of microcomputers into basic education, with the aim of ensuring the social and occupational reintegration of participants. How is this accomplished? What do microcomputers add to this process? What initial changes are required? What are the results? The answers to these questions will be of great interest to both our Québec and European readers.

Based on the CUEEP case study in northern France (see *ALPHA 88*), Bernard Obled envisions the "multimedia open education" model and systematically analyzes all the changes and innovations in teaching methods that it necessitates. He focusses in particular on how this training model addresses new requirements in the area of vocational training and human resource development in industry. The objective of developing the learner's independence is central to this mode. Individualization becomes more a strategic than an ideological concept, and all allusions to therapies disappear. We find ourselves on the threshold of a new philosophy of education where "illiteracy" is perceived as a means to survival. Interesting developments are surely forthcoming in this field!

---

* *Expérimentations du traitement de texte en alphabétisation*, J.-P. Hautecœur, ed., Ministère de l'Éducation du Québec, 1989. A follow-up to this report is currently being prepared.

FUNCTIONAL ILLITERACY AND THE "NEW LITERACY"*

Jean-Pierre Vélis
UNESCO, Paris

* Excerpt from *Through a Glass, Darkly: Functional Illiteracy in Industrialized Countries*, UNESCO, Paris, 1990 [title and some subtitles by J.-P. Hautecoeur].

FROM THE CAMPSITE TO THE STREET

"Literacy is the hook, life is the focus."[1] This short sentence encapsulates better than any long speech could ever do the thinking behind "Beat the Street," a program which was launched in Toronto, Canada, in 1985 and has now been extended to Winnipeg and Regina with the support of the Canadian Employment and Immigration Commission.

One morning in April 1989, I met Martina, Joyce, Linda and Tess in a simple room on the ground floor of a small house not far from the centre of Toronto, where Beat the Street has set up headquarters. They described to me what they are doing and explained their aims, which are quite straightforward and practical and involve coming to the aid of boys and girls over the age of 16 who have left the school system altogether and are now just "kicking around." Their world is the street, where they live among their own kind, either alone or in gangs, without homes or jobs, having broken with their families. They have opted out of society and live on the borderline of delinquency, drug addiction and prostitution, if they have not already taken the plunge. There are estimated to be some 25 000 young people leading this sort of life in Toronto. Many of them are functionally illiterate, although this in no way prevents them from knowing how to fend for themselves in a large modern city. They have devised their own frames of reference and means of survival.

They are apparently very good at passing on information among themselves by word of mouth. This is how they come to learn about Beat the Street and that there is a place somewhere in town that is open to receive them from 9 o'clock in the morning to 4 o'clock in the afternoon, Mondays to Fridays, where they can come in complete confidence (nobody is going to ask them anything or try to "assess" them). They will find all kinds of material there, even computers. One boy comes because he needs to read a brochure and cannot manage it; there is a girl who wants help in passing her grade 10 exams; another boy would like to pass his driving test, and so on. In short, if they can bring themselves to cross the threshold, it means that they need help.

Martina, Linda, Joyce and the coordinator, Tess, welcome them, listen to what they have to say and suggest putting them in touch with somebody — a volunteer — who will become their "tutor." The idea is not to start off any form of training in the conventional sense, but merely to establish an absolutely informal one-to-one relationship between two people from the same environment. Indeed, as Jack C. Pearpoint, President of Frontier College, has explained on numerous occasions: "Beat the Street is a literacy program that uses homeless street people to tutor street people. There are a few 'straights' around, but fundamentally it is a program conceived and operated by street people for street people." The meetings between the young person and his or her "tutor" take place outside in the street or in parks — when the temperature is not 30 below — or in shopping centres, in short, anywhere in their regular everyday world. The "learning" material is borrowed from the same environment and consists of newspapers, shop signs, graffiti, restaurant menus, bus maps, car registration plates, and so on. The thirty-odd volunteer tutors were first introduced to the "learner-focussed teaching methods" which the College tested for a number of years and which are now printed in the form of a handbook. [2] Monthly meetings are held to enable them to come together to exchange ideas and discuss any difficulties they may have had.

Since this program came into being, it has helped several hundred young people; about 200 were participating in it at the time of my visit. Some of them have gone back to their homes, while others have been taken in by foster families. Some have enrolled in correspondence courses, so that they can pursue the effort they have made, while yet others have found their first jobs. Some have left the street; others have died.

When I asked Martina how she saw the future, she said: "My problem is not to know whether I am optimistic or pessimistic, but to get on with my job. If I have helped somebody to make it, that's enough for me." Incidentally, Martina is a former "street kid," as they call them in Toronto.

Beat the Street is one of the ongoing programs of Frontier College, a Canadian institution whose origins date back to the end of the last century, when Alfred Fitzpatrick, a former Presbyterian minister from Nova Scotia, recruited students and sent them to live in logging, mining and railway camps where they could help the workers to learn to read, write and count, among other things. Since it was common for these activities to take place under canvas, the volunteer organization was known as the Reading Tent Association. It was not until 1922 that it took the name of Frontier College.

From one generation to the next, an army of Fitzpatrick's disciples have taken up the torch and extended the activities of Frontier College in many directions, adapting them as required to the workers' new living conditions and helping them to cope with the changing demands imposed by an evolving society. In 1977 the College received a Literacy Prize, an honorary distinction awarded by UNESCO. In 1988, on International Literacy Day, Canadian Prime Minister Brian Mulroney and his wife came to read to a group of children assembled in a tent which had been erected for the occasion in remembrance of the pioneer era, in front of the splendid, greystone building in which Frontier College and its recently created Frontier College Learning Foundation now have their headquarters.

I have chosen to dwell on this institution not so much out of a taste for sensation-mongering (there is no doubt that it is because of the people it sets out to help that Beat the Street has already been highly publicized in the press and has attracted many journalists and aroused the interest of a large number of television networks) as because I feel that its history and above all the way it is now evolving are a clear pointer to the current trends in literacy work in the industrialized countries. Indeed, they are almost symbolic.

Beat the Street is only one of a number of programs run by Frontier College. "Independent Studies," for example, is a venture that is comparable in all respects to what is being done by a very large number of other voluntary organizations in many other countries, whereby adult literacy training is provided by volunteers working in a one-to-one relationship with learners, with the backing of a methodology, the SCIL (Student Centred Individualized Learning) programs, and supervision (one coordinator for every 40 volunteers and their "pupils"). "Prison Literacy Initiatives" was created in 1983 at the request of the Correctional Services of Canada, which estimated that more than 50 percent of the prison population was functionally illiterate. Here again, literacy work in the penitentiaries is done by volunteers, as well as by other prisoners. The system is in effect in other places as well.

The HELP program is much more original. It stemmed from an idea launched in 1977 by a former inmate who sought to help people released from prison by setting up a sort of specific employment agency designed for and run by ex-offenders who are employed there full time. Frontier College became associated with the project in 1980. Through the representations it makes to prospective employers, HELP now manages to find more than 5000 jobs a year for ex-prisoners in Ontario. In addition, thanks to the "Street Readiness Program," before prisoners are released they can now attend a two-week session to prepare them for life outside.

New strategies

All these programs tie in directly with Fitzpatrick's original goals. He was convinced that "whenever and wherever people shall congregate, there should be the time, place and means of their education." It is not surprising, therefore, that the most recent of the programs set up by Frontier College should be called "Learning in the Workplace."

What does come as a surprise is the way in which the program is presented. It is a far cry from the heroic days when a handful of volunteers ventured into the lumber camps and shared the life and work of the people they had come to help, thereby inventing the concept of the "labourer-teacher." Nowadays, in approaching employers to propose its services, Frontier College uses a video or prospectus of a standard equal to any of the advertising material used in marketing campaigns. With the confidence born of its 90 years' existence, and with its reputation, experience and know-how behind it, Frontier College now sells a specialized product which might be called "corporate literacy consultancy." Like any commercial training consultants, Frontier College offers employers a two-day workshop at a cost of C$350 per person (meals included) to help them design and implement in-house literacy programs. The workshop's prospectus, *Workplace Literacy,* which is intended for personnel and training directors, describes its aims as follows: "This workshop is designed to help you organize, implement and maintain a self-sustaining literacy component within your company's overall training scheme. Through recruiting, training and matching volunteer tutors and learners from all areas of your workplace, you can establish a program which responds to the needs of the company and its work force."

It is clear that the gap separating Beat the Street and *Workplace Literacy* is quite large, in spite of the common thinking behind them.

The case of Frontier College is by no means unique. Such approaches as the introduction of a new and resolutely more modern and "competitive" language, the development of new strategies that are geared to attracting what can only be called "customers" and, above all, the priority given to economic arguments over overriding humanitarian considerations or even merely social ones, can now all be found in many other countries.

In France, for example, one of the main workers' education movements, the Fédération Léo Lagrange, bore witness to this trend when it organized a workshop in Paris in June 1988 on the subject of "Functional Illiteracy — The Responses of Business." The points it made in its arguments included the following:

> The automation of production lines and the redefinition of jobs and qualifications hinge on the know-how, experience and knowledge of all the people working in the company, without exception. Cutting back production costs, forestalling breakdowns, reducing the number of industrial accidents: all these objectives entail drawing up a staff training strategy and dealing with functional illiteracy. All companies

will have to contend with technological and organizational changes. Some of those exposed to fierce competition have already begun to implement organization and training strategies, including specific measures for functionally illiterate personnel.

Functional illiteracy is now the subject of a new discourse being addressed to the world of industry with the support of some political decision-makers such as Brian Mulroney, who, in addressing his best wishes to the 1987 Toronto conference, wrote: "Our unquestioned principal challenge, now and in the future, is to provide an enabled work force to meet the needs of industrialized societies. Through the planning and implementation of educational programs to service youth and to train or retrain adults, nations will be better equipped to meet the opportunities of the future." A year later, on International Literacy Day, he declared that "the time is long since past when government can sit on the sidelines and leave the issue of illiteracy to the efforts of the voluntary sector," and announced his government's decision to invest C$110 million in the following five years "to combat illiteracy."

In France, André Laignel, Secretary of State for Vocational Training, in an address delivered on 12 January 1989, went so far as to say that "the scale of the task calls for a veritable 'national crusade.' I intend to ensure that training activities designed to combat functional illiteracy are rid of the secretive atmosphere in which they are all too often shrouded and become one of the main concerns of the training schemes introduced for people whose low standards of knowledge currently exclude them from the labour market...This campaign is all the more pressing since such exclusion is a threat to progress and spells the ruin of development in the long run. It is economically necessary for us to win the battle and it would be socially unjust not to fight it." Some weeks later, the French Council of Ministers identified a number of priorities, covering: an unprecedented increase in the volume of training activities devoted to the struggle against functional illiteracy (at the end of 1989, a 65 percent increase in government credits compared with 1988; efforts to be continued in 1990); an improvement in the quality of instructors (with, in particular, the implementation of a national specialist training program); the opening of the major national training programs to functional illiterates (with 10 percent of the places being set aside for them in the training courses directly managed by the state); strengthening of interministerial cooperation (with the aim, for example, of training several thousand young men called up for military service); and the mobilization of public opinion (especially in connection with International Literacy Year).

You may be wondering how a relatively limited and barely acknowledged problem, which was long confined to the poor, the underprivileged and the rejected of industrial societies, should have managed to become in the space of a few years "probably the most important problem, the biggest problem facing the United States," as Bill Goodling, an American congressman has said, to take only one example.[3] This development is all the more surprising in that what I am tempted to call the "basic" functional illiterates are, in their vast majority, still "missing persons," with no voice of their own.

What sparked off this passionate and fighting response? It may have been people's need to take a fresh look at the problem and to show their clear-cut determination to seek out functional illiterates in their hiding-places, or even to coin a new term. In any case, it is a matter of conviction. Jack C. Pearpoint showed the way in 1987, when he said: "Literacy is essential to full participation of citizens, thus the appropriate technology solutions to the literacy issue of the 1990s will be to take education to the people, on issues they deem important, wherever they are. Hopefully by then they will be called 'management' or 'communication,' or other names that are not as demeaning as 'illiteracy.' "[4]

That is more or less what is now starting to happen.

The spectacular and alarmist figures produced by the Canadian Business Task Force on Literacy[5] are one of the main reference points featured in the prospectuses of both Frontier College and Laubach Literacy of Canada (the Canadian branch of one of the largest American voluntary organizations, Laubach Literacy Action, which has been engaged in literacy work in the United States for several years). An advertising brochure entitled *How Employees Become More Valuable to Employers*, which Laubach has sent out to employers to vaunt the merits of its new Industrial Tutoring Project, cites the Southam News Survey, and describes illiteracy as being "the hidden problem that costs Canadian industry more than $4 billion each year." What a far cry this appears to be from promoting literacy for reasons of social justice or simply of solidarity.

This fashionable talk of the "new literacy," which is visualized as being "the basics of growth"[6] and is being imposed in order to grapple with the technological challenges of industrial societies, can now be heard all over North America. In January 1988, the Business Council for Effective Literacy (BCEL) reviewed the commitment of private companies to literacy work in the United States. Among the information it gave was the fact that, between 1984 and the end of 1987, new nationwide or regional adult literacy programs were carried out with funding from private companies amounting to some $10 million. Over the same period, BCEL received 128 grants from 78 different sources, mainly from business, to replenish the resources of its own development program. The rate at which the number of these grants increased — ranging from six in 1984 to 22 in 1985, 42 in 1986 and 58 in 1987 — reflects the growing interest in the problem. Of these donor companies, 40 percent belong to or are associated with the publishing sector, while the remaining 60 percent are represented by banks or financing agencies, communications firms, and oil or insurance companies.[7]

There is no reason to be surprised that everything involving publishing and the printed word in general should be heavily represented. As Jack C. Pearpoint has written: "Book publishers, booksellers and others concerned with the printed media have come to see that promoting reading for a broader public is more than social welfare — it is good business."[8] In the United States, a large number of newspaper publishers have come together to form the particularly active American Newspaper Publishers Association (ANPA) Foundation. Jerry W. Friedheim, the Foundation's Executive Vice-President, leaves us in no doubt when he writes: "We must make reading in America our number one priority... not just because it's right, but because our future depends on it."[9] At a symposium held in Washington in May 1988, William Hohns, Executive Vice-President of Waldman Graphics Inc., was even more down-to-earth when he said to the participants: "Imagine for a moment how General Motors or Ford might react if one-third of their potential market was unable to utilize their product." It is true that, shortly afterwards, he raised the debate to the level of ideals and added: "What good is a free press that only half of America can read?"[10] This argument and the risks it implies for democracy justified the support given by Barbara Bush to ANPA, and her words: "Newspapers depend on literacy. Our precious freedom of the press has limited meaning for the tens of millions of Americans who lack the basic literacy skills that would give them access to the written word. We must work together for literacy, so that all may read and better share in the world around them."

The fact remains that more wide-ranging economic considerations appear to be coming to the fore and to be taking over the leading role. The argument is that if functional illiteracy continues to spread, the future of the national economy will be in jeopardy and the United States' position in worldwide economic competition will be called into question.

Considering that 75 percent of the people who will form the working population in the United States in the year 2000 are already outside any formal education system and that they include a very substantial proportion (between 20 and 30 million people at least, depending on the criteria adopted) without a command of the basic skills they need to cope with and adapt to technological changes, many public figures have voiced their concern, as did Bill Goodling who has said: "Members of Congress are beginning to understand that, as a matter of fact, illiteracy is going to determine whether we are competitive or not competitive in years to come."[11] Others have echoed the latter-day Cassandras who are predicting that, sooner or later "the United States will become a second-rate nation, fulfilling the predictions of historical doomsayers that we will follow the path of other great powers towards national decline."[12]

In Europe, a game of hunt the slipper

European continuing education specialists attending their second congress in West Berlin in October 1988 affirmed that illiteracy was a serious problem in the United States while it virtually did not exist in Japan; as for Europe, people just buried their heads in the sand.[13] This is harsh criticism. Is it justified?

If this statement means that functional illiteracy has not unleashed the same spate of discussion on both sides of the Atlantic, then it is undoubtedly true. But if it means that most of the people responsible for dealing with the problem in Europe are casting the problem out of their minds after having duly acknowledged that a large number of adults in their working population are poorly trained — or are compelled to remain inactive because of unemployment — then it is just as undoubtedly wrong. Here again, it is a matter of definition. We have to ask where literacy stops and the upgrading of skills begins. In North America, it has now been decided to cast the net wide, but most of the other industrialized countries are still at the stage of setting priorities. What we see depends on which end of the binoculars we look through. But does this mean that the real-life situation we are looking at is any different?

In France, for example, attempts have also been made to cost academic failure rather than illiteracy. In a report submitted to the Economic and Social Council in October 1987, Jean Andrieu, the former President of the Fédération des conseils des parents d'élèves (FCPE) estimated the cost of academic failure at 100 billion francs (60 billion francs representing expenditure on children having left the school system without a certificate, 25 billion francs on children having to repeat a year, etc.), or 2 percent of the country's gross domestic product (GDP) and almost one-quarter of all expenditure on education. In spite of the approximate nature of these figures, the Economic and Social Council approved the report. There was no mention of the fact that it specifically concerned functional illiteracy.

Likewise in France, it has been known for a long time that about 100 000 young people leave school every year without any recognized qualification. Nobody ever suggested they were all functionally illiterate.

According to a survey carried out in 1982 by the French Institut national de la statistique et des études économiques (INSEE), 64 percent of all French people have a general level of training equal to or lower than a primary school leaving certificate. The Association française pour la lecture (AFL) is virtually the only organization to claim that this level is precisely that of functional illiteracy.

The growing obsolescence of knowledge is often regarded as being partly responsible for unemployment. According to a commonly acknowledged argument, hundreds of thousands of adults are, or will be, debarred from the labour market because their skills are too poor or their level of training is too low. When Philippe Séguin was the French Minister of Social Affairs and Employment, he even coined the phrase "the new selectivity of labour" for the phenomenon, which he saw as being unavoidable. Yet nobody got up to say that the workers concerned were all functional illiterates.

This certainly does not mean that nothing is being done. Efforts are being made; but in compartmented sectors where functional illiteracy — in the North American sense of the term, I am tempted to write — is not necessarily identified as such or as an exclusive feature.

To summarize, two main options are being opened up, between which the precise place occupied by adult literacy has not been very clearly determined. The first option involves preventing functional illiteracy from the very first years at school, while the second involves providing vocational training in adulthood. In other words, we could talk of preventive action within the school system and efforts to upgrade the basic skills and vocational training of job-seekers — especially young people fresh out of the school system and, to a lesser extent, the long-term unemployed. Of these two main tendencies, the former depends on the steps taken by national education systems, such as the Interministerial Program for the Promotion of Success at School in Portugal, while the second depends on the measures adopted to gradually reduce unemployment. Between these two extremes, adult literacy, with the notable exception of the Netherlands and Portugal, is still, to a very great extent, dependent on the goodwill of voluntary or other organizations whose size is relatively small compared with the purported scale of the problem.

Even today, on-the-job literacy activities are exceptional enough to warrant singling out, although an increasing number have been introduced and are being funded by private companies under their training programs. To be truthful, there are many more companies that have not contemplated such activities either because they have not identified the problem or do not have the resources, or because they are absolutely opposed to them. It is true that, in view of the ready availability of labour on the market, it is much simpler, in the absence of specific protection measures, to dispense with the services of an employee whose skills no longer give satisfaction and to require a secondary school leaving certificate for a manual labourer's job which does not require any academic knowledge. This

obviously cannot be readily measured. Jacques Lesourne claims, for
example: "The structure of a country's production is the outcome not only
of the skills on offer but of the prices of the goods and the (explicit and
implicit) cost to the employer of the different job categories (thus, the fact
that some young people are jobless is due less to their level of training than
to the refusal of French society to countenance a freer-flowing labour
market)."[14] You can well imagine the discrimination that this represents for
functionally illiterate workers.

This twofold approach, entailing the prevention of functional illiteracy at school and the provision of vocational training for adults, can again
be seen when it comes to considering international cooperation. In the
European Community, the programs dealing specifically with "the fight
against illiteracy" for the most part only envisage its prevention in the
context of school. This seems quite normal inasmuch as this concern
emerged from the meeting of the EEC Council and the Ministers of
Education on 4 June 1984. As is only logical, the group of national
officials which was subsequently set up is composed of delegates from
Ministries of Education and a few independent experts. Its aims are quite
explicit and chiefly cover preventive action that can be taken by the
education system at the preschool, primary and early secondary levels. The
group is also required to consider adult literacy whenever that problem
comes under the Ministries of Education.[15] To judge from the different
activities undertaken to date (study tours, symposia, research, etc.),
priority is, in fact, still being given to school and prevention. For example,
the summer university held in Toulouse, France, in July 1988 was
concerned with "writing and first contacts with the written word" while the
combined research and practical action launched in the same year was
conducted in pilot schools in several of the member states, with a view to
testing some of the proposed measures in nursery and primary schools and
the lower grades of secondary school.

If that is so, then what did the 150 delegates who attended the
meeting convened by the Commission of the European Communities in
Seville, Spain, in May 1987, talk about when they discussed the development of human resources in regions undergoing economic conversion with
the financial support of the Community?[16] Literacy was apparently not on
their agenda. Yet when those experts described the situation in the
different regions involved,[17] they were unable to avoid a number of
conclusions, including the fact that there is a large population of unemployed and poorly skilled young people and a population of adults with
skills that are inadequate for coping with the ongoing technological
changes, who have either been without work for periods that are tending to
become ever longer or else are in danger of losing the jobs they currently
occupy. These people are, in other words, a ready-made clientele for the
"new literacy."

A pervasive problem

In a good many industrialized countries, illiteracy is so well concealed that it is everywhere to be found. It is not so much a question of people burying their heads in the sand as of their not being able to see further than their noses. Moreover, if it is a question of waging a "battle," the battle order has not yet been drawn up in all these countries. According to Gerald Bogart,[18] in the current crisis situation the European countries are faced with common challenges; each country is endeavouring to meet them by means of methodologies, approaches to issues and institutional tools mobilized within its own traditions and resources but which could be transferred. Here again, these views do not apply to a problem primarily designated as being that of functional illiteracy but to the difficulties being experienced by the long-term unemployed in becoming integrated into a constantly evolving social and economic environment in 18 member countries of the Council of Europe.[19]

We are warned that the population involved is not clearly defined, yet we know a number of things about it: the long-term unemployed have a negative experience of school, which has often left them without any real and adequately structured basic knowledge (problems of absolute and functional illiteracy), without any job qualification (or with skills that have become obsolete) and, if they have any work experience, the jobs they do are repetitive, monotonous and unappealing. There is a relationship between the low level of qualifications and unemployment. The long-term unemployed create their own cultural models: with their lack of confidence leading to feelings of despair, as individuals they are often defeatist and have given up hope of receiving any help whatsoever from present-day society. They can be said to have become adapted to a new jobless culture. The state of shock engendered by unemployment results in mental deconstruction in relation to the habitual settings of everyday life. The future is no longer regarded as being a whole series of varied possibilities that can be put in some sort of order, but is left to the vagaries of fortune. Day-to-day time management and, indeed, space management break down. In some cases, the countryside starts turning into desert, as in the case of Cyprus, while elsewhere, in the United Kingdom for example, whole city areas are emptied of their inhabitants. In some instances, as in the Netherlands, networks are organized in terms of survival. According to the Italian project, the problems of demoralization are also those of delinquency, alcoholism and illness. On the one hand, the long-term unemployed have a negative experience of education, from which they have often been debarred: on the other hand, they prefer to look for another job rather than undergo training. In North America, the documents on functional illiteracy are full of descriptions like these. In Europe, this apocalyptic picture comes under the heading of "adult education and social change."

You will note that some countries, such as Denmark, which only a short time ago did not readily admit to the existence of illiteracy, now find themselves in the same boat as the others. One of the Danish pilot projects on behalf of the long-term unemployed is taking place in the canton of Strostrøms, which has one of the country's highest jobless rates (8.6 percent among men and 14.9 percent among women, in January 1988). And what is it we hear? "A special-risk group is the work force of non-skilled women with less formal schooling. A great part of the unemployed belong to this group. This group needs better basic skills and qualifications if they are going to have new jobs or if they are going to start an education which, in the long run, will make it possible for them to change their situation." Yet there is no reference anywhere to the fact that these women are functionally illiterate.

This is something that would probably come as a surprise to many North American experts who, in the wake of the Canadian Prime Minister, share the view of John Kenneth Galbraith that "we are coming to realize that there is a certain sterility in economic monuments that stand alone in a sea of illiteracy." The issue has apparently by no means run its full course in North America. Indeed, the pace has quickened considerably in recent months and it has even passed another turning point.

In January 1989, the Southport Institute for Policy Analysis stirred up the debate by bringing out a document entitled *Jump Start*, by Forrest P. Chisman,[20] which openly challenges the United States Federal Administration, while experts in the behavioural and cognitive sciences, following their meeting in San Diego, California, have published the results of their thinking and exchanges of ideas in *Making the Nation Smarter*,[21] in which they go straight to the point and recommend that new approaches be tried out. Both documents are highly critical of the action that has been taken so far. In some respects, *Jump Start* has all the makings of a firebrand.

Forrest P. Chisman is a model of pragmatism. He does not set the day of reckoning in the abstract, as being sometime at the beginning of the next century, but points precisely to the year 2010, the time when the baby-boom generation, representing some 75 million people in the United States, will begin to retire. "America must do a great many things to avoid that unhappy rendez-vous with demographic destiny. And among the most important things it must do is ensure that the twenty-million-plus adults who are seriously deficient in basic skills become fully productive workers and citizens well before the rendez-vous occurs. Without their best efforts over the next 20 years, there is little hope for the economic and social future of this country."

Jump Start claims that educational reform cannot solve the problem (since the adults involved have already left school) and that neither unpaid voluntary activities nor companies can manage by themselves. It goes on to put forward a number of proposals for legislation (in particular through the adoption of an Adult Basic Skills Act) and financial support (which is estimated to amount to 3 percent of current federal investment in education and training). The feature which all these measures have in common is that they have to be taken and paid for by the federal government following a personal pledge by the President: "In the early months of his term of office, the President should clearly establish the enhancement of adult basic skills as a major priority of his administration." This is followed by a detailed proposal for an action program.

There is a fortunate coincidence in the fact that at the very time when *Jump Start* has forcefully underscored the need for adult education and training policy to take off in a new direction, experts in the cognitive sciences are proposing a way of "making the nation smarter," while doubling the effectiveness of every dollar currently invested in basic education. This goes by the rather learned name of Intergenerational Transfer of Cognitive Ability.

Please excuse the rather cursory oversimplification: roughly speaking, the mistake that has been made with all the programs that have been launched in the United States in recent years is that they have focussed on specific age groups (for example, "Head Start" and "Chapter I" on children, Job Corps on young people, and the Adult Basic Education Act on adults). With hindsight, they can be seen not to have produced the results expected. By contrast, the "intergenerational" programs, based on contributions by a host of different disciplines (such as anthropology, sociology, psychology, data processing applied to artificial intelligence, behavioural genetics, neurology, linguistics and philosophy) look upon the family, or adults and children taken together, as a closely combined learning unit. The outcome consists of educational practices in which different groups, and especially children and parents, become partners in a joint approach.

This new approach is still too recent for it to be possible to evaluate its effects with any certainty, but it can be noted that it has already created a definite wave of enthusiasm. The announcement of the creation, on 6 March 1989, of the Barbara Bush Foundation for Family Literacy is undoubtedly the clearest indication of this development. Among its objectives, the Foundation plans to provide grants to existing literacy programs having already proved their effectiveness, with a view to introducing "intergenerational" dimensions into them. Whether this is the beginning of an answer, only time will tell.

By a cruel stroke of fortune, international solidarity turns up in places where people would prefer not to see it. Everything suggests, in fact, that functional illiteracy is not an exclusive speciality of the industrialized countries. In Brazil, for example, where 66 percent of the population live — or survive — in urban areas, 53 million of the 83.5 million people over 15 years of age have not completed the eight years' compulsory schooling which they are guaranteed by the Constitution, 35 million have not even completed four years and, of that number, 20 million are illiterate. Lêda Maria C. Tajra, president of the EDUCAR foundation, who presented these figures at the 24th Session of the General Conference of UNESCO held in Paris in November 1987, went on to say:

> For several reasons, it is this same segment of the population which has most difficulty in obtaining access to education. It is composed of workers, most of whom are engaged on the informal labour market. Their earnings are among the lowest of the low and are often not sufficient to cover their basic needs, such as housing, food, transport, clothing, health care and leisure-time activities [in 1987, the minimum monthly wage in Brazil corresponded to less than 50 dollars]. It is also composed of migrants, who are victims of the sharp deterioration in the demographic situation that has occurred in Brazil in recent decades. Their wholesale flight from the countryside has brought them to the fringes of the main urban centres or to the frontiers of agricultural expansion. Their experience of academic failure has left them with indelible feelings of individual guilt, when in fact the fault lies in the social policies that were adopted [the average length of time pupils spend in the first year of primary school is 2.7 years, owing to the vast number of them who have to repeat it].

To listen to her, you say to yourself that she could just as well deliver her paper at some of the proceedings of the Council of Europe.

More recently, in May 1988, at a regional workshop organized by UNESCO in Apia, Western Samoa, the participants, who came from six countries in the Pacific Region, revealed the existence of very large numbers of young people who, although having duly attended school, have proved incapable of making effective use of reading, writing and arithmetic in their everyday lives.

They did not say that these were cases of "functional illiteracy." They did not speak of the "new literacy." Instead, they talked about "hidden illiteracy."

NOTES

1. Marsha Forest, with Bruce Kappel, *It's About Learning*, Toronto, Frontier College Press, 1988.

2. Tracy Carpenter, *The Right to Read — Tutor's Handbook for the Frontier College SCIL (Student Centred Individualized Learning) Program*, Toronto, Frontier College, 1986.

3. At the Symposium on the Image of Print Media and the Problem of Functional Illiteracy in the United States, organized at the Capital Hilton Hotel, Washington, D.C., on 25 May 1988, by the Research and Engineering Council of the Graphic Arts Industry and cosponsored by the Academic Advisory Council (AAC) to the Public Printer, the Government Printing Office and the Department of Education.

4. Jack C. Pearpoint, "Frontier College: Literacy Education since 1899," *Prospects* (Paris, UNESCO), Vol. 17, No. 2, 1987, pp. 227-86.

5. *The Cost of Illiteracy to Business in Canada*, Toronto, Canadian Business Task Force on Literacy February 1988.

6. Ministry of Skills Development, *Literacy — The Basics of Growth/L'alphabétisation — base de la croissance*, Ministry of Skills Development, Ontario.

7. Business Council for Effective Literacy, *BCEL Newsletter for the Business Community*, New York, BCEL, January 1988.

8. Pearpoint, op. cit.

9. American Newspaper Publishers Association Foundation, *Newspapers Meet the Challenge: Literacy Handbook*, Washington, D.C., ANPA, 1987.

10. See note 3.

11. See note 3.

12. American Newspaper Publishers Association Foundation, op. cit.

13. Report on the second European congress on continuing training, held in West Berlin, 27-28 October 1988, *CEDEFOP Flash*, No. 6, West Berlin, European Centre for the Development of Vocational Training, 1988.

14. Jacques Lesourne, "Enseignement: les défis de l'an 2000," in Minelle Verdié (ed.), *L'état de la France et de ses habitants*, Paris, Éditions La Découverte, 1989.

15. Commission of the European Communities, Directorate-General for Employment, Social Affairs and Education, *Report on the Fight Against Illiteracy*, Luxembourg, Office for Official Publications of the European Communities, 1988 (Social Europe, Supplements, 2).

16. See "Report on the Forum on Regional Development and Professional Training: Developing Human Resources in Regions Undergoing Economic Conversion with the Financial Support of the Community, convened in Seville, Spain, 25-27 May 1987," *CEDEFOP Flash*, West Berlin, European Centre for the Development of Vocational Training, 1987.

17. Danish Jutland, the northern Netherlands, northern England, southwest Ireland, the Belgian Limburg province, Saarland, the Nord-Pas-de-Calais and Lorraine regions of France, Liguria in Italy, Akhaïa in Greece, Andalusia in Spain, and northern Portugal.

18. Gerald Bogart, *Adult Education and Social Change — Report*, prepared for the Council of Europe, Council for Cultural Cooperation, Topic Group on the Long-Term Unemployed, Strasbourg, 13-14 October 1988.

19. Austria, Cyprus, Denmark, Finland, France, Greece, Iceland, Ireland, Italy, Malta, Netherlands, Norway, Portugal, Spain, Sweden, Turkey, United Kingdom and Yugoslavia.

20. Forrest P. Chisman, *Jump Start — The Federal Role in Adult Literacy*, Southport, Southport Institute for Policy Analysis, January 1989. (Final Report on the Project on Adult Literacy.)

21. Thomas G. Sticht and Barbara A. McDonald, *Making the Nation Smarter; The Intergenerational Transfer of Cognitive Ability*, San Diego, Calif., Applied Behavioral and Cognitive Sciences Inc., 1989.

LITERACY POLICY IN QUÉBEC: AN HISTORICAL OVERVIEW

Jean-Paul Hautecoeur
Ministère de l'Éducation
du Québec

This overview of the political status of the literacy dossier and the action plans developed by the Québec government was prompted by a speech on literacy given by the Minister of Education on 9 August 1989. It is a very important document inasmuch as it is the current government's only official text on literacy. This clarification of the government's position ended the seeming political lethargy and inaction within the adult education portfolio, which itself had been in a state of disarray since 1984. The Minister's speech stimulated my interest in conducting an historical study of the question from the perspective of literacy policy by returning to the source: the Parent Report.

The opportunity to conduct the study came about through a request by the Conseil supérieur de l'éducation for a consultation on the problems raised by the current literacy portfolio and the proposed solutions. Once I had made my observations to the Conseil, basing my remarks on my notes and hypotheses, it remained for me to carry out a careful review of the government's policies in order to write a critical analysis and justify the positions taken. It seemed to me particularly important to establish a basis for drawing conclusions in order to avoid an impasse. The focus of this overview was not to be politics (the ideology of the government apparatus) or the literacy movement (popular and academic ideologies); rather, it was to be a bringing together of the fragments, the visible traces, the directions that literacy training has taken, now that enough time has elapsed that we can learn from it. I also took into consideration other documents and the experiences of other countries in order to treat alternative courses of development.

A RECENT CONCEPT

The concept of literacy training as a unique social phenomenon rather than a specialized area of education is relatively recent. Although some volunteer work in literacy training was done well before the formal organization of lifelong education in 1967 (in the 1950s, missionary sisters with literacy training experience acquired in Africa worked sporadically with illiterate adult Quebecers and immigrants), the first organized attempts to provide literacy training date back barely 10 years.

The first official mention of "a systematic offensive against illiteracy" appeared in a 1980 government policy statement on schools in economically disadvantaged areas.[1] Before this, basic education was part of a federal-provincial vocational education program, the objective of which was to "reschool" undereducated workers in order to enable them to acquire occupational skills. From this point on, literacy training was perceived as being distinct from academic upgrading and vocational education programs. The existence of an illiterate population outside the scope of the adult education structure was recognized, as was the need to implement various literacy training measures. A new concept had emerged.

This recognition served to validate an existing literacy movement supported by research, experimentation, associations and demands for action. Nevertheless, public awareness of the movement came only shortly before official government recognition. Three socially significant events occurred in 1978: a provincial seminar, called ALPHA 78, which can be considered the true beginning of the literacy movement,[2] the publication of a report on illiteracy and literacy training in Québec,[3] and the broadcasting of a National Film Board documentary on national television.[4] Another seminar on the theme of popular literacy training, ALPHA 80, took place in 1980, marking the creation of an independent, popular literacy movement, which became known as the Regroupement des groupes populaires en alphabétisation the following year.[5]

Undoubtedly the greatest contribution to the literacy movement's public visibility, direct representation in all regions, and discussion of its aims and significance within the context of a lifelong education policy was made by the Commission d'étude sur la formation des adultes, which was active from 1980 to 1982. Following the example of UNESCO, in the Third World, and taking into account the more recent experience of Great Britain, it popularized what was, at the time, a highly motivating symbol of the literacy movement: the national campaign against illiteracy. In its report to the government, the Commission established the creation of a five-year literacy campaign as a priority of basic education.[6]

The follow-up proved disappointing in that the chief recommendations of the Commission were not carried out and the focus was placed on "harmonizing" the youth and adult sectors. With respect to literacy training, this meant the integration of basic education into the general education program of the ministère de l'Éducation du Québec (MEQ) and the gradual marginalization of the social, militant and popular movement, which had greatly contributed to defining a comprehensive approach to literacy training. Thus, there was no literacy campaign; in fact, there has been no further official indication of government or even departmental policy in literacy training since this time.

Apart from this limited action by the Québec government, the literacy movement was represented in the regions and municipalities by popular organizations and associations, and gained recognition through awareness campaigns, special events such as "Alpha-fête," "Grande rencontre," "Colloque des apprenants,"[7] publications, press conferences (especially popular on International Literacy Day, every 8 September), documentaries, surveys and media coverage.[8] The growth of literacy activities in adult education centres, as well as the development of local networks supporting these activities (the community approach) confirmed the movement's duality, visible through its academic and social, institutional and popular, and professional and volunteer aspects. The entire history of the literacy movement bears witness to the tensions, contradictions, competition and links inherent in this duality.

THE CANADIAN AND INTERNATIONAL CONTEXTS

Now that we have observed the historical origins of the literacy phenomenon and seen how it became rooted in the public consciousness, we must attempt to situate and explain it. Some myths must be dispelled, particularly that of Québec's insularity and the notion that literacy was a "new" concern in the province.

Beginning in the 1960s, a massive literacy movement occurred in several regions in the form of adult reschooling, which, as mentioned above, was preceded by the sporadic efforts of missionary sisters. In the late 1960s, a group of nuns founded the first specialized basic education centre.[9] The 1970s were also good years for basic education, which, as a prerequisite to vocational education, played an important role in adult education activities. Training benefits encouraged (or forced) the unemployed to enrol with school boards. The urban popular education movement, for its part, experimented with various basic education approaches.[10]

This era paved the way for the literacy movement, which differed from basic education in name, and through its search for an identity, its special events, relative independence, new provincial and international solidarity, creation of a professional category, etc. This social movement was not limited to Québec: similar movements could be observed elsewhere in Canada (especially in British Columbia and Ontario) and in Europe.

In Ontario a national conference organized by World Literacy of Canada, a Third World aid agency which had just become active in literacy training on a national scale, was held for the first time in Toronto. A conference with the same theme took place the following year in Ottawa, with a view to incorporating the budding movement into a national organization called "The Movement for Canadian Literacy."[11] In British Columbia, a conference on basic education (ABE: Adult Basic

Education) took place in 1976. The following year a report was made to the government proposing a comprehensive literacy action plan, which resulted in the formulation of an official policy in 1980. [12]

Although cooperation between these provinces and Québec was limited, and the events occurring in the different provinces cannot be assessed on the same basis, there was a common denominator. Essentially, it was federal manpower training policies, especially the Canadian government's gradual withdrawal from basic education (culminating in 1977, when the provinces assumed responsibility for basic education), which revealed the prevalence of illiteracy.

In 1977 a symbolic event linked Canada to other countries active in the struggle against illiteracy: Toronto's Frontier College received an honorary award from UNESCO for its work in the field of literacy. This event revealed two important facts: that Canada was not a newcomer to literacy training, and that UNESCO now recognized a problem of "functional illiteracy" in industrialized nations in addition to the problem of Third World illiteracy. UNESCO also sponsored the first seminar on illiteracy in industrialized countries, held in 1981 in Great Britain, then the European leader in literacy activities because of its massive literacy campaign begun in 1974. Another European event which had an influence on Canadian policy was a 1982 resolution on the struggle against illiteracy adopted by the European Parliament. [13]

Although the courses of local and international events varied depending on their level of implementation (local, provincial or national), there were certainly many common elements. An attempt must be made to explain Québec's particular situation, keeping in mind that it may resemble that of other provinces and countries.

THE QUÉBEC CONTEXT

As observed above, the development of specific literacy concepts and activities was triggered by the federal government's gradual withdrawal (1972-1977) of basic education programs for the work force. These programs, which in theory were to have facilitated vocational education, instead revealed the existence of widespread illiteracy. For the most part they were directed at those on the fringes of the regular labour force who lived permanently below the poverty line. Such were the findings of the Standing Senate Committee on National Finance in 1975. Indeed, over half the money spent on manpower training programs went to training individuals living below the poverty line; one-third went to basic education. [14]

For 10 years the federal government had been involved in laying the groundwork for a literacy training infrastructure in Québec, focussing on underdeveloped regions where education levels were lowest. When basic education was dropped from vocational education programs, it had to be implemented as a separate provincial program (literacy training) and adapted to local illiterate populations. The time was ripe and the conditions ideal for such a program. These favourable conditions can be summed up as follows:

— Illiteracy had been recognized as a widespread social problem.

— Literacy had appeared as a new concern of adult education.

— A militant wing of popular education was prepared to convert a training program into a social movement.

— The nationalist, social democratic government in power at the time and the trend toward expanding government services encouraged the development of this movement.

What follows is a brief overview of each of these points.

• In the 1970s there were no statistics on illiteracy; rather, it was lumped in with the problem of undereducation, and adults who had not completed five years of schooling were considered illiterate. This level stood at 13 percent in Québec in 1961, dropping to 8.3 percent in 1971 and 7.5 percent in 1976. At the national level, Québec ranked third for the cumulative indices of illiteracy, unemployment and poverty, behind the Atlantic provinces and the Northwest Territories. Regional statistics, published by the MEQ in 1976 (1971 census), were alarming for some regions: the Outaouais registered an illiteracy rate of close to 20 percent and the Gaspésie rate was 16 percent, compared with a rate of less than 1 percent for one of Montréal's anglophone districts. [15]

Several conclusions were drawn from these statistics. Obviously, greater attention needed to be devoted to education in Québec if it was to catch up to the other provinces and overcome its problems of underdevelopment. Also, since illiteracy rates were seen to decrease from one census to the next, it was felt that education could all but eradicate the problem. Finally, there was a call for appropriate action and special measures to address the situation of the poorest segments of the population.

• Adult education was at the experimental stage. Extracurricular measures were being developed (community activities, popular education), enrolment was up and activities were being expanded, more people were being reached, and, in cultural terms, there was a great push on for development and social justice. The expansion of adult education services in the school boards compensated for the drop in enrolment and activities at the regular elementary and secondary levels. From an administrative point of view, it was an ideal time to replace the former basic education program with a provincial program that would ensure a comparable level of activity. Literacy training was perfect because of the vast population to be drawn upon.

For adult educators and community activity leaders, literacy training raised a stimulating challenge with respect to pedagogical approaches, academic upgrading, justice and social change, and the expansion of extracurricular popular education and community activities. Once those receiving basic education were no longer directed toward academic upgrading by manpower officers or motivated by training allowances, other incentives and recruitment methods had to be established to bring educators and the illiterate together. Not only were these experiments attractive to the educators, but they also opened up a new occupational field and created jobs. Moreover, contact with the illiterate was perceived as an enriching human experience, as a vocation, a religious calling, as it were.

• The independent popular education movement (which received government funding and is not to be confused with volunteer organizations) had experimented with literacy training in the working class districts of Montréal and in a number of immigrant communities. Although these activities were limited in number compared with the basic education programs offered in institutions, they were part of a militant tradition that perceived the objectives and conditions of literacy training as part of the more comprehensive popular education and organization process, formulated specific pedagogical methods, created support service networks ranging from the local neighbourhood to organizations similar to those in other countries (namely Latin America), and formed political alliances.

When the time came to convert basic education into a provincial literacy program, the popular education movement was prepared to invest in it, demand official recognition of its special skills in this area, and claim education rights for the illiterate. Conditions were right for developing a social movement that combined various sociocultural approaches to education under the banner of literacy training, offering competition to professional educators, who saw it as a new branch of adult education. This competition to dominate a single market was both reinforced through opposing ideologies and camouflaged through participation in the general movement to promote literacy.

- From the government's perspective, conditions could not have been more favourable for the development of literacy activities. The nationalist government of the Parti Québécois wished to "repatriate" control over manpower policy and, in more general terms, formulate an independent lifelong education policy. Ottawa's relinquishing of basic education jurisdiction meant that it was now up to the MEQ to take action.

The main priority of the Parti Québécois was to democratize education and adapt the school to local communities, particularly in disadvantaged areas. Extracurricular activities, such as community activities and independent popular education, were strongly encouraged in the adult education field. Support was available both for school boards and independent agencies. This emphasis on research, experimentation and evaluation could not help but foster innovation.

With respect to resources, it must be remembered that the 1970s were still a time of large-scale spending. Education was not affected by budget cuts until the early 1980s, and then it was mainly sectors outside the school system, such as popular education, which felt the pinch. In short, the sky was the limit when it came to literacy...

A QUARTER CENTURY OF POLICIES

But if "the sky was the limit" then, what has happened since? In this section, we will limit ourselves to adult education strategies and action plans, which reveal an important change in 1984. Because less was written around this time, and the issue was less the object of political discussion, we will look elsewhere for indications of current strategies and trends.

To understand the present state of affairs, it is useful to refer to the first record of adult education, the Parent Report (1966). This founding document of lifelong education is, in effect, closer to current directions in literacy training than are subsequent policies dealing specifically with the subject.

The *Report of the Royal Commission of Inquiry on Education in the Province of Quebec* analyzed the undereducation of French Canadians, a major cause of Québec's industrial backwardness and of French Canadians' limited role in the economy. Obviously, the most pressing objective was to make up for lost time by upgrading workers' skills and providing the most widespread access to secondary-level education possible. A sense of urgency and need produced a mood of optimism:

> The rise in the attendance rates of secondary educa-
> tion is, at the moment, extremely rapid, as a result
> of new popular attitudes toward education. The op-
> timum goal will perhaps not be reached much later
> than 1970. [16]

"Illiteracy" does not figure greatly in the Royal Commission's analysis of the state of education in Québec; rather, the authors of the report view the development of education in terms of universal accessibility. The few passages in which illiteracy is mentioned refer to 19th-century, preindustrial Québec. [17] The lines that come closest to defining measures resembling literacy training recommend that undereducated adults be provided with "further education":

> As a first step, they should be offered courses which
> will help them to express themselves better in their
> own and, if possible, in a second language. They
> also need a good knowledge of elementary mathe-
> matics and some instruction in the natural and the
> social sciences. (Vol. 2, p. 329)

Only a first step, to be sure, but one which approaches the aims of literacy training. With respect to the mother tongue, the report does not specify whether the targeted improvement is in written or oral expression. Literacy was not yet perceived as a concept in itself, just as illiteracy had not yet been diagnosed in a large part of the population. Faith in the powers of education was unbounded, and merely providing standardized services was considered enough to change the world.

It was not until 1980 that an MEQ policy statement acknowledged the existence of an illiteracy problem and announced that a "systematic offensive against illiteracy" would be a top priority in a series of education measures designed for the "disadvantaged classes." The policy statement observed that "important classes of society are excluded" from educational services, and that "the current education system does not succeed in reaching them" because it "is not adapted to their needs and expectations." [18] Thus, the major orientations of the policy consisted in giving priority to the most disadvantaged areas ("positive discrimination"), promoting "greater responsibility for local-level agencies," and recommending "experimental action" monitored by the local agencies and evaluated jointly with the MEQ. These orientations reveal:

> A spirit of openness and an attitude that is receptive
> with respect to local drives, the desires of the group
> concerned and diversity in the implementation of the
> programs recommended in the policy. (p. 115)

In literacy training, the measures announced stressed the importance of local initiatives in raising public awareness, enlisting local
agencies and implementing new approaches. Emphasis was placed on
informal measures such as educational services for parents, community
activities and popular education. Objectives such as developing new
approaches, conducting experiments, and "deschooling" (although the term
is never used) educational services, replaced academic upgrading. For the
first time, those involved "were committing themselves completely to
major community action programs...intended to help residents take charge
of their community" (p. 16).

The 1982 report of the Commission d'étude sur la formation des
adultes takes a similar line in granting a fundamental role to basic
education. Inspired by practical American concepts of functional literacy,
basic education emphasizes "the four languages considered essential for a
person to function in a society like ours. These are audiovisual language,
informative language, technical language, and politico-economic language."[19] The acquisition of these languages presupposes proficiency in
speaking, reading and writing skills, in a word, literacy.

The Commission acknowledged, as did the preceding MEQ policy
statement, the existence of a "pure illiteracy" problem in 6.75 percent of
the adult population, and recommended a "literacy campaign" to address
their needs. This campaign was, however, conceived on a short-term basis
(five years) and designed for a minority: the small number of illiterate
adults willing to undergo literacy training. The Commission focussed more
on the problem of "functional illiteracy," which affected a greater number
of adults ("difficult to target"), and thus on the long-term mandate of basic
education, which called for joint action by several partners, such as
businesses, schools, unions, volunteer associations and libraries.

Thus, this report by the "Jean Commission" took the MEQ's action
plan a step further by recommending a systematic, short-term literacy
campaign, carried out in large part by local agencies who were equipped to
"develop independent alternatives to complement current school structures." It went still further by developing a functional literacy concept
different from that of the general education provided by the schools. This
basic education was specific to adult education; it could not be lumped in
with reschooling or confined to the exclusive jurisdiction of school boards.
Apparently, this was going too far too fast.

The next government statement, published two years later, bears witness to this. The 1984 *Continuing Education Program: Policy Statement and Plan of Action* considerably reduced the population of "genuine illiterates," estimating it at 93 000. [20] Of this number, half were likely to enrol in literacy activities, to ensure that they could "earn a living and function in society." [21] Literacy training was perceived as a "functional" survival measure, and thus a priority in popular education (an area which, in the years preceding the report, had suffered drastic budget cuts), along with special programs designed for unemployed or inactive youth, disadvantaged women and the disabled. The action plan focussed not on a literacy campaign but on a learning activity program divided between the public and private sectors "backed by distance education agencies...and by Radio-Québec." The government's educational television network was given the job of raising public awareness, a task which, up until that time, had been carried out by community groups.

As for basic education, after considerable discussion, it was declared equivalent to the secondary school diploma: "the 'vital minimum' of education for each person that we must strive towards" (p. 13). The main priority of this policy was occupational skills training. Even literacy training had its place, constituting "the key to this basic education" (p. 19). However, in the context of the policy, literacy training was considered a special program, outside the usual occupational skills streams. Its status was ambiguous: to teach reading, writing and counting, but from a functional rather than an occupational skills perspective. Independent popular education organizations still played a very important role in literacy training, but their productive association with public institutions was also encouraged.

This policy statement on continuing education, which combines an education policy, a vocational training policy and priority targets (popular education), marked the transition between a specific concept of adult education (Jean Commission) and the concept of "harmonization" between youth and adult education. It also marked the transition between a comprehensive social vision of literacy training, developed in large part outside the school system, and its integration into this system through general education. The ambiguity raised in the policy statement was resolved shortly after its publication, at the implementation stage. The literacy program was integrated into the MEQ's general education program, but a minor role was reserved for independent popular education. The situation remains the same today.

The final document dealing with the harmonization of the youth and adult sectors is the Education Act (Bill 107, 1989), which states that:

> 3. The educational services...shall be provided free
> to residents of Québec...Literacy services and the

> other training services prescribed by the basic school
> regulations (régime pédagogique) shall be provided
> free to residents of Québec...

The basic school regulations, which must be modified for adult education, have not yet been published. However, the speech given by the Minister of Education outlined literacy strategies:

> Publicly financed literacy programs must be goal-oriented...Basic education is provided with the specific objective of enabling adults to acquire skills through secondary-level education.[22]

Popular education is also defined as a socioeducational approach to attaining the same objective. As for the questions and problems specific to literacy training, such as identifying persons in need of assistance and offering better-adapted services, the solutions are not in finding alternatives to the school but in joint action by qualified institutions and associations. In response to the federal government, which would like to intervene in the province's literacy affairs, the Minister stated that "government policy must focus more on development and reinforcement of existing resources than on innovation at any price."

Political discussion on adult education had never been as true to the spirit of the 1966 Parent Report, which recommended widespread (and ideally universal) schooling of Québec adults by the 1970s. In the intervening years other policies and action plans were formulated. Of particular note were the discovery of illiteracy, numerous literacy experiments, and a literacy movement lobbying for a comprehensive joint action plan.[23] A new Act was created, pairing literacy services with universal accessibility to education, a recommendation made by the Jean Commission and which most countries would be financially incapable of implementing today. Considerable budgets and resources were also allocated and their continuing availability is ensured by the current service network...All this boils down to a simple, categorical equation: literacy training equals schooling, and vice versa!

If information were available on the number of former illiterate individuals who now possess a secondary school diploma or who are working towards one, or on the illiterate and semiliterate individuals who plan to do so, it would be obvious that schooling is not the solution to illiteracy, and that literacy training, in the reality of popular cultures, meets other needs and desires, both real and imagined, than academic qualification. This realization is shared by most of those involved in literacy training, although it has not yet been confirmed by studies. Perhaps this lack of statistical proof explains the still widespread belief, 20 years after the Parent Report, that the only way to stamp out illiteracy is through public education.

CURRENT TRENDS

To complement this historical overview of literacy in policy documents, we must enlarge our field of observation, move from theory to practice, and determine linking elements. Although the policies are often definitive, they sometimes bypass the objectives originally targeted to focus on secondary ones.

We are a long way from having accurate figures on the size of the illiterate population and the concept of illiteracy varies from one region to another, so that it is perceived as a mysterious phenomenon rather than a familiar social element. Differences in the numbers determined by separate studies, not to mention the range between minimum and maximum rates found within the same study have done little to dispel the uncertainty concerning the reported extent of the phenomenon.[24] The general public, and this includes the most well-informed groups (journalists, for example), reveals a certain incredulity regarding the prevalence of illiteracy and the danger it represents.

Where illiteracy is still understood in a literal sense and associated with lack of schooling or academic failure, it follows that it would be seen to affect only a minority and not close to one-third of Quebecers, as estimated in a Southam News poll.[25] In other words, literacy training pertains to a limited segment of the population and in no way justifies a specific policy or national campaign. Moreover, the place to provide literacy training is in a school for adults. This is still a far cry from the mass phenomenon of functional illiteracy ("illettrisme"), as interpreted and measured in France, based on the criteria of reading efficiency and speed, and from the concept of functional literacy found in English-speaking countries, based on a skills criterion applied to different communication contexts and not exclusively to rudimentary writing skills in the mother tongue. These differences may explain the fact that Ottawa and Québec City do not always have the same concept of illiteracy and do not attach the same political significance to it.

This leads to the observation that illiteracy is not yet perceived by politicians as a question of national and governmental interest. Rather, it is a concern of education departments, much like certain special education programs for the disabled (in fact, the two are often confused in practice). We have seen this in policy papers; even in the area of education, the issue seemingly does not justify being made a departmental priority worthy of separate treatment. The important issue appears to be youth and adult undereducation, of which illiteracy is merely an extreme case.

The literacy movement, particularly the popular education branch, has lobbied hard to have illiteracy recognized as a problem that goes beyond the confines of education by linking it to employment, social rights, poverty-related policies, etc. It has been all for naught since 1984-1985, however, for the question appears to have been shelved. [26]

The current situation is comparable to that of the 1970s, when the federal government decided to transfer its basic education investments to occupational skills training, leaving literacy training to the provinces. After 10 years of literacy training development in Québec, the tendency was to focus on academic qualification and leave basic literacy training to popular organizations and volunteer associations. Ironically, in 1988, the federal government came out with a national literacy program to assist provincial organizations that were not receiving aid from the provincial governments.

One of the consequences of political noninvolvement is that decisions fall to the administrators of the education structure, who must operate within the limits and in the best interests of their administrative territory, while dealing with decreasing government services. A clearly sector-based portfolio such as literacy has little opportunity to make headway outside of education (in the areas of immigration, social work, manpower, culture, etc.); in fact, it runs the risk of being incorporated into an already existing program that is easily monitored and managed. This is what occurred when literacy training was removed from the marginal popular education context and incorporated into general education.

This had far-reaching consequences for literacy activities as a whole. Popular education suffered severe budget restrictions (activity resources were cut and the independent popular education aid program was frozen), while the budget for training literacy workers increased considerably, in proportion to enrolment. A program management decision would have had a much greater impact on literacy development strategies than a policy document (1984), which, in any case, was invalidated by this decision.

The consequences were inevitable. Once all the resources are invested in a single education program whose sole objective is schooling, the only choices are to subscribe to it or take the volunteer route. A third possibility is to completely ignore other areas and assume that education is the only viable alternative.

One example concerns the independent popular literacy movement. To briefly describe the situation, the popular organizations often have no other choice but to do subcontracting work for educational institutions (literacy activities or training in rural regions, working with immigrants, etc.). There are still very few truly independent organizations that can, for example, offer literacy training in Spanish to recent immigrants and refugees from Central America while enabling them to practise spoken French. It would appear that this is not in keeping with conventional educational practices.

Another example concerns the unions, which have implemented various literacy projects for the benefit of their members or even for the general public. These organizations have their own training services and can thus operate relatively independently. Given that they are not a part of the current network of literacy services, they are not eligible for provincial or federal education grants which are administered by the MEQ. They must be self-financing. Few attempts have been made in this direction, despite the fact that the potential for on-the-job training appears great. School boards, however, are attracted to this market and are attempting to penetrate it.

A final example concerns the immigration phenomenon, although the public library network could also be mentioned. The entire apparatus for providing immigrants with information and training is geared to francization and cultural integration, without taking into account immigrant illiteracy (only a 5 percent rate of illiteracy is recognized) or interculturality, and thus does not include an organization specifically adapted to literacy services in the cultural communities. This responsibility is assigned to the MEQ, whose services are, by definition, universal and nondiscriminatory.

There are few possibilities for diversification with respect to the locations where literacy training is provided, to the literacy trainers themselves or to the types of literacy training provided, although such diversification appears essential if services are to be adapted to widely varying populations, contexts, needs, expectations, and other social programs such as work skills education for young people.[27] **Paradoxically, the new Education Act makes literacy training accessible to all, but its incorporation into the school system is likely to discourage those who would benefit most from it**. This problem is recognized by school board educators; the door is open, but few people make the effort to enter; those who enter rarely stay; and of those who stay, how many have the necessary motivation to continue?[28]

CONCLUSION

For the time being, this fragmented history of literacy training has reached an impasse. Or, like the projects, ideals and developments begun during the Quiet Revolution with the Parent Report, we have come to the end of the story, a story we did not read in terms of illiteracy at the beginning, and which we still avoid reading in terms of literacy training, or "basic education," as the Jean Commission refers to it. "We" in this instance is used in a purely political sense, and this general overview concerns above all policy documents and orientations, not the other powers, participants and instances of literacy training which have contributed to the current situation. They, too, changed history, including politics. Predicting the future necessarily implies taking into account these sociological and political aspects.

From a sociological perspective, the definition of illiteracy, its appellation and boundaries can only be made clearer, either in the radical, literal and pauperist sense of the term, to designate a marginal population (roughly estimated at 10 percent of the adult population) generally excluded not just from language exchanges but also from social exchanges; or, in a broader sense, to include populations unskilled in various communication contexts (professional, civil, private), whether in writing or data processing (in this case, up to one-third of the adult population is illiterate). The second case seems to call for a different designation that better represents the new social perception of a phenomenon which corresponds neither to lack of schooling, academic failure nor social isolation.

The French, UNESCO and many industrialized countries (including Canada) speak of "functional illiteracy"; the term "semiliteracy" has been proposed to refer to those who are minimally literate but who lack writing skills; the term "new illiteracy" has also been used, just as one speaks of "new poverty." Indeed, this recent social phenomenon, which seems to be growing rather than disappearing, is inherent to the postindustrial, or "information" society. [29] It is rarely analyzed, little known (and therefore referred to incorrectly and not easily recognized), and Québec has not yet fully grasped its consequences, made it a major political concern, or searched for new, efficient solutions adapted to the problem.

The narrow definition by which literacy was initially understood gave rise to numerous experiments, both in adult education centres and directly in the adults' environment through popular education. It was here that the literacy movement concentrated its efforts by putting pressure on the government to support and coordinate all the required measures. Ten years later, the political response given — the schooling solution — seems to target eradication of illiteracy through institutionalization, which in turn will result in a higher number of dropouts and the social integration of some, but also a greater number of activities for the school and rationalized system management. Politically speaking, there are no indications of rapid change.

The broader concept of functional literacy, which takes a practical approach to teaching communication skills ("alphabétique," or "literacy for communication"), is just now being introduced. This trend, also known as "new literacy,"[30] is geared more toward vocational education than multi-purpose social action. The current basic literacy program practically excludes it, and it has not yet been included in the various vocational education approaches. This experimental trend requires the investment of several social partners, such as businesses, unions, educational organizations and institutions, universities, community organizations and public authorities. A number of experiments have been attempted outside Québec, notably, in Ontario. Organizations specializing in this type of service have been created; government policies support and promote them; lobby groups from industry have raised the government's awareness of the socioeconomic stakes of this "new literacy"...

We have not yet reached this stage, either sociologically (perceptions, concepts, knowledge and organized action) or politically. But we have come close: the Commission d'étude sur la formation des adultes has already raised the problem in these terms, and has even proposed a method for administering this type of unstructured education: the training credit.[31] The Canadian Institute of Adult Education has also drawn up a highly critical report of Québec's one-dimensional approach, and has recommended a comprehensive literacy plan which could include the two dimensions and the various target populations briefly examined in this document.[32]

From a political point of view, the development of these approaches implies the twofold socioeconomic choice of linking literacy training to a group of control measures against social isolation and to work skills training and lifelong education. First, we could define such an orientation and create experimentation possibilities where needed. In practical terms, the current climate outside the province is favourable to exploration, research, experimentation and contact with new partners and measures: financial aid from the federal government, International Literacy Year, the new literacy strategies which are being formulated on an international level (UNESCO)...Within the province, general sociological conditions constitute a reason for reexamining a theme which has fallen out of favour, despite the spectacular spending increases perpetually invoked by the government as tangible proof of its action. In Québec, a policy remains to be chosen, but as we have seen, opinions vary widely as to the direction such a policy should take.

NOTES

1. *Adapting Schools to Their Milieux, Policy Statement for Schools in Economically Disadvantaged Areas*, Québec City, Ministère de l'Éducation, 1980, p. 100.

2. *ALPHA 78 Compte rendu du séminaire*, Québec City, Ministère de l'Éducation, 1979.

3. Jean-Paul Hautecœur, *Analphabétisme et alphabétisation au Québec*, Québec City, Ministère de l'Éducation, 1978.

4. Robert Verge, *J'ai pas mes lunettes*, Montréal, National Film Board of Canada, 1978.

5. *ALPHA 80 Compte rendu du séminaire*, Québec City, Ministère de l'Éducation, 1981; Regroupement des groupes populaires en alphabétisation, *L'alphabétisation au Québec, situations, recommandations*, report presented to the Commission d'étude sur la formation des adultes, Montréal, 1981.

6. Commission d'étude sur la formation des adultes, *Learning: A Voluntary and Responsible Action, Summary Report*, Gouvernement du Québec, 1982.

7. Regroupement des groupes populaires en alphabétisation au Québec, *La Grande Rencontre-Cahier Alpha-Souvenir*, Montréal, RGPAQ, 1985.

8. Jean-Paul Hautecœur, "Topographie de l'alphabétisation au Québec," *Revue internationale de pédagogie*, (publication in 1990).

9. Jean-Paul Hautecœur, "Historique des pratiques et des politiques en alphabétisation au Québec," *Introduction aux pratiques et politiques en alphabétisation*, J.-P. Hautecœur, ed., Édition André Dugas, Université du Québec à Montréal, 1987.

10. Serge Wagner, "De l'alphabétisation à l'éducation populaire: L'expérience du Carrefour d'éducation populaire de Pointe-St-Charles," *ALPHA 78*, Québec City, Ministère de l'Éducation, 1978.

11. Audrey Thomas, *Adult Basic Education and Literacy Activities in Canada*, Toronto, World Literacy of Canada, 1976; *Adult Literacy in the Seventies: Conference Report*, Toronto, The Movement for Canadian Literacy, 1978.

12. Audrey Thomas, *Adult Illiteracy in Canada — A Challenge*, Ottawa, Canadian Commission for UNESCO, 1983.

13. Reprinted in *Introduction aux pratiques et politiques en alphabétisation*, op. cit., p. 272-76. This resolution was followed in 1984 by specific measures as part of a policy to stamp out illiteracy: "Conclusions du Conseil et des ministres de l'Éducation réunis au sein du Conseil du 4 juin 1984," Annexe XII de *Europe Sociale, Rapport sur la lutte contre l'analphabétisme*, Supplément 2/88, Luxembourg, Office des publications officielles des Communautés européennes, 1988.

    Concerning the 1981 Eastbourne seminar, see Serge Wagner, "L'alphabétisation et les pays industrialisés," *ALPHA 82*, J.-P. Hautecœur, ed., Québec City, Ministère de l'Éducation, 1982.

14. *L'analphabétisme chez les adultes au Canada*, op. cit., p. 71.

15. Jean-Paul Hautecœur, "Le point sur l'alphabétisation au Québec," *Revue internationale d'action communautaire*, 3/43, 1980.

16. *Report of the Royal Commission of Inquiry on Education in the Province of Québec*, Gouvernement du Québec, 1966, vol. 5, p. 45.

17. "School instruction was not necessary in these [manufacturing] trades...At this technological stage, the economy could easily make use of a population with little education, or even one that was illiterate. The 1871 census tells us that in Québec 40 per cent of the men over twenty could neither read nor write." Ibid., 1963, vol. 1, p. 61.

18. *Adapting Schools to Their Milieux*, op. cit., p. 5-16.

19. *Learning: A Voluntary and Responsible Action*, op. cit., p. 16.

20. These estimates, which differ from previous estimates based on the declared enrolment figures, are taken from an MEQ survey by Robert Maheu and Claude St-Germain: *L'analphabétisme au Québec, résultats d'un sondage*, Québec City, Ministère de l'Éducation, 1984. The publication of this survey aroused bitter disputes. For a critical analysis, see Jean-Paul Hautecœur, "Sondage léger, conclusions lourdes," *ALPHA 86*, J.-P. Hautecœur, ed., Québec City, Ministère de l'Éducation, 1986.

21. *Continuing Education Program: Policy Statement and Plan of Action*, Gouvernement du Québec, 1984 (p. 13).

22. *L'alphabétisation, facteur de développement*, speech given by Claude Ryan, Minister of Education, at the annual convention of the Association canadienne d'éducation de langue française, Québec City, 9 August 1989.

23. Andrée Boucher, *En toutes lettres et en français. L'analphabétisme et l'alphabétisation des francophones au Canada*, Montréal, Institut canadien d'éducation des adultes, 1989.

24. The Minister of Education expressed this doubt as follows: "The trend toward easy demagogy and alarmism should be avoided...Certain illiteracy statistics which are often cited should be examined with some reservations. For example, when it is stated that illiteracy affects close to one-third of Québec's population, I remain skeptical." *L'alphabétisation, facteur de développement*," op. cit.

25. *Literacy in Canada — A Research Report*, prepared for Southam News, Ottawa, by the Creative Research Group, Toronto, 1987.

26. The report of the Canadian Institute of Adult Education sees this as being the Québec literacy movement's chief obstacle: "the political will must be there if the current situation is to improve." *En toutes lettres et en français*, op. cit., p. 75.

27. The Canadian Institute reached a similar conclusion: "There is no excuse for not using all available means to reach illiterate adults in their life environment, such as offering various training locations. The narrow-minded attitude toward new, important partners (such as trade unions) is completely incomprehensible." Ibid., p. 79.

28. Jean-Paul Hautecœur, "Generous Supply, Barred Demand: The Current Paradox of Literacy," *Adult Literacy Perspectives*, Maurice Taylor and James Draper, eds., Toronto, Culture Concept Inc., 1988, p. 129-41.

29. This fact is now acknowledged by political leaders, although not long ago it was believed that the problem of illiteracy would solve itself. See the Québec Minister of Education's speech, cited earlier, and that of André Laignel, French Secretary of State for Vocational Training, given before the Standing Committee on the Struggle Against Illiteracy, 25 October 1988: "Not only have we not stamped out illiteracy, but we are likely to witness the growth of this phenomenon in our society, along with all the dangers inherent in it."

30. "Literacy no longer simply means the ability to read and write. Now it means the ability to meet demands new technologies place on us: for increasingly sophisticated reading, writing and numeracy skills." *Literacy: The Basics of Growth*, Toronto, Ministry of Skills Development, Government of Ontario, 1989, (p. 5). See also Jean Pierre Vélis' article in this volume.

31. France is moving toward this type of educational organization, linking the social and vocational phases through a training credit. "The struggle against illiteracy requires a comprehensive skills development policy developed for the population in their environment...The struggle against isolation in any shape or form could be considered our social phase, which alone would justify our action. It is all the more important that such action be taken as isolation threatens progress. This struggle is a social necessity; not to carry it out would be a social injustice...Within this complex strategy, lifelong vocational education plays a major role..." André Laignel, op. cit.

32. "Insufficient in Québec, the sole strategy of quantitative resource allocation in a single network, without a global plan, limits access to literacy training...It appears important to us to consider diversified strategies adapted to the environments we wish to reach, and which take into account the various *categories* of illiterate persons." *En toutes lettres et en français*, op. cit., p. 136-37.

LITERACY AND THE ASSIMILATION OF MINORITIES: THE CASE OF FRANCOPHONES IN CANADA

Serge Wagner
Université du Québec à Montréal

Adult literacy training is a recent phenomenon that began to develop in industrialized countries during the 1980s. Many nations initially focussed on providing literacy services to recent immigrants, but quickly realized that a portion of their native population was also illiterate, despite the fact that education was compulsory and had been made widely accessible.

To date a number of studies have shed light on the relationship between class division and illiteracy. However, little attention has been given to the phenomenon of industrialized countries that have ethnolinguistic minorities among which the percentage of illiteracy is proportionally higher than in the majority group. In many cases these minorities find it extremely difficult to preserve their cultural and linguistic heritage, especially because the school system often contributes to their children's assimilation. Fewer studies have concentrated on the relationship between adult literacy training and the assimilation of minorities, particularly minorities who enjoy some type of official status. While illiteracy and literacy provision among ethnolinguistic minorities appear to be a major aspect of the phenomenon of illiteracy observed in several industrialized countries, they do not seem to have been the focus of detailed national studies. (In fact "national" studies tend to deal primarily with the situation of the dominant majority group and give only partial or incidental consideration to that of minorities.)

In industrialized countries literacy is generally provided in the dominant language, i.e., the language of political life and, perhaps above all, of social, cultural and economic life. It is significant that the UNESCO position on the primacy of mother-tongue literacy has had very little impact in industrialized countries, where the desire to integrate and the demands of economic survival make literacy in the dominant language a premise that is rarely questioned.

It is interesting to note the place reserved for Canada's francophone minority in the policies and practices of jurisdictions other than Québec. Canadian francophones constitute an official minority under the Constitution and accordingly enjoy constitutional protection with respect to the education of children. This protection does not, however, extend to adult education and literacy. Francophones participate proportionally less than anglophones in adult literacy activities, since these are for the most part conducted in English. *Systemic discrimination* at least partially explains this situation, and some provinces are beginning to address the need for affirmative action under certain programs.

It should also be noted that language and culture are the main distinguishing features of most francophones in Canada. Unlike visible minorities (Amerindians, Inuit, blacks, etc.) they do not share common physical features which set them apart from the anglophone majority.

Linguistic affiliation is therefore a distinctive characteristic that determines their cultural reality — a situation which further underscores the importance of providing mother-tongue literacy services.

In this paper we will examine the situation in Canada as a whole. We will then look more specifically at Ontario, which has the largest francophone population outside Québec. We will see how preserving one's mother tongue can be a complex undertaking and how several factors jointly contribute to the assimilation process. We will also take a look at Ontario's recent policy on literacy training, which recognizes the right to community-based literacy programs that respect the language and culture of the French-speaking minority, and will give an overview of the development of an original literacy model.

THE SITUATION IN CANADA AS A WHOLE

Overview

Although Canada has been populated for thousands of years by Amerindians and Inuit, the country was officially discovered by the French in 1534 and came under British rule in 1760. Settlement by francophones occurred primarily in the 16th and 17th centuries. Canada's French-speaking minority is therefore a well-established society that became a minority during the 19th century, when it acquired certain constitutional rights. To some extent Confederation (1867) set the tone for relations between Canada's two main linguistic communities. Francophones form a minority in all Canadian provinces except Québec, where they are increasingly concentrated.[1] In addition, because education is a matter of provincial jurisdiction, the francophones in this country have had to wage, and continue to wage, tremendous battles over schooling. In the 19th and 20th centuries, francophones gradually lost political and legal power, particularly in the field of education. In several of the provinces with anglophone majorities, the rights of francophones in educational matters have been abolished, restricted or simply not recognized.[2]

In 1987 the federal Commissioner of Official Languages observed that demographic data from successive censuses confirmed the "steady erosion" of French-language society:

> There is no doubt that French has been steadily losing ground to English in Canada since the Second World War. From some 29 percent of the mother-tongue population in 1951, it had dwindled to roughly 25 percent in 1986 and looks likely to fall even further by the year 2000 (p. 12).

The Commissioner also noted that French seemed to maintain a solid position only in Québec and northern New Brunswick, while francophone minorities seemed to be on the decline "virtually everywhere else" (p. 13). It is therefore not surprising that illiteracy rates are relatively higher within the French-speaking community.

Data on illiteracy among francophones

The definition of illiteracy and the question of related statistics have been the focus of discussion and controversy both in Canada and around the world. Regardless of the data considered, however, the statistics point to a difficult situation for francophones in Canada.

In 1987 the Creative Research Group conducted a survey of 2398 Canadians in which the subjects took aptitude tests in reading, writing and arithmetic. The survey was based on an American study carried out by National Assessment of Education Progress (1986). The results of the Canadian survey showed a major illiteracy problem among francophones.

— The rate of illiteracy among francophones is 29 percent, compared with 23 percent among anglophones (p. 61).

— Québec accounts for 26 percent of the Canadian population, but 31 percent of illiterate Canadians (ibid).

— Francophones "perform" at 88 percent of the level of anglophones (p. 28).

Other statistics focus more on the schooling of individuals. Data based on these criteria also confirm the extent of illiteracy among francophones.

Table 1

Canada. Population 15 Years and Over Not Attending School Full Time, by Mother Tongue and Highest Level of Schooling, 1981
(Based on 20 % Sample Data)

	Did Not Complete Grade 5		Grades 5-8	
English	195 215	2.0 %	1 224 870	12.7 %
French	276 070	6.4 %	1 014 350	23.7 %
Native languages	24 585	28.8 %	28 570	33.4 %
Non-status Indians	3 075	21.1 %	4 085	28.1 %
Other mother tongues	276 700	11.3 %	617 240	25.2 %
TOTAL	775 650	4.7 %	2 889 115	17.5 %

Source: Statistics Canada SPC81B92

According to these data the gap between the schooling of francophones and anglophones is even greater than indicated in the Southam poll on literacy skills. It should also be noted that, even in Québec, where francophones form the majority, the francophone group is much less educated than the English-speaking minority, as indicated by Table 2.

Table 2

Québec. Population 15 Years and Over Not Attending School Full Time, by Mother Tongue and Highest Level of Schooling, 1981 (Percentage) (Based on 20% Sample Data)

	Did Not Complete Grade 5	Grades 5-8
English	3.3 %	15.3 %
French	6.2 %	23.6 %
Total population	6.6 %	22.9 %

Source: Statistics Canada SPC81B92

This overview of the illiteracy and education level of Canadian francophones indicates major gaps and thus emphasizes the pressing need for literacy and basic education programs for this group. These gaps also mask another reality, particularly important outside Québec: large numbers of francophones attend English-language schools, and this contributes heavily to their assimilation. A study by the Commission nationale des parents francophones showed that outside New Brunswick, Ontario and Manitoba "only 8.4 percent of francophone students...[were] currently enrolled in French schools" (quoted in Commissioner of Official Languages, 1987: 202). The study also showed that half of all young francophones outside Québec were not being educated in French as guaranteed by the *Canadian Charter of Rights and Freedoms* (*La Presse*, February 27, 1989).

Combination of factors

A number of studies in Canada and other countries have demonstrated that illiteracy has more than one cause. It is also clear that schools must be considered both a factor and a symptom of illiteracy.

The economic inferiority of French Canadians is one of the major historical factors which explain the poor development of educational services. French Canadian society was rural, and even in the urban and primarily French Québec of the 1960s, economic power was concentrated among the anglophone minority.[3] In both rural and urban areas employment was distributed among the classes in a way that partially corresponded to the ethnolinguistic division of society. If francophones were less educated, this was also a reflection of the social position that most of them occupied.[4]

Alone, however, the situation of French Canadians in relation to the dominant anglophone group does not account for this state of affairs. One of the main features of traditional francophone society was the polarization between an educated, middle-class clerical elite and a largely uneducated majority. School was not perceived as a fundamental necessity for the "people" and, historically, was valued by the elite primarily because of the role it could play in preserving religion. The traditional francophone elite was greatly concerned with preserving the Catholic faith and viewed the French language mainly as an instrument to this end. (This attitude was not unique to francophone society, and has been noted by Cippola [1969] and others[5] in various Western Catholic societies.) It seems significant for French Canadian society that the law making education compulsory was not passed in Québec until 1942; Québec was probably one of the last industrialized societies to enact such legislation.

Illiteracy and lack of schooling among francophones can also be seen as the result of opposition to and rejection of a dominant culture (usually English in Canada) that did not mesh with the social, cultural and linguistic vision of the "French Canadian people" (Wagner 1987: 11; Boucher 1989). In their frequent struggles to obtain education in French, many francophones chose to keep their children at home rather than send them to English-language schools, where in some cases government and educational authorities had outlawed the use of French.

Constitutional and educational rights (late)

Since education is a matter of provincial jurisdiction in Canada, francophones have had the greatest difficulty gaining access to French-language schools in provinces other than Québec. Although the *Constitution Act, 1867* and other fundamental laws such as the *Manitoba Act* of 1870, the *Northwest Territories Act* of 1891 and the *Saskatchewan Act* of 1905 recognized that francophones in some provinces had certain political and educational rights, these rights were either abolished or simply not respected. It was not until 1985 that the Supreme Court of Canada, about to rule on Québec's recent Bill 101 (which made French the official language of that province), "discovered" the almost-century-old illegality of laws limiting the use of French in some provinces.

The objective educational difficulties of francophones in Canada were noted by the OECD in its *Examination of National Policies for Education* (1976):

> The essential difficulty stems from the fact that, although French is considered on an equal footing with English as one of Canada's two official languages, it does not enjoy equal standing. Implicitly or explicitly, the francophone minority in Canada, faced with the risk of anglicization, requires special protection greater than that afforded by official equality (p. 65). [Free translation]

In any event the *Canadian Charter of Rights and Freedoms* (1982), which is entrenched in Canada's new constitution, guarantees English and French linguistic minorities the right to education in the minority language (section 23). This provision invalidated certain provisions of Québec's Bill 101, but at the same time granted rights to the francophone minority outside Québec.

As stated earlier, even with the legislation passed in 1982, Canada's francophones were still not assured of universal access to education in French. But francophones are increasingly demanding all-French schools, i.e., schools that serve only francophone students, thus calling into question the services of "immersion" schools that offer instruction in French to student populations often composed of a majority of young anglophones. As these students use English as the language of communication in school, immersion schools may be hastening the anglicization of the francophones who attend them (Bordeleau 1988; Churchill et al. 1987; Cummins 1983).

Hoping to make French-language schools true institutions of cultural development in French, francophone communities outside Québec are increasingly demanding not only all-French schools, but also control over these schools and the boards that manage them. These demands are currently before the Supreme Court of Canada.

Ironically rights are being accorded to francophones at a time when the assimilation process is largely complete, as life in French has disappeared in many communities and modern Canadian society is literally inundated with English culture and communications media.

Education and adult literacy

Given the ground that must be made up, the development of French-language literacy programs is a necessary complement to French-language elementary and secondary education. For some adults whose mother tongue is French but who received a minimal education in English, French-language literacy activities constitute a relearning of the French language.

From this perspective francophone adults are discriminated against on two counts. First, current literacy programs are not widely available except perhaps in Québec. A 1985 study by the Department of the Secretary of State of Canada confirmed that the rate of participation in adult education programs increased with the level of schooling already completed. In 1983 only 5 percent of those with less than grade 9 took adult education courses (p. 13).

The same study showed that francophone access to adult education was also limited: at 21 percent, anglophones recorded the highest rate of participation, compared with 19 percent for francophones and 18 percent for francophones outside Québec. And access to literacy training *in French* is even more limited, as French-language literacy programs are still very rare outside Québec, Ontario and New Brunswick. This was noted by the Fédération des francophones hors Québec (FFHQ) as early as 1983, when there were practically no French-language literacy activities at all outside Québec. More recently Andrée Boucher, in her study on French-language literacy activities in Canada (1989), confirms my own findings (Wagner 1988a: 15): these activities are available for the most part in Québec, Ontario and New Brunswick. As for the other provinces, there are

> absolutely no French-language literacy programs in Nova Scotia, British Columbia, the Northwest Territories, the Yukon and, until very recently, Saskatchewan; local development projects are very limited in Manitoba, Newfoundland, Alberta and, until very recently, Prince Edward Island (p. 357). [Free translation]

The constitutional right of young people to elementary and secondary education in French does not extend to adult education. It is obvious that, where provinces fail to offer French-language literacy services, there is *de facto* discrimination against francophones. But even where such services are offered, to date they have not been designed to meet the needs of illiterate francophones. Many provinces say they are willing to provide literacy services in French, but claim there is no demand. This situation suggests the existence of systemic discrimination, which is generally defined as a form of unintentional discrimination that is rooted in the management system and management practices; these may appear neutral but actually have potentially discriminatory effects on the members of a particular social group. A recent development resulting from antidiscrimination studies and policies is the use of statistical methods to demonstrate unlawful discrimination, in particular systemic discrimination (Knopff 1986). Needless to say systemic discrimination is just as unacceptable as intentional discrimination against individuals.

Whether discrimination is intentional or systemic, the solution lies in *affirmative action* programs. These are needed for illiterate people in general but, for ethnolinguistic minorities, they are essential. A recent study on the educational needs of Franco-Ontarians accurately defined the problem.

> People who did not go beyond elementary school are the most difficult to reach with the methods current- ly used for adult education in community colleges and other institutions: since almost all these individ- uals are unaccustomed to studying, instruction must be geared to their specific aptitudes. A "neutral" approach, providing services only to those who come forward to request them, is tantamount to a refusal to provide assistance: discouragement and a fatalistic view of the formal education system are so common they cannot be ignored. We can easily see the value of an active approach if we consider the costs society must assume because some of its mem- bers lack a certain level of education. These costs relate especially to unemployment (which affects the illiterate population first): unemployment insurance benefits, welfare, health care, etc. For the well- being of the individuals concerned and of society as a whole, it is important to adopt community- development methods and to coordinate all types of educational and social services in each region or community (Churchill et al. 1987: 162-63). [Free translation]

While the situation of illiterate francophones outside Québec ap- pears tragic, recent initiatives suggest an imminent change in the area of French-language literacy programming. Literacy activities have been developed in French for Franco-Ontarians and New Brunswick Acadians, while projects are getting under way in other provinces. This change is primarily the result of the French-speaking community taking greater responsibility for illiteracy (especially in French Ontario and New Bruns- wick). Further, francophones in Canada are trying to work together to deal with this issue (the study by the Institut canadien d'éducation des adultes and the FFHQ is a particularly good example of this). Finally, since 1987, when the Department of the Secretary of State became involved in literacy, francophones outside Québec have been assured of vital support in this area.

ILLITERACY AND LITERACY PROGRAMMING IN FRENCH ONTARIO

Ontario has the largest francophone population outside Québec and has been the site of the greatest developments in the areas of illiteracy and literacy programming. In many respects the development of literacy in French Ontario seems to be indicative of the problems facing francophone communities throughout Canada. But we also view Ontario as an excellent example of how a community can decide to take action and find innovative ways of initiating literacy programs.

The following is a brief outline of the historical context of illiteracy and the first attempts to provide literacy training.

Historical context

Ontario's French-speaking minority is among the national minorities in Canada that have experienced difficulties in the 20th century.[6] While Ontario's francophone community can trace its roots to the earliest days of settlement in Canada, and while it increased considerably in size in the 19th century, its very existence was called into doubt in the late 19th and early 20th centuries. *Instruction Circular 17*, also known as **Regulation 17**, which in 1912 made English the chief language of education in Ontario, represents only one episode in a series of conflicts between the French minority and an Anglo-Saxon majority determined to limit the rights of that minority. In Ontario education accounted for most of the battles that were waged in public. It is interesting to note that the main Franco-Ontarian movement, the Association canadienne-française d'éducation de l'Ontario (ACFEO), founded in 1910, saw its concerns as relating primarily to education, and that it was not until 1969 that its name was changed to the Association canadienne-française de l'Ontario (ACFO), thus reflecting a desire to consider the minority situation in a broader context.

Generally the struggle for "French survival" lost ground as, owing to unjust laws and the pressure of market forces, a significant proportion of the francophone population became anglicized and assimilated into the English-speaking majority. The minority status of Franco-Ontarians intensified in the second half of the century. By 1981 the French-mother-tongue population represented only 5.5 percent of the total population of Ontario, and in reality only 3.9 percent of Ontarians habitually spoke French (*Les francophones tels qu'ils sont*, 1985). (The francophone population fell to 5.3 percent in 1986, whereas francophones had accounted for approximately 15 percent of the Ontario population in the 1950s.) Today Franco-Ontarians are concentrated primarily in outlying regions of the province (particularly in the East and North), where they account for a considerable proportion of the regional populations.

Precisely when the francophone community was declining in numbers, it experienced a burst of renewed vitality. At first this was no more than the normal reaction of a minority under attack and using every ounce of its strength to resist assimilation and extinction. In the 1970s in particular the Franco-Ontarian minority began to make gains. Initially federal government interest in French-speaking Canadians led the Ontario government to focus concern on Franco-Ontarians and to grant this group certain rights. Federal initiatives included the Royal Commission of Inquiry on Bilingualism and Biculturalism (1963-1981), the *Official Languages Act* of 1969, and major involvement of the Department of the Secretary of State in cultural and linguistic matters beginning in the mid-1960s, etc.

Changes in Ontario's policies were fewer and slower to come about. Francophones were recognized as an official minority by the federal government, but the Ontario government refused to follow suit. The past 20 years have been marked by legal and political battles, and by gradual victories for the recognition of the French fact and the rights of francophones. In 1961, for example, a number of secondary school boards were given permission to teach Latin in French on an experimental basis. It was not until 1963 that French was authorized as the language of instruction in grades 9 and 10 — "at the discretion of the school principal"! And it was only in 1965 that the Minister of Education announced that French-language curriculums could be used for Latin, History and Geography throughout the secondary school system — at the discretion of local school boards (Choquette 1980: 202). In Ontario today there are more immersion schools for anglophones than French schools for francophones.

Since the mid-1970s, however, a veritable "Quiet Revolution" has been taking place within the francophone community. This evolutionary process first took root in the field of education.[7] The French minority fought for access to education, first at the elementary level, then at the secondary. Nor did the fight end there, for the current goal is to obtain access at the postsecondary level (colleges and universities). Very rapidly francophones demanded not only access to French-language education and counselling services, but also the right to manage their own education services. They officially contested the existence of bilingual institutions (certain colleges of applied arts and technology, commonly referred to as "community colleges"). Franco-Ontarians only recently obtained a commitment on the creation of the first francophone community college, with a major financial contribution from the federal government.

The struggle has also spread into areas other than education. In 1983-1984 ACFO adopted a development plan for the francophone community, setting out community development objectives in 12 different sectors of activity. The plan called for the right to live and obtain services in French in all aspects of life in Ontario. This right was to be partially recognized by the *French Language Services Act, 1986* and the creation of a French-language TVOntario network in 1987.

Franco-Ontarians are thus currently faced with a one-step-at-a-time attitude on the part of government, just when they are taking a broader and more clearly defined view of their overall development.

Illiteracy and literacy programs

Illiteracy is a major problem in French Ontario. The limited access for francophones to a full system of French-language education, combined with other factors which we are unable to examine in this paper, has resulted in a very high number of illiterate and undereducated people among the francophone population (see Table 3).

Table 3

Francophones (Mother Tongue) and Non-francophones (Mother Tongue other than French) 15 Years and Over, by Level of Schooling

| | Francophones | | Non-francophones | |
	Total	%	Total	%
Total all schooling	383 305	100.0	6 266 410	100.0
Less than grade 5	21 120	5.5	219 555	3.5
Grades 5-8	78 575	20.5	841 080	13.4
Grades 9-10	64 920	17.0	987 580	15.8
Grades 11-13	92 720	24.1	1 701 235	27.1
Postsecondary (other than university)	76 675	20.0	1 442 640	23.0
University degree	49 295	12.9	1 074 320	17.1

Source: 1981 Census, data published by Ministry of Citizenship and Culture

We have already referred to a number of factors that underlie the high rate of illiteracy among Franco-Ontarians. The combination of these factors is largely responsible for the low rate of schooling and the high dropout rate for this population group.

Table 4

Comparison of Populations with Fewer than 9 Years of Schooling in 1981, Ontario and Regions: Francophones and Non-francophones (Language Spoken at Home) Aged 25 to 64

	Francophones		Non-francophones	
	Total	%	Total	%
Ontario	50 355	31.2	685 966	16.8
East	18 436	25.2	66 744	13.1
Northeast	21 665	39.5	44 330	20.5
Centre	6 305	26.9	448 635	16.8
Southwest	2 395	33.8	103 680	17.5
Northwest	1 290	45.7	22 200	20.8

Source: 1981 Census, quoted in Churchill (1987: 184), based on the data in Guindon (1985: 30)

More is involved, of course, than just the general situation of Franco-Ontarians. Factors more specific to each region, and sometimes to each community, help explain the phenomenon of illiteracy and undereducation. The specific situation in each region must be analyzed because the variance in some instances is considerable, as shown in Table 4.

It was stated earlier that, in most industrialized countries, illiterate people occupy the lower ranks of the social scale and are often marginalized with respect to their society. Various effects of this nature have already resulted from illiteracy and undereducation among Franco-Ontarians. A recent ACFO study, *Les francophones tels qu'ils sont* (1986), explores the consequences of illiteracy.

> **Low education reduces the chances of finding a job**. Only 50 percent of francophone men 15 years of age and older with less than grade 9 worked full time in 1980, compared with 74 percent of those with grade 9 or higher. The gap is even wider among francophone women: barely 15 percent of illiterate women held full-time jobs in 1980, compared with 42 percent of those with more education (p. 31). [Free translation]

A June 1987 survey done for the Ontario government revealed that 37 percent of the respondents of French origin stated that the need for literacy was a "serious problem" in Ontario, compared with 30 percent of the respondents of British origin. In addition 44 percent of the respondents of French origin reported knowing someone who had difficulty reading and writing in everyday life, compared with 34 percent of the respondents of British origin (Environics Research Group 1987).

Illiteracy and undereducation are without question the biggest adult education problems within the francophone minority, yet awareness of the nature and scope of the problem is recent and still limited.

Considering Ontario society as a whole the issue of illiteracy among francophones has never been addressed in general studies on adult education. For example, the 1981 report *Continuing Education: The Third System* raised the problem of basic training in the province, provided quantitative data and noted the high percentages of people with little education in communities like Sudbury (p. 39), without mentioning the extent of illiteracy in certain ethnocultural communities. References to the situation of francophones were limited to a brief, separate section which stated in general terms that the lack of programs in French was a major linguistic and cultural obstacle for Ontario francophones (p. 80). It was not until 1986 that a government document (*For Adults Only*) accurately described the problem of illiteracy among Franco-Ontarians and the limited access to French-language basic education services from either the Ministry of Education or the Ministry of Colleges and Universities.

Until very recently the Franco-Ontarian community had also largely glossed over the problem of illiteracy and the need for a sustained literacy effort. This doubtless stems from the fact that Franco-Ontarian community organizations have traditionally been involved primarily in formal education. Another reason may be that much of the community's effort was devoted to the struggle for elementary and secondary education and, in latter years, postsecondary education. This disinterest may also be a manifestation of embarrassment about illiteracy and the fact that francophones are behind in terms of basic education; francophone organizations have more readily highlighted the deficiencies in college and university education. It should also be added that the elite within the minority have historically shown little interest in the fate of those with less education. Yet another reason for the minimal concern for literacy is the nature of illiteracy itself and the complexity of literacy activities. Illiteracy is a problem entailing more than education; there are linguistic, social, cultural and political aspects to consider as well. It is now known that the key to literacy does not lie in education alone (i.e., illiteracy cannot be solved by formal education systems alone) - and this is especially true for ethnic minorities.

Limited initiatives

In recent years there has been some effort in Ontario to provide literacy activities in French for francophones. The last 10 years have seen a series of social agencies take an interest in the matter. First, a number of

school boards offered basic education activities in French for several years but never succeeded in reaching a significant number of francophones. Data compiled by the Ministry of Education in 1983 and referred to in the report *For Adults Only* showed that in the fall of 1983 only 100 people were enrolled in French-language basic education classes offered by school boards, compared with an enrollment of 6562 in English-language classes (p. 45). In other words the school boards were reaching only about 1.2 percent of the French-speaking population, although francophones accounted for more than 5 percent of the total population of the province and functional illiteracy was twice as high among francophones as among anglophones (ibid.).

Among **community colleges** (most of which are anglophone and none of which are francophone) Algonquin College was apparently the only one offering basic education in French in the 1970s. Only after francophone employees of the **Ministry of Colleges and Universities** intervened was an experimental program set up in six community colleges in 1982-1983. The program, however, remained experimental and was influenced by the one-to-one approach of the "Anglo-Saxon" model; it never managed to reach a significant number of francophones.

Next to become involved in literacy was the **Franco-Ontarian community movement**. An experimental community project independent of the community colleges was set up in Hawkesbury in 1982. The Comité d'alphabétisation Prescott-Russell was established and set about defining illiteracy as a primarily sociocultural problem requiring a popular socioeducational approach. The project was influenced by the model being tested at the time by popular literacy groups in Québec. The committee took the name Alfa-Action and planned to organize a literacy campaign in eastern Ontario, bringing the problem of illiteracy among Franco-Ontarians to the attention of community leaders and the general public. Alfa-Action's legacy included *Le Monde des mots*, a project at Algonquin College in Ottawa which in reality had been introduced in 1978 as the "French version" of the College's English-language basic education program *People, Words and Change*. *Le Monde des mots* adopted a more community-oriented structure in 1984 and subsequently changed its name to *La Magie des lettres*. For many years, however, these community-based/popular initiatives also remained outside the mainstream.

In the mid-1980s literacy provision among Franco-Ontarians reached a plateau. Three models were tested, but none was developed to a significant degree.

A new policy

In September 1986 the Ontario government unveiled a five-year **basic adult literacy action plan**, under which $20 million was to be spent each year. The initiative involved 14 government ministries and agencies in all, although three key players were identified: the Ministry of Citizenship and Culture was given primary responsibility for the overall government initiative and was to administer the new Ontario Community Literacy program (OCL); the Ministry of Skills Development was to organize literacy activities geared to vocational training (provided by community colleges), while the Ministry of Education (through school boards) was to continue offering basic and presecondary programs.

As for the **language of literacy** the new policy stated that the government's aim was to promote literacy in both of Canada's official languages and that the linguistic and cultural reality of the province's francophone population would be recognized in all provincial literacy programs.

The new OCL program had two components: Component A, for literacy projects, was restricted to groups that had been offering literacy activities for more than a year; Component B was designed specifically for developing groups. This program structure potentially put francophone groups at a disadvantage (no more than three groups could meet the Component A criterion) in relation to anglophone groups, which were considerably more numerous and had been involved in literacy for many years.

Francophones held public demonstrations immediately after the government's policy was announced. In January 1987 the Ministry of Citizenship and Culture hired a francophone coordinator for the OCL program (and then a female Amerindian coordinator). The result was an astounding combination of the community model that had begun to materialize in eastern Ontario and the resources that had been made possible through the French aspect of the OCL program.

In only a few months a number of seed groups were created. The francophone coordinator accomplished a great deal in terms of organization and development. A number of regional ACFO groups became involved in literacy programming (particularly in northern, eastern and southwestern Ontario). The survival of a number of literacy projects created under the special Ministry of Colleges and Universities program in community colleges is to some extent due to the OCL program!

The number of local groups funded through the program increased rapidly:

1986-1987:   4 groups
1987-1988: 18 groups
1988-1989: 20 groups

Reluctance in government and among francophones

Since most French-language activities are organized on a grass-roots basis, government ministries are somewhat hesitant about the growing scope of the francophone program. Should the program not confine itself to providing funds for groups? Is it necessary to design and set up support programs (documentation, teacher training, etc.) that would also be geared to the francophone community? Are Ontario's literacy coalitions not officially bilingual, and would it not therefore be appropriate to refuse funding for the unilingual French groups that have begun to form?

The French-speaking community is equally surprised with the rapid growth of the literacy movement. Local community groups are beginning to work together on a regional basis. Isolated in widely separated regions francophone organizers are demanding adapted resources and a specific forum in which to cooperate. A first methodological publication has appeared, and the groups are carrying out and publishing their own community studies.

After the provincial election in 1987 the Ontario government announced that primary responsibility for literacy in Ontario and for the OCL program was being transferred from the Ministry of Citizenship and Culture to the Ministry of Skills Development. This change, planned for the winter of 1988, raised a great deal of concern both for community-based literacy activities in general and for literacy activities among Franco-Ontarians in particular. While the Ministry of Citizenship and Culture had traditionally been involved in local communities, often in a relatively informal way, and had proven relatively sensitive to the aspirations of francophones, the Ministry of Skills Development seemed to have stronger ties with private enterprise and appeared rather insensitive to the needs of the French-language minority.

The "Alpha-Partage '88" symposium

Early in 1988 the Ministry of Skills Development agreed in principle to a francophone symposium that would be arranged jointly with the ACFO and supported by an organizing committee made up of community representatives. "Alpha-Partage '88" was held in Ottawa in May 1988 and attracted more than 175 participants.

The numerous workshops held as part of the symposium provided an opportunity to reflect on all aspects of illiteracy and literacy programming. More generally the participants considered the objectives and meaning of French-language literacy, the methods, approaches and content of literacy programs, and the future of the community movement, which was still very much feeling its way.

The symposium was open to everyone concerned by literacy, but was dominated by community groups. In their final recommendations, the participants sought to ensure follow-up, particularly at the community network level. Specifically, there were calls for:

— the creation of a community network of francophone groups;

— greater commitment from the francophone community and the ACFO;

— a greater contribution from the French-language network of TVOntario;

— the creation of a Franco-Ontarian literacy resource centre;

— pay for OCL teachers;

— another "Alpha-Partage" symposium for 1989.

The participants elected a follow-up committee of regional representatives to act on their recommendations.

Learner participation

More than a dozen learners, enrolled in community group literacy workshops, took part in "Alpha-Partage '88." At the end of the symposium some of them joined together to prepare an evaluation. They expressed satisfaction at having had the opportunity to attend the meeting, but were critical of the fact that they had been given a very small role. They made specific demands for the next symposium, asking that learners be identified, that they have greater representation and that a half day be devoted to them. They also requested that a learners' group be formed and that a representative be appointed to speak on their behalf. One learner was therefore elected to the follow-up committee.

A busy fall

The weeks following the symposium were extremely busy. In June, at the 39th general meeting of the ACFO, literacy advocates won general approval in principle for the 12 points in the summary report on "Alpha-Partage"! In September TVOntario launched a series of videos on literacy. In August community groups organized a postcard campaign to protest the low level of funding they received. On 8 September, International Literacy Day, francophone groups demonstrated during the announcement of the Canadian literacy policy by the Prime Minister of Canada; they also held discussions with the Secretary of State and marched in front of Queen's

Park (seat of the Ontario government). In October production began on a series of methodological documents.

And in December 1988 the groups formed the Regroupement des groupes d'alphabétisation populaire en Ontario.

ACCOMPLISHMENTS TO DATE

It is still early to give a full account of the Franco-Ontarian experience. We can, however, make a number of observations.

Recognition of illiteracy and the right to literacy

The Ontario government has for a number of years shown an interest in the question of illiteracy. Within the context of the last year, the largely Anglo-Saxon government was to a certain extent forced to grant some official recognition to the unique aspects of illiteracy and of literacy needs among francophones.

ACFO, which officially represents the interests and demands of the Franco-Ontarian community, has gradually become involved in the literacy debate. This involvement implies that the traditional Franco-Ontarian elite has formally, if only recently, recognized the problem of illiteracy within their community. Until very recently literacy was not considered a priority issue for the francophone community by that community's main "national" organizations, ACFO included. Militant literacy advocates have taken up the cause over the past few years and have succeeded in bringing the matter to the attention of various players in the Franco-Ontarian community.

Recognizing the importance of literacy among Franco-Ontarians also means acknowledging the fact that academic upgrading programs for young people (undertaken recently) are not enough and that it would be better to adopt the dual strategy of educating young people and providing literacy training for adults.

Recognizing the reality of illiteracy and undereducation and, in corollary, the necessity of making a commitment to promoting adult literacy, means concretely recognizing the significant portion of the Franco-Ontarian minority that has historically been marginalized not only by the state but also by its own elite. Encouraging the Franco-Ontarian minority to accept some of the responsibility for increasing literacy among its members entails a new, demanding commitment — very different to the lobbying of government agencies. Taking an active part in literacy means becoming directly involved, right in the core of that silent segment of the population that we are trying to reach in its everyday reality and in its own language. Becoming involved in literacy means working to promote both

French language and culture, and the largely misunderstood local and regional culture.

Recognition of the unique aspects of Franco-Ontarian literacy

Like many provincial programs the OCL was designed as one single program which would nonetheless take the specific needs of native people and francophones into consideration. The scope of this "consideration" was not entirely clear: for the most part, it meant hiring a francophone coordinator and a female Amerindian coordinator. Less than two years after the program was introduced, it was being implemented by the Franco-Ontarian community in a very different way.

Francophone literacy organizers quickly demanded a program that would take the unique characteristics of Franco-Ontarians into account at all stages of policy-making; they also asked to be consulted on the entire process. The main players were not only asking that services be offered in French; they wanted the whole francophone literacy programming process to be thought out in French, designed in French and geared to the linguistic and cultural needs of the francophone community.

The government was very soon faced with specific demands from a militant core of francophones. In August 1987, just when the Ministry of Citizenship and Culture had developed a bilingual "clearinghouse" project, francophones demanded special consultation and asked for a separate centre for Franco-Ontarians. As plans were being made to translate and adapt for francophones material that had been produced for anglophones, a request for separate francophone material was made and a first document produced. On the other hand, in 1987-1988, the ministry responsible refused to provide funding for a coalition of francophone organizations in eastern Ontario on the grounds that it was already funding an officially bilingual coalition (which was in fact anglophone).

Government action therefore caused concern at two basic levels. First, the prevailing tendency to devise global solutions blocked the development of a genuinely francophone program. In addition OCL funding was largely monopolized by anglophones, so that new francophone groups risked being frozen out of a program whose level of funding would remain the same over the coming years.

Literacy advocates

Recent events have also shown that it is possible for the various players to work together. The "Alpha-Partage" symposium was attended by people connected with a number of literacy networks: institutional (school boards, community colleges), community, etc.

The greatest cooperation, however, has been between groups under the community-based program wishing to distance themselves from institutional practices.

The illiterate

Some community literacy groups had tried to encourage learners enrolled in literacy workshops to become involved in the management and development of their organizations. Some learners attended the "Alpha-Partage" symposium, but their presence caused some discomfort as the symposium was designed primarily with literate participants in mind! The result was a paradoxical situation: the community movement, which was trying to make a place for itself in the field of literacy in Ontario, was unable to provide an adequate place for the illiterate. With the founding of the Regroupement des groupes d'alphabétisation populaire in December 1988, the situation changed dramatically. Provision had been made for the statutory participation of learners (one-quarter of the delegates) and, with the assistance of these representatives, their integration into the future organization was ensured. This was probably the first time in Canada (perhaps in the world) that learners were directly involved in the establishment of a community-based literacy organization.

Franco-Ontarian literacy organizers were isolated in various regions of the province. Some communities had begun to collaborate but this had proven problematic, mainly because travel costs were prohibitive for a number of representatives (especially for northern Ontarians). Community network members realized that they had to be able to meet, to discuss their practices and reflect on problems common to all the groups.

Basis for a community-based/popular model

The network was made up of groups which for the most part had not yet organized literacy activities per se or were only just beginning to do so. In other words the content of the literacy activities had by and large yet to be determined. Many groups, on a local or regional basis, had expressed a desire to adopt a literacy model that would differ from the school-based model, which in itself differed from the "community-based" model prevalent among anglophone literacy groups (model characterized by one-to-one instruction provided by volunteer tutors). A number of the francophone literacy groups expressed interest in the "popular" model developed by volunteer literacy organizations in Québec.

The OCL model is decentralized and gives considerable autonomy to local literacy groups, but francophone literacy organizers (community representatives) wanted to explore the possibility of outlining a **community** action program that would apply to the Franco-Ontarian community in its entirety, while simultaneously addressing local and regional concerns.

The groups eventually opted for a "popular" model, with all the ambiguity the term comprises. They thus dissociated themselves from the "community-based" program which is their main source of funding. They have yet to define this potential model in terms of everyday practice and local conditions.

The "bilingual" literacy model has been categorically rejected (this adult model is somewhat similar to immersion schools for young people).

CONCLUSIONS AND OUTLOOK

The Franco-Ontarian experience of community-based literacy training is proving to be dynamic and interesting, but the development of French-language literacy programs for the minority in Ontario and for the francophone minorities in the rest of Canada is still subject to several basic restrictions and raises a number of issues. To conclude I will mention a few of these: the first relates to the recent developments in French-language literacy programming in Ontario, while the others apply to all francophone minorities in Canada, although these should be considered in light, not only of the facts presented in the first part of this paper, but also of the experience in Ontario.

Ontario

Most of the current community-based/popular literacy programs are taking place in the outlying regions of the province, where a significant percentage of the population is francophone and a certain level of "life in French" has been maintained. In central and southern regions, where francophones are dispersed in isolated pockets, program implementation constitutes a much greater challenge and actually raises doubt as to the feasibility of French-language literacy activities in areas with very few francophones.

At the same time the relative success of the community network seems to have been followed by a withdrawal on the part of public institutions, which, under provincial policy, are officially responsible for literacy programming. Recently the school boards accounted for only 284 registrations (Boucher 1989: 244), while a survey of the province's community colleges revealed that 89.6 percent of work-related training activities were being offered in a bilingual context (Ogilvie 1988).

Limited involvement on the part of educational institutions has serious ramifications, as the community-based/popular network alone cannot meet all literacy needs. The manifest success and vitality of this network should not be used as either a pretext or as justification for inaction on the part of public authorities. Overreliance on the francophone community-based programs may end up masking the lack of French-language activities in the *other* literacy and basic education programs. If, as is currently the case, the majority or all of the French-language literacy activities are offered through community-based programs, French-language literacy provision will have to be summed up as an *overall* failure.

Basically the relative success of community-based literacy programs and the low profile of French-language literacy services in the other literacy programs are a reflection of the progressive repression of French in regions other than Québec. Even in areas and municipalities where francophones constitute a major segment of the population (and are sometimes in the majority), their public life (i.e., life outside the home: work, recreation, services, etc.) increasingly takes place in English, while French is apparently relegated to the private sphere (home, Church and a few community groups). From this perspective, the relative success of community-based French-language literacy programs seems to reflect and confirm the trend towards both greater community involvement and the privitization of the French language.

French Canada outside Québec

The right to French-language literacy training should be accorded as soon as possible by all the provinces and territories in Canada — where this right is not currently accorded. The current predominant trend towards offering English-language literacy training to francophones can be countered only through an energetic head-on attempt to alter policies and practices.

Recognition of the right to French-language literacy training should itself come under the larger recognition of the right to lifelong education in French.

Policies affecting French-language literacy and adult education programs should address the objective needs of francophones in the area of academic upgrading, as well as the vulnerability of several French communities which are on the verge of disappearing. The content of these literacy activities should on the whole be defined by the French communities themselves. They should be planned and carried out over a long period of time. French-language literacy programs are penalized by current five-year plans: they have barely gotten off the ground, while English-language projects are soaring.

Given the widespread difficulties experienced by francophones in attaining concrete recognition of their children's right to education in French — a right nonetheless laid down in the Canadian Constitution, it will be uphill work to obtain significant French-language literacy programming in the territories and provinces other than New Brunswick and

Ontario. Only explicit federal policy, implemented through the literacy resources of the Secretary of State, could — perhaps — incite provincial authorities to become receptive to the need for such services. Must we repeat that an overview of literacy activities in Canada has revealed that francophones enrol primarily in *English-language* programs? This is evident in the dearth of activities *in French* over the past two decades.

At the same time we must not delude ourselves as to the possible impact of literacy programming in French. To date, in Canada as in other industrialized countries, only a very small percentage of the so-called "illiterate" population has enrolled in literacy activities. And, as all the literacy studies agree that the participation rate for minorities is even lower than that for majority groups, we must not rely only on French-language literacy programming.

The major long-term solution to the educational problems of francophones is to provide a solid basic education *in French* to francophone children.

From a larger perspective, however, even ensuring French-language instruction for young francophones will not be enough. Data from the most recent Canadian censuses show that francophones outside Québec are gradually being assimilated (at varying rates), a process which accentuates the current linguistic polarization in Canada: francophones are concentrated primarily in Québec and ultimately will not survive outside this province (other, perhaps, than in New Brunswick and certain outlying areas of Ontario).

Educational initiatives alone will not reverse the process of francophone assimilation. While providing instruction in French to both young people and adults is fundamental to the survival of French life outside Québec, it appears to be insufficient. Other urgent measures must be introduced: these are in the hands of our political and judicial leaders and, at a deeper level, they depend on the dominant anglophone society agreeing to make room for the francophone minorities living in the "English" provinces and ensuring them of viable conditions.

The history of Canada, particularly in the past 20 years, underscores the difficult relations between the two linguistic communities of this country, and it is primarily the French minorities outside Québec who have borne the brunt of the tension. If we do not radically rethink the current demographic and linguistic division, we may one day look back and see our current struggle for the right to literacy programming in French as having been our final convulsive effort, all the more pathetic for having come too late. History abounds with examples of minorities deluding themselves while in the terminal phase of their extinction.

NOTES

1. This concentration of French Canadians in Québec (and the attendant reduction of their numbers elsewhere in Canada) has taken place gradually over the 19th and 20th centuries.

2. Several authors have documented the fight for schools by French minorities outside Québec, among them L. Groulx (1933).

3. This sense of inferiority among francophones was publicly addressed in the preliminary report of the Royal Commission of Inquiry on Bilingualism and Biculturalism (1967).

4. The relationship between social standing (rural workers and urban proletariat) and illiteracy noted in American and British studies has been confirmed in Canada, with the difference that, here, the ethnolinguistic dimension must also be taken into account (see J. Kozol 1985).

5. This theory was also advanced by Oxenham (1980) and cited by Max Weber in *The Protestant Ethic and the Spirit of Capitalism* (Paris: Pion, 1964).

6. Regarding the history of Franco-Ontarians, refer in particular to the monograph by Robert Choquette (1980) entitled *L'Ontario français, historique*.

7. A basic study of the whole issue of education for Franco-Ontarians has been published: Churchill, Quazi and Frenette (1985).

REFERENCES

Bordeleau, L.-G., P. Calvé, L. Desjarlais and J. Séguin. *L'éducation française en Ontario à l'heure de l'immersion.* Toronto: Conseil de l'éducation franco-ontarienne, 1988.

Boucher, A. *En toutes lettres et en français: l'alphabétisation des francophones au Canada.* Montréal: Institut canadien d'éducation des adultes in cooperation with the Fédération des francophones hors Québec, 1989 (references are to the preliminary edition).

Choquette, Robert. *L'Ontario français, historique.* Montréal: Éditions Études vivantes, 1980 (Collection l'Ontario français).

Churchill, S., S. Quazi and N. Frenette. *Éducation et besoins des Franco-Ontariens,* 2 vol. Toronto: Conseil de l'éducation franco-ontarienne, 1985.

Cippola, C. *Literacy and Development in the West.* Harmondsworth: Pelican, 1969.

Commissioner of Official Languages. *1987 Annual Report.* Ottawa: Minister of Supply and Services, 1987.

_____. *1988 Annual Report.* Ottawa: Minister of Supply and Services, 1988.

Continuing Education: The Third System. Toronto: Ministry of Education and Ministry of Colleges and Universities, 1981.

Creative Research Group. *Literacy in Canada. A Research Report.* Ottawa, 1987.

Cummins, J. "Research Findings from French Immersion Programs Across Canada: A Parents' Guide." *CPF Special Report,* 1983.

Department of the Secretary of State of Canada. *One In Every Five: Survey of Adult Education in Canada.* Ottawa: Minister of Supply and Services, 1985.

Environics Research Group. *Focus Ontario Omnibus Service, June 8 to June 21, 1987.* Toronto, 1987.

FFHQ. *Analphabétisme chez les francophones hors Québec.* Report of a mini-seminar on illiteracy and approaches to literacy held 28-30 March 1983, in Val-Morin. Ottawa: Fédération des francophones hors Québec, 1983.

Les francophones tels qu'ils sont. Regard sur le monde du travail franco-ontarien. Ottawa: ACFO, 1985.

Groulx, L. *L'enseignement français au Canada. Les écoles des minorités.* Montréal: Granger Frères, 1933.

Kirsh, I. and A. Jungeblut. *Literacy: Profiles of America's Young Adults.* Princeton, N.J.: National Assessment of Educational Programs, 1986.

Knopff, R. "On proving discrimination: Statistical methods and unfolding policy logics." In *Canadian Public Policy,* XII, pp. 573-83, 1986.

Kozol, J. *Illiterate America.* New York: Anchor Press/Doubleday, 1985.

Marchand, J.-P. *Maudits Anglais! Lettre ouverte aux Québécois d'un Franco-Ontarien indigné,* 1989.

OECD. *Examination of National Policies for Education: Canada.* Paris, 1976.

Ogilvie, Ogilvie & Company. *A Survey of Literacy Training in the Colleges of Applied Arts and Technology*. Toronto, 1988.

Oxenham, J. *Literacy: Writing, Reading and Social Organization*. London: Routledge & Kegan Paul, 1980.

Royal Commission of Inquiry on Bilingualism and Biculturalism. *Preliminary Report*. Ottawa: Queen's Printer, 1967.

Wagner, S. *Étude du milieu et analyse des besoins en alphabétisation des adultes*. Toronto: Queen's Printer, 1987.

_____. *Enjeux actuels pour l'alphabétisation au Nouveau-Brunswick*. Dieppe, N.B.: Community College, 1988 (1988a).

_____. *Alpha-Partage '88. L'alphabétisation et nous les Franco-Ontariens. Compte rendu du colloque*. Vanier: Association canadienne-française de l'Ontario, 1988 (1988b).

_____. "Naissance de l'alphabétisation populaire en Ontario français. Un aperçu du colloque 'Nouvelle Orientation.' December 1988." *Notes*, special issue, May 1989, pp. 1-24.

Weber, M. *The Protestant Ethic and the Spirit of Capitalism*, Paris: Pion, 1964.

Wright, G.W. *For Adults Only* (study on continuing education). Toronto: Ministry of Colleges and Universities, 1986.

ADULT ILLITERACY IN THE UNITED STATES: RHETORIC, RECIPES AND REALITY

Mike Fox
Catherine Baker
PLAN,* Washington, D.C.

* Push Literacy Action Now

One would have to be totally tuned out of current events to not know that illiteracy is one of the United States' major ills, sharing top billing with homelessness, child abuse and drugs. Since Kozol's passionate and eloquent book, *Illiterate America*, broke open the topic in 1986, educators, grass-roots workers, business leaders, governors and even the nation's First Lady have been voicing the message that too many adult Americans cannot read, creating serious problems for the individuals involved and for the country as a whole.[1]

Unfortunately, much of the current rhetoric about America's literacy problem is misleading, suggesting that the problem is larger than it is (that, for example, there are tens of millions of American adults who cannot read well enough to perform basic tasks like taking a bus across town or filling out a social security form) and simpler than it is (that the baseline problem of all these people is that they lack reading, writing and computing skills) and easier to solve than it is (that all we need to do is get people into programs that will teach them to read).

In reality, illiteracy should be viewed as a continuum of undereducation, stretching from those who cannot read at all at the low end, to those who have less than high school education at the high end. People at different points along this continuum have different needs, which may differ greatly from the needs existing literacy programs are trying to meet. We say "may" because at this point there are virtually no national data to indicate how people are spread out along the literacy continuum or how they view their own functioning and needs. We do know that the track record of existing literacy programs is not strong. In many instances, outcome data are unavailable; when they do exist they show that the vast majority of educationally disadvantaged adults are not being reached by programs and that the people in the programs do not stay.

Furthermore, there is little evidence that improving a person's literacy in and of itself helps that person get off welfare, find a job, get a better job or perform better on the job - even though these may be the things that "illiterate" people want literacy for (and this is the claim being made for literacy instruction). The research indicates that people tend to seek specific strategies to deal with specific self-defined reading problems, not just assistance in learning to encode and decode written language.

They tend to rely on reading tutors or school-based programs. In fact, school is possibly the last place a person with a history of failure and alienation in an academic environment will choose to go.

Volunteer tutors paired one-to-one with students, ploughing through workbook after workbook (if the student lasts that long), are not the only solution. A literacy training and support program offering a range of services and learner-oriented assistance provides a much more viable service to people who have reading problems. Programs must also concentrate on getting illiterate and marginally literate parents the help they need to ensure that their children do not inherit their problem. They must promote collective action to, among other things, encourage and demand that public and private organizations produce their written informational materials at a level that is accessible to marginally literate readers. Only through these multiple approaches will we be able to "solve" the literacy problem in the United States.

WHAT IS THE PROBLEM?

In many Third World nations the literacy problem is relatively clear-cut: a given percentage of the adult population has not been given the opportunity to learn to read, write and compute. But the United States has 12-year school systems, publicly funded adult education programs and a literate culture. At one point, and not too many years back, the nation's leaders congratulated themselves on having a 95-percent literacy rate. What is going on here?[2]

First of all, it should be said that something is certainly going on. Various studies and surveys have determined that there are between 50 and 70 million Americans aged 17 and older considered to be "educationally disadvantaged." This term generally refers to adults who have not completed high school, though some studies have attempted to further break down this category into illiterate, functionally illiterate or marginally literate adults.

Despite some rather arbitrary approaches to "counting the numbers" and some questionable definitions of literacy, these studies *do* show that:

— 23 million adults cannot perform such tasks as reading a paycheque stub, filling out a tax form, addressing an envelope or reading an equal opportunity announcement. An additional 34 million have some difficulty in performing the same tasks;[3]

— 13 percent of American adults (somewhere between 17 and 21 million) cannot answer 20 of 26 multiple-choice questions on material considered to be written at a fourth-grade level;[4]

— among young adults aged 21 to 25, 5 percent (1 million) cannot read above the level typical of the average fourth grader; 20 percent (4 million) cannot read much better than the average eighth grader; and 40 percent (8 million) are unable to read beyond the level of the average 11th-grade student;[5]

— about 50 million persons aged 17 and older have not completed high school, and approximately half of these dropouts have not completed eighth grade;[6]

— 700 000 young people graduate each year functionally illiterate;[7]

— 700 000 young people drop out of school each year. In at least 15 states, dropout rates range from 26 to 42 percent and, in many of our major cities, the rate is closer to 50 percent;[8]

— an estimated 1 million low-literate immigrants enter the U.S. each year.[9]

What we do not know, and none of the studies thus far has shown us, is the nature and extent of literacy *as a problem*, either for the individuals who are themselves educationally disadvantaged or for society as a whole. The data we have do not tell us:

— how those who "flunk" a pen-and-pencil functional skills test (which many of the above studies used) actually function (or are unable to function) as consumers, workers, parents, citizens and community members, among other roles;

— whether or not, and in what percentages, adults who have not completed a particular grade in school are illiterate, functionally illiterate, marginally literate, or literate — if in fact these can be considered discrete or meaningful categories to begin with;

— what literacy means and what skills are needed *as perceived by* the particular individuals or groups being measured;

— what types of training and support services would best help those who are considered "lacking" in skills, or would best benefit the country as a whole;

— how many persons even want to improve their ability to read and write;

— what changes might be expected as a result of improving an individual's literacy skills.

We do not know, in other words, whether the inability to read a classified ad makes one less apt to find a job, or whether the inability to read bureaucratese limits access to social services. We do not know what literacy or lack of literacy means within a particular situation or context.

From the available data it is evident that tens of millions of Americans are in some way educationally disadvantaged and fall somewhere on a continuum of undereducation. The continuum ranges from the illiterate who cannot read or write at all, to the functionally illiterate who are unable to function or cope in certain socially accepted ways as defined by the researchers, to those who are marginally literate, that is, who have not graduated from high school but are able to pass the functional tests.

The data also show very clearly that those who fall on the continuum are concentrated among the poor, the unemployed, the imprisoned and among racial and ethnic minorities. [10] Despite this evidence, the tendency among politicians, corporate leaders and some education professionals is to say that the problem cuts across class lines. And the numbers themselves have been used irresponsibly, to indicate, for example, that:

— "Illiteracy weakens the U.S. defence posture because it affects the recruiting base...it affects our country's ability to compete in foreign trade...it is one explanation for poor voter turnout... its costs to society range from $100 billion to $220 billion a year." [11]

— "23 million Americans have reading problems so serious that they have difficulty in competently handling the minimal demands of daily living" (U.S. Department of Education, *National Adult Literacy Project Overview*). [12]

— "72 million essentially nonliterate people...that results in lower productivity, poor product quality, lost management and supervisory time and restricted mobility and promotability of employees...that costs the corporate world and the nation billions of dollars a year." [13]

— "27 million Americans can't read and guess who pays the price — the top 120 U.S. corporations....By the year 2000, two out of three Americans could be illiterate....There's an epidemic, with 27 million victims and no visible symptoms..." [14]

— 23 million Americans "cannot read, write, reckon and reason well enough to solve problems, to make sensible decisions or to make reasonable judgments in the fast-changing, high technology of America in the 1980s."[15]

— "Of the 100 million [members of today's work force], tens of millions are seriously handicapped in their work and in their everyday lives by a lack of basic skills. They cannot read, write, compute, solve problems, communicate, or perform other basic intellectual functions well enough to gain or hold good jobs, to participate effectively in public life, or to meet many of the challenges of everyday living in an increasingly complex world."[16]

Exploitation of the numbers has also fuelled blitzkrieg-style efforts, from literacy crusades to massive media campaigns. First Lady Barbara Bush appears almost daily in newspapers and on television, drawing attention to one literacy program or another. Her name graces a new foundation to support family literacy programs.[17] A multimillion dollar billboard campaign sports the slogan "Erase Illiteracy" — it is merely the latest "awareness" campaign that has sprouted up in various media outlets.[18] UPS, Coca-Cola and the Southland Corporation (through its 7-11 stores) are just a few of the expanding number of agencies and corporations that have pledged financial support, spurred in part by the promotional efforts of a foundation called the Business World for Effective Literacy.[19] The United Way (the major charitable fund-raising agency in the United States) has launched a new campaign to promote literacy.[20] Newspapers try to outdo each other in the grandness of the literacy project they have taken on. The American Bar Association is among several professional organizations prodding their members to "do something."[21]

Federal funding for the Adult Basic Education program, which enables many school systems and junior colleges to operate adult literacy classes, has increased over the past few years.[22] Congress has adopted new measures for funding training efforts in the workplace, family programs, early childhood education programs, "workfare" welfare programs and English-as-a-Second-Language programs. (It should be noted, however, that overall government spending on adult literacy, compared to pre-Reagan levels, has remained virtually stagnant.)[23]

Several governors and mayors have launched state and local initiatives, and broadly supported legislation calls for nationally networked support centres. Players at all levels have joined coalitions designed to coordinate action; one product of these coalitions is a nationwide 800 number to recruit resources, volunteers and potential learners.[24]

The heightened awareness generated by these activities has vastly increased the number of persons seeking tutors and people offering to volunteer.[25] These people are being absorbed by the adult literacy programs run by school systems, community-based groups, churches, businesses, labour unions, libraries, civic clubs, YMCAs, community and neighbourhood associations, nationally affiliated tutor-based programs and a variety of other private groups. But is all this well-meant activity having any effect? It is hard to say but, from all indications, the answer is unfortunately no.

The message being sent by all these groups misrepresents the "illiterate" and "illiteracy," and misleads the public. Much of the current rhetoric suggests that the problem has a solution:

— The problem is that there are 20, 40, 60 — or more — millions of adults hidden somewhere in this country who cannot read street signs, get across town on a bus, fill out a job application or function in a number of other ways.

— Their inability to read causes poverty, crime, unemployment, welfare dependency, and loss of productivity for American business.

— The solution, for the individual and the country, is for these millions to learn how to read.

— There is a "safety net" in the country in the form of adult basic education (ABE) and voluntary literacy programs that can teach adult illiterates how to read.

— The threads (programs, resources and volunteers) of the safety net need to be increased and more closely knit.

— The federal initiatives, voluntary coalitions, business council and the two national volunteer/student brokering organizations (Laubach Literacy and Literacy Volunteers of America), with the help of the media, will do the knitting.

— Outcomes can only be positive.

The reality behind the rhetoric is very different. In practice, the safety net of national literacy programs leaves some very big gaps:

— The total number of educationally disadvantaged adults caught in the net each year by all programs does not exceed 10 million.[26]

— More than 50 percent of these people slip through the net (drop out) in six months to a year — too little time to make any significant learning gains. [27]

— Those caught by the net tend not to be representative of the educationally disadvantaged population as a whole. More than 50 percent are not on welfare, unemployed, minority or at the lower end of the illiteracy-literacy continuum. [28]

— There is little data to back up claims of positive outcomes from these programs. In fact, as discussed below, very little data exists at all, and what does exist is not encouraging.

Study after study, year after year, the United States has been told that its approach to adult education in general, and adult literacy in particular, has been a failure — or at minimum, that there is little proof of success. Most of those who claim to have programs, methods and materials that work have not been held accountable for such claims. Harman and Hunter, for example, having evaluated various categories of adult education and adult literacy programs, concluded that "One thing is apparent: publicly proclaimed program goals and actual achievements are far apart." [29]

The many claims of "touching and reaching" the lives of people are not backed up by proof that people are learning to read. According to Wurzbacher, who made a study of five U.S. and one Canadian Laubach Literacy programs, the simple, direct lesson is that "Do-gooders must learn to do better." [30]

McGrail, in a summary of existing data on literacy programs, concluded: "It is not possible to provide a complete and accurate picture of literacy programs in the 1980s using existing data. Most of the needed information is not available." [31] McCune found much the same situation: "[We do not know] who is delivering these programs, what they do, how many are being served, how well they work, what unmet needs they might have. Student data are equally short in supply. [We do not know] levels of performance, rate of growth and benefits [students] derive from various instructional approaches." [32]

When data are available, in program after program the same results are evident: a high dropout rate, a low progress rate and a lot of disappointed people.

WHAT IS WRONG?

The mistake made consistently over the years by educators and literacy workers is to view literacy solely as an educational problem, solvable by simply "teaching people how to read." The solution has always been to launch a literacy program. It is simple: those who can read will teach those who cannot. Get the recipe from one of the national literacy groups and follow it. [33] Use volunteers — they are cheap. Basic resources such as space, books and staff will somehow take care of themselves. And forget about planning, resource development, experimenting with new ideas, providing adequate training for teachers and accountability to learners — there is neither time nor money for any of that. One other thing you should do, particularly if you want to recruit volunteers, is to ignore the reality that there is no "quick fix" for literacy.

This mindset has led us through too many campaigns, initiatives, programs, approaches and instructional methods that have failed to make any significant difference for those who have the problem. For the fact is that reading is a complex communication process that requires the reader to *bring meaning to* as well as *get meaning from* print. The ability to process print relies heavily on background knowledge and familiarity with how words interact to make sense. Most undereducated adults do not have the prereading vocabulary and concepts in history, science, geography, current events and a myriad of other subject areas that help bring meaning to print. Thus they often have a doubly difficult and time-consuming task: learning the mechanical and organizational skills of the reading process *and* acquiring the background knowledge needed for comprehension of the text.

It is a plain truth that those at the lower end of the literacy continuum — nonreaders and poor readers usually with life histories of failure in school and out — need a major investment of their time, a major supply of teacher time and skill, and a lot of hard work to become even marginally better at reading. It is neither a simple nor a quick accomplishment, and many adults with family and job are not able to do it.

Most certainly another reason why learning is slow and why many adult learners give up before they get very far is that they are bored, alienated or both by the learning materials they must work with. Adults — even low-level students still struggling to sound out and recognize words — want to read material that interests them. They want material with conflict, material that stresses emotions, material that allows them to reflect on their own lives or to escape into other people's. This is not found in books designed to teach sound-symbol correspondence or in books designed for children.

Unfortunately, most programs do not invest very much time or money in building a varied resource collection from nontraditional sources. Instead, they buy into a set of phonics-building workbooks and materials, such as those published by Laubach's New Reader's Press. Much of the content is of the This-is-a-bird-This-is-a-cup order, with story content playing second fiddle to the phonics lesson.[34] While the material may be expedient for use with volunteer tutors, the end result is that students are not expected to think or feel, much less be inspired or challenged.

Beyond the specific problems that can be found in mainstream U.S. literacy training methodology, the nation's simplistic approach to illiteracy has a more serious and dangerous flaw in that the very people who are supposed to be helped become scapegoats for the problems that afflict them. As Frank Smith writes, "When literacy is promoted as the solution to all economic, social and educational problems, it is easy to assume that inability to read and write creates those same economic, social and educational problems. Literacy becomes a caste mark, and those who haven't got it are discriminated against...The language that is used to describe people who don't read and write well is often reminiscent of some of the most prejudiced ways in which handicapped people or racial and other minorities are discussed."[35]

Arlene Fingeret, associate professor of adult and community college education at North Carolina State University says, "Today's political talk about literacy is not about empowerment of people who are poor and disenfranchised. It's really about maintaining the present distribution of wealth and power in America and, even more...maintaining that distribution across the entire planet...The talk today is not about literacy for social mobility but it is about literacy for basic, entry-level employment. These arguments focus only secondarily on improving the quality of life for individuals and communities. Primarily they emphasize maintaining the preexisting standard of living in America."[36]

Clyde Taylor, an associate professor of English at Tufts University, charges that literacy is used as a "credential of entitlement" to maintain the oppression of minority and other underclass groups.[37]

In the ways described above and more, programs are failing because they are based on false assumptions about learners and their needs. With few exceptions, the people who create the programs in the first place have not taken time to talk to the learners and other illiterate adults themselves, to find out what it is they want and need.

If people were asked what they needed and wanted as a "solution" to their so-called literacy problems; if they were included in the testimony, the conferences and the boards of adult education and literacy programs; if the nation were *really* committed to responding to *their* needs; then the approaches that satisfy politicians, national literacy programs and "back-to-basics" educators would most likely join the history of the windmills.

In summary, to question and challenge the ways in which "illiter-ates" have been counted, how literacy has been defined, how study results have been used and how the United States is responding to its so-called "literacy crisis," is not to deny the fact that there are millions of educationally disadvantaged adults in the U.S. who need our attention. It is rather to emphasize that the data tell us very little about exactly where these millions of people fall on the illiteracy-literacy continuum, what their needs are and what type of services would best help them. To describe the basic problem all along the continuum as lack of reading and writing skills oversimplifies a complex problem and tends to suggest solutions based on the notion of "helping people learn to read." Alternative ways of looking at the "problem" can lead to quite different solutions.

TOWARD A DIFFERENT MODEL

Needless to say, there are many reasons for "illiteracy," and the complex nature of the problem means that solving it will require a continuum of strategies including not only remedial teaching but also increased learner participation in the process, creation of a system of support services, a change in educational policies, and action for social change. Some of these alternative strategies are addressed below.

Training

According to some researchers, the teaching approaches that seem to work best are the ones that have the learners define their own objectives, and then provide instruction to match. "We must distinguish between external standards that define minimum literacy requirements for functioning in daily life, and internal standards people set for themselves which define their hopes, choices and ambitions," conclude the authors of the 1979 book, *Adult Illiteracy in the United States.*[38] In the words of a prominent education consultant, "When students don't like what they get, they'll walk." If learners define "what they get," they are more likely to persevere.[39]

A successful literacy program must be based on respect for how learners see their world, respect for what they can contribute, and respect for what they may wish to learn (as opposed to what teachers may wish to teach). A learner-centred emphasis has many implications for programs:

  — It requires an approach that gives learners what they want and need. In many cases this necessitates greater flexibility in program design — for example, in providing functional skills training focussed on the skills that learners want to develop.

— It requires an approach that is participatory rather than didactic, eclectic rather than preprogrammed. Learners must be included in the decision-making process.

— It requires that teachers and tutors have a high degree of familiarity with the materials and techniques available to literacy education, and a willingness to experiment. It is unlikely that the average, unsupervised volunteer could successfully adopt such an approach without extensive training, support from professional staff and access to a varied resource collection.

— It requires, above all, listening. Adults often know why they failed to learn in school, and are aware of what they need to know now. What they need most from a literacy program is help in working out strategies for obtaining their perceived goals.

Fingeret, in a 1985 "Overview" paper, places the program implications of literacy assumptions into a useful framework, making a distinction between individually oriented programs and community-oriented programs. (The term "community-oriented" as used by Fingeret is distinct from the term "community-based," a term so widely used and variously defined that it confuses more than it elucidates.) The distinctions between the two types of programs can be shown as follows:

	Individually oriented	Community-oriented
Planning	Based on legislative mandate, tradition	Based on community evaluation of wants and needs
Objectives	Teach reading; grade level advancement for individual	Situational and contextual; improvement in quality of life for the community
Evaluation	Grade levels attained; competencies gained. What can the program do better?	Affective change; anecdotal accounts of progress. What can you (learners) do better?

Instructors	Credentialled or trained	Advocate, facilitator, change agent, resource person
Instruction	Generally top-down, instructor — learner, diagnostic/prescriptive	Generally lateral; holistic
Curriculum	Generally prescribed; predeveloped and commercially produced; skill-oriented	Typically situational; program-developed; issue and problem-oriented. Often includes nonliteracy components
Materials	Commercial skill books; level-oriented; workbooks; vocabulary building	Chosen or developed for content, context and meaning

Both individually and community-oriented programs are concerned with empowering adults, that is, with assisting adults to develop a greater sense of control over their lives. Individually oriented programs focus on individual action for personal development, while community-oriented programs advocate collective action for community development. Neither approach is, by definition, right or wrong. However, it appears that the community-oriented approach offers greater potential for effecting positive change in students. Some of the reasons include:

— Community-oriented programs enjoy links with the community and the involvement of people from the community in teaching, administration and governance. This makes the program seem more comfortable and less threatening to students "turned off" by the school-like nature of ABE and other programs.

— Community-oriented programs emphasize meeting a full range of learner needs. This leads to more flexible, learner-oriented programming, with an emphasis on much-needed counselling support.

— Community-oriented programs emphasize dealing with the person within the community. This allows more broadly constituted programs and advocacy activities to take place (parenting education, for example). [40]

Because such programs seek to meet a full range of needs, they are more likely to provide counselling support and are more open to taking up broader literacy-related activities that can improve the community as a whole — such as parenting education and advocacy described below.

However, while some evidence suggests that community-oriented programs have more potential for serving adult learners — particularly those at the lower end of the literacy continuum — than school-based or tutorial programs, they may also become too flexible, too participatory and too eclectic to meet the needs of learners seeking a credential such as a high school equivalency degree. It is up to each program to strike a balance between the two approaches, based on its own learners' needs.

Last but not least, no one teaching method will work for every program in every situation. As David Harman suggests in *Illiteracy: A National Dilemma*, "The successful programs should not be blindly copied; they should serve only as a source of ideas that might be useful. By combining sensitivity to the needs of the learners, understanding of the process of adult learning, and knowledge of appropriate methods, programs can be vastly improved. The result will not be a uniform system of adult education, but a variety of activities that reflect the variety of American life."[41]

Support services and advocacy

> Employers know which workers can't read; the emergency room staff knows whose children got the wrong medicine because the parents couldn't read the label; the welfare workers know why the forms don't get filled out right; and we (in literacy programs) know most of all. Yet most establishment people are forever telling us that more might be done if the illiterate were more visible. Now that, in the words of our students, is a truly hurting thing.
>
> Mike Fox[42]

Fingeret (1983), in studying nonreaders in their communities for a year, found a web of social relations around each person she studied. Included in these relations were several "readers" of varying skill levels, with the "helper" being chosen by the degree of intimacy and the skill that fitted the need. Each of the participants in the study had at least one such reader in his or her life.

Fingeret argues that "illiterate adults do not necessarily see themselves as dependent simply because they lack reading and writing skills." She also reminds us that adult educators ought to know from their experience, research and review of the literature on adult illiteracy that "many illiterate adults are far from the stereotypical dependent, incompetent individuals associated with the term 'illiterate.'"[43]

Stephen Reder, in another significant study, also highlights the value of informal "literacy helping networks." Reder has found that helping networks exist in many different forms in most communities with significant numbers of nonreaders. In *Giving Literacy Away*, Reder claims that these networks offer a key to attracting and keeping students in formal literacy programs. He also suggests that for the many nonreaders who will never want to participate in training programs, the networks should be nurtured as an end in themselves. [44]

With the support of the findings of Fingeret, Reder and others regarding helping networks for adult illiterates, and with some further study of where and how these networks operate, perhaps much more help for educationally disadvantaged adults can be forthcoming through these networks. Certainly, use of nonformal networks is an effort that ought to be encouraged and funded. Meanwhile, there are many helping services that can be provided using existing public and private community services, networks and opportunities.

Programs wanting to provide formal literacy training have had little success in simply opening their doors and waiting for people to come in. The research suggests that they would do better if they reached out to where people are: to the local church, the head start program, to tenants' groups and legal services offices, to the informal helping networks that may already exist. In reaching out, programs may find that in some areas there is less need for a formal literacy program than there is for a support mechanism that would reinforce and expand existing networks and helping services.

Every literacy program, and every staff member or volunteer who has worked in literacy for at least six months, knows many ways in which the program itself or others might "make a readable difference." Here are just a few suggestions that literacy programs working with illiterate and low-reading-level populations might consider:

— Create self-help groups that could in turn become a helping service.

— Use volunteers to walk people through the employment, school or community services maze. Do not require that people learn how to read well enough to walk it alone; chances are that this is simply not going to happen.

— Use voter assistance volunteers to help the concerned but illiterate voter. Federal law allows voters to take the "reader" in their lives into the voting booth with them.

— Let parents whose children are having problems in school know that they are welcome to bring their problems to the literacy programs.

— Set up watchdog committees to monitor plain English, schools, job training programs, judicial services and community services.

— Have volunteer readers on call for those who find themselves in a sudden "literacy crisis."

— Above all, develop and advertise the existence of helping services. Let the community know they are available, that short-term needs will be met, that a literacy program can be more than a group of tutors who are trained in the art of phonics and using their good hearts in unproductive ways.

An extension of the above is the idea of community/neighbourhood literacy support centres that would provide information, testing, counselling and referral, among other things. Such a program would base its literacy training objectives on what people themselves believe they need (a class in tax form preparation, driver's examinations, parenting, job applications, etc.). And to extend the vision further, each centre could have a bookstore, a library, a PTA,* a parent-child reading program, self-help groups: in short, it would be a literacy place.

A final point, but an important one: such centres would be grass-roots places where for every educator there is a social worker; where for every professional there are, say, six "literacy paraprofessionals" with a strong connection to the community; and where volunteers are interested in more than drilling people to build encoding/decoding skills — they are interested in the local hospital's current admission and consent processes, in the complexities of voter registration forms, in the neighbourhood school's special education program for children with reading problems, and much, much more. The idea is certainly worth trying.

Intergenerational literacy training and advocacy

It is no secret. Children who grow up in a world of books and reading tend to become good readers; those who grow up without family support for reading do not. A supportive family setting not only gives the child the opportunity to develop reading skills, but gives reading a practical value and a deep social meaning. Children learn primarily through participating in challenging learning activities with those whom

---

* Parent-Teacher Association

they love and admire most: parents, grandparents and siblings. The children of illiterate parents are deprived of these activities.

The National Commission on Excellence in Education, the Commission on Reading, and the "A Nation at Risk" report all stress the importance of parents participating in their children's education, reading to their children, encouraging them to learn letters and words, taking them to the library. [45] Former Secretary of Education William Bennett echoed this theme in testifying before Congress: "Parental involvement and the informal curriculum of the home have got to play a part in promoting literacy." [46]

For literate parents, involvement is demanding and time-consuming, but realistic. It is not so for low-literate parents who tend to see themselves as lacking the skills, confidence and power it takes to be a model for their children.

So how do we get illiterate parents involved in reading to children, teaching through discussion, taking part in games or activities related to school work, creating learning materials for and with their children? How can we help these parents give their children an even start?

First, let us define "even start."

— An even start for the child of an illiterate parent begins when the parent (or grandparent or sibling or whoever) leaves the ward of the maternity hospital able to read the low-level reading materials the hospital or the Red Cross provides on parenting. It starts when the mother rocks the 6-month-old baby and reads aloud as she rocks. It starts when the father points out the parts of the body to the baby sitting in the bathtub, knowing that this may lead to better reading later.

— An even start begins when the mother knows where the local library is, gets a library card and checks out books; when she learns not to be intimidated by the library system, despite her own reading level; when she finds out when and where the children's programs are.

— An even start begins when the father knows how to go into the local bookstore and select books that he and his child can read.

— An even start begins when the parents know how their existing abilities and skills, no matter how low, can be put to use in working with a child that has not yet begun to walk or talk.

— An even start continues when the parents know how day care, head-start preschool and the public education system work; know how to communicate with these systems; know how to (at a minimum) read school notices, progress reports and report cards.

The first hurdle to involvement — motivation — is in the case of parent-child programs surprisingly easy. A number of studies confirm that low-income and minority families are very much interested in the present education and future success of their children. Cross, for example, found in a five-state survey high aspirations for children among both high and low socioeconomic status parents and among both blacks and whites. Cross concluded that "lack of school success cannot generally be attributed to the notion that poor and minority parents do not value education."[47]

The second hurdle — the frustration of parents who do not know what to do or how to do it — can also be overcome. Existing adult education agencies and adult literacy programs could provide structured programs, materials, modelling techniques and other support services to educationally disadvantaged parents. The key is to set goals that are specific, realistic, short-run and tangible; to get to the people that children most love and admire — family members; to support the already supportive family setting; and to teach parents and other family members vigilance, participation strategies, the nuts and bolts of teaching first lessons, and the strategies others have discovered for communicating with, nurturing and stimulating children.

A growing number of programs, somewhat creative but nonetheless traditional, are providing opportunities for parent and child to "go to school together." In this way, the parent, as a literacy student, becomes a leading role model for the child. The two share the learning experience, and are encouraged to read together.[48]

A few radical programs go even further. They focus not on teaching the parents how to read, but rather on providing the parents with some *teaching skills* so that they can coach their own children in language skills development. The training includes basic instruction in child development and the learning activities that can be used at various ages to promote intellectual and motor growth. Such programs also bring families into the network of community programs: libraries, local bookstores, school and cultural programs, and other community-oriented organizations that can provide support and learning opportunities. Another goal of these programs is to raise the consciousness of educators and social service professionals so that they more effectively communicate with and provide support to parents with limited education.

This is not a pie-in-the-sky idea that will cost millions. It does not need to be researched to death or monitored by government overseers and education professionals. It is being done now, by more and more community-oriented literacy groups, and is proving to be a common-sense, practical way to use volunteers creatively, while offering parents literacy training that will serve their immediate needs and provide creative, positive outcomes.

Plain language writing

The majority of the United States' 40 million so-called "illiterates" are denied access to crucial information about personal, political, social and economic issues that affect their lives. The cause of this injustice? The fact that institutions in American society generally do not consider whether or how the educational and promotional information they publish is received by the general public, and that writers are too often more preoccupied with the medium than the message. As a result, tens of millions of Americans who read at a fifth- to ninth-grade level cannot read basic public materials, such as tax forms, warnings on medical bottles, memos on factory bulletin boards and notices sent home from their children's schools. Writers and document designers, by not writing what is important in a way that can be read and understood by marginally literate adults, keep the reader alienated from, and deprived of, crucial information, services and, in some cases, their civil rights.

Those doing the writing are oftentimes the very people who are most concerned about civil liberties, justice and empowerment — although some argue that the difficult language used in many informational documents is a deliberate gatekeeping mechanism. In the words of one educator, "It can be argued that the most efficient means of discriminating against individuals within our society is to make sure that their facility to receive written language (to read) is not sufficient to meet general public need."[49]

Dozens of studies have documented the startling disparity between the readability of basic public information materials and the reading abilities of millions of Americans who need them. Local governments, utilities, banks, social and political advocacy groups, businesses and health agencies produce information with little awareness of its readability. State and federal documents render even the most skilled readers functionally illiterate; ironically, the overly complicated language used in such documents serves as the model for the language used in much public information.

A seemingly radical, but in reality relatively simple, solution to this issue is for institutions to create and disseminate written materials that are accessible to marginally literate readers. As long as the reading level of most materials is determined by the education of the writer, a campaign to make such information more readable could be as effective as a massive teach-them-how-to-read campaign.

Literacy groups could work to:

— set up watchdog groups of volunteers to monitor public communications by government agencies, utilities, corporations and other groups, and challenge the reading level of the materials — in the courts, if necessary;

— develop organizing strategies to draw attention and support to the issue;

— solicit commitment by public and private organizations to address readability in preparing their own materials, and provide readability assessments and assistance in rewriting;

— tie in with consumer organizations and other groups to promote demand for readability;

— prepare and distribute guidelines that community groups can use for assessing, challenging and improving readability at the local level;

— hold training workshops for writers of public information and for community-based education groups.

All of this could be accomplished through a national "write to read" program and campaign, patterned after other successful consumer rights efforts. The benefits would be several: millions of marginally literate adults would have greater access to information and documents that directly affect their lives, and institutions would benefit from improved response from and/or participation by the people they seek to serve and with whom they wish to communicate.

Ironically, several so-called document design centres are already providing some of these "readability" services and activities for clients such as banks and computer companies serving the more educated, affluent class. Yet when the suggestion is made that the same be done for the marginally literate, less affluent population, there is resistance to "dummying-down" — another manifestation of the blame-the-victim mentality.

FROM THEORY TO PRACTICE

Providing a "continuum of strategies" is the objective that governs Push Literacy Action Now (PLAN). PLAN is a privately funded, nonprofit adult literacy program in the District of Columbia. Over the past 17 years we have provided comprehensive services to low-literate adults in the Washington area and championed alternative viewpoints in the national literacy debate.

These are our goals:

— to meet the training, support and advocacy needs of low-literate adults;

— to conduct activities that promote change in the systems and institutions that cause and perpetuate illiteracy;

— to pursue an agenda that challenges the educational, social, political and economic barriers to literacy development.

Our activities reflect an understanding that illiteracy is more than an educational problem. It is also a social, economic and political issue. This philosophy underlies our approach to literacy training, our other community-based activities such as family literacy, and our advocacy.

Training

PLAN provides literacy training for adults aged 18 and over. Classes, conducted at PLAN's offices in two adjacent townhouses, cover basic literacy through high school equivalency test preparation. Students are placed in classes following an intake interview and inventory of their skills, reading level and needs. Instruction is ongoing, depending on learner goals and objectives; these goals and objectives are defined and redefined on a semester basis.

Students attend classes twice a week; generally, one class concentrates on reading and the other on writing; students may also opt to work on computers. Classes are offered in the morning and evening, to accommodate various work and family schedules. In a few instances, one-to-one tutoring is provided for students who have special needs such as job-related or parent-child tasks and activities.

Students are charged a tuition of $25 per month (the equivalent of $1 per hour of instruction). A sliding scale is used for students who cannot meet this tuition, and students who receive public assistance are encouraged to apply for stipends that cover their transportation and day-care costs. Students are expected to attend regularly, to complete their assigned homework and to find ways to incorporate reading and writing activities into their everyday life, whether by deciphering street signs, looking at the newspaper, going to the library or whatever. Some students cannot make these commitments; some leave the program temporarily, while others drop out permanently. Many such ex-students, however, continue to call on the staff as an informal "helping network" for problems with job applications, deciphering medical information, or dealing with their children's school, etc. Overall, PLAN's first-year retention rate is about 80 percent.

PLAN does not have a set, prescribed approach for classroom instruction. Teachers attempt to develop a variety of skills: comprehension, use of context, word analysis, phonics. They use a variety of materials rather than a single text, and students are encouraged to understand what they are reading. Exercises and activities vary from class to class. PLAN's approach, in short, is eclectic. Volunteers are guided in their selection of texts and activities by more experienced full-time staff.

The consistent theme underlying the mix of activities at PLAN is the development of students' understanding that reading is a meaningful process. Teachers try to make students aware of the reasons why different skills are important, why understanding is more important than correct spelling or pronunciation. All of the program's different activities are thus focussed on a common end, understood by students as well as staff.

PLAN's approach to lesson design incorporates any specific objectives learners may have. Often one of the two classes each week focusses on special "functional" or "survival" skills identified by the students. The class may work on completing forms, deciphering bank statements or phone bills, writing cheques. Or there may be a discussion/reading session on tenants' rights or parents' obligations.

Volunteer teachers are trained using the experiential and participatory approaches that teachers are expected to use in their own classes. New volunteers begin by becoming familiar with the PLAN approach: observing classes, looking through materials in the resource centre, talking through lesson plans with staff and, above all, coming to understand that reading is a thinking process. Less-experienced teachers are provided lesson plans and materials to assist them. All volunteers attend periodic inservice workshops on topics they identify. At these workshops, PLAN staff facilitate "lateral learning" between teachers, who share their problems, concerns and strategies. Because classes are taught in PLAN's headquarters, staff are able to offer ongoing support: to observe classes, offer comments or suggestions, and be available should questions or problems arise.

PLAN measures student progress qualitatively on an eight-week basis, and quantitatively on a yearly basis. Should one group or individual be progressing more slowly than expected, the class is observed closely. Suggestions may be made for different class activities, for example, or different materials may be introduced. In some cases, regrouping or a change of teacher may be required.

At PLAN, volunteers outnumber paid staff 10 to one, but not every volunteer is expected or encouraged to teach. PLAN staff consider each potential volunteer according to the applicant's skills and experience, what he or she wants to do, and our needs. Volunteers raise funds, provide administrative support, conduct research, monitor federal and city agencies, and write and edit PLAN's newsletter. Whatever the volunteers' roles at PLAN, they are viewed as staff. They are involved in the program's decision-making, consulted as knowledgeable, informed professionals and expected to treat their volunteer commitment as seriously as any paid position. Evidence that most of the volunteers see their role the way PLAN does is the average length of time a volunteer continues with PLAN: close to three years.

Family literacy

On average, 25 percent of the adults enrolled in classes at PLAN each year are parents of children in grades 1 to 4. More than half of these children are in special education or are at least two grade levels behind in reading. About half of the parents are themselves reading below the fourth-grade level. In addition, of every five phone calls that come in to PLAN from people with literacy problems, one is from a parent whose child has a reading problem.

These statistics caused us to look at the city in which we operate. In Washington, D.C., nearly two-thirds of all female heads of family living below the poverty line have not completed high school. Of these, approximately 20 000 are 18- to 26-year-old parents of more than 35 000 children considered to be educationally at risk.

As we examined these facts, it became obvious that we could not serve the adults in our program without addressing their literacy needs *as parents*. It also became obvious that, unless we began to address the literacy needs of parents who do not read well and are currently *not* in any literacy training program, we would be guaranteeing ourselves a growing supply of students for several generations to come. And that is not our intent.

This thinking is at the heart of our family literacy project, Take Up Reading Now (TURN), which has three components: Take PART (Parents as Reading Teachers), Take CARE (Child Advocacy for Reading Education) and Take a BOOK. Through these three components, TURN seeks to involve the parent, the community and the child.

Take PART

One-hour, hands-on reading workshops for parents with children below age 3 are conducted by TURN parent coordinators who are themselves marginally literate parents. These workshops, which focus on the specific learning activities their children need to practise at their particular stage of development, have been offered through a health clinic's child life program, a prenatal program for expectant teenagers, a housing program, a community centre, a hospital Handicapped Intervention Program, a Head Start program and two WIC nutrition programs.

At the workshops, each parent is also given a parent-child learning kit, containing information about library activities for children (including the library's Dial-a-Story number), books, and a child development toy (specific books and toys vary, depending upon the age of the child). The kit also includes an easy-to-read book which was developed by PLAN staff and parents, and evolved out of the early workshops. *Read to Me* is a collection of rhymes and a story line that moves from the opening phrase, "Read to me...," to the conclusion, "And someday I will learn new things all by myself." *Read to Me* is accompanied by a cassette tape of the story, so that children and their low-literate parents can learn the words with ease and pleasure. At workshops, parents and children also put together a type of scrapbook, *All About Me*, and discuss parenting issues using as a guide *Reading and Learning Tips for Parents*, an illustrated brochure describing how parents can help their children learn. *All About Me* and *Reading and Learning Tips* were both developed by TURN staff, with parent involvement.

Take CARE

This project is for low-literate parents whose in-school children are experiencing learning problems. In other words, it involves parents who want and need to intervene and negotiate a resolution to school-related problems, but who are not comfortable with confronting the school system alone. When students first come to PLAN, we ask whether they have school-age children and if they know how their children are doing in school. For parents whose children are experiencing "a reading problem," we offer assistance for improving the situation both at home and at school. For example, we offer to test the child and review the report card and school testing scores, advise parents of their rights and options, and go with them to meet school officials.

In addition, PLAN presents community workshops at which parents come together to read and interpret their children's report cards and progress reports, discuss what questions to ask school officials, and share advice on any other action they should take to improve their children's learning situation. One parent, for example, whose son had extremely poor eyesight, received help in having the child declared legally blind so that he would be eligible for special instruction. Another parent who received support and advice succeeded in persuading his son's school system to test his child, determine the nature of his learning disability and place him in special education.

Take a BOOK

Take a BOOK is a low-cost, common-sense way to get easy-to-read books into the hands of low-income parents and their preschool children. PLAN has enlisted the help of individuals and local professionals and volunteer groups to collect new and good-condition used books. The books are distributed directly to parents and children at local neighbourhood centres and public housing complexes.

In addition, PLAN has teamed up with the D.C. public library to distribute 1000 donated copies of the children's classic *Where the Wild Things Are*. These books are being distributed to families at two prenatal clinics. At these events parents and children together learn two easy at-home book-related activities: they make paper bag "Wild Things" puppets and they role-play the "Wild Things" as a children's librarian reads the story. The librarian also uses this opportunity to introduce families to the library's services for children.

TURN staff has provided training, librarians and early childhood teachers, in effective outreach to low-literate parents. In 1989 TURN staff trained librarians from five northeastern states. TURN cosponsored Washington D.C'S first Family Literacy Conference in December 1988. Out of this conference have come several collaborations for family literacy activities involving PLAN, the library, local clinics and a local education program serving Spanish-speaking immigrants. In addition, TURN staff and parents were selected to script and participate in two video training programs on parent-child literacy issues; these videos are being distributed by Project PLUS, the national literacy awareness campaign.

Through the experience gained from the first years of the TURN project, in late 1988 the staff developed "Laying the Foundations," a first-of-its-kind parent-child literacy training kit for professionals who work with low-literate parents and their children. [50] Within just six months this kit was being used by more than 300 educational programs nationwide and in Canada; users include libraries, adult literacy programs, YMCAs and a women's prison, along with Head Start, child care and early intervention programs. This kit includes information on: how to teach parents the basics of child development and reading skills; how to teach a nonreader to read a children's book; a parent-child reading workshop curriculum; writing to reach parents; utilizing community education resources; and supporting advocacy and parent involvement. The kit also includes three model books for families: *Read to Me*, *Read All About Me* and *Reading and Learning Tips for Parents* (described above). Programs are encouraged to copy or emulate these books for distribution in their own communities. Such activities have enabled TURN not only to provide meaningful educational support to hundreds of families in Washington, D.C., but also to positively affect the approach used by thousands of professionals nationwide who serve low-literate parents and their children.

Advocacy

We believe that advocacy is essential because it is only through political, social and educational action that needed changes will come about. PLAN's call for advocacy has its voice through our newsletter, *The Ladder*, which started as an in-house newsletter but now has more than 500 subscribers in the U.S. and Canada — primarily community-based literacy programs. The bimonthly newsletter provides commentary on issues, events, practices and ideas in the field of literacy. It is *not* objective. Our writers (all volunteers) call it like they see it. The issues that *The Ladder* has spoken out on and, we believe, exerted a positive influence on include: intergenerational literacy activities, workplace literacy, literacy campaigns and volunteer drives, "mandatory" literacy programs, learner involvement in defining the "problem" and "solution," accountability of programs, volunteer/tutor brokers, publishers of instructional materials, and other players in the movement, etc.

Locally, we are vocal advocates for plain language writing. Among other activities, PLAN has:

— worked with the D.C. Board of Elections to radically revise the city's mail-in voter registration form. The new version is a simpler form and set of instructions; it eliminates legal language, confusing design elements and excessive background information that interferes with what people need to know in order to register properly;

— worked with the local electric utility to analyze memos, forms and customer publications for readability. PLAN also provided workshops on clear writing for the company's managers;

— reviewed, analyzed and rewrote the local phone company's consumer affairs materials, including the introductory pages to the "White Pages" telephone directory (which include instructions on using the telephone for various types of calls, and emergency information).

Our newest and most exciting advocacy project is the "Literacy and Justice for All" campaign, for which we just recently received a seed grant. Our intention is to build an alliance of social action groups and community-based adult literacy programs, for the purpose of providing access to information on social action issues to marginally literate adults. The project will do this by giving social action groups an active voice and presence in the adult basic education classroom and by assisting literacy programs in becoming more sensitive to the need for and benefits of a political context to reading instruction.

The project will begin with a collection and analysis of existing written materials produced by social action groups, to discover the extent to which such materials are accessible to marginally literate readers. The project will develop and disseminate an annotated bibliography of materials suitable for immediate use in the adult basic education classroom. Project staff will work with social action groups to develop new materials or to produce easy-to-read versions of current materials including brochures, posters, newsletters, position papers, etc. From the research and initial experiences working with social action groups and literacy programs, project staff will create a handbook on readability to be disseminated both in the social action and education communities.

By positive example and aggressive outreach, we hope to encourage local literacy programs and the social action groups operating in their communities to collaborate on educational activities. The project will attempt to inculcate across the board in society a respect for the abilities of marginally literate persons, particularly in contributing to endeavours that seek social justice and enable literate and marginally literate adults to become fully enfranchised in their education and political life.

* * *

Push Literacy Action Now (PLAN) is a nonprofit, voluntary adult literacy program in the District of Columbia. Since 1972 PLAN has provided reading and writing instruction to more than 3000 low-literate adults. Its training and advocacy reflect the position that illiteracy is a social, economic and political issue, as well as educational.

PLAN's activities include general literacy training, literacy helping services, advocacy for Plain English, consulting services and the publication of a nationally-distributed newsletter, *The Ladder*.

In 1984 PLAN established Take Up Reading Now (TURN), a training and advocacy program for low-literate parents and their educationally at-risk children. Through the TURN project, PLAN has spearheaded cooperative activities among a variety of agencies including the D.C. Public Schools and the D.C. Public Library, to support low-literate parents and their children. Through its parent-child literacy training kit for professionals, "Laying the Foundations," PLAN has influenced the development and direction of more than 300 educational programs in the U.S. and Canada.

In the field of workplace literacy, PLAN activities include literacy and Graduate Equivalency Degree (GED) classes for workers, workplace literacy audits, writing workshops for managers and supervisors, and the analysis, redesign and rewriting of job-related and consumer-related reading materials.

In 1984 the National Adult Literacy Project, a federally-funded survey of 225 adult literacy programs throughout the nation, cited PLAN as one of 31 "outstanding adult literacy programs." PLAN was also a featured program throughout Jonathan Kozol's book, *Illiterate America*, and has been the subject of many radio, television and newspaper features around the nation.

NOTES

1. Jonathan Kozol, *Illiterate America* (New York: Anchor Press/Doubleday, 1985).

2. U.S. Bureau of the Census, fifth estimate: "Literacy: Current Problems and Current Research," *Fifth Report of the National Council on Educational Research* (Washington, D.C.: National Institute of Education, 1979).

3. Adult Performance Level Project, *Final Report: The Adult Performance Level Study* (Austin, Texas: University of Texas at Austin, 1977).

4. U.S. Department of Education, *The English Language Proficiency Survey* (Washington, D.C.: U.S. Department of Labor, 1986).

5. Irwin S. Kirsch and Anne Jungeblut, *Literacy: Profiles of America's Young Adults* (Princeton, N.J.: Educational Testing Service, 1986).

6. Division of Adult Education and Literacy, Office of Vocational and Adult Education, U.S. Department of Education, unpublished statistical summaries, October 1989.

7. Estimates of the Adult Literacy Initiative (now the Division of Adult Education and Literacy, Office of Vocational and Adult Education, U.S. Department of Education).

8. Ibid.

9. Ibid.

10. Carmen Hunter and David Harman, *Adult Literacy in the United States* (New York: McGraw Hill, 1979).

11. ABC/PBS, press releases of the Project Literacy U.S. (PLUS) campaign, 1985.

12. Renee S. Lerche, ed., *Effective Adult Literacy Programs: A Practitioner's Guide* (Cambridge: Cambridge Books, 1985), p. 1.

13. Business Council for Effective Literacy, *BCEL Newsletter*, 9, September 1984.

14. Coalition for Literacy/Ad Council, public relations material.

15. Barbara Bush, "Our Reading Problem," *The Washington Post*, August 1, 1984.

16. Forrest Chisman, *Jumpstart: The Federal Role in Adult Literacy* (Southport, Conn.: The Southport Institute for Policy Analysis, January 1989), p. 1.

17. Barbara Bush Foundation for Family Literacy, c/o Community Foundation of Greater Washington, 1002 Wisconsin Ave., N.W., Washington, D.C. 20007.

18. "Erase Illiteracy" campaign, sponsored by the Outdoor Advertising Association of America, Inc., 1212 New York Ave., N.W., Suite 1210, Washington, D.C. 20005.

19. Many of these corporate efforts are documented in the *BCEL Newsletter*, published by the Business Council for Effective Literacy, 1221 Avenue of the Americas, New York, NY 10020.

20. See David Spights, ed., "United Way, UPS Foundation Announce $700,000 in Literacy Grant Awards," *Report on Literacy Programs*, Vol. 1, No. 7 (30 November 1989), p. 54.

21. American Bar Association, *Lawyers for Literacy: A Bar Leadership Manual* (Washington, D.C.: American Bar Association, 1987). Also, American Newspaper Publishers Association, *Newspapers and Literacy: "...that all may read"* (Washington, D.C.: American Newspaper Publishers Association, 1989).

22. Division of Adult Education and Literacy, op. cit.

23. For a summary of Congressional action on literacy, see Paul M. Irwin, "Adult Literacy Issues, Programs, and Options" (Washington, D.C.: Education and Public Welfare Division, Congressional Research Service), updates 1/6/86 and 1/5/87.

24. Contact Center, Inc., Lincoln, Nebraska, 1-800-228-8813.

25. See, for example, recent annual reports from Laubach Literacy Action, Box 131, Syracuse, NY 13210 and Literacy Volunteers of America, 5795 Widewaters Parkway, Syracuse, NY 13214.

26. Division of Adult Education and Literacy, op. cit.

27. Ibid.

28. Ibid.

29. Hunter and Harman, op. cit., p. 57.

30. Mark F. Wurzbacher and Christine Yeannakis, *A Summary of Volunteer Adult Basic Literacy Organizations in the United States and Canada* (Philadelphia: Lutheran Church Women, 1983) p. 147.

31. J. McGrail, *Adult Illiterates and Adult Illiteracy Programs: A Summary of Descriptive Data* [ED 253 775] (Columbus, Ohio: ERIC Clearinghouse on Adult, Career and Vocational Education, 1984), p. 26.

32. Kathleen J. Philips, quoting D. McCune, *Affective Aspects of Adult Literacy Programs: A Look at the Types of Support Systems, Teacher Behavior and Materials that Characterize Effective Literacy Programs* (Washington, D.C.: National Institute of Education, 1985), p. 6.

33. "Recipes" are available from Laubach Literacy Action, Literacy Action of America, from many of the state literacy coalitions, and others.

34. See, for example, Frank C. Laubach, Elizabeth Mooney Kirk and Robert S. Laubach, *Laubach Way to Reading: Skill Book 1-5* (Syracuse, NY: New Reader's Press, 1981).

35. Frank Smith, "Overselling Literacy," *Phi Beta Kappan*, January 1989, p. 355.

36. Arlene Fingeret, "The Politics of Adult Literacy Education" (speech), Urban Literacy Conference, Washington, D.C., January 1988.

37. Clyde Taylor, "The Politics of Illiteracy," *ISEP Monitor*, Vol. 7, No. 3-4 (Special Edition), 1983.

38. Carmen Hunter and David Harman, *Adult Illiteracy in the United States* (New York: McGraw Hill, 1985), paperback edition, p. xii.

39. Tom Sticht (Applied Behavioral and Cognitive Sciences, Inc.), interview with Catherine Baker, quoted in "All Americans Should Read, Right?" *Public Citizen*, March/April 1988, p. 16.

40. Arlene Fingeret, *Adult Literacy Education: Current and Future Directions* (Columbus, Ohio: ERIC Clearinghouse on Adult, Career and Vocational Education [ED 246 308], 1984).

41. David Harman, *Illiteracy: A National Dilemma* (Cambridge, Mass.: Cambridge Book Co., 1987), p. 89.

42. Mike Fox, "Plain Talk," *The Ladder*, January/February 1983, p. 2.

43. Arlene Fingeret, "Social Network: A New Perspective on Independence and Illiterate Adults," *Adult Education Quarterly*, Vol. 33, No. 3 (Spring 1983), p. 133.

44. Stephen Reder, *Giving Literacy Away: Alternative Strategies for Increasing Adult Literacy Development* (Columbus, Ohio: ERIC Clearinghouse on Adult, Career and Vocational Education [ED 253 775], 1985.

45. National Commission on Excellence in Education, *A Nation at Risk: The Imperative for Educational Reform* (Washington, D.C.: National Commission on Excellence in Education, 1983).

46. William Bennett, testimony before the Education and Labor Committee, U.S. Congress.

47. M. Cross, ed., *What You Always Wanted to Know About Research Findings: Families as Educators* (Washington, D.C.: National Institute of Education, Reading and Language Studies Division, 1984), p. 3.

48. See, for example, Barbara Bush Foundation for Family Literacy, *First Teachers* (Washington, D.C.: Barbara Bush Foundation for Family Literacy, 1989) and M. Conlon McIvor, ed., *Family Literacy in Action: A Survey of Successful Programs* (Syracuse, NY: New Reader's Press, 1990).

49. Yetta Goodman and Carolyn Burke, "Language and Psycholinguistic Bases," *Teaching Reading Foundations and Strategies* (Belmont, California: Wadsworth Publishing, 1980), p. 89.

50. PLAN, Inc., *Laying the Foundations: A Parent-Child Literacy Training Kit* (Washington, D.C.: PLAN, Inc., 1989).

GENEROUS SUPPLY, FLAGGING DEMAND: THE CURRENT PARADOX OF LITERACY

Jean-Paul Hautecoeur
Ministère de l'Éducation
du Québec

*The measure of success [of literacy] should be the
number of adults who become involved in learning
and the number of successful readers who have won
the tools by which to alter the condition of their
lives.*

Jonathan Kozol

THE GAP BETWEEN SUPPLY AND DEMAND

Those who support the fight against illiteracy are quick to cite
figures to show the magnitude of the problem. They may also draw
attention to the distressing psychological and social condition of the
"victims" of illiteracy or, then again, may deplore the huge economic and
social cost of widespread illiteracy in Canada. Whatever their battle cry,
literacy advocates loudly sound the alarm, speak of a critical situation or
deplore the fact that public and private authorities are not taking the issue
seriously enough. They call for recognition of the scale of the "drama,"
"crisis" or "danger" and make demands for adequate funding, a national
plan of action, mobilization of the business community, and so forth.

This, in a nutshell, is a description of the battle against illiteracy in
Canada. It often unites professional educators, literacy volunteers, social
activists, a few politicians and the private sector (especially the pulp and
paper, printing and publishing industries) as partners in literacy efforts.
The situation in Québec is comparable, with the exception that professional educators are more heavily involved and the private sector and volunteer
organizations, less so. In fact, in Québec virtually all literacy programs are
in one way or another associated with the ministère de l'Éducation (MEQ).

It is now estimated that one Canadian adult in four is functionally
illiterate; the corresponding estimate for Québec and the rest of Canada's
francophone population is almost one in three.[1] Although this situation is
comparable to that in the United States,[2] the illiteracy rate is not as high as
in France, where 50 to 70 percent of the adult population is considered
functionally illiterate.[3]

Whether the validity of these data is questionable is irrelevant at this time. What is important, however, is that these statistics are widely circulated by the media, virtually endorsed by government, and as such carry even greater weight when cited for dramatic effect. As a result, the deprived population is seen as being in urgent "need" of literacy training, while young people of school age are perceived as having a no-less-urgent need for "preventive measures." As the figures inflate, the need follows; and the necessity for intervention becomes more pressing as the diagnoses become more alarmist.[4]

Demands made on various fronts by increasingly influential pressure groups normally result in a stronger commitment from government, the allocation of more resources and the development of services. This is where we stand at present in Québec and Canada. Governments have been made aware of the problem, are setting up mechanisms for intervention and are allocating more resources for information, organization and training. While these efforts are uneven, growth is progressive, which is not the case in most social and educational sectors.

In Québec, the MEQ has established a literacy program which, in theory, provides school boards with the means to expand their training services in keeping with demand. The model is rigid: it imposes universal administrative standards, gives the school boards virtually monopolistic regional power over literacy, etc. Québec's literacy program, which is far from possessing all the virtues readily ascribed to it by outside observers, nonetheless ensures that — in principle — adults have the same access to education as school-aged children. This is an important step in terms of the formal right to education.

Despite this, there appears to be a major problem, not within the system but in connection with the way it is being used: supply, i.e., currently available literacy services, is greater than demand. The people presumed to have an imperative and urgent "need" are simply not showing up. The fact that the costs involved in offering literacy services continue to increase at a considerable rate is due less to an actual increase in literacy enrolment than to a growth effect endogenous to the system. Adult literacy students are not coming forth: it is precisely this recruitment problem upon which this paper will focus.

We must first define the problem and examine how various groups concerned by illiteracy perceive it. A 1986 survey involving most of the literacy groups in Québec will provide the background information to help us understand the reasons for the lack of demand for literacy services and the conclusions that can be drawn from this. The question is to determine what can be done in order to ensure a more effective use of the resources which have been made available for literacy training. Although this paper does suggest possible solutions to certain problems, it does not constitute a new plan of action for Québec. Such a plan must be the fruit of a collective effort, following more stringent evaluation of current programs. We have not yet reached this stage.

THE ESSENCE OF THE PROBLEM

In a survey designed to inventory all the literacy activities in Québec,[5] respondents were asked to evaluate their work, i.e., to list what they considered to be their successes and failures. The following information is drawn from an analysis of some 180 questionnaires.[6]

According to Lucie Lépine, "It is at the recruitment level that our failure to extend literacy services ["opening the network," in educational jargon] is felt most keenly." While many literacy groups consider government and public recognition of illiteracy as one of their evident successes — along with the increased awareness of educational institutions as to the "urgent need for literacy" and, in some cases, the priority now being given to these services in adult education — many also acknowledge that screening and recruitment remain a "major challenge." "Reaching those who constitute the hidden part of the iceberg poses a considerable problem." This implies that the submerged portion of the proverbial iceberg, much more massive than the tip, remains untouched.

With regard to the presumed pool of "needy" people in the various regions, it is acknowledged that enrolment rates are low. "Most agencies have not reached the estimated number of candidates in their area." Failure is patent in some instances: local anglophone literacy groups easily recruit volunteer tutors, but few candidates for literacy training. The result is that literacy organizers sometimes discontinue the services or redirect their efforts to offering preventive measures within the school system.

In rural areas, enrolment drops if recruitment efforts are not maintained. It is also recognized that "enrolment does not reflect the amount of energy expended in recruiting." "The extreme difficulty of recruiting 'truly' illiterate adults who are isolated psychologically, socially and geographically is a common feature across the evaluations." In some cases, "training centres have been closed because of low recruitment and the impossibility of merging with groups in other municipalities."

"Creaming" or the "exclusion of the most needy," a phenomenon long observed in the schools, has also been observed in literacy work. Many literacy organizers admit that "the most needy are not the population they reach most easily." The use of an overly academic approach has resulted in a certain selection among candidates for literacy training and has consequently eliminated certain groups of illiterates.

Furthermore the fact that it is easier to recruit young people for academic upgrading (with financial incentives) and specific minority groups such as the mentally retarded, or allophone immigrants, has compensated for the drop in enrolment by "regular illiterates." Many school boards have aimed their efforts at providing functional education for the handicapped. Literacy training was a promising area for this student population, just as it was for allophones wanting to learn written French. Without these and many other compensations, it is to be feared that enrolment rates would have dropped in many instances, leaving school boards with serious financial loss, reduced employability, etc.

Clearly the supply is far from creating the expected demand. In 1989-1990, the cost of Québec's literacy program was estimated at $25 million, while the number of people reached was estimated at 16 000. It is also known that enrolment figures are high, compared to the number of students who actually attend literacy classes.

Given that about 1.5 million adults (29 percent of the adult population) have been identified as illiterate or functionally illiterate,[7] the literacy program is reaching only 1 percent per year. This rate is not unusual, and compares with estimates for the United States and Europe. We may find it unacceptable, but we must try to understand the underlying causes.

WHY ARE LEARNERS NOT COMING FORWARD?

There are several possible explanations for low enrolment, each of which would warrant further analysis. I will first give an overview of these explanations, before going on to expand on each.

- First, one might say — and some do not hesitate to do so — that if so few people have shown up after the massive effort to promote and offer literacy services, it is because the problem did not exist in the first place. The extent of illiteracy has been exaggerated out of all proportion, and it is time to take a hard look at the facts and to invest in educational projects which produce results.

- Literacy professionals suggest that current resources are insufficient, particularly in the crucial area of preliteracy, which includes promotion, recruitment and community action. The program developed by the MEQ has emphasized training at the expense of popular education activities — hence lagging recruitment.

- A more critical or down-to-earth appraisal of the situation might bring one to question the adequacy of the services offered. If they are not attracting anyone, then perhaps they are not attractive! The school-based literacy program is being called into question here — an issue with both technical and political ramifications.

- One frequently heard argument ascribes recruitment difficulties (the "broken date") to the very nature of illiteracy: it is an invisible reality because it is hidden, shameful, private and repressed. Strategies, services and human resources must be adapted to the distressing nature of the phenomenon. This requires mechanisms, favourable conditions and, above all, competent organizers with solutions tailored to learners' needs.

- Lastly, the failure of the traditional approach to literacy is due to its archaism, and to the noninvolvement of business and government. The pressing need is to provide basic education that will enable workers to keep up with modern communications technology and a changing work environment. Efforts must be channelled away from recruiting and into providing adequate services. This is the point of view of the business sector.

Each of these possible explanations ties in with a specific ideology of literacy provision, which is in turn connected to a specific social group. What Lae and Noisette have said of the situation in France could very well apply to Québec: "What is said and done in the fight against illiteracy reveals much more about those who are talking or doing than about a subject which none of them has managed to grasp."[8]

The problem is exaggerated

This is a conservative, even reactionary, argument, according to which everyone or almost everyone has had the chance to go to school, so that the only illiterate people left today are undereducated older people, certain Third World immigrants and a few unlucky individuals (the sick, handicapped, mentally deficient or maladjusted).

In French this prejudice is reinforced by the word used to designate an illiterate person, *analphabète*, and by its original meaning, literally, "a person who does not know the alphabet." The stereotype of the illiterate is that of an odd individual, who cannot find his way about town and is scarcely able to sign his name: the hybrid mixture of an idiot, a peasant, a handicapped person, a miserable beggar and a simple-minded stranger.

In Québec one generic term, *analphabétisme* (illiteracy), is used to designate the range of situations that involve a lack of writing skills or the inability to use them. The French have recently begun to use the term *illettrisme* (functional illiteracy) to refer to this variety of situations and usages, while anglophones qualify illiteracy in various ways ("basic," "functional," "cultural," "technical," etc.). The use of one blanket term, i.e., *analphabétisme*, can cause a great deal of confusion.

The definition of illiteracy could be debated endlessly. If we stop at the literal or strict sense of the word, that of zero written communication for a population or individual, all ambiguity disappears and the number of Canadians to whom one might apply the term is minute. But for the concept of functional illiteracy or, as I proposed following the survey on illiteracy in Canada, *semi-alphabétisme* (semiliteracy),[9] there is no scientific definition: how we perceive, understand and define the phenomenon at any given time depends above all on social context, as do the categories of people designated and the numbers involved.

These perceptions and categories vary. Only 10 years ago, for example, it would have been unthinkable to say that one-quarter to one-third of the adult population was illiterate. The situation has changed considerably, as have the words and numbers. Within a relatively short time, the concept has been popularized and its definition extended. The phenomenon is no longer seen as "pathological" or exceptional, but now seems normal, even familiar. The history of illiteracy has not yet been completed.

From a semantic or terminological point of view, we may question the extensive use of one concept. We may also be tempted, in the name of effective communication or an elitist principle, to raise considerably the "acceptable" threshold of language performance. We must nonetheless take into consideration the popular definition of illiteracy, the definition on which the major institutions have agreed and which, for a time, becomes the widely-accepted meaning. From this perspective, neither the problem nor the rate of illiteracy has been inflated: both correspond to reality.

Illiteracy, like mental illness, is what society defines it to be at a given point in history. In North America today, and in an increasing number of European countries, the illiteracy rate varies between one adult in five and one in three. This is a fact. Which leaves us with our problem: why are so few learners coming forward?

Resources for preliteracy are insufficient

This is the assessment of literacy tutors, who blame the new literacy program for at least some of the recruitment problems. In actual fact the problems date back to the first budget cuts in community-based education (which served as a springboard for literacy work in Québec).

But they have been exacerbated by the new program, particularly in rural and semirural areas.

Administrators were delighted when the new management model was implemented: it meant that the school network would be opened to adults; it meant "unlimited funding" and the integration of literacy training into the MEQ's general education program. Management was streamlined, resources were to increase, there was a shift from short-term to medium- and long-term planning, while accessibility was guaranteed for everyone. In addition literacy training was once again considered as the learner's first step towards a secondary school diploma.

But this model can be implemented only when the learners have shown up. It excludes virtually all community action. It divides literacy provision into training, which is standardized and subsidized, and recruiting, which is left entirely up to volunteers. This model discourages grassroots work in favour of quantitative management of student numbers and internal system resources.[10] It is easier to implement in urban centres, where population density reduces the need for community involvement in recruitment.

The paradox is that, at a time when supply is abundant, demand has stagnated. Student enrolment in school-based literacy programs can be maintained, and even increased, by incorporating community-based education groups and offering to pay their instructors, or by adapting instruction to the needs of the new "special" groups (young people in academic upgrading programs, the handicapped, allophones) or by making literacy training widely available to students in personal and social development courses (previously called "community-based education").[11]

Thus, while it is true that resources allocated for promotional activities are insufficient, increasing them would not necessarily solve the problem of recruitment. Literacy training has undergone a transformation: it has evolved from community action and community-based education into a school-based program providing academic upgrading and remedial education. The stagnation in the demand for adult literacy services can be attributed as much to this systemic tendency as to the lack of resources.

Services are inadequate

For this point I will borrow from Jonathan Kozol, as the proponents of the alternative, community-based approach to literacy provision have been less vocal in Québec in recent years. This is partly due to the situation described above: the new adult literacy program gave more power to the school boards, which have absorbed (or created) a large number of independent agencies. In the shift towards a school-based approach, the proponents of community-based literacy work have lost their voice as critics and can no longer offer an alternative.

According to Kozol the answers to the following three questions will determine whether or not literacy training is rooted in the community and, hence, able to ensure the participation of the adults concerned:

- "Who calls the shots in setting up the structure and the goals of actual recruitment and instruction?

- "Who is involved in the recruiting work and what tone does it assume?

- "Where do recruitment and instruction finally take place?"[12]

Community action which mobilizes local resources and people should be remunerated and not based on volunteerism. This is the only way to motivate and involve community personnel from the same group as the literacy students. According to Kozol, "Many who live on welfare checks today would be ideal candidates as literacy teachers, organizers and recruiters." This echoes the *Declaration of Persepolis* (1975):

> [Literacy teachers] should not form a specialized and permanent professional body, but should be recruited as close as possible to the masses undergoing literacy training and should belong to the same or to a related social and professional group in order to make dialogue easier.

> The effectiveness of this mobilization will be increased if greater respect is paid to the initiative of the populations concerned and to consultation with them, instead of abiding by bureaucratic decisions imposed from outside and above. The motivation of those involved will be stronger if each community is itself given the opportunity of carrying out the literacy project.

We have learned from experience that the most effective recruiters are literacy students themselves, provided they are satisfied with their literacy program. We know that the best promotional method is word-of-mouth and friendly conversation, as opposed to the Fuller Brush approach and television advertising. We know that we must go looking for literacy candidates on their own turf, where they feel free from outside constraints (a long-time tutor told me he recruited a lot of young people in Montréal's East-end parks). We also know that meeting places such as neighbourhood houses, community centres or drop-in centres are ideal for literacy activities, etc.

Québec has chosen to support the development of school-based rather than community-based literacy services (although "chosen" is perhaps not the best word: traditions, structures and organizational concerns were undoubtedly important determining factors). From the point of view of administrators and teachers' union leaders, this policy has obvious advantages. It also ensures access to educational infrastructures and the services of the school system. On the other hand, it has marginalized the independent community education movement. As mentioned earlier, for several years now, the new policy has allowed local school boards to absorb community groups.

It is not surprising, then, that public response to the services offered by school boards has been no more than lukewarm. The shift to a school-based approach has not been conducive to massive recruitment among the working classes, who are culturally far-removed from the school-based organization of services.

We must also ask ourselves to what extent literacy provision is attaining the objective of providing "academic upgrading" (access to secondary education), at least to undereducated young people. We have no data concerning this theoretical objective, which was added to the literacy program in 1984 (when it was decided to integrate literacy training into the general education program rather than community-based education). It is becoming indispensable to evaluate this aspect of the program, since increased investments have not created an increased demand for services, and it is possible that stated objectives are not being attained.

The nature of illiteracy explains the absence and the silence

One of the arguments most frequently used to justify the special treatment reserved for the illiterate population, i.e., the provision of literacy training, is that these people are invisible and stigmatized. They are invisible because they are hiding, afraid of being found out and ashamed of the poor image society has of them. They will not come out unless discovered or unless the pressure to come out becomes unbearable. Consequently literacy services, much like individual or small-group therapy,[13] must be adapted and tailored to the learners' needs and abilities.

To attain this objective, anglophone literacy organizers use a one-to-one approach, while others, both in their ideology and preliteracy activities, stress the importance of using individualized teaching strategies. In this context, one should not take "preliteracy" to mean "all-purpose"[14] community action or community-based education, but something more along the lines of an office consultation between a patient and a healer. Where pathology is diagnosed, curative and preventive treatment is required,[15] hence the services of reeducation specialists. And, just as volunteers play an important role within the health system, a number of kindly people must be available to work alongside professional literacy workers. Everything takes place in an institution, a place far removed from learners' everyday lives and day-to-day communication needs (although the institutions use teaching strategies based on stereotyped everyday situations, i.e., the functional approach).

It is not surprising that, in keeping with this logic, literacy training has come to be associated with special, curative treatment; literacy students, with the physically and/or mentally handicapped; and the school, with a rehabilitation centre requiring qualified staff, appropriate administrative measures and additional funding. As there is a tendency to define the illiterate population in terms of its most disadvantaged members, the special care is used to explain the low recruitment. The problem with demand is certainly not due to the poor quality of the services offered, but to the fact that illiteracy is perceived as a symptom of individual psychosis.

Perceptions of the problem and attempted solutions are outdated

In a recent editorial a group with considerable influence on Canadian thought expressed a position it feels is timely, responsible — and nationalistic:

> [M]ake no mistake, as long as literacy is mired in the donations committees of the country, it won't be making headway on the shop floor or in the steno pool. At the moment, literacy is yet another raised voice with upraised palm competing for funds with orchestras, community centres and diseases.
>
> While these are all worthy causes, literacy is different. Literacy in the workplace is a profoundly self-interested goal for any corporation. It's a bottom-line issue for every company, as our soon-to-be-released study on the costs of illiteracy will show.
>
> ...If we love our country and would like to see it prosper, literacy in the workplace must become a top priority.[16]

In another editorial, the president of this business group suggests that literacy training should be called by another name, since this term has archaic connotations which discourage workers from acknowledging their lack of skills, employers from investing in worker training and governments from making literacy a national priority. The concept and the activities it designates must be updated and revamped in order to get literacy out of its rut in the social and health services sector, where it has been impossible to adapt services to labour market requirements or to stimulate growth in demand.

When defined in this way, i.e., in terms of the need to adapt to technological changes in the workplace, being literate means having a range of information-processing skills which may be applied to different tasks in a variety of situations.[17] This is a far cry from the ABCs of school-based literacy or the clinical rehabilitative approach aimed at developing learners' autonomy; a far cry, too, from the ideals of social justice and reform that inspired militant literacy advocates. Henceforth literacy strategies are to be determined by the historic and synchronic laws of the job market, as is now being widely proclaimed throughout Canada:

> It is clear...that both the rate of technological innovation and the level of competitive advantage achieved among Canada's major trading partners will depend upon the availability of a well-educated, skilled and adaptable work force... As the OECD notes, "Even where specific jobs may not demand a full range of qualifications, a contingent reserve of skills is needed to give a worker the flexibility and adaptability needed to function in a full range of tasks over time."[18]

While we may doubt that this training imperative should bear the name of "literacy training," it does concern a very large pool of workers who could be recruited directly within industry and at employment centres. All we have to do is raise job requirements, pressure the work force to undertake training or upgrading and offer adequate on-the-job programs. We must also obtain the cooperation of government, of businesses that offer training and retraining programs, and of the unions — which may eventually take on the task of upgrading the work force to meet the needs of the changing job market.

Such an agenda is not without problems. But, as we are dealing with the work force of a business or country, recruitment is no longer a major stumbling block: potential candidates, being dependent and under pressure, have little choice. The challenge is to offer training which adequately and effectively addresses the new demand.

This increasingly popular position is mainly concerned with workers who are already in the workplace and have little or no qualifications. From this stance, literacy skills are made more complex and technical, to emphasize the importance of the basic requirements for employment. By raising minimum performance criteria, this definition of literacy considerably increases the number of people considered illiterate. Training programs are designed only for workers who are already in the job market and are said to be illiterate because of an inability to keep up with advancing technology rather than because of social marginalization. The chronically illiterate, consistently excluded from socioeconomic activity, are again left waiting on the sidelines. Obviously, the problem of the demand for training is far from settled. On the contrary, offering services to a select group may widen the social gap still more.

COUNTING ON THE AVAILABILITY OF SERVICES TO UP THE DEMAND: A RISK

Most of the above attempts to define the problem also comprise solutions to the lagging demand for literacy services. I would like to conclude by turning the problem around, to look at the situation through the eyes, not of literacy professionals and organizers, but of the much-sought-after "illiterate population" — the victims.

Having analyzed available services in an attempt to determine why demand is so weak, we must now ask ourselves how those considered the victims actually experience illiteracy. How, in fact, does illiteracy affect everyday life? In answering this question, we must take care to avoid alarmist interpretations which exaggerate the scope and gravity of the problem. It may well be that the widespread phenomenon we deplore today and loudly claim to have "discovered" was actually created before being scrupulously recorded. We may have counted on supply creating a demand. Is our problem then simply one of marketing, or of upping the pressure?

It is often said that there is a "hard core" of illiteracy, composed of people stigmatized by their inability to write, an inability which generalizes to more or less all forms of communication with the outside world. We tend to associate this group with the dramatic stereotype painted in clinical terms and expect to meet these "typical" illiterates in literacy centres (where journalists also go hunting for them). As these are the people most immediately affected by illiteracy, they are theoretically the ones for whom literacy services were set up in the first place. It is difficult to put an exact number on this group, but a cross-check of the surveys enables us to estimate it at some 10 percent of the adult population, i.e., at about 500 000 individuals.[19]

Theoretically, the "need" for literacy training should be strongest among people in this group because it is most keenly felt and suffered by them. In actual fact this is not necessarily the case. The need for literacy or normal communication is normative: society imposes it, the school makes it a categorical imperative and literacy organizers project it onto a target population. This population, however, is elusive. Its needs do not correspond to perceived needs, nor its characteristics to the stereotype.

There comes a time when exclusion from society becomes normal, comfortable. The illiterate person interiorizes, assumes and adapts his condition to the point of playing a role both in public and private. "Ultimately, illiteracy and failure become part of the individual's social status and character," writes J.-P. Vélis. Quoting a psychologist, Vélis continues, "There are those who willingly put themselves in the position of welfare recipient. It is not unusual to find young people and adults who tell you right out 'I am illiterate' and who will prove it any way they can! Illiteracy is their banner, and it also justifies their not finding work…"[20] For these people, a change of status may be perceived as threatening, so that undertaking any kind of training is out of the question.

Delinquency may also be adopted as a way of life in which illiteracy is seen not only as normal, but as a mark of distinction. This trademark of rebellion is learned from peers at school and follows these young people when they move on to the underground. Delinquency may be cultivated through the use of other means of communication such as slang or music (for a picture of this, see the lovable Ti Pit who, like so many others, ends up as a recluse[21]). Labov describes these subcultures in minute detail, including their language and values, and shows how these groups overcome exclusion by refusing to participate or assimilate in any way, and by ostentatiously and aggressively asserting their difference.[22]

Although we can draw a profile for certain groups within the illiterate population, most do not match any specific profile. The further we move from the "hard core" of illiteracy, or from radical exclusion, the harder it becomes to recognize illiterates. While social differences are indeed perceived as inequalities, they are not attributed to "illiteracy." People must be educated or have climbed the socioprofessional ladder to recognize the value of written objects and graphic communication. They must recognize the value of this type of social advancement before they can see themselves as illiterate or wish to improve their situation. They must know or believe that learning to write will change their lives and enable them to open the door to a new adventure in learning.

This is not the case for the majority of people the surveys have been able to identify as illiterate.

According to the survey on illiteracy in Canada, half the respondents in Québec did not consider it very important to know how to read well, write well or even speak well; they did not find it very important to have attended secondary school. Sixty percent felt that it was not important to read to children; 44 percent stated that they had not read a book during the previous six months; 62 percent had never written a letter of more than one page; 77 percent had never been inside a library; 38 percent did not feel that reading and writing are essential in their line of work; 89 percent declared that they had never been penalized because of reading and writing...

It should be noted that literacy surveys show a wide gap between men and women. The studies confirm that illiteracy is more prevalent among men than among women.[23]

Thus, we are far from being a society in which everyone writes, just as we are far from reaching a consensus within our culture as to the importance of literacy. Many people do not seem to perceive illiteracy or functional illiteracy as a handicap. Whereas 37 percent of respondents acknowledged that they need help with reading or writing (M: 41 percent; W: 33 percent), only 11 percent admitted they felt penalized by their illiteracy. Turning to another person for help with reading and/or writing is not always perceived as being in a position of inferiority or dependence.

These few observations help us to see that the much-discussed "need" for literacy (which, for many organizers, justifies offering appropriate services), rather than being an actual fact of daily life for one-third of the adult population, has arisen primarily because of outside pressure. Illiteracy is first and foremost a definition formulated by the cultured or moderately educated classes. The division of society along this sociolinguistic line is a middle-class perception. But, while the division is very real and is recognized by the poorer classes,[24] it does not necessarily lead to literacy training.

It should not be assumed that people will perceive the offer of training or the chance to go back to school as desirable or as a means to attain personal advancement. In fact people participate in the training activities organized by their society to the extent that they play an active role in that society and share the values of its working members (who produce, communicate and write). Québec's Conseil supérieur de l'éducation recalls this oft-forgotten fact:

> The ratio of adults involved in training activities is one in 20 for those with an elementary school education and four out of 10 for those with a university education.

> There is a direct link between a person's involve-
> ment in adult education activities and his employ-
> ment status: if he has regular work, his participation
> in training activities will be greater.
>
> It is almost essential to have a certain level of basic
> education before developing an interest in the train-
> ing process, or even being able to appreciate its
> importance.
>
> The undeniable fact is that the imposing apparatus of
> adult education is far from reaching those segments
> of the population whose training needs are most
> urgent.[25]

And here we are, back at square one — having nonetheless explored the lagging demand for literacy services. We have established that there is a lack and have at least partially explained it. Now what should our next step be, whether our stated objective is to "fight illiteracy" or to ensure that the greatest number of people possible share in our cultural, economic and social life?

Essentially, there are only two possible courses of action: we can use marketing strategies to up the demand, or we can return to grass roots and determine optimum conditions for the joint development (co-management) of the supply of services and the demand. I greatly fear that at present we are on the former track: we are "fighting illiteracy" rather than working towards a more balanced development of resources and skills.

NOTES

1. The Creative Research Group, *Literacy in Canada: A Research Report*, prepared for Southam News, Ottawa, 1987; *Literacy in Quebec: A Research Report*, prepared for the Gouvernement du Québec, Ministère de l'Éducation, Québec City, 1987.

2. Kozol notes that "Twenty-five million American adults cannot read the poison warning on a can of pesticide, a letter from their child's teacher, or the front page of a daily paper. An additional 35 million read only at a level which is less than equal to the full survival needs of our society. Together, these 60 million people represent more than one-third of the entire adult population." *Illiterate America* (New York: Anchor Press/Doubleday, 1985), p. 4.

3. The Association française pour la lecture (AFL) estimates that between 50 and 70 percent of the population is excluded from all forms of written communication. Quoted by Jean-Pierre Vélis, *La France illettrée* (Paris: Éditions du Seuil, 1988). [Free translation].

4. Here, for example, is what the National Advisory Board on Science and Technology had to say: "...it is essential that the Government of Canada maintain its leadership in order to ensure that this problem is resolved with extreme urgency. There is no excuse for a country like Canada, with its resources and talents, to be tolerating the level of illiteracy which exists at present." *Technological Advance and Social Change: A Report by the Industry Committee of the National Advisory Board on Science and Technology* (Ottawa, 1988).

5. *Recherche-action sur le développement de l'alphabétisation au Québec* (Québec City: Ministère de l'Éducation du Québec, Direction générale de l'éducation des adultes, 1987).

6. Hélène Blais, Jean-Paul Hautecoeur and Lucie Lépine, *Recherche-action sur le développement de l'alphabétisation au Québec: Évaluations* (Québec City: Ministère de l'Éducation, Direction générale de l'éducation des adultes, 1988). All subsequent citations are from Lucie Lépine's section, "Jeu de pistes dans les autoévaluations."

7. Jean-Paul Hautecoeur, "Poids et mesures de l'alphabétisation au Québec," *ALPHA 88*, J.-P. Hautecoeur, ed. (Québec City: Ministère de l'Éducation, 1988).

8. Jean-François Lae and Patrice Noisette, *Je tu il elle apprend, Étude documentaire sur quelques aspects de l'illetrisme* (Paris: La Documentation française, 1985). [Free translation].

9. "Poids et mesures....," op. cit. Also François Furet and Jacques Ozouf, *Lire et Écrire* (Paris: Éditions de Minuit, 1977).

10. Despite this, teachers now sometimes do campaigning and recruiting work, in addition to their regular tasks. The maintenance of student enrolment, and thus of student commitment, depends on these nonacademic activities. Seven teachers working for the same school board made the following statement: "It is easy to contact mentally retarded students, but regular students are much more difficult to find. It is not easy to admit that we have difficulties with reading and writing. This is why, *in literacy work, we must keep constantly involved in awareness campaigns, recruiting and marketing activities....*," *Alpha Liaison*, Vol. 9, No. 1 (October 1988). [J.-P. Hautecoeur's italics].

11. The problem of recruiting regular students and the solution of replacing them with more willing student groups have also been observed in Belgium: "In the city, the immigrants are not ashamed, for they know why they have language problems. In rural areas, organizers turn too readily to those who are — or think they are — weak in spelling, or to the mentally retarded....," *Le Journal de l'Alpha*, 1-2/89, Lire et Écrire, Brussels. [Free translation].

12. Jonathan Kozol, *Where Stands the Republic? Illiteracy: A Warning and a Challenge to the Nation's Press*, Cox Newspapers, Atlanta, U.S.A., 1986.

13. For an official example of this, see the *Guide d'intervention sur mesure en formation de base*, Document 1 (Québec City: Ministère de l'Éducation, Direction générale de l'éducation des adultes, 1987), pp. 33-34.

14. "Le CECQ donne gratuitement au public des cours d'alphabétisation," *Le Soleil*, 9 September 1988.

15. See Hélène Blais, "Des mots et des maux, discours qui soignent," *Recherche-action...*, op. cit.

16. Extracts from the editorial, *Newsletter: Business Task Force on Literacy*, Vol. 1, No. 2 (January 1988).

17. In the United States, a Council of Employers for the Development of Literacy (connected with the McGraw-Hill Group) defines literacy as "the ability to process information, understand it, and apply it to defined tasks...14 million workers have a reading level equivalent to grade 4, and 23 million (20 percent) only have a grade 8 level. However, studies indicate that 70 percent of the reading material required for a sample of jobs across the nation require a level of comprehension corresponding to at least grade 9...," "Illiteracy Seen as a Threat to U.S. Economic Edge," *The New York Times*, 7 August 1988.

18. *A National Literacy Skill Assessment: Planning Report* (Ottawa: Statistics Canada, Special Projects Group, 1988), p. v.

19. Other estimates include: those unable to read newspapers, 8 percent; the adult population declaring less than five years of schooling, 6 percent; the failure rate for the most elementary test on language skills, 8 percent; the rate for adults who admit that being unable to read and write has penalized them at work or in their lives, 11 percent; the average failure rate in a series of seven simple tests on language skills, 12 percent.

20. *La France illettrée*, op. cit., pp. 146-47. (Free translation).

21. Jean-Paul Hautecoeur, *Anonymus Autoportraits* (Montréal: Éditions Saint-Martin, 1984).

22. William Labov, *Le parler ordinaire* (Paris: Éditions de Minuit, 1978).

23. "Poids et mesures...," op. cit.

24. Vivian Labrie, *Alphabétisées! Quatre essais sur le savoir lire* (Québec City: Institut québécois de recherche sur la culture, 1987), pp. 41-44.

25. *Des priorités en éducation des adultes* (Québec City: Conseil supérieur de l'éducation, February 1987). [Free translation].

THOSE INDIANS ARE TROUBLE...

Noëlla McKenzie
Maliotenam, Québec

As far back as I can remember, my parents always lived on their hunting ground, called **Mineik***, while I, their first child, lived on the reserve at a boarding school. This was between 1953 and 1963, when the government wanted all of us to go to school, French school.*

But the Montagnais Indians of the Lower North Shore came to resent sending their children off to school.

It was probably around this time that the Indians began to experience serious problems. They were no longer self-governing; they were governed by others.

"Your father is a hunter. It's all I know. I was born a hunter. I hunted and trapped so that you and your mother could eat — caribou and beaver, Indian meat. Not once did you go hungry," he used to tell me when alcohol loosened his tongue and turned our conversation into a monologue on the past.

"Look at your father, Noëlla. I'm an honest man. When the Indian was his own master, it was not his way to be separated from his children, and he was always able to kill enough to feed them, even if he had a large family. When I was 16 years old, I helped your grandfather and grandmother, even after I married your mother and could hunt alone."

It's easy to understand why my father did not want his children taken away from him and sent to the boarding school on the **Maliotenam** *reserve to be educated by strangers.*

"I stopped spending 10 months a year in the bush, my child, because I was worried about you. This is what I think. I believe school has no value for the **Innu***,* * *and that the white man built the school and the reserve to trap us into a sedentary way of life while he makes a living off our land. When he built the railroad and the boarding school, it was to destroy more than it was to build. Remember, your father is an honest man.*

---

* Innu: Montagnais

"*The government never gave us any compensation for* **Caniapiscau**,** *where 100 000 caribou were drowned because of the white man's dam. But if the government had given us 100 000 cows and they'd all died, then you can be sure we would've had to pay for them! The government can do that, you know. And as if that wasn't enough, we had to remove all the dead caribou from the river. It was our meat they stole from us.*

"*The white man wants to build more dams on our rivers. He's probably talking about it right now behind our backs.*

"*Our rivers...where every summer we fished for salmon before returning to the bush to hunt.*

"*Now it's dangerous in the bush. Think of last year, when they confiscated your brother's guns and the game he had taken and put him in prison in Newfoundland. The gamekeeper can hide all he wants in the bush, I know it and its inhabitants well.*"

I watched him. He had calmed down now and was sleeping on the couch.

And I knew, without having lived in the bush, that what he said was true, not only for us but for all the other families on the reserve.

In the 1950s, at the boarding school, I wasn't allowed to speak our language or I would get the strap. Once, at nap time, I said in Indian, "It's already daylight," and all the children laughed. I don't know what the nun thought I said. I think we weren't allowed to speak Indian even in the schoolyard among ourselves. That's hard for a 7- or 8-year-old, especially when the only tongue you know is your mother tongue.

What would the white man think if my parents brought his children into the bush and forbade them to speak French or English? What would he do if the Indian beat white children because they knew nothing of our way of life?

For 10 years, I was forced to receive a "white" education, in addition to being separated from my mother, father, aunts and uncles. All those years, I spent only two months out of the year with them.

Now, 22 years later, I think of the white man. He does not seem concerned over what has happened to us. Not once has he said, "I'm sorry. It was wrong of me to do you wrong."

** Caniapiscau: former hunting ground

The white man never said to the Indian, "I am taking your hunting grounds away from you and you will move to another place I have prepared for you." The school officials never said to us, "You will lose your culture. Your children will go to our school."

When I listen to my father, I think that my culture is good and sound. It did everything it could to help us live off our hunting and fishing. That's what "making a living" meant to the Montagnais.

I can still speak my mother tongue, but I do not eat Indian food and I do not live in the bush. Those of my people who are my age no longer make a living the Indian way, nor do they know how to work like the white man. And still the white man says, "Those Indians are trouble."

"Those Indians are trouble," says the white man when he talks about us. "They have no education and they do not want to live in the bush. All they do is sit around."

TOWARD A EUROPEAN SPACE FOR ADULT LITERACY AND BASIC EDUCATION

Pierre Freynet
Université d'Angers

Most of the European contributors to this volume met at working conferences organized by the Centre universitaire de formation continue (CUFCO). It therefore seems relevant at this point to discuss the significance of, reasons for and dynamics of these conferences.

A PRAGMATIC APPROACH

It is for very pragmatic reasons that the first pan-European conferences on adult literacy education were organized, at CUFCO's instigation. Although CUFCO had already established ties with the international adult education community, it had not yet had reason to look into the problem of adult illiteracy. In 1983 or thereabouts, a local association working with illiterate adults asked CUFCO for help in training its instructors. This was not an easy task: like many other organizations, CUFCO was just becoming aware of the extent of adult illiteracy and of an even more serious problem, i.e., that little was being done in France in the way of literacy work.

CUFCO naturally turned to organizations in other countries such as Great Britain and Germany, which, in turn, were interested in knowing more about the situation in France. A number of European and international conferences provided other opportunities to continue making contacts, and from these exchanges came the idea of organizing a European conference, not on the broad subject of illiteracy (which had already been extensively discussed), but on a more specific topic. After much thought, it was decided that the conference would focus on what seemed to be one of the most pressing and urgent needs, i.e., the training of literacy instructors. Thus, the first European conference, made possible by funding from the Commission of the European Communities, was held in May 1987 at the Université d'Angers.

NEEDS

From the first meeting held in January 1987 in Angers to plan the conference, it was clear not only that such a conference filled a need but also that such meetings should be held on a regular basis and not merely as the result of an organization's wish to hold a one-time event on a particular theme. The need to create some kind of pan-European "network" with a focus on adult illiteracy and basic education was already emerging and would continue to be felt at subsequent meetings of European practitioners.

Meetings were held each year for three consecutive years under the auspices of CUFCO, with funding from the Commission of the European Communities. Practitioners, researchers, instructors, policy-makers, and learners involved in adult literacy and basic education came together to share their findings and experiences.

— The 1987 meeting was devoted to instructor training.

— The 1988 meeting was devoted to discussing instructor training in greater depth. Research was also on the agenda, but discussions focussed on the organizational problems inherent to setting up a pan-European network.

— The 1989 meeting, a seminar held at the Université d'Angers in April, was devoted to research.

Three years gives time to mature projects. It also gives time to take stock. However, assessments are realistic only if their initial objectives are kept in perspective. At the outset, our objectives were quite modest. We were venturing into vast uncharted territory and it was very clear to us that we had to restrain our ambition and set objectives that were within our reach. Given our limited resources and the scope of our venture, our policy has been to work towards modest, yet realistic objectives. Specifically, it has always been our concern to publish, to give our work a concrete dimension.

Among the publications released to date are:

— an overview, in French and English, of the adult illiteracy problem and of adult literacy initiatives in member states of the European Economic Community;

— the proceedings, in French and English, of the European seminar on adult education and literacy instructor training, held in Angers in May 1987;

— a paper giving a "profile of the perfect instructor";

— a proposal for a program to ensure minimum training for novice adult education and literacy instructors.

These documents provide a yardstick against which to measure our progress so far but, most significantly, they are the result of a collaborative effort by individuals who do not speak the same language, share the same cultural background nor live in the same context.

This is another aspect to consider when reviewing past and present achievements. Besides providing an opportunity to produce knowledge, sometimes shaped into articles and papers, these meetings brought together more than 60 people, creating a truly "European" nucleus of professionals from different countries who know each other, have worked together, and are at least familiar with the problems that exist in other European countries besides their own. This nucleus is still small, but represents a good core around which we can build, and this, we feel, is a major achievement in itself.

Another of our initial objectives was to find ways of facilitating exchanges within this nucleus and to reflect on how a truly pan-European network could operate. Needless to say, this is quite a challenge!

TOWARD A EUROPEAN NETWORK?

While it was generally recognized that a permanent mechanism for exchange and cooperation had become a necessity in Europe, how it would actually work was still very much unclear. It had to satisfy a number of requirements that seemed totally irreconcilable at first glance, among which:

— to ensure efficiency without becoming bureaucratic;

— to ensure adequate funding without compromising its political independence;

— to bring together representative individuals from various groups without becoming elitist;

— to define its geographical boundaries without limiting itself to that territory.

Of course, the mechanism to be set up would also have to address the problems posed by language and distance.

Several meetings were devoted to discussing these problems and examining possible solutions.

— Should we create an entirely new structure or link up with an existing body?

— Should it be a single, central structure or should it distribute responsibilities among various branches?

— Should its geographic location be permanent or should it rotate?

— Should it establish direct links with local organizations and practitioners (in which case the vast number of these becomes a problem) or indirect links through regional and national organizations (in which case, the selection of these intermediaries becomes a problem)?

These and other questions had to be answered before a structure could be proposed. It is at a meeting in Lille that the groundwork for this structure was laid. A number of concerns influenced the decisions made at this meeting, among which the concern to:

— avoid creating a duplicate structure;

— avoid creating a cumbersome bureaucratic structure;

— create a structure that would give a voice to local practitioners and not only to their "official" representatives;

— create a structure independent of official authorities.

The proposal was to create a "European network for research, action, and training in adult literacy and basic education."

The use of the term "network" is deliberate, as it suggests a body composed of members who are on an equal footing and communicate with each other directly, as opposed to a vertical hierarchy.

In the same vein, the term "European" should be taken in its broadest sense, meaning that the network's point of reference is Europe and that members must not necessarily go through intermediate levels, such as national or regional organizations. (This does not, however, imply that these intermediaries are unnecessary.) It was decided to define "Europe" as meaning the "European Community," although this does not exclude representatives of non-European countries from joining the network.

As for the network's objectives, they are:

— to support and promote adult literacy and basic education;

— to promote the sharing of information;

— to promote cooperation (joint projects, exchanges, etc.);

— to put out documents, surveys and other various publications.

In order to achieve these objectives, it might be tempting to set up a new infrastructure whose role would be to organize conferences, seminars, and study trips, and seek sources of funding. However, in addition to having to jockey for position among existing organizations with a similar role, such a structure might quickly turn into a bureaucracy.

It seemed more in keeping with the philosophy underlying the network to let its members take initiatives and to set up a skeleton executive office that would simply help coordinate members' efforts. The program assessment and review group was designated to fill this role by participants at the first conference in Angers. CUFCO, of the Université d'Angers, is temporarily assuming administrative duties.

The executive office disseminates information through its newsletter, which is published in French and English.

As for projects, they are numerous, of course, given the extent of the problems to be resolved. Among current projects are a European summer university program planned for July 1990 with the aim of situating the illiteracy problem within a broader perspective.

PROBLEMS

A number of problems must be considered when setting up such a network, for example:

— geographical distance, with all the travel and expense it involves;

— the linguistic problems involved not only in communicating with people of different languages, but also in making important documents available to all;

— institutional problems. It is not always easy to have people from different institutions work together on a project. One must make allowances for personal interests. (No sooner was the network set up that the person in charge of analyzing how it could structure its activities tried to use his position to advance his own interests.)

Yet the need to create a "European space" for adult literacy and basic education has never been so great. The institutional problems mentioned above only serve to underline the importance of the stakes involved. In creating this space, two key elements must be considered.

International Literacy Year

By declaring 1990 International Literacy Year, the UN kicked off many international events, the most important of which is no doubt the World Conference on Education for All in Thailand in March 1990. Among other events held at this conference is the publication of a charter on the universal right to education. It is therefore important that Europe clearly define its position on these issues. With respect to world adult literacy and basic education, it is important that European countries identify their distinctive characteristics. Two positions were voiced at the meeting held in Strasbourg in late October to plan the world conference.

— Illiteracy is not a problem in European countries. All literacy efforts should focus on developing countries.

— The best — if not the only — way to fight illiteracy in developing countries is to make general elementary schooling compulsory.

The current situation in European countries belies both positions. It is therefore vital that Europe share the lessons it has learned from experience.

Any thought on the situation in European countries should be directed along the following lines:

— It is evident that all European countries must contend with the problem of adult illiteracy. Almost all of them have officially recognized its existence and some report significantly high rates. However, because many countries thought they had eradicated adult illiteracy, they have lost whatever practice and experience they had in this area. Hence, they could certainly benefit from the expertise gained by developing countries. For example, the British literacy campaign was modelled after the Cuban experience. Similarly, leaders like Paolo Freire have strongly influenced European educators.

— Nonetheless, while developing countries and European countries have many problems in common, the latter have a number of specific characteristics that must be considered:

— European countries are highly industrialized, with highly diversified economies.

— Communications in these countries are highly sophisticated (print and electronic media, telephone systems, computer systems, telecommunications).

— They have universal elementary and even secondary school systems (and in some countries, this has long been the case).

Any analysis of the illiteracy problem in a European country and any policy statement regarding literacy programming must take into account these distinctive characteristics.

Europe: Which Definition?

We have already discussed the need to define the differences that characterize European countries as regards adult illiteracy. But just what "Europe" are we talking about? The 12 member states of the European Community? The 23 countries of the European Council? Europe as defined by UNESCO (i.e., all of Europe, the U.S.S.R., North America, and Israel)? Europe in its strict geographical sense (i.e., "from the Atlantic to the Ural mountains")?

"From the Atlantic to the Ural mountains" is indeed a nice formula but, in reality, it is politically meaningless. Physical and human geography do not necessarily overlap. The Ural mountains do not form a natural barrier, much less a human one. The Cossacks crossed them long ago. The question is whether or not the U.S.S.R. should be considered part of Europe. If it is included, we should speak of Europe as stretching "from the Atlantic to the Pacific."

According to recent declarations by President Bush, the United States has no wish to be left out in the cold. Are we then moving toward a Europe as defined by UNESCO, i.e., all industrialized countries of the northern hemisphere? Will the East-West division give way to a North-South division? Such questions may seem premature or even simplistic. Still, the accelerating pace of change in Eastern Europe is reason enough to give this matter careful consideration.

In each of these definitions of Europe, what becomes of adult basic education? What role can it play? What role must it play? These questions are not purely academic. To be relevant and move with the times, European policy on adult education must not merely keep up with developments but anticipate them.

LINKING RESEARCH AND PRACTICE: TEN EXAMPLES OF ADULT LITERACY RESEARCH IN BRITAIN[1]

David Barton, University of Lancaster
Sally Murphy, Bradford Literacy Group

In Britain, the importance of adult literacy and basic education[2] has been recognized for the past 15 years and there has been a wide variety of provision with innovative teaching methods and approaches. More recently there has been an interest in research. In many cases the approach taken to research has reflected the philosophy which has developed in basic education: it is learner-centred and based on practice.

It is hard to get an overview of literacy research in Britain for several reasons. Firstly, research activities are spread thinly across the country. They are carried out in quite different places and are often hidden away in dissertations and project reports which are not easily available. Secondly, the general approach to literacy teaching in Britain (learner-centred and generally suspicious of traditional research) goes counter to the idea of large-scale high-profile research programs. Thirdly, adult literacy and basic education is a low-prestige, underfunded area of education where little research funding is available.

For these reasons, there is no central coordination of research. Although the government-funded Adult Literacy and Basic Skills Unit (ALBSU) has been crucial in the development of teaching provision, it has not been primarily concerned with research. It has funded a few research projects, some of which are described below, and its publications report on a wide range of activities.

What we will describe here are some of the developments in Britain which have led to higher-profile research. The viewpoint is that of the researchers who have been involved in the Research and Practice in Adult Literacy Group (RAPAL).

CONFERENCES

In 1984 we were involved in a conference entitled "Research and Practice in Adult Literacy." Held at Lancaster University, it was aimed at making links between researchers and practitioners and at getting an overview of research in Britain at that time. The report of that conference is listed below as Report 1.

Discussion at the conference generated many ideas and showed that there is widespread interest in linking research and practice. Specific areas were recommended for research. These include: identifying barriers to effective participation in groups; writing in basic education; how basic skills get transferred and used from one situation to another; comparative descriptions of adult basic education work; better understanding of the social context of literacy and numeracy, and their uses in everyday life.

Equally important were the questions about what counted as research.

> People were continually questioning what is meant by research, and they were criticizing traditional models of research. This was seen to be as important as generating specific research questions. There was a very clear idea of people's typical view of what research is, and people were very critical of much research. On the other hand, a very clear idea also emerged of what we would like research to achieve. Most practitioners' view of research is the traditional, dominant model that derives from psychology, and originally from the natural sciences such as physics. There are all sorts of metaphors for this research: the one we like best is the "parachute" model, where an outsider parachutes in from, apparently, nowhere brandishing a questionnaire. This external observer collects data, reaps the facts and disappears, never to be heard of again.

> The criticisms people have of this model are not just minor ones of technique, such as preferring interviews over surveys, but they are *basic* dissatisfactions:

> — Is this *all* you can call research? Is this what research is?

> — Who in fact does research? Who should do it?

> — Who should benefit from it?

> — What is the relationship between the funder and those who are affected by research?

> Barton and Hamilton, Report 2

With this enthusiasm and questioning, a second conference was organized in London by the Inner London Education Authority (ILEA) in February 1985. At this conference there were overview talks about what counts as research, along with workshops and poster displays of current research. The report of the conference (Report 2) ends with concrete proposals about how to relate research activity to practical issues of literacy provision in London. A year later, in July 1986, the ILEA organized another conference, again with a mixture of different types of sessions (Report 3). The RAPAL group was launched at this conference.

A fourth conference entitled "Literacy Research in the U.K.: Adult and School Perspectives" was organized at Sussex University in 1987 and the proceedings have been published by the RAPAL group (Report 4). This conference provided a comparative perspective on literacy, linking in both school and historical issues. All four of these conferences were attended by a wide variety of people including literacy practitioners and students. There have been changes during this time: gradually, different partnerships in the research process have been explored; a broader range of questions have been posed; and more basic education students have become involved.

LINKING RESEARCH AND PRACTICE

People's ideas have developed from conference to conference. In between the two London conferences, several of us from London, Lancaster and Bradford got together and decided that one way to keep in touch would be to start a group. We called ourselves the Research and Practice in Adult Literacy Group (RAPAL).

The three aims of the group are to:

— improve communication between practitioners and researchers in adult basic education;

— explore broader ideas of what research is;

— encourage research in this area.

We have been busy pursuing all three aims. Our main activity has been bringing out the RAPAL Bulletin. (Subscription details are available from RAPAL, Bolton Royd Centre, Manningham Lane, Bradford BD8 8DD.) There have been eight issues of the Bulletin containing short articles, reviews, reports and news, along with a digest of publications we know about. In addition to the conferences, we have been involved in training courses, including research methods courses for tutors and students, and locally based events. The results of a course on doing research, organized by the Lee Community Education Centre, London, have been written up (Report 5).

EXAMPLES OF CURRENT RESEARCH

Rather than attempt a comprehensive overview of research in Britain, we have decided to give brief details of 10 research projects. This should provide an idea of the range of activities currently going on in Britain. We have chosen them to demonstrate the variety of approaches rather than attempt to cover everything that is being done. The projects are all ongoing or have been completed recently; they are not necessarily linked to the RAPAL group. A fuller account of current research can be found in the four reports listed at the end of this paper and in the nine issues of RAPAL Bulletin.

Afro-Caribbean project

This project was set up to improve language and literacy provision for students in London who have an Afro-Caribbean language background. A small number of tutors were given a few hours relief from teaching to undertake their own projects. There have been many different projects, including: using information about the history of English to help students develop a positive attitude to their own variety of language and developing students' own written language histories. By means of these projects, practitioners were given some time to stand back and look at their work, to identify ways of improving it, to try these ways out and to make the results available to others.

Surveys carried out in 1984 revealed negative and generally confused attitudes to the languages of the Caribbean among students and tutors: "Black English is bad English," "Is it a dialect or a creole?" Students with the lowest level of literacy held the most negative and ill-informed attitudes to their own languages.

From this information, language awareness became the major thrust of the project. It was realized that this is an extremely delicate issue with potential for great harm. It was decided that heightened consciousness about language would be to everyone's advantage, not only those from an Afro-Caribbean language background. Approaches that have been employed are:

— using passages of literature by black writers;

— collecting information about the history of English;

— focussing on students' own language histories;

— translating spoken language into writing for publication;

— gathering and disseminating detailed information about African and Caribbean languages, including French Creole.

Future work is likely to include projects to train black literacy tutors, to focus on literacy for specific jobs, to pilot materials and to set up a centre in Hackney for French Creole.

Information and copies of reports are available for the Afro-Caribbean Language and Literacy Project, 1 Gerridge Street, London SE1 7QT. The Afro-Caribbean Project has been funded by ILEA and brief details can be found in RAPAL Bulletin 2: 1-2.

Student involvement in research

This work arose from two 24-hour workshops held in London in September and November 1987 with the aim of involving ABE students in research.

At the first meeting 22 students from around the country decided what they wanted to discover about students' needs in ABE. From numerous wide-ranging questions, they finally decided on "How do people decide to join classes?" The students then devised a 16-point questionnaire, and were asked to interview students in their own centre or area within the following two months.

The students used different methods to collect their information. Some used individual and private interviews, while others asked everyone in a class to complete the survey or mailed the questionnaires to a tutor. Some questions did not work well. For example, on choice of class (such as one-to-one, group, single-sex group), the information was inconclusive.

In November the group met again to compile their findings. To the question "What made you decide to come?" most people checked confidence and hope, which the group took to mean "wanting to gain more confidence" and "hope for the future." They found wide discrepancies in fee levels across the country and almost no accommodation for people with disabilities. They also noted that they had mostly interviewed men between the ages of 25 and 40.

This research was designed and carried out by tutors and students, and was organized by the National Federation for Voluntary Literacy Schemes. A full report can be obtained from Jane Mace, Lee Community Centre, 1 Aislibie Road, London SE12 8QH. A short report of this research can be found in RAPAL Bulletin 5: 2-3.

Basic skills project

This project examined the literacy problems of a cross section of Britain's population: 12 500 23-year-olds. More than 10 percent reported having problems with reading, writing or spelling since leaving school. Among the many results, it was found that two-thirds of the people who reported problems had no educational qualifications, while one-third did.

There were more likely to be problems with writing than reading. These problems could often be summed up as a general feeling of not meeting a standard expected by themselves or others. When the problems were specific, they were mostly related to jobs. Numeracy, however, was more often related to home, and women's responses emphasized home and children's needs more often.

The project highlighted gender differences: 12 percent of the men and 9 percent of the women had literacy problems, but numeracy problems were evenly distributed. However, men were twice as likely to seek literacy help and four times as likely to seek numeracy help. Although 46 percent overall received no training, this represented 39 percent of the men and 57 percent of the women. Seven percent of the women were single parents and, in general, the women were poorer than the men.

As for the early identification of problems, 7 percent of the basic skills group had been in special schools by age 11 and 36 percent had received help by age 16. However, 40 percent of the group never received any special help and found that school-based definitions of competence were at odds with what mattered to people in their daily lives.

The project is at pains to highlight that these findings indicate "a structural problem that needs to be understood in a broad cultural context and not simply a remedial problem that can be solved on an individual basis."

This project was funded by the Adult Literacy and Basic Skills Unit and the Manpower Services Commission. The research was carried out at Lancaster University and a report by M. Hamilton, entitled "Literacy, Numeracy and Adults" is available from ALBSU, 229 High Holborn, London WC1V 7DA. A discussion of the report appears in RAPAL Bulletin 3: 1-3.

Understanding public information

This project studied the problems people experience in obtaining, understanding and using information about public services. Most of the project is a case study of the Housing Department in Brighton and the public information it provides. Tenants' views on the written material were discussed with housing officers in order to improve the information provided.

Researcher Rachel Lickiss interviewed approximately 30 tenants identified by the Housing Department. The sample was known to include some with good and some with poor relationships with the Housing Department. Lickiss also attended information sessions to get a fuller picture of the Department's relationships with tenants.

Tenants found that written information was not useful if too detailed. If the written information was about an unfamiliar subject, they found it very difficult to "get the hang of it." They preferred an A5-sized sheet which gave broad outlines and indicated where to get more detailed, spoken information. Tenants also preferred to have one Housing Officer whom they could get to know as a person and ask for spoken information. The Housing Assistants also preferred spending some of their time in local offices, where they could get alongside local tenants and work with them.

A report on this project can be obtained from the Lewis Cohen Urban Studies Centre, 68 Grand Parade, Brighton BN2 2JY. Further details can also be obtained from Rachel Lickiss, 49 Firle Crescent, Lewes, East Sussex BN7 1QG. There are brief details in RAPAL Bulletin 5: 9.

Student control

In 1987 students and tutors in the Blackfriars Literacy Scheme in London decided to examine what was meant by "student control." Did the term mean "participation" rather than "control"? Did it mean control over what was learned or how their scheme was organized, or both? Could students have control if organizers were accountable to funding agencies? It was decided to develop a definition which learners and workers shared.

To this end 24 students completed two questionnaires, one about student control of learning, the other about student involvement in the organization of the Blackfriars Scheme. One of the groups within the centre took responsibility for collating the data.

Control over learning:

Most students seemed satisfied with the amount of control they had over their own learning. Two students wanted more control but only three of the 24 thought that control was shared 50:50. Being involved in the preparation of materials, helping each other, leading workshops and groups were good examples of control. Bad exemples were: being hurried or forced, suffering patronizing volunteers, or being told to write something and then having it ignored. Interestingly, some students regarded "control" as negative and preferred to think in terms of "student responsibility."

Control of the scheme:

Three-quarters of the sample were satisfied with the amount of control they had. However, while attendance at scheme meetings was seen as a way to participate in control of the scheme, only four students regularly attended.

This in-house research has led to the rotation of scheme meetings (with increased attendance) and opened a debate about control versus responsibility. This is an example of a group of students doing research as part of their learning. A report of their findings appears in RAPAL Bulletin 6: 4-5.

Literacy in the community

This research aims to investigate people's everyday uses of literacy and to build up a notion of "community literacy," as distinct from school views of literacy or work views of literacy. People in Lancaster have been interviewed about how literacy fits into everyday activities. The interview covers subjects as diverse as: what happens to junk mail; who controls the family newspaper; whom people go to locally for advice. It is an oral history or an "ethnography" of literacy. We are interested in everyone's uses of literacy. To begin with, we are interviewing basic education students. We hope to be more detailed and systematic than is possible when analyzing students' needs in a literacy class. Students find it valuable: some who have been interviewed are interested in going out and doing similar interviews themselves. We are finding that the interview starts discussions about the value of literacy, support networks, different literacy roles people have, access to information, and more.

In addition to the interviews, three other sorts of information are being collected: firstly, detailed case studies of families going about their daily lives, with observation of how home uses of literacy fit in with the demands of children at school, how there are differing demands at home and at work, seeing what people do when they identify reading and writing problems; secondly, general observations of reading and writing in the local community, in shops, post offices, hospitals, etc.; thirdly, collection of recorded data on access points for literacy, on libraries, bookshops, schools, etc.

This project is funded by the University of Lancaster and the Economic and Social Research Council. There are brief details in RAPAL

Bulletin 6: 11 and more can be obtained from David Barton, Department of Linguistics, Lancaster University, LA1 4YT.

Management in adult basic education

This work-in-progress is examining teams of managers (including two adult basic education teams) and how they carry out the job of managing. Several sources are being examined to establish how the teams manage: minutes of meetings, programs which teams produced, individual team member's repertory grids about adult education and members' answers to open-ended questions about the nature of teamwork. Although the study is not yet concluded, it appears that:

— The educational goals of individuals within teams are often divorced from the work they must do to be managers.

— The goals of individuals in relation to effectiveness are likely to be more ambitious than external goals.

— There is a pattern to the job of managing: planning projects are divided between those implied by the managers' brief/goals and those arising from the demands of the work; planning is one of the managers' tasks as well as organizing facilities, working out procedures to get things done, and staff work. Although the time spent on these activities varies according to the managers' interpretations of their jobs, the season and the length of time they have been managing, it may be that a concrete awareness of the tasks could make managing easier.

— What managers think they are doing changes all the time but, because they are involved in the activities, they are often unaware of the changes in their thinking.

Further details can be obtained from Mandy McMahon, 18 Thackley Old Road, Shipley, Bradford BD18 1DD, West Yorkshire. There are details in RAPAL Bulletin 6: 12-13.

Assessment of student progress

This project is reviewing assessment techniques currently used in literacy schemes and other areas of education. This information is being used to develop assessment models which are appropriate to adult literacy, emphasize participation and are of use to the learners. One current aim of the project is to prepare a booklet on assessment which will be useful to those interested in taking a critical look at their own practice in the field. A draft booklet has been produced and is being piloted.

The project is funded by ALBSU. For more information, contact research worker Deryn Holland, Adult Education Research Centre, Cherry Tree Buildings, University of Nottingham, Nottingham. There are brief details in RAPAL Bulletin 6: 11-12.

The U.S.-U.K. exchange

In June 1988, 75 American and 40 British participants met in New York to begin a process of information exchange, research and report. Initially, the participants met in groups which were assigned themes, including: assessment, work-related education, literacy for community action, learner-centred education, tutor training and funding. During the week in New York, the groups met daily and considered proposals for collaborative projects; in the process, they explored similarities and differences in basic education in the two countries.

People worked on their projects during the year and about 40 Americans took part in a return meeting in Britain in July 1989. The groups varied a great deal in what they achieved but several of them, such as the Literacy in Prison group, have decided to stay in regular contact.

Details in RAPAL Bulletin 7: 13-15; 8: 12-14 and from ALBSU, 229 High Holborn, London WC1V 7DA.

The all-Wales student writing project

This project aims to develop student writing in both English and Welsh, and to develop tutors' confidence and abilities in initiating a variety of opportunities for writing and in understanding the different processes involved in writing. There is a regular newsletter with articles written by students and tutors on ideas for writing and group work, as well as reports of writing workshops and writing weekends.

For details, contact Margaret Morris, Room 22, Llyn-y-bryn School, Walter Road, Swansea, West Glamorgan, Wales. There is a brief report in RAPAL Bulletin 8: 9.

CONCLUSION

The diversity of these 10 examples of research should be obvious. Firstly, many different participants in literacy activities (tutors, students, managers and full-time researchers) have been involved. Secondly, the projects have been funded in quite different ways, some locally, some nationally. Thirdly, they have been carried out in quite different institutions with different forms of collaboration. In some, groups of basic education students have done the research themselves, while full-time researchers have been involved in others. To some extent, these differences reflect the different aims of the research.

We hope these examples of research will prove to be a springboard for discussions about what research is and how it links with practice. There is a strong interest in making research relevant to the teaching situation and in involving all participants, including learners, in the research process. However, the teaching situation is not the only point of research. There is a need to go beyond this: other aspects, like management issues in basic education, need research; people are situating teaching in the broader context of everyday use, and are asking basic questions about what literacy is and about its value in contemporary society.

Britain is undergoing major changes in the legal framework and funding of education at all levels. Basic education is particularly vulnerable, and it is increasingly important that we continue to record and reflect upon our activities.

NOTES

1. A shorter version of this paper was prepared for the European Community conferences: "Research as a Tool in Literacy Practice and Adult Basic Education," London, December 11-13, 1988 and "Writing in Adult Basic Education," Angers, April 23-27, 1989.

2. In English we have a terminology problem. In this paper we use the terms *literacy* and *basic education* interchangeably, although we are aware of the issues and problems raised. We also use the words *teacher*, *tutor* and *practitioner* to mean the same person, i.e., the person doing the teaching. The person "receiving" the teaching is referred to as a *student* or *learner*. We do not use the term *illiterate*, which is both inappropriate and pejorative.

CONFERENCE REPORTS

Report 1: M. Hamilton and D. Barton, *Research and Practice in Adult Literacy*. 1985. Published by the Association for Recurrent Education, Cherry Tree Buildings, University of Nottingham, Nottingham.

Report 2: M. Baynham and R. Ivanic, *Research and Practice in Adult Literacy*. ILEA Language and Literacy Unit. Occasional Paper No. 1, September 1985. Published by The Language and Literacy Unit, 1 Gerridge Street, London SE1 7QT.

Report 3: G. Lobley, *Work in Progress*. ILEA Language and Literacy Unit. Occasional Paper No. 4, July 1988. Published by The Language and Literacy Unit, 1 Gerridge Street, London SE1 7QT.

Report 4: J. MacCaffery and B. Street, *Literacy Research in the U.K.: Adult and School Perspectives*. 1988. RAPAL Publications. Distributed by Avanti Books, 1 Wellington Road, Stevenage SG2 9HR.

Report 5: M. Baynham and J. Mace, *Doing Research: Interviews, Tapes and Transcriptions*. 1986. Published by The Lee Community Education Centre, 1 Aislibie Road, London SE12 8QH.

UNDERSTANDING EVERYDAY LITERACY[1]

David Barton
University of Lancaster

Many new views of literacy are being developed. My own work has been concerned with making sense of what people read and write in their everyday lives. In this paper I want to spell out the framework that is needed to understand everyday reading and writing, and to demonstrate that a social view of reading and writing is an essential part of our understanding of literacy. There are three aspects to a social view. Firstly, to describe people's everyday literacy, we must refer to *literacy practices* and *literacy events*. Secondly, it is useful to see everyday literacy as being one of several *domains* of reading and writing. And, thirdly, we must see literacy practices as *social practices* involving the roles people adopt, the networks they are part of, and the values and attitudes they hold.

Everyday literacy is a very rich area to explore. We can see this clearly with an example. In going about their daily life, people today are constantly placed in situations requiring literacy. For people waking up in Lancaster, England (where I live), the first voice heard in the morning might well be that of someone reading a written text to them: a news reader on the radio. Going downstairs, they find a newspaper on the doormat along with some mail, and they at least glance at these. Even before the first cup of English tea, there have been two literacy events quite different from each other. We could continue through the day, from shopping, consulting a calendar, following the instructions for using a new watch and writing a cheque, on through to leaving a note for the milkman last thing at night. The activities involving literacy in some way are many and varied.

We can use this short example to demonstrate what a comprehensive view of literacy must include. The first point is that literacy is embedded in these everyday activities. It is not something done just at school or at work. In fact several of the activities seem quite unlike those which are focussed on in our educational system. For example, making notes or consulting a calendar may not sound like skills typically taught in school, while listening to the news may not be thought of as having anything to do with literacy.

Secondly, we can also see that there are many different ways of using the written word. Listening to the news being read, scanning through the junk mail or leaving a note for the milkman are all very different activities; in each, literacy has a distinct use. These uses are very different and it may not be very advantageous to think of writing as one activity which is the same across all situations. Approaches using broader terms such as "literacy events" or "literacy practices" are important here. We also find we need to talk in terms of "literacies," not just literacy. There are many ways of writing, just as there are many ways of reading or "taking meaning from the text."

These examples are also particular to a specific community at a given point in history. It is only in some cultures that newspaper, milk and mail are delivered to the door early in the morning. It is only in some cultures that it is thought normal to start the day sitting at a table and simultaneously listening to a radio, reading a newspaper and drinking a cup of tea.

The social settings in which literacy occurs are particular to individual societies and have developed over time. Like other cultural activities, ways of being literate are passed on from generation to generation. They are reorganized and reinvented by each succeeding generation. We therefore also need a relativistic view which includes a historical perspective.

The early morning scene we have described could include people of all ages, from young children to elderly people. People learn about literacy throughout life, not just during one age range, and all activities are forms of learning. To take account of this we need a view of literacy which allows change, a dynamic view of constantly developing literacy, rather than a static model. The literacy demands on people fluctuate during their lifetime.

It is individual people who participate in literacy events: they are actively involved with literacy and are aware of it; it makes sense to them, and holds meaning and value for them. This meaning and this value then act as guides to and constraints on action. People have purposes. They have their own purposes and at the same time live in a society which makes demands upon them. Most of the above examples refer to people's direct participation in literacy in their everyday lives. While they are varied, they nevertheless cover only a narrow view of literacy: the example of listening to a radio news reader indicates how literacy is part of much broader activities requiring understanding of what is going on about us, and requiring that we make sense of the world. As a communication medium, literacy structures certain social relations.

We have already made several observations not covered by the most common views of literacy. Most theories of literacy start out from the educational settings in which literacy is typically taught, so that the dominant definitions of literacy are school-based and, to a lesser extent, work-based. These views of literacy are often at odds with what people experience in their everyday lives. The discrepancy can be very straightforward, in that the reading and writing which people do in their everyday lives is different from that done in school. It can also relate to more general conceptions of literacy. An example of this is that society's view of illiteracy may be quite different from the perceptions of a person with reading and writing difficulties. We assume that school, work and community are different domains of literacy. We must develop ways of talking about literacy in these different domains.

If we look outside the educational domain, different issues arise and phenomena not highlighted in a school-based view of literacy suddenly become prominent. For example, we see that people learn from each other and that, as adults, people continue to learn about how to use their language. We see that people can have different roles in a literacy event. A much wider range of activities count as writing and reading, and we get a far richer view of what literacy is.

EVENTS AND PRACTICES

Reading and writing are carried out in everyday life. Our starting point is everyday life and we need ways of talking about everyday activities. As already stated, it may not be very useful to think of writing as one activity which is the same across all situations. It is probably not very useful to try to abstract some general skill from them and it is important to get away from something residing in the individual or in the product. We need to talk in broader terms and it is here that the concepts of "practices" and "events" are helpful. Several people have been using these terms. (Others have made "activity" the central unit.) We can start by drawing on other people's characterizations of literacy practices and events. These terms are part of newer conceptions of literacy which are being articulated in different ways by linguists, sociologists, anthropologists, psychologists and others converging on the same problem.

Firstly, what is meant by "practices"? The term is used in several disciplines, and several researchers have applied it directly to literacy. Street, an anthropologist, speaks of an "ideological" model of literacy which assumes that "the meaning of literacy depends on the social institutions in which it is embedded" and that "the particular practices of reading and writing...taught in any context depend upon such aspects of social structure as stratification...and the role of educational institutions" (1985: 8).

Coming from a psychological perspective, Scribner and Cole (1981) move away from a skills explanation of reading and writing. They are edging towards their alternative notion of a "practice account" of literacy, arguing that literacy can only be understood in the context of the social practices in which it is acquired and used. They conclude their study of Vai literacy:

> Instead of focussing exclusively on the technology of a writing system and its reputed consequences... we approach literacy as a set of socially organized practices which make use of a symbol system and a technology for producing and disseminating it. Literacy is not simply knowing how to read and write a particular script but applying this knowledge for specific purposes in specific contexts of use. The nature of these practices, including, of course, their technological aspects, will determine the kinds of skills ("consequences") associated with literacy (1981: 236).

Their discussion expands on this and they discuss how practices can be seen as ways of using literacy which are carried across situations (234-38).

The other general term which has become a basic unit of analysis is that of "event." The notion of literacy event has its roots in the sociolinguistic idea of speech events. It has had its most detailed use in Heath's study of communities in the United States; she refers to a literacy event as being "when talk revolves around a piece of writing" (1983: 386). Elsewhere, she talks of literacy events more generally, as being communicative situations where literacy has an integral role in people's interactions and their interpretive processes (1982). This is important in demonstrating that literacy has a role in so many communicative activities. Identifying and describing these events is important in understanding children's (and adults') learning of literacy.

There are two terms to use here. "Literacy events" are the particular activities where literacy has a role; they may be regular, repeated activities. "Literacy practices" are the general cultural ways of utilizing literacy which people draw upon in a literacy event. For example, leaving a note for the milkman is a *literacy event*. In deciding to do it, finding a pen and paper, deciding what to write and where to leave it, we make use of our *literacy practices*.

DOMAINS OF WRITING

There may be different literacy practices in different *domains* of social life. The term "domain" has been used in the study of language for some time. It is useful when talking about everyday reading and writing, as it enables us to contrast home, school and work situations. School and work are two obvious domains which have been studied and where there may be distinct literacy practices. To this we are adding the domain of everyday literacy. For the moment, home and community are being treated as one homogeneous domain. However, different breakdowns are possible. The decision that something constitutes a separate domain is based partly on sociological considerations (i.e., a distinct social situation) but more on the fact that identifiably different types and uses of literacy are involved.

Particular institutions support these distinct domains of home, school and work. They support particular definitions of literacy and nurture associated literacy practices. There are certain definition-sustaining institutions. It is probably true that different institutions define and control or influence different areas of literacy. For example, it may be true in a particular culture that religion influences ritual aspects of literacy; the family has an effect on habits of personal communication; and work and school influence public and formal aspects of communication. To some extent these different institutions may be supporting conflicting literacy practices. It follows from this that domains are not equal, that they overlap and that there is movement between them.

Documenting and understanding everyday literacy is an essential part of understanding the learning of literacy. One reason for identifying the everyday as a distinct domain is the belief that the key to learning is in everyday activities and in how people make sense of them. Beginning from everyday contexts and later moving out to study school and work situations should contribute to our understanding of learning and may give us different insights from those provided by studies which start from school or work.

The home domain

In mainstream culture, the household is an ecological niche in which literacy survives, is sustained and flourishes. In many households literacy is part of the web of home life. In addition to the example already given many everyday activities require the use of literacy in some way. Sometimes, it is central and its role obvious; at other times this is not so. There is a great deal of print in the house: on packaging and notice boards, in instructions, junk mail, magazines and books. Cooking, eating, shopping, keeping records and celebrating all make use of literacy in some way. Literacy is not the aim of these activities. Their aim is something else — to survive, to consume, to act in the world — and literacy is an integral part of achieving these other aims.

In many households, literacy is an essential part of these everyday activities and, in many ways, the household is structured around literacy, which mediates family activities. There are many ways of putting this.

Heath locates literacy in the ways families use space and time, and describes how literate traditions

> ...are interwoven in different ways with oral uses of language, ways of negotiating meaning, deciding on action, and achieving status. Patterns of using reading and writing in each community are interdependent with ways of using space (having bookshelves, decorating walls, displaying telephone numbers), and using time (bedtime, meal hours, and homework sessions).

This is true of very literate households, but literacy has a significant role even in less literate households. Where researchers have taken very simple measures, such as the number of books in the home, it is very easy to find wide disparities — and to be shaken in one's own literate world by the high number of homes containing almost no books. However, all homes in Britain and North America are touched by literacy. There are still consumer packaging to get through, bills to pay, junk mail to sort and various official forms and notices to deal with. Junk mail cannot be avoided; you have to do something with it and people develop individual solutions to cope with the continuous tide (Taylor 1983: 27).

It is not a question of households being literate or not. It is not adequate to characterize this as a simple dimension of amount of literacy. What we can see from Heath's study and others is that households are part of whole communities which are oriented to literacy differently. This reflects not only on literacy but on the whole dynamics of the households. For the moment, it is enough to emphasize that, in Heath's Trackton, despite being unlike mainstream culture and being in many ways oral, literacy still impinges a great deal.

WRITING AS SOCIAL PRACTICE

We are assuming that how literacy is used in everyday life in the home and the wider community constitutes a coherent domain. It is a distinct domain in that literacy has its own uses and is sustained in particular ways; we expect to see distinctive practices which we can then draw upon to provide insights into understanding other domains such as school.

If everyday literacy is a distinct domain with its own practices, then these must be documented. In doing this we come across several themes which provide a richer way of talking about literacy and which help us identify significant aspects of the context of literacy which must be incorporated into any theory of literacy learning. Firstly, we must situate people's *literacy practices* as being part of their *social practices*. Next, there are particular *roles* people take and *networks* of support they participate in. This leads on to the sense people make of reading and writing and the *value* literacy holds for them. A theme which seems very rich when discussing writing is *literacy and change*. The last theme to mention is that of how everyday *processes of learning* are revealed in the home and community. Here, I will focus on what is meant by these themes. For a concrete example of how this framework has been applied to understanding a particular community, see Barton and Padmore (1990).

Literacy practices as social practices

There are common patterns in reading and writing activities in any community. These literacy practices must be seen as social practices. People do things for a reason; they have purposes. Literacy serves other purposes. In general, people do not read in order to read, nor write in order to write; rather, they read and write to do other things, to achieve other ends. People want to know what time the train leaves or how a new watch or video works; they want to keep in contact with a friend; they want to make their voice heard. They must pay the bills or bake a birthday cake. Reading and writing can be part of these social activities. They fit in in different ways. They can be an integral part of the activity, or the relationship may be more complex.

Reading and writing are often one option among others for achieving a given communicative goal: to find out when the train leaves, there may be a choice between asking someone, phoning someone or looking in a timetable. Each of these involves reading and writing in different ways. Patterns of choice may vary from one individual to another, as people trust these forms of communication in differing amounts. The importance of viewing reading and writing in terms of social practices is that we see the purpose behind the activities; we also see how intertwined the written word is with other forms of communication, especially spoken language.

Roles and networks

Who does what? There are appropriate roles and forbidden ones. Not everyone does everything. We can examine the asymmetry of literacy roles as well as people's assumptions about what are appropriate or proscribed activities for themselves and others. The headline in a British newspaper, "Wives write Xmas cards...Husbands write cheques," sums up a common role division. In couples, women often write in the personal sphere, keeping in contact with friends and relations, while men deal with the business world. These roles can be maintained to the extent that men are unable to write a personal letter and women do not know how to write a cheque. However, the division is not hard and fast and the roles not always obvious. Difficulties with reading and writing, or with particular skills in this area, can affect the roles people assume.

Roles are much broader than this and, in any social event, people adopt particular roles. The importance of talking in terms of roles is that we see people's literacy practices as being related, not just to *abilities*, but rather to what is or is not *appropriate*. There are appropriate roles and inappropriate roles. To move away from describing people's actions just in terms of abilities is a significant step in our understanding of literacy.

Roles exist within networks. We can map the social networks of support which exist and the informal learning which takes place. These networks have broad functions covering work, child rearing and other areas of social activity. Sometimes there is support where people identify problems with literacy-related activities. Where people have problems, their roles can be very different. Another aspect of these networks is that, since they exist, problems do not arise: people have networks of support which help them avoid problems.

Thinking in terms of roles and networks, and realizing that every-one has appropriate and inappropriate roles, emphasizes the relative nature of difficulties. People do not need to identify literacy "problems" in order to get a friend to help them with their tax form or to have the railway official write out some train times. Specific people who provide support can be regarded as brokers for literacy activities. They may be neighbours or friends who deal with figures or fill in the forms. Support may also be institutionalized: the railway officials who look up train times, the travel agents who fill in holiday forms for customers.

The notion of networks is important in trying to push our under-standing of literacy beyond the standard accounts; it also emphasizes that reading and writing are not just an individual affair: often a literate activity involves the contribution of several people. Networks are also important for people's attitudes to education and the possibilities it can provide. Outside the immediate family, other relatives can be very influential. How people with literacy problems make use of social networks is described by Fingeret (1983).

Values

People make sense of literacy as a social phenomenon, and their social construction of literacy lies at the root of their attitudes towards literacy and their actions. It follows from this that people's views of literacy are important in how and what they learn. A parent's attitudes and actions influence a child's behaviour at school. We are trying to develop a way of talking about literacy which can encompass this. Saying that literacy has a social meaning is going further than saying that it has social dimensions or that it exists within a social context. The act of reading or writing becomes symbolic: it takes on a social meaning; it can be an act of defiance, solidarity, or conforming; it can be a symbol of change.

One way in which people express the values they attach to literacy is in their moral attitudes. There is a range of moral and social values attached to writing. People have values, attitudes and feelings associated with literacy and these values underlie their practices, affect what they do. It is in practices that values are expressed. For example, people often have strong views about reading at the meal table or writing in books. This is also reflected in views about censorship of literacy materials.

Another aspect of this is that values are also clearly expressed in the relative value attached to literacy as compared with other domains, such as practical and physical activities. Sometimes reading and writing are contrasted with work; at other times they are equated with leisure. In our historical study, for instance, we got the impression that people felt it is better to be reading than to be doing nothing, but better still to be doing some "real" work rather than reading (see Barton 1988 for examples). Writing is not just a cognitive activity; feelings run through it.

Change and access

There are several ways in which literacy is bound up with changes in people's lives. Firstly, people write at particular times in their lives. The demands of life change: there are times in people's lives when they need to write more and times when they feel this need less. This can result from changes at work or in their personal lives. For example, parents may experience changing demands when their young children grow up and go to school. It is often at points like these that adults decide to return to education. People want to make changes in their lives, and reading and writing enable them to make changes. Access to basic education classes and other forums for writing provides new possibilities for change. People vary in the extent to which they have this access to literacy.

A second notion of change is in tracing links from the past to the present. From generation to generation people pass on a culture. In our studies of literacy in Lancaster we can compare different generations and see how practices are passed on from generation to generation. Historically, there are links with the earlier generations and, in our current study, we can see ways in which the people we interviewed want life to be different for their own children. These people are passing on a culture in a changing environment.

Another aspect of change is the current, rapid social evolution, in which new technologies and political developments are altering the demands on people. New social practices are paving the way for new possibilities, so that paying bills by installments is easier, while new systems of paying by cheque in supermarkets require less literacy. Some social changes increase literacy demands; others reduce them. Another example from modern technology is the choice between sending messages by mail or by telephone or, where people have access to them, by fax, telex or electronic mail. The path to a choice in any particular instance is very complicated, involving availability, cost, technical ability, reliability and other factors — possibilities which are all changing rapidly.

Processes

Reading and writing have often been seen just in terms of the processes involved, and these have been studied in formal educational settings. However, processes are situated in a context, and informal learning in home and community situations is important. In our study of literacy in the community there were several examples of everyday theories of learning, where people articulated parts of the theories of learning they were operating with. These were concerned with how to learn and how to remember. One person hung lists of words around the house in order to memorize them — although reporting that this turned out to be completely ineffective. Another person writes new words on scraps of paper, "to take them out of the jumble on the page." The theories of learning which people take to school and college stem to some extent from their experiences at home with everyday theories of learning.

SUMMARY

All of the above topics contribute towards providing us with a coherent way of describing home and community literacy events, so that in any event we can identify phenomena such as roles, networks and values. Briefly summarized, the social view of literacy means that, if we are to understand reading and writing, we must talk in terms of "literacies," not just one literacy. The literacies vary by social context from one domain to another and from one event to another. They are best described as practices, rather than as skills. This gives a dynamic and relativistic view, where a historical perspective is essential, rather than a static model. The dominant school-based and work-based definitions of literacy are often at odds with what people do in their everyday lives. Home, school and work are different domains of literacy supported by definition-sustaining institutions. We must continue to develop ways of talking about literacy in these different domains.

NOTES

1. A more detailed version of this paper appears as a chapter, "The Social Nature of Writing," in D. Barton and R. Ivanic (eds.), *Writing in the Community*. The ideas have been developed in association with Mary Hamilton, Roz Ivanic and Sarah Padmore.

REFERENCES

Barton, D. "Exploring the Historical Basis of Contemporary Literacy." *Quarterly News-letter of the Laboratory of Comparative Human Cognition*, 10(3), 70-76, 1988.

Barton, D. and S. Padmore. "Roles, Networks and Values in Everyday Writing." In D. Barton and R. Ivanic (eds.), *Writing in the Community*. Sage, 1990.

Fingeret, A. "Social Network: A New Perspective on Independence and Illiterate Adults." *Adult Education Quarterly*, 33(3), 133-46, 1983.

Heath, S.B. "What No Bedtime Story Means: Narrative Skills at Home and School." *Language in Society*, 11, 49-76, 1982.

—————. *Ways With Words*. Cambridge University Press, 1983.

Scribner, S. and M. Cole. *The Psychology of Literacy*. Harvard University Press, 1981.

Street, B. *Literacy in Theory and Practice*. Cambridge University Press, 1985.

Taylor, D. *Family Literacy*. Heinemann, 1983.

IS THERE AN ILLITERATE CULTURE?

Dominique Brunetière
Jeannette Metay
Thierry Sylvestre
CUFCO, Université d'Angers

AN ACTION-RESEARCH TRAINING PROJECT

Instructor training

From October 1985 to December 1988 the Centre universitaire de formation continue (CUFCO) of the Université d'Angers ran a training program for literacy instructors working with francophone adults. The program took the form of an action-research project and was aimed at identifying cultural characteristics specific to the francophone adult population. Various approaches were incorporated into the program (linguistic, sociological, psychological, etc.), which was designed to encourage participants to reflect on the problem of illiteracy and our conceptions of this phenomenon.

In April, May and June 1985 CUFCO held a training session entitled "Illiteracy and Literacy Practices." The session was open to all literacy instructors in the department but only those at the Angers literacy centre expressed an interest. The session was led by a psychosociologist, an ethnosociologist, a psychosociologist specialized in literacy training and a linguist. It took place in two phases: the first allowed participants to discuss illiteracy and various reading methods used with children and adults (the latter at the instructors' insistence). This phase made it possible to identify facets of the illiterate populations with which the instructors were not fully familiar and revealed that instructors' understanding of illiteracy and illiterates varied according to their own individual motivation, experience and practices. The second phase enabled the session leaders to determine the instructors' training needs, as these were to serve as the basis for an action-research training program.

Illiteracy: a linguistic and cultural problem

The goal of the training program was not only to help the instructors reach a better understanding of the problems they encountered in their work with literacy students, but also to improve their working conditions by providing them with new perspectives. The instructors' expressed expectations and questions enabled us to delimit two major areas for study, i.e., the possibility of identifying cultural traits specific to the illiterate population and the difficulties raised by the strictly oral nature of their language.

A second training session began in October 1985. The goals were: first, to describe the use of language by the instructors' literacy students and to use this description toward more effective learning and, second, to identify the cultural environment in which literacy practices occur. To this end two course options were proposed: one on language and literacy, the other on illiteracy and culture.

Is there an illiterate culture?

The objective of the course on illiteracy and culture was to identify the cultural environment in which literacy practices occur by attempting to establish pertinent criteria. The session was structured along three main lines of exploration:

— **Research**, carried out with the collaboration of the literacy instructors and, if possible, their students. The purpose of the research was to study the group identity and the negative identity of the literacy students. The research was to be based on the observation and description of the homelife and everyday activities of the students, and would require a comparative study of the literate and illiterate cultures.

— **Clarifying the instructors' own relationship with culture**, by exploring their cultural identity and references, and their acceptance or rejection of popular culture.

— **Studying the concept of culture**, by examining the oppositions between popular and learned culture, oral and written culture, and dominant and dominated culture.

The central hypothesis of the study was that **there is an illiterate culture which is distinct from literate culture**. The main lines of exploration which had been determined for the training program roused the instructors' interest in research procedures (observation, interview and documentation methods), thus resulting in an action-research project.

Basic and working hypotheses

Once we had defined the central hypothesis of the study we attempted to develop a methodology which would enable us to verify it with members of the illiterate population of Maine-et-Loire. After discussing popular culture, the group proposed that everyday life be used as a criterion for identifying culture. It was assumed that popular culture is distinct from learned culture, that it comprises illiterate culture, and that it is characterized by uniformity of standards and values rather than of everyday practices and behaviour.

We also hoped to confirm the following hypotheses during our study, although this was not our major goal:

— **Urban illiterate culture is different from rural illiterate culture**. As we had grouped illiterate culture with popular culture our research was geared to the study of the urban population. It could not be assumed however that illiteracy is similar in urban and rural environments.

— **Some types of knowledge are legitimate, or recognized, while others are not**. The knowledge of illiterates, recognized by instructors who do not have negative preconceived ideas about illiteracy, is not academic, was not acquired at school and does not lead to certification. Our study was aimed at revealing this unrecognized knowledge through questions about the subjects' work and school history.

— **The process of acquiring and building up knowledge is different in literate and illiterate individuals**. Illiterate people derive their knowledge implicitly from evidence and experience; it is based on a perception of time and space which sidesteps the concept of future plans.

The study tool: preliminary analysis and reflections

Having carried out an initial series of interviews with 40 illiterate and five literate respondents between January and September 1987 the members of the research team attempted to develop a study methodology. They tested several hypotheses that had been proposed during preparation of the interview questionnaire, including the relationships between illiteracy and dependence on the family, illiteracy and sibling relationships, and illiteracy and isolation. The preliminary results seemed to invalidate the widely accepted belief that illiteracy is a stigma.

As the questionnaire items turned out to be geared more to literate than to illiterate respondents, both the literate control group and the study methodology were modified to allow for their limitations. Using an article on survey methods the group compiled an analytical grid which took into account nonresponses, respondent comprehension, difficulty in responding, multiple responses, and response affectivity and subjectivity.

To conclude we would like to note that the study had a certain impact on literacy training, as the instructor-researchers began to question their own understanding of illiteracy and the illiterate population. They were able to relativize the experience derived from their double relationship with "their" literacy students. After identifying and discussing the positive aspects of the illiterate environment — which we have called the "illiterate culture" — the instructors and researchers in our group no longer saw illiteracy as a stigma.

CUFCO'S STUDY

The subjects

The illiterate respondents:

Forty illiterates were interviewed. As shown in the following table they can be classified according to age, sex, rural or urban origins, family situation, ownership or nonownership of their home, and occupation.

AGE	16-29		30-49	>50
	21		16	3
SEX	male		female	
	25		15	
ORIGIN	urban		rural	
	20		20	
FAMILY SITUATION	alone	with their parents	with their children	in a home
	9	19	10	2
HOME	tenant		owner	
	28		12	
OCCUPATION	11 labourers 8 clerks 1 retiree 12 with no occupation		3 odd jobbers 5 handicapped	

* Two are in this situation because of illness.

The occupations of the respondents differed markedly from those of their parents. Their fathers included 28 labourers, five clerks, two craftsmen and three farmers. Two respondents were unable to answer this question. The mothers included five labourers, 10 clerks and three farmers. Sixteen mothers had no occupation and one was handicapped. Five respondents were unable to answer this question.

As shown in the table the 40 respondents were primarily young men, equally divided as to urban or rural origins. One-third had no occupation and five were handicapped. This group is not typical of the illiterate population in Maine-et-Loire, but does represent those who come forward for training.

Illiterates usually hide their handicap but it soon becomes apparent when they are forced to deal with health and social services. The Agence nationale pour l'emploi (ANPE), which offers on-the-job training to young people with no occupational qualifications, has been made aware of this problem (which doubtless explains the high proportion of young people among the survey subjects). Through intermediaries like ANPE illiterates are put into contact with literacy groups. The learners who took part in our survey came from various literacy groups within our department.

The literate control group:

We used a literate control group to verify some of our hypotheses by determining the differences and similarities between the literate and illiterate groups. Normally the control group should have been similar to the illiterate study group, but this was not entirely possible.

The literate control group was composed of 17 people. The table below provides a breakdown of their characteristics similar to that done for the study group.

AGE	16-29		30-49	>50
	4		10	3
SEX	male		female	
	8		9	
ORIGIN	urban		rural	
	16		1	
FAMILY SITUATION	alone with their parents		with their in a children home	
	4		13	
HOME	tenant		owner	
	11		6	
OCCUPATION	6 labourers 1 TUC* 9 with no occupation		1 seasonal worker	

* Travail d'utilité publique, a French government program providing work to unemployed students.

Because of the conditions under which the study was done it was impossible to compare the two groups in terms of employment. The members of the literate control group were unemployed and involved in on-the-job training or in upgrading programs.

Verifying the hypotheses

Illiteracy and family dependence:

Comparison of the numbers of subjects living with their families showed a marked difference in the family situations of the two groups:

	Living with parents	**Living with children**
Percentage of illiterate group	42.5 %	25 %
Percentage of literate group	23 %	77 %

This table does not include the 22.5 % of the illiterate group who did not answer this question.

There is an obvious dissimilarity between the two groups, as nearly half of the illiterates live with their parents, while three out of four literates live with their children. It would thus seem that illiterates are more dependent on their family and that this is inherent to their status as individuals in need of financial aid. (We would like to point out that this dependence on the family has no negative implications as far as we are concerned.)

Illiteracy and isolation:

Family data (concerning father, mother and siblings) revealed a number of characteristics which tend to isolate the illiterate person even within his own family.

— **Illiterates come from large families**. In the study group only nine illiterates came from families with three children or fewer, while the other 31 came from families of four children or more (15 of which counted eight children or more).

Five members of the literate control group came from families of fewer than four children, and only four from families with eight children or more (this bears out department statistics).

— **Illiterates have literate siblings**. One might logically think that, in a family where one child is illiterate, several or all of his siblings will also be illiterate.

The study data showed that 33 families had only one illiterate child. All the siblings were illiterate in only three families out of 40, and most of the siblings were illiterate in only one family. We thus concluded that illiteracy does not necessarily occur in all siblings, and that the illiterate person may be isolated within his own family.

— **Illiterates are eldest children**. In light of the observations made in the two preceding paragraphs we wanted to determine if there was a link between illiteracy and family environment, and wondered if this handicap is related to the child's position within the family. It was felt that illiterates were often eldest children.

As it turned out 31 members of the illiterate survey group were eldest children or could be considered as such. For our purposes the eldest was the first-born in a family of fewer than four children, the first and second in a family of fewer than eight, the first three in a family of fewer than 12, and the first four in a family of more than 12.

Our hypothesis was thus fully confirmed by the study.

The dependence of illiterates — from a physical to a psychosocial handicap:

We noted in the interviews that a number of the illiterates did not work because they were disabled. It is important to clarify the concept of "disability" in relation to social and family environments, and more specifically in relation to the child's school career.

In France there are many possibilities for students with learning difficulties. Starting at the age of 7, if a child fails his preparatory year* a second time, he may leave the regular school program. At the elementary level (ages 6 to 11) remedial classes are provided for children with a low level of failure, only slight or no intellectual deficiencies and no visual, auditory, motor or behavioural disabilities. Children showing signs of such deficiencies or disabilities are sent to either a child guidance centre (abbreviated in French as IMP) or a rehabilitative medical institute (IME). Children may stay in the IMP until the age of 14.

---

* Reading and writing are taught in this class, which is equivalent to grade 1.

For the first cycle of secondary education (ages 11 to 16) children from remedial classes move on to a high school specialized education section (SES) or to a state vocational school (ENP). Those leaving an IMP are directed toward a vocational medical institute (IMPROs).

Half of our survey group of 40 illiterates had received their education at an IMP or IMPRO. Uncovering this fact during the structured interview proved difficult for those of us who were not familiar with these institutions. Illiterates rarely mention where they were educated, sometimes because there are painful memories attached, but often because they simply do not know the names of the classes they attended. It is particularly important in cases such as this that the interviewers be thoroughly familiar with all the educational institutions within the system.

For many illiterates an academic handicap may easily result in a social handicap. When a disabled person leaves an IMPRO he may go to a workshop (CATs), where he will receive a "salary" (actually a type of allowance). Five people in the illiterate survey group were in a CAT and one was under guardianship. Eighteen of the other illiterate subjects were unemployed. This is not surprising, as one of the principal reasons why illiterates undertake training is that they have lost their jobs because of a lack of skills. This number is nonetheless high.

Ten illiterates had a steady job, three did odd jobs and three were mothers at home.

Rural or urban: integration or isolation?

One of our research hypotheses was that there is a difference between rural and urban illiteracy, and that this difference might be reflected in specific cultural traits. Before attempting to verify the hypothesis it was important to clarify our definition of "rural environment" for the researchers participating in the study.

The criteria of having been born and educated in a rural area are not sufficient to identify the rural population. People may meet these criteria and not be of rural origin. Because of this we included the criterion of **stability**, so that, to be considered of rural origin, subjects had to have been born in a rural area and have received their education (or at least have lived) there up to age 16; their parents also had to come from the same area.

Our survey subjects were divided into two groups: one composed of 20 urban illiterates living in Angers and the other of 20 rural illiterates living in Baugé, Beaupréau, Saumur and Segré.

Having identified these two groups we determined criteria that would enable us to measure an isolation index: our hypothesis was that rural illiterates are less isolated than urban illiterates because they are more fully integrated into their environment. Our criteria were: ownership of a home (only two urban illiterates owned homes for every 10 of rural origin), frequency of moves, occupational activity and family environment.

Using these criteria the illiterate respondents were classified according to their isolation index.

Isolation index	Urban	Rural
High	6	2
Fairly high	9	3
Fairly low	5	7
Low	0	8

The urban illiterate subjects had a higher isolation index (the highest numbers appear in the two upper levels) while the rural illiterate subjects had a lower isolation index (the highest numbers appear in the two lower levels). The data concerning the disabilities described above (IMP, IMPRO, CAT and guardianship) confirm these findings, as seven out of 20 rural illiterate subjects (35 percent) were disabled compared to 13 of the 20 urban illiterate subjects (65 percent).

We thus concluded that rural illiterates are more fully integrated than urban illiterates, because they are more familiar with their environment, more strongly attached to their place of origin, and are more stable; they also have a lower geographical and psychosocial isolation index. This higher level of integration among rural illiterates would suggest that their culture is distinct from that of urban illiterates.

CULTURAL CHARACTERISTICS OF ILLITERATES

Our study of the cultural characteristics of illiterates was aimed at identifying cognitive processes which would distinguish this group from literates. To this end we felt it was more important to identify value judgements (ways of thinking) than fundamental behavioural patterns (ways of doing). Our analysis targeted the identification of ways of thinking based on what the illiterates said about their experiences at work and school, on their conceptions of reading, writing and arithmetic, and on how they talked about these things and structured their speech.

The analysis of how the illiterate subjects organized their speech was based on Schatzmann and Strauss' theories of the interview and experiment organization. It therefore had to take into account what the illiterates said and how they said it, and especially how they reacted to questions drawn up and asked by literates in the artificial context of a structured interview.

The interview set-up represented a group-to-group contact between literates and illiterates, using literate communication techniques. In such a situation the illiterate subjects might react in a variety of ways: by being conformist, displaying noncomprehension, refusing to answer, shutting themselves off or otherwise blocking the questions. In this intergroup exchange we had to focus attention on the nonresponses, which proved highly significant. We were also watching for signs that the academic model of literacy had been assimilated by the illiterate subjects as the dominant model (these signs included the sense of inferiority experienced by illiterate individuals because of their social stigmatization).

The hierarchy of skills and knowledge:

We established a hierarchy of reading and writing skills in order to assess the knowledge of the illiterate survey subjects and to characterize them as accurately as possible.

	Arithmetic	Reading	Writing
Level 0	Can count money	Decoding	Copying
Level 1	Can add and subtract (abstraction: level 1)	Minimal	Copying
Level 2	Can multiply and divide (abstraction: level 2)	Decoding	Minimal
Level 3		Minimal	Minimal

Before classifying the illiterate respondents according to these levels we asked several questions about their conceptions of reading, writing, arithmetic and the acquisition of these skills. The responses did not enable us to classify their skills, and we were obliged to question our own conceptions in this regard.

Reading, writing and arithmetic
— pragmatism vs. rationalism:

The questions "What does knowing how to read mean to you?" and "What interested you most when you were learning to read, write and do arithmetic? Why?" were not understood in the same way by the literate and illiterate respondents. Because they have mastered these socially recognized skills the literate group perceived them as knowledge and used classifications when answering. The illiterate subjects, who did not objectify in this way, responded in terms of action. For example, the illiterate subjects in our survey answered the first question, a typically literate question which refers to knowledge, as though they had been asked "What is reading?"

This led us to reconsider the meaning of our question. As literates and researchers we had based this question on reading levels we had determined prior to the study. The answers we received indicated that these questions were not valid for determining the illiteracy level of the respondents. "What does knowing how to read mean to you?" met with the following responses from two illiterate subjects:

It's for the papers and in the stores.

It's to pass the time, for something to do.

These responses are representative of those given by the majority of the illiterates interviewed and, as we can see, are expressed in terms of action rather than knowledge. Reading is perceived as either a necessity or a useless activity.

"What interested you most when you were learning how to read, write and do arithmetic? Why?" drew these answers from the same respondents:

All three, because they're part of everyday life.

Reading. Arithmetic too, because you have to add and subtract.

The illiterate respondents had difficulty establishing categories and classifying skills which call for considerable self-investment. These answers are very utilitarian: "...they're part of everyday life," "...you have to add and subtract." In this respect there was a marked difference between the responses of the literate and the illiterate subjects. The literates answered this question in much more abstract terms. They rationalized their experience with reading skills, whereas the illiterates had given very practical responses. This can be illustrated with two responses to the question "What does knowing how to read mean to you?"

> Understanding what is said in books and on television.

> One feels intelligent, a part of society.

These are abstract responses. "Understanding" and "[feeling] a part of society" link reading skills with otherwise unrelated elements which nonetheless determine the significance of reading and its social role.

"I only need reading for roadsigns." This response from an illiterate, like the others quoted above, is in direct opposition to the concept of reading held by literates. Reading is seen as a mere technique ("reading roadsigns") and is useful only on an individual level (repeated use of the personal pronoun).

Know-how vs. knowledge:

A number of questions in the structured interview were designed to identify formal conceptions of learning and to verify the hypothesis that some knowledge is legitimate and recognized, while other knowledge is not. In terms of the theory of knowledge, this refers to the opposition between learning and teaching, between experience and instruction. The illiterates' responses to "How did you learn the occupation or occupations you have worked at?" indicated that they had not integrated the literate models. For them learning does not take place in the classroom.

> I learned on the job with the other workers.

> By working.

> By doing what everyone else was doing.

> When I left school I got a job. I watched what the others did and soaked it all in.

> By following people's advice and by doing.

These responses indicate that their experience was often acquired by watching others work and by imitating them. The only "schools" mentioned are vocational institutions (IMPROs) that provide work-oriented training.

Illiterates learn in other ways:

Based on Schatzmann and Strauss' analyses of communication sociology, the differences between the speech and thought processes of the working classes and those of the middle classes may be attributed to the distinction between literates and illiterates, particularly in relation to:

> the number of points of view adopted during communication,
>
> the ability to empathize with the listener,
>
> the number and types of classifications,
>
> the contexts of speech organization and stylistic procedures (enumeration and repetition; rarely, development).

Reaction to questions designed for literates:

An analysis of the responses to misinterpreted or misunderstood questions enabled us to identify the reactions of the illiterate subjects to questions designed for literates. For the most part their answers were either vague or took the form of concrete enumerations or a battery of images.

For example the question "Can you describe a very happy memory?" — a question which involves the respondent emotionally — met with responses such as: "I've lived a happy life since I married D." or "Surrounded by many people. A happy day." The first response avoids the question, while the second refers to a concrete, vivid situation.

Responses to the question "If you could buy your furniture anywhere, where would you go?" also demonstrate this reaction to literate questions. "I would choose antique furniture." "In a store." "I don't know. We bought ours at Pascal's on Pouancé Street." The first two answers are vague, while the third is very concrete.

Classification:

The last question mentioned provides another indication of the types of classification used by illiterates. Comparing interviews with a literate subject and an illiterate one makes it possible to assess the difference in the number and type of classifications used. When asked "If you could buy your furniture anywhere, where would you go?" a literate subject gave the following answer: "The kitchen and bedroom furniture I'd buy at Morin's and the living room set at Mobis'. If I had to buy right now I'd probably go to But's."

This answer distinctly classifies the stores, as Morin's is the most "chic," followed by Mobis', while But's is a more run-of-the-mill store. The speaker's point of view is easily understood: he makes a distinction between what he would purchase if he had the means and what he could buy at the present moment ("If I had to buy right now...").

The same question put to an illiterate subject met with the following answer, also mentioning Morin's but from a different point of view: "I'd buy at Morin's. I went there one day to have a look around. Their furniture is beautiful, but it costs a lot." This answer constitutes a value judgement. The individual does not classify the stores based on what he can or cannot afford ("...it costs a lot").

Personalization of social relations:

To analyze how the illiterate subjects perceived work the following question was asked:

What do you think is most important in your line of work? (by order of importance)

— learning the job

— interest in your work

— work atmosphere

— work schedule

— wages

— possibilities for promotion

— other

The priorities of most of the illiterates interviewed were work atmosphere, learning the job and interest in their work. (They also mentioned wages, but in conjunction with these three.) The literates felt that possibilities for promotion, work schedule and wages were most important.

As concerns work and social relations the illiterates focussed on the group and the literates on the job to be done. This is also demonstrated in the fact that the illiterates tended to refer to their co-workers by name rather than by job title.

Illiteracy and change

During the structured interview the illiterate subjects were asked if they planned to make any changes in their homes. The objective was to verify the hypothesis according to which illiterates live a polychronic existence, characterized by the absence of plans or projects.

"If you could change something in your home, what would it be?" met with responses like "Nothing." "It's not my home, I can't change anything." "Nothing, I like things just the way they are." "I don't know." "My mother is the one who looks after that." "In my room? No, the house is fine as it is. I'm not complaining."

These answers display a high level of conformity. What matters seems to be the present, perceived as unchangeable. This is clearly illustrated in the answer: "I like it a lot better than where I was before."

Responses given by the literates, on the other hand, indicate a desire for change, linked to a particular project:

My daughter's room: a bed and a dresser.

I'd install more shelves in my kitchen to make room for all the kitchen appliances. I'd like more comfort in my kitchen.

Even the responses which resembled those of the illiterates differed in meaning: "I can't think of what I would want to change. One gets used to what one has, even the oldest furniture." The literate who gave this response is attached to the objects because of their history, as demonstrated by his response concerning the choice of furniture: "I'd buy old furniture in an antique shop. I like period furniture." Again this response indicates the existence of a project.

Challenging the interview questions

Above and beyond what we discovered during this study on illiteracy and on our conceptions of the phenomenon, we feel that our major revelation was the fact that the interview process, based on questions which we — researchers and instructor-researchers — had formulated ourselves, was not suited to the study group in question.

Naturally more importance is attached to the right answer than to the right question, as even the right question does not necessarily elicit **the** right answer. The origins of the respondent must be taken into account. Communication between social groups is not without its difficulties, as

Schatzmann and Strauss have warned: "Anything that has any bearing on the interview situation must be taken into account if we want to give a correct interpretation to the differences between the social classes."

Our interview questions, designed for and by literates, were not suitable for use with illiterate subjects.

THE THEORETICAL AND IDEOLOGICAL PREMISES OF A STUDY ON ILLITERACY

(Dominique Brunetière)

> What is said and done in the fight against illiteracy reveals much more about those who are talking or doing than about a subject which none of them has managed to grasp.

Lae and Noisette

Our attempt to update the ideological and theoretical foundations of our empirical study fell into line with a comment by Jean-François Lae and Patrice Noisette: "It is impossible to give an unequivocal interpretation to any remark about illiteracy. It is possible, however, to determine the underlying meanings and values by taking the source of the remark into direct consideration." This source is what we will be discussing here.

Self-evident facts

At the beginning of the study the research team was confronted with pressing questions about the fight against illiteracy. How many illiterates are there? Who are they? What can be done to help them alter their situation? For the instructor-researchers the existence of illiteracy was self-evident, and their needs were expressed essentially through concerns of a more technical nature, such as: "What is the quickest way to teach them division?" "Let's find the most effective strategy for teaching them to read the newspaper." "How can we help them to write a few sentences in a few months?" The central question of the study, "Is there an illiterate culture?" did not directly correspond to the instructors' concerns and questions; it had an interrogative, closed structure, and was inductive and highly provocative.

From the outset it seemed clear that opposing the negative image of illiteracy as a handicap or stigma (Goffman) with a positive image of illiteracy attained through cultural recognition, boiled down to balancing one self-evident fact against another.

The main objective of the study was not so much to identify the causes or consequences of illiteracy as to describe the cultural traits of the population in question. Parallel to this there was a desire to study the mechanisms which come into play in the transition from oral communication to written, to develop innovative teaching strategies and methodology, and to heighten our awareness of our conceptions of illiteracy and the motives which underlie the fight against illiteracy.

These objectives, formulated by the instructor-researchers, were based on three main lines of exploration: studying the concept of culture, comparing the literate and illiterate cultures, and exploring the relationship with one's own culture and with culture in general.

For the purposes of our research group culture was provisionally defined as a set of ways of doing, feeling and thinking. Given the scope of this initial definition we had to adopt an anthropological approach, with all the methodological implications.

The paradox of culture

Culture is an ambiguous concept: invisible to the naked eye, it is both an abstraction and a construct. The basis for the presumed existence of an illiterate culture was the hypothesis that there is an illiterate reality distinct from the literate. The presumed uniformity of the illiterate population overrode the diversity of individual situations by asserting that there was one single culture.

A given culture may contain and camouflage one or several others, whose existence it recognizes only in terms of its own criteria, thus making it very difficult to objectively identify the characteristics of these other cultures. Our study questions, typically literate (like the reading levels we had identified or the writing skills), were asked in the context of a structured interview, a purely literate technique. The illiterate respondents had difficulty understanding a number of questions, despite our many precautions. Answering the questions required a minimum of literate skills, although the main problem was that certain questions were simply not suitable for illiterate subjects.

A study of illiterate culture conveys its own presuppositions. To the supposed uniformity of common values is added the belief that experience is a source of ongoing self-training, a premise which ignores the fact that occupational or paraoccupational experience can be as much a source of regression as of intellectual development.

The three implicit premises

The first premise consisted in presuming that modes of communication are determined by skills or means of communication. These modes of communication or thinking were seen as mentalities, systems of logic or cultures. Consequently writing and speaking were both considered as specific communication techniques, each involving a particular mode of thinking.

The second premise was based on the traditional opposition between popular culture and learned culture. This opposition includes the relationship between the dominant and the dominated culture, and the distinction between knowledge which is considered legitimate and knowledge which is not recognized (know-how). From the beginning of the study illiterate culture was implicitly considered to be an integral part of popular culture.

The third premise was based on the distinction between concrete and abstract thought, which is continued and theoretically justified in the opposition between analogical and numerical thought. Its justification is found in the two-brain theory (cf. Paul Watzlawick).

This dichotomy is not new and dates back to the early days of anthropology, namely to Levy-Bruhl and the opposition between prelogical and logical thought. Early anthropologists were quick to realize that there is a type of reasoning which differs from our own rationality, and whose logic escapes us. The difficulty of conceiving of a mode of reasoning different from our own led them to consider this other mode of reasoning as illogical or at least prelogical.

Among our near-contemporaries, J. Goody raises the question, "Are there intellectuals in primitive societies?" W.J. Ong poses the same pertinent question in other terms: "Illiterate subjects (in an oral society) identify geometrical figures using the names of objects rather than abstract terms such as circle, square, etc. Instead of circle, they say plate, sieve, bucket, watch, moon; instead of square, they say mirror, door, house, apricot pit. [They] identify the drawings as representations of familiar objects. They never refer to abstract circles or squares, but rather to concrete things" (W.J. Ong, *Orality and Literacy*).

Working hypotheses

The premise opposing concrete and abstract thought, when applied to the question of the existence of an illiterate popular culture, focussed our study on two hypotheses: first, that it was less important to identify types of knowledge specific to literate and illiterate groups than to determine the different processes by which people acquire knowledge;

second, that the illiterate popular culture should be described in terms of the uniformity of its values rather than of its practices. This hypothesis was based on R. Hoggart's analysis of the "poor man's culture," in which he states that, while it is difficult to find uniformity in the attitudes and everyday activities of members of the working classes, it is no doubt possible to detect uniformity in their perceptions of "what should be done" to conform to standards. As the author explains, "There are standards which are not always respected, but which should be" (*The Poor Man's Culture*: 48).

One of the first projects undertaken by the research team consisted in compiling data from the proceedings of a conference on "popular culture." The major characteristics thus identified for the popular culture were social customs relating to the family, group activities, special occasions and leisure activities, namely gardening and handiwork. Other characteristics were pinpointed, particularly in relation to blue-collar workers. They included frequent moves and the instability of couples. Within the popular culture writing was seen as meeting certain needs, and as being a pleasant activity or a tool for militancy, while reading was not perceived as being useful: most saw it as an almost clandestine diversion, a waste of time and even a source of evil thoughts.

These observations led to the hypothesis that urban illiterate culture and rural illiterate culture are two separate entities. Underlying this hypothesis was the idea that the immediate sociocultural environment of illiterate individuals contributes to integration in rural areas and to isolation in the urban environment.

As a result of the anthropological approach and the tentative definition of culture which had been adopted, the research team soon decided to study culture by observing everyday life and activities. Everyday culture seemed one of the best access routes to the illiterate mode of thought. Through everyday behaviours (observed in the workplace, during leisure activities, in transit, personal relationships and food habits) we hoped to identify a specifically illiterate relationship with time and space. Everyday cultural practices would give a perfect reflection of the cultural values and models which had been assimilated by the subjects.

Everyday cultural practices were observed in two phases by the team members. A preliminary study of our own food habits allowed us to reflect on our conceptions of right and wrong, good and evil, and to arrive at a better understanding of our own culture. The goal was to help us understand where we stood in relation to our own culture and cultural references.

Observation of the illiterate subjects' home environment by their literacy instructors was the next step in the study. This participatory observation did not give the hoped-for results because of material difficulties, constraints and biases created by the situation. Data gathered through documentary research and observation enabled the group to verify the proposed hypotheses.

The anthropological approach manifest in the central study question "Is there an illiterate culture?" should have led to a qualitative approach based on participatory observation. However the concrete realities of the observation site, the difficulties involved in using the observation tools, the extended scope and vagueness of the concepts used, along with the nature of our working hypotheses were such that our study was oriented more towards classic investigative methods, such as interviews and questionnaires. By necessity the quantitative approach took precedence over the qualitative, as a contradiction in our topic became apparent and persisted until the end of the study.

The interplay of key concepts

The basic concept of culture included a whole series of oppositions, i.e., that between illiterate and literate culture, between oral and written culture, and between popular and learned culture. The use of spoken language could not replace or compensate for writing skills. For one thing spoken language does not serve the same purpose for illiterates as for literates. Limited access to writing is often a result of limited mastery of spoken language as a means of communication. At the same time the structure of the spoken language in a society with writing skills is more or less subject to writing standards and differs from the structure of spoken language in a society without such writing skills.

The second key concept corresponded more to the notion of knowledge. This notion is typically literate, so that discussing knowledge with an illiterate is rather senseless. Knowledge, as a group of objectified, transmittable facts, is as different from know-how as night from day. Here we see the distinction between speech, which is an action, and the word, which is an object. This notion of knowledge refers to legitimate knowledge, which results from instruction, as opposed to unrecognized knowledge, which results from experience and practice.

The notion of thought constitutes the last key concept which, implicit in all the others, has a global aspect. It was used in relation to the opposition between concrete and abstract thought and is based on the two-brain theory in relation to the opposition between analogical and numerical thought. In this context thought is taken to mean a mode of communication or a mentality. The following diagram represents the relationships between the various concepts.

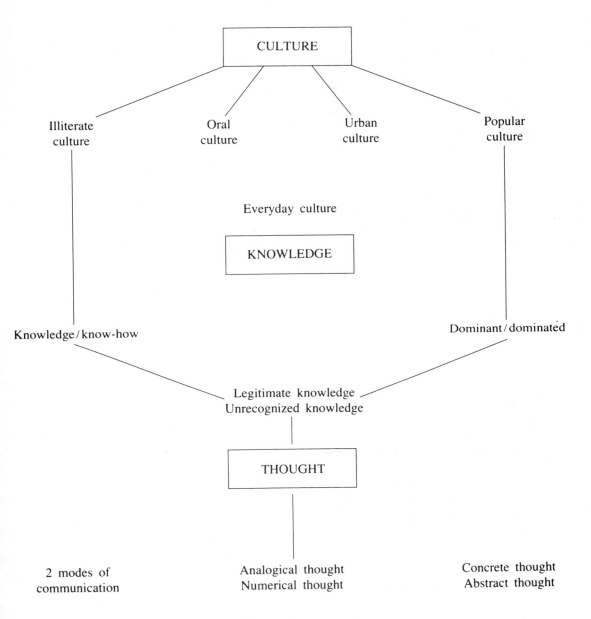

Towards a theory of knowledge

The theory of the two hemispheres of the brain — the left, seat of analytical skills and rationality, and the right, seat of universality and intuition — can be used to formulate a communication theory. These two modes of communication or ways of thinking correspond to two distinct cognitive processes which exist within each individual.

The dominance of one mode of communication over the other depends largely on the individual's background, on his socialization and on the dominant mode in which he was raised — in short it depends on his culture of origin.

Reading, writing and arithmetic skills apparently favour development of the left hemisphere. Writing skills considerably develop the individual's capacity for abstract thought by harnessing his logical reasoning (Goody). Everyday experiences, where the individual learns through imitation, repetition and initiation are also a source of knowledge very different from that of literate individuals. Experience, as a body of empirical knowledge acquired through practical experiences, relies primarily on the development of the right hemisphere or on the simultaneous development of both hemispheres.

The artificial opposition between oral and written culture stems from ambiguity surrounding the functions of the ear and eye, particularly the latter. In simply defining oral and written language as different communication skills or cognitive processes we do not clarify their respective functions in relation to speech and writing.

The ear is located in the centre of the auditory field; we can hear even with our eyes closed. The ear suggests a certain interiority and occupies a multidimensional space. The eye is much more paradoxical. The visual field is always in front of us and creates something of a distance between the object and ourselves. The eye suggests a certain exteriority and occupies two-dimensional space.

In relation to written logic (with writing considered as the support tool of experimental reasoning) the eye is used in deciphering letters, words, groups of words and the spaces between words. According to analyses by Goody the spatial structure of words in a list or distributed in a table suggests an objective meaning: a hierarchy in the case of the list, a closed symmetry in the case of the table. These basic graphic techniques result in a type of reasoning and mode of thought which Goody considers typically literate.

In relation to oral logic the eye (through observation) is the indispensable support tool of empirical reasoning based on social practices or personal experience. In this case visual perception is global and plays a role in the production and construction of images.

Oral language depends above all on context for its meaning and interpretation; time and personalization are essential components. Conversely writing is timeless and impersonal; written works often survive their authors and some are even anonymous. (If we transpose the Japanese analogy of time, represented by a circle, and space, represented by a square, it could be said that oral language is round and written language square.)

The importance of context in oral language led us to explore the difference between analogical and numerical thought, referring to E.T.

Hall's work on culture, specifically to the concepts of weak or strong contexts, monochronic or polychronic time, and fast or slow messages. The context is deemed "strong" or "rich" when frequently referred to during the communication, and "weak" when there are no references or infrequent references. In communication systems based on polychronic time, individuals are able to carry out several tasks simultaneously. In monochronic systems individuals plan their time, establish priorities and can do only one thing at a time.

The two-brain theory, systematic and sometimes exaggerated, constituted one of the pivots of our study. As the study progressed we were able to deepen our understanding of the basic dichotomy between analogical and numerical thought. The following diagram indicates the essential points:

Cognitive Processes and Modes of Communication

(Table based on the diagram of the two hemispheres by P. Babin and M.F. Kouloumdjan)

ANALOGICAL THOUGHT (Global)	NUMERICAL THOUGHT (Sequential)
Learning	Teaching
Experience	Instruction
Comprehension logic	Explanation logic
Teaching by example	Teaching by demonstration
Know-how	knowledge
Empiricism	Rationality
Practice (Manual)	Theory (Intellectual)
Oral	Written
Interiority	Exteriority
Image and symbol (link between concrete object and immediate referent)	Written word (distance between signifier and signified)
Implicit	Explicit
Fast message	Slow message
Strong context	Weak context
Psychological time	Mathematical time
Polychronic time	Monochronic time
Multidimensional space	Two-dimensional space
Ear	Eye

The various theoretical elements and working hypotheses led to the development of a questionnaire for the structured interview. The working hypotheses could not be systematically verified, primarily because of the nonexhaustive and nonrepresentative nature of the study groups; instead, they guided the study and helped us formulate new hypotheses.

The interview questions centred around three themes. The first, the subject's background, was chosen to help us describe sociocultural traits specific to the illiterate study group, and the processes by which they had acquired their knowledge.

The remaining themes, one focussed on conceptions of reading, writing and arithmetic, the other on everyday cultural practices, were aimed at helping us identify the cultural characteristics of the illiterate group.

THE STRUCTURED INTERVIEW

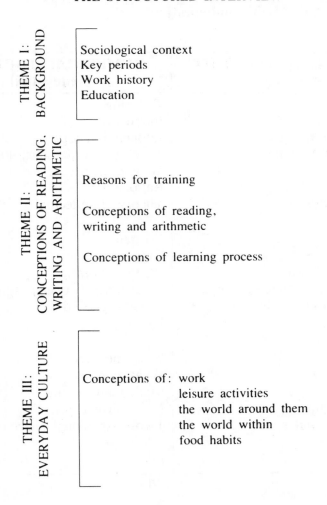

THEME I: BACKGROUND

Sociological context
Key periods
Work history
Education

THEME II: CONCEPTIONS OF READING, WRITING AND ARITHMETIC

Reasons for training

Conceptions of reading, writing and arithmetic

Conceptions of learning process

THEME III: EVERYDAY CULTURE

Conceptions of: work
                 leisure activities
                 the world around them
                 the world within
                 food habits

CONCLUSION: ON THE THEORY OF CULTURAL DOMINATION

At the outset most of the instructor-researchers had what could be called a "legitimist" attitude toward illiteracy. They found it scandalous that illiteracy should exist in a society where education has been free and compulsory for a century. Given the urgency of the situation, they felt that any means possible should be used to aid illiterates, whom they perceived as lacking an essential minimum of culture. This paternalistic attitude was reinforced by the way in which the illiterate participants had assimilated their inferiority.

A different position was adopted by a small number of instructor-researchers, who relativized the values inherent in the fight against illiteracy by distancing themselves from the dominant literate culture. For them the question "why" replaced the question "how." Their relativist attitude was aimed at legitimizing popular culture, and found its raison d'être in the study premise. While the legitimists risked falling into the trap of negativism, the relativists came dangerously close to populism. Acknowledging the illiterate culture in an outburst of humble fraternalism produces the same end result as helping the poor through high-minded paternalism. These opposing attitudes both ignore the true nature of the illiterate culture and basically reinstate literate culture as the only legitimate one.

Beyond the paradox of ideologies studying illiterate culture makes it possible to measure the gap between two worlds which are too close to ignore each other, yet too far apart to understand one another. A study such as CUFCO's, with all its inherent contradictions, no doubt constitutes a first step towards linking the effort to read, write and count to the discovery of a collective identity (Dumazedier and de Gisors).

REFERENCES

Les cultures populaires, proceedings from a conference held 9-10 June 1983, Société française de sociologie, Société d'ethnologie française, Université de Nantes.

Analphabétisme et pauvreté dans les pays industrialisés. Paris: UNESCO, February 1983.

Babin, P. and M.F. Kouloumdjian. *Les nouveaux modes de comprendre*. Paris: Éditions du Centurion, 1983.

Dumazedier, Joffre and H. de Gisors. "Français analphabètes ou illettrés?" in *Revue française de pédagogie*, No. 69, 1984.

Goffman, Erving. *Stigmates, les usages sociaux des handicapés*. Paris: Éditions de Minuit, 1975.

Goody, Jack. *La raison graphique. La domestication de la pensée sauvage*. Paris: Éditions de Minuit, 1979.

Hall, E.T. *Au-delà de la culture*. Paris: Éditions du Seuil, 1979.

Hoggart, Richard. *La culture du pauvre*. Paris: Éditions de Minuit, 1970.

Lae, F. and P. Noisette. *Je, tu, il, elle apprend — Étude documentaire sur quelques aspects de l'illettrisme*. Paris: la Documentation française, 1985.

Ong, W.J. *Orality and Literacy*. New York: Routledge-Champson & Hall, 1982.

Pharo, Patrick. *Savoirs paysans et ordre social, l'apprentissage du métier d'agriculteur*. Centre d'études et de recherches sur les qualifications, January 1975.

Schatzmann, L. and A. Strauss. "L'entretien et les formes d'organisation de l'expérience," from *Le métier de sociologue*, Bourdieu, Chamboredon & Passeron, Paris: Éditions de Minuit, 1973.

Watzlawick, Paul. *Le langage du changement — éléments de communication thérapeutique*. Paris: Éditions du Seuil, 1980.

WOMEN AND ILLITERACY

Fie van Dijk
University of Amsterdam

Teach a woman letters? A terrible mistake:
Like feeding extra venom to a horrifying snake.

Menander (c. 342-291 B.C.)
cited by Levine

Sociologists of education have proven that our education system reproduces the social class structure. Even today, most school dropouts (or rather, school outcasts) belong to the lower classes. One of the most important means of selection relates to *language*: theory and abstraction are in high favour at school; the students' everyday experiences are not really relevant; language use and communication acts that do not conform to the requirements of middle class usage (like speaking dialect or slang, doing instead of talking, or remaining silent, etc.) are neglected or condemned. Even interactions between students, between students and teachers, and between parents and the school are dominated by middle class language standards. Baudelot and Establet (1979) have clearly demonstrated that, at least in French schools, the literacy process causes the greatest number of victims among working class children. This is also true in the Netherlands, as shown by the fact that most students in adult literacy classes are from the lower classes.

Research done by the Adult Education Project (abbreviated as PVE in Dutch) of the University of Amsterdam has shown that many learners in adult literacy classes dropped out of primary school before Christmas of their first year, in the sense that they never again took an active part in the education process. They passed through primary school without receiving any attention from teachers, except the negative attention apparent in questions such as "What am I to do with you?" or in suggestions such as "You may draw if you like..." These students were no longer asked questions and simply spent their time watering the flowers, making coffee for the teachers or cleaning out cupboards. Some were referred to a special school, where they generally did not learn much, but later felt stigmatized for having been a pupil at that kind of institution (van Caspel 1983).

There are approximately 800 000 illiterates in the Netherlands. The ratio between men and women has not been clearly established, but some publications and our own pilot study reveal that 60 percent of the learners in adult literacy classes are men and 40 percent women. Women dominate in Amsterdam, while the number of female learners is increasing in the rest of the country.

In Amsterdam, a random survey on women's progress in literacy class showed that *more than one-third dropped out without having learned to read and write*. We asked ourselves two questions, one about the eradication of illiteracy, the other about its prevention:

— Why do women drop out, even from literacy classes?

— How can we prevent illiteracy?

LITERACY AND ILLITERACY

Literacy and illiteracy are defined in many different ways, depending on one's approach to reading and writing, and on one's interests (government, multinationals). For the school, you are literate if you passed a number of reading and writing tests, but some people consider themselves literate if they can sign their name, while Brazilian pedagogue Paulo Friere associates the process of learning to read and write with the acquisition of a critical view of society and a movement towards action that will "humanize the world" (Friere 1978).

Social anthropologist Brian Street distinguishes two models for the analysis of literacy: the *autonomous* model and the *ideological* model. The autonomous model represents literacy as a "neutral technology that can be detached from specific social contexts." The ideological model "stresses the significance of the socialization process in the construction of the meaning of literacy for participants and is therefore concerned with the general social institutions through which this process takes place" (Street 1984). Adult literacy work in the Netherlands tends to follow the ideological model, liberally inspired by the theory and practice of Paulo Friere and of French pedagogue Célestin Freinet (Freinet 1961).

In this article, I will call illiterate anyone who looks upon him or herself as being illiterate. Literacy teachers working with both male and female groups know from experience that women are more likely than men to call themselves illiterate, even when they master more literacy skills.

MOTHERS AND SCHOOL

The dropping out of working class children is a complicated issue. Empirical research on children with serious reading and writing problems shows that *the mother* is in a key position if:

— she is from the lower classes;

— her formal education ended in primary school;

— she has neither trade nor profession;

— she has more children than mothers in a control group who come from the same social class but whose children do not have reading and writing problems (Valtin 1974).

It is clear that middle and upper class parents (mothers) are in a better position to help their children with school matters. They read books and articles, participate in symposia about dyslexia, and spend a lot of money for remedial teachers, physiotherapists, speech therapists — or corrective lenses — precisely to ensure that their children receive an education and do not remain illiterate. Lower class parents obviously do not want their children to be illiterate either, but they simply do not have the means and instruments to cope with school problems.

The educational journal *Didaktief* published the results of research on the role of parents in the development of their children's attitude to and performance in reading (Lierop 1986). Based on 20 interviews with parents, it was stated that "the higher the professional level of the parents, the better the overall reading atmosphere within the family. This applies even more if both parents are professionals, and even if only the mother is a professional...Reading is also encouraged in families where the parents have little formal schooling. In all families, people read aloud and all children have their own books. But the parents of lower class families generally read less frequently than more educated parents, and the books they read are different."

Research like this raises some questions in my mind: What does "less frequently" mean? Or "different" books? Perhaps these vague terms are explained in the research report (different = worse? = no literature?), but I am quoting this journal because it is widely read by teachers and other educators. "In all families, people read aloud"? Some parents do not even dare to go to parents' evenings at their children's school because once they were asked unexpectedly to write — and could not. Middle class teachers are unaware of this problem, yet complain that many lower class parents show no interest in their children's school career. I know mothers who are totally embarrassed when teachers ask them to help their children with reading or to be a "reading mother" at school: they simply cannot read themselves. It is still taken for granted that everyone in the "civilized" Western world is able to read and write, perhaps because illiteracy does not fit well with the ideology of "equal opportunity."

As long as educational researchers and classroom teachers remain such strangers to the social context of literacy, it will be impossible to prevent illiteracy.

We have two options for improving the chances of "deprived" children (deprived at school, as compared to middle class pupils). One would be to provide remedial courses for their mothers. Such courses are already offered, now and again, to adult education groups. But many women feel very anxious about joining this kind of group. Moreover, the government's retrenchment policy and conservative approach to education (priority to traditional adult education, with creation of secondary schools for adults and emphasis on vocational training) reduce the chances of forming adult education groups adapted to the educational needs of the population. Apart from this, it is quite inadmissible to blame mothers for their children's failure at school. The school is at fault, since it does not acknowledge the personal baggage that each child brings to the classroom: his or her own culture, language behaviour and way of learning (for more in-depth discussion, see Holt, 1984 and Kohl, 1973).

The second possibility for improving the chances of children with reading and writing problems is to *change the school*. The school's requirements in reading and writing are standardized in countless tests that measure skills, level, speed, comprehension, etc., and in primary school readers and writing books.

The approach to literacy manifest in these tests and textbooks conforms to Street's autonomous model: the process of learning to read and write is divided into various separate skills that can each be practised in isolation. A distinction is also made between technical reading, reading for comprehension and critical reading — skills that are supposed to be mastered in a certain order. The underlying hypothesis is that learning to read and write is a continuous process from A to B, from easy to difficult, in the same order and at the same pace for everyone. Text content is irrelevant, as is the meaningfulness of given reading or writing situations.

The content of most textbooks is conformist, promoting traditional sex roles, among other things. Situations and language use are middle class; occasionally, they are archaic. Men and boys play the leading roles:

> Loes sits by the cradle.
> Mother puts the pan on the cooker.
> The bell rings.
> Here are Father and Wim.

(from the AVI Test, Level 1A)

In the garden next door, we see a girl with long pigtails. She sits on a swing and looks shyly at Wies and Joop. Her little brother is bolder and cries: "Are you our new neighbours?" They soon make friends with one another.

(ibid., Level 8A)

In the primer used in 90 percent of Dutch schools, we find:

Mother is in the kitchen.
Joep is in the kitchen.
I am cooking, Joep!
I am cooking soup for Joep.
Mother is cooking for Father
and for Kies and Miep.
Mother gets the strainer.
Mother strains the soup.

Nice, boring texts. Small wonder that many children see reading as something you do only at school — a "no-fun" activity.

The question of changing the school, of switching from the autonomous approach to literacy to the ideological one, is political. Changing the school would require not only that we replace methods and textbooks, but also that we alter social conditions. In this article, I simply want to plead for dialogue between the traditional school (pupils, parents and teachers) on the one hand, and adult literacy classes (learners and teachers) on the other. The confrontation must be led by the learners in literacy classes, for they alone are deeply concerned about changing the school because of their own negative experiences and because they want to see their children fare better than themselves. In the Netherlands, dialogue sometimes occurs between students at teachers' college and learners in a literacy class. Teachers in traditional schools, however, see such dialogue as threatening...How can the school possibly be changed when teachers do not understand the problem?

BOYS, GIRLS AND READING

Another aspect of the question of women and illiteracy is the difference in reading performance between boys and girls. It is not known whether there are more illiterate men than women. We are not unduly concerned with the statistics, but would like to know if there is more hidden illiteracy among women than among men. The answer to this question could be of interest to those recruiting literacy students. Women who do not work outside the home are able to hide their illiteracy better than men, although this does not imply that their "secret" causes any less suffering.

Most studies on sex differences in reading performance mention the fact that girls read better than boys, but there is much contradiction and inconsistency among the studies. According to one, for each girl with reading problems there are 15 boys. Another reports equal reading performance for boys and girls. The dissimilar results are due to different approaches to reading, different ways of measuring reading performance (tests or observation) and the diversity of academic disciplines that are studying the question.

So much is published about sex differences in reading performance that I will mention only aspects that are often cited in the literature:

— Girls are exposed to more prereading activities than boys.

— Girls identify more easily with female primary school teachers.

— Higher demands and pressure are placed on boys, so that when they fall behind it is noticed earlier.

— Boys are more vulnerable to stress than girls.

— Girls have greater aptitude for intellectual activities, and boys for physical activities.

— Abstract reading methods are less motivating for boys than for girls.

— Boys develop more slowly.

Publications about abstract reading methods (methods that do not connect reading to the everyday experiences of working class children) link attention and behaviour in the classroom to reading performance (Samuels and Turnure 1974). Both ideas have gender-specific aspects: boys are more active and enterprising than girls, and working class boys who fail at school become rebellious or play truant. Friedlander also reports that the Language Experience Approach is much more appealing to active children (1981: 330).

I have a collection of postcards that show people and animals reading and writing. They reflect the Western, male approach to literacy: reading is mainly done by sweet, white girls and women. What are they reading? Dime novels, poems (while gazing adoringly upon their lovers), women's magazines, gossip papers, letters and recipe books. While demure girls are reading (underline: "A book makes a wise boyfriend" or "Silence is golden"), little boys explore the world. Boys hardly ever read. Mothers and grandmothers (often represented as mice) read aloud to children. Men read thick books, learned books, books with sex in them and, above all, newspapers and *Playboy*.

The women on the postcards are dressed romantically or are naked. They are reading aloud to children or a sick woman. They are knitting or watching over a baby, surrounded by flowers and trees. The men are never naked, not even when represented as pigs. They are shown with a pipe or cigarettes, a radio, a typewritter, a computer or a robot. Some are reading their books and newspapers in a library or cafe.

There are far fewer postcards about writing but, even in the ones that I have, men are busy working on impressive books, while women write letters… "Au cher absent. Loin de toi, seule avec ma pensée/Mon coeur est près de toi, mon cher aimé!"

A SECOND CHANCE FOR WOMEN?

In the novel *Monsieur Saint-Anne* by Belle van Zuylen (1740-1805), Madame d'Estival says to her prospective son-in-law: "Today, [my daughter] is illiterate and she loves you and you love her. Do not make her literate or learned. Change is fundamentally wrong. You love her as she is now, so leave it at that. Add to this, that I remember some lines of poetry — the only ones I ever learned. My uncle, the school teacher, made me recite them so often I have never forgotten them. But he would not teach me the alphabet, no matter how I begged and entreated. He said: 'A woman who knows the alphabet would want to learn to read; and when she could read, she could learn to write of her own accord. But I agree with the words of the wise man, who said:

> When a woman is bored at home,
> the man must hide pen and ink from her.
> He talks, he writes, and it is his word
> we read and hear through all the ages
> (as it has always been).'"

(van Zuylen 1986: 92)

Van Zuylen clearly depicts the contradictory feelings of Madame d'Estival: she who had begged to learn the alphabet repeats what learned men have said about a woman's role. Is this story valid only for the 18th century?

A pilot study on women who dropped out of literacy classes brought to light that, even today, a woman's social position plays an important role in the process of dropping out (van Bemmel and Helsloot 1987):

— The simple fact that a woman starts to learn again means that her position within the family is called into question.

— Women often get little or no support from their housemates or family ("You're fine the way you are."). This is often because of the family's dependence on the mother, and because of the values and beliefs of the milieu — shared by the women themselves — about what it is to be "a good daughter," "a good wife," "a good mother," etc.

— Women often live in straitened circumstances because of a tight financial situation.

— Women have neither the time nor the money to join a literacy class: if the plumber or a visitor is expected, if a child or any member of the family falls ill, then the woman is expected to stay at home.

— Day care is not always available at literacy courses and, if a woman is obliged to arrange for a babysitter herself, she must either invent a poor excuse or admit to being illiterate.

— Sometimes social workers refer women to literacy classes: when there are too many problems, illiteracy may appear to be the only one that can be solved but, in this instance, the women themselves are not very motivated to join the class.

— When women are swamped by problems, they stay away from literacy class; when the problems lessen, they often return.

Literacy teachers who work with both male and female groups feel that men have similar problems but are less troubled by their families. Levine warns against stereotyping that generates "well-meaning but ultimately fanciful pictures of the dependency and vulnerability of the illiterate" (1986: 96). He and many other academic literacy researchers do not take into account the gender-specific aspects of illiteracy. Our experience is that an illiterate woman is more dependent on her father, husband or other family member than an illiterate man on his wife or other family members. The man remains the "head of the household," controlling money and property. More research in this area is required, of course.

> Bep (30) had been going to literacy class for two years at a rate of one evening per week: "I dropped the course because I had a breakdown. My family and work got to be too much for me." When asked about going back, she replied: "One minute, I'd like

to go back and the next, I wouldn't. It means so much stress for me. I'm so afraid it will be too much. I have three boys. Maybe I could take classes in the morning but not in the evening...Not in the evening anymore. My husband comes home quite late. But in the morning, I could take classes for two hours. I learn more than when I just drink coffee." (Five months after this interview, Bep went back to literacy class.)

Astrid (30) dropped her literacy class after four years. Born in Suriname, she had come to Holland when she was 24. She had three children and worked as a cleaning lady. "In the evening, at the literacy class, I was dead tired. During the last series of courses, I was very busy. I didn't see much progress." Her children say to her: "You went to school for so many years and you still can't write? You're too stupid. You're too scared to do anything and you can't think properly." But Astrid says: "I'm glad I took the course. Before, I just didn't dare talk to anybody or go anywhere on my own, or even look for a street. Now I can manage that sort of thing" (Boelens 1988).

These are only two examples, but even they demonstrate the complexity of the dropout phenomenon among women. The learners themselves stress the fact that "progress" means more than scoring on a reading or writing test. Sometimes they come up against such huge barriers to learning that their progress is less obvious for some years. Some drop out. Others persist and are rewarded with a sudden breakthrough. Women have special problems stemming from their social position: if they can learn instead of drinking coffee, they need not feel guilty towards their husbands and sons. As for children who call their mother stupid, who can tell how inconvenient it is when Mother claims time for herself!

MORE RESEARCH

If we want to understand why some women drop out of literacy class, we must investigate why others come and stay. What kind of literacy training do women need? In what kind of situation? Do these needs alter as women learn to read and write? What kind of services do they need?

The Adult Education Project, in collaboration with learners and tutors, is attempting to find answers to questions like these. We talk with women attending literacy classes about the role reading and writing play in their lives, at home, at work, in their free time and on holiday. I record our discussions in simple words and make little books that we can read together and discuss again and again. We can add to them or alter them as need be.

Our objective is to identify the various literacy practices of women and to relate these to their social reality, in hopes of improving literacy work in the Netherlands. The interviews also help the learners and tutors to become more aware of the process of learning to read and write.

> My Father is my last hope.
> My husband says it's okay
> but he never asks for anything.
> He didn't want to listen
> when I wanted to read aloud.
> He started to read it for himself.
> He allows my sister-in-law
> to tell me "Shut up!"
> because I cannot read or write.
> If ever I have to miss my Father,
> I'll hang myself.

(Donna)

> I wanted something of my own.
> I did not want to be dependent.
> I wanted to be free.
> If you can do things on your own,
> you will do them on your own.
> Sports and that sort of thing.
> Reading directions.
> Filling in forms.
> Signing your name on a marriage certificate.
> For the first time, we'll travel to Italy
> on our own. By train.
> I want to learn Italian.
> I want to learn to drive the car.
> I want freedom.
> Then I can take a book
> and make my own clothes.
> Now, I say: "I am doing this for my children, too."
> But first and foremost, I am doing this for me.

(Petra)

REFERENCES

Baudelot, Christian and Roger Establet. *L'Ecole capitaliste en France*. Paris, 1979.

Bemmel, L. van and Y. Helsloot. "Eerst nog even... een onder- zoek naar het afhaken van vrouwen in lees — en schrijfgroepen." Amsterdam, doct. scriptie, PVE, 1987.

Boelens, Amandus. "Toen ben ik gestopt. Een onderzoek naar het voortijdig beeindigen van deelname aan lees — en schrijfgroepen." Amsterdam, doct. scriptie andragogy, PVE, 1988.

Caspel, Tamar van. "Nel Hofmeester en Rutger Hueting, Wat doe ik hier eigenlijk? Afvallers van het lees — en scrijfonderwijs aan het woord." Amsterdam, 1983.

Freinet, Célestin. *Méthode naturelle de lecture*. Cannes, 1961.

Freire, Paulo. *Cultural Action for Freedom*. Harmondsworth. Penguin, 1972.

Holt, John. *How Children Fail*. Harmondsworth. Penguin, 1984.

—————. *How Children Learn*. Harmondsworth. Penguin, 1984.

Kohl, Herbert. *Reading: How To*. Harmondsworth. Penguin, 1974.

Friedlander, Janet. *Early Reading Development: A Bibliography*. London, 1981.

Levine, Kenneth. *The Social Context of Literacy*. London/Boston, 1986.

Lierop-Debrauwer, Helma van. "Ouders kunnen een belangrijke rol spelen bij het lezen van kinderen." In *Didaktief*, 7, 1986.

Samuels, S. Jay and James E. Turnure. "Attention and Reading Achievement in First-Grade Boys and Girls." In *Journal of Educational Psychology*, 1, 1974.

Street, Brian V. *Literacy in Theory and Practice*. Cambridge, 1984.

Valtin, Renate. "Legasthenie: Therapie ohne Grundlagen. Bericht ueber eine empirische Untersuchung." In *Thema: Grundschule*. Weinheim/Basel, 1984.

Zuylen, Belle van. *Mijnheer Sainte-Anne*. Amsterdam, 1986.

THE ADULT LITERACY MOVEMENT IN IRELAND

Noel Dalton
Jenny Derbyshire
Geraldine Mernagh
Mairead Wrynn
National Adult Literacy
Agency, Dublin

In this article we will describe the development of literacy work in Ireland overall and in County Offaly specifically. The first part will focus on how literacy provision has emerged as a separate practice from mainstream education. There will be a description of significant facts in relation to the evolution of this "alternative system," with a discussion of the strengths and weaknesses of present literacy provision under this system. The article will then focus on the emergence of a policy document formulated by the National Adult Literacy Agency (NALA). This section will discuss the key principles of good-quality literacy provision as they have evolved over the last 15 years. The third part of the article will apply the discussion of the first two parts to the Literacy Scheme in County Offaly, which has been the subject of an action-research project carried out by NALA.

We will examine the research methodology which is most suitable to promoting the aims of good-quality literacy provision, along with significant developments which took place within the Literacy Scheme during and after the research project. We will also consider how to translate into practice the principles discussed in the second part of the article.

DEVELOPMENT OF THE ADULT LITERACY MOVEMENT IN IRELAND

We propose to look at the factors which have been most influential in developing the character of the adult literacy service in the Republic of Ireland.

A tenacious myth

Ireland, like many Western countries in the postwar period, accepted that economic growth could be achieved only through a major investment in the educational system. In that period, and especially in the 1960s, a lot of new initiatives were introduced: free secondary schooling, establishment of third-level technological colleges, grants for third-level education, etc. Built into this major expansion was the accepted wisdom that everyone would benefit from this improved service. To both professional educators and laymen it seemed logical to assume that, at the very minimum, illiteracy as a major problem would be swept aside in the rising tide of increased mass education.

With the "discovery" (or rediscovery) of the adult literacy problem from the mid-1970s on, the truth began to dawn on many people that school in all its forms still fails for a significant proportion of our population. So far this awakening has led to very little debate on school reform or on alternative strategies to a school system that is dominated by the academic approach, examinations and competition. Unfortunately, many educationalists believe there is nothing fundamentally wrong with the traditional education system and that only superficial changes are required, such as developing alternative forms of certification or emphasizing the need for more remedial teachers. Very few mainline educationalists are calling for a root and branch review of our educational institutions, especially as these relate to the section of the population that they fail to assist in acquiring the most fundamental of all educational rights: the right to read and write. Unfortunately, the myth that school is good for all still persists in Ireland.

The early literacy movement

The most startling feature in the discovery of the literacy problem in the 1970s was that the issue was brought to the attention of both the State and the public by nonprofessional volunteers (mostly women), rather than by people in the field.

A collection of concerned individuals from a wide variety of backgrounds (housewives, community-based workers, volunteer tutors, retired teachers, etc.) took the initiative of helping adults with reading and writing difficulties. It was these people who organized themselves under NALA in 1977, in what was none other than the early stages of the adult literacy movement in Ireland. NALA is a national support agency for literacy work in Ireland. It is a membership organization and its 400 members include individual literacy students, tutors and organizers, as well as voluntary group members, local education authorities, libraries and trade unions. The main task of the Agency is to promote literacy work at a local level.

In 1973 the State first officially recognized[1] the adult literacy problem, suggesting that there were over 100 000 people in the Republic of Ireland with reading and writing difficulties. More recently, in 1986, the Department of Education's discussion document on adult literacy[2] put this figure at 400 000 (18 percent of the population). However, of the 400 000 who would have some difficulty in reading and writing, there are about 150 000 who would be considered unable to carry out functional reading and writing activities. There is also growing concern about the numbers of young people who still leave school with some level of difficulty in reading and writing. A 1987 NALA survey[3] showed that 63 percent of those availing themselves of Ireland's adult literacy service were between 16 and 25 years of age. Ireland is not unique among Western industrialized countries in the length of time it has taken to obtain official recognition for the problem and in the alarming indications that the problem is ongoing, as young people continue to leave school requiring help with reading and writing.

The key role which voluntary help played in initiating the adult literacy movement determined the voluntary aspect of this work. The allocation in 1985 of a special budget for adult literacy and community education has led to some development. Where funding is allocated to literacy work, through local educational authorities, it is directed to local literacy schemes and has allowed for minimal payment of part-time organizers and salaried tutors.

Outside the school system

It is significant that the energy for change came from grass-roots workers and learners, who were all largely located outside the formal school network. It is this central feature which accounts for both the strengths and weaknesses of the literacy service in Ireland. Let us look first at some of the positive benefits:

— The development of services outside the formal school system has been of great benefit in the attempt to develop a genuine alternative which is based on a sound philosophy of adult education. In areas where conditions have been conducive to growth (i.e., where proper funding, V.E.C.* support, commitment from adult education services, etc. are available), good adult literacy provision is beginning to emerge.

— Student participation at all levels of provision has always been a natural and integral part of good adult literacy practice in Ireland. This reflects both democratic principles of organization and the informal and intimate nature of much literacy provision in this country.

Closely linked with this are such widespread practices as the publication of student writings and specialized learner events like writing weekends.

— Being on the outside has also meant that we are not tied by the heavy bureaucracy of the school system, with all the attendant

---

* Vocational Education Committee, equivalent to a Local Education Authority.

barriers to learning such as set curricula, qualifications, institutional demands, etc. Despite many difficulties, there is still a sense of freshness, freedom and spontaneity about much of the adult literacy work in Ireland.

While being located largely outside the formal school system is the source of our strength, it is nonetheless also the basis of many of our weaknesses. The chief of these might be summarized as follows:

— Many areas of the country still have no acceptable level of provision.

— There is still too great a reliance on volunteers, with the consequence that, when the volunteer energy dries up, literacy provision collapses. In most schemes, well over 75 percent of the work is still done on a voluntary basis. Many schemes, especially in rural areas, are able to provide only one-to-one tuition and have no group tuition for students.

— Adult literacy, which is a central part of government policy, attracts only a minimum amount of resources. In 1988 it was estimated that £268 000* were spent directly on adult literacy. This represents 0.02 percent of the total education budget. Put more starkly, this means that approximately £0.60 was spent on every adult with literacy problems.

THE PRINCIPLES OF GOOD ADULT LITERACY PROVISION

Urgent need for guidelines

One consequence of official recognition for the literacy problem was that literacy courses began to be offered in a wider range of settings. Literacy work, which had largely been carried out within voluntary literacy schemes, was extended to other areas. Courses are now available in training workshops for young people and the disabled, in prisons, a few psychiatric hospitals and some unemployment centres set up by trade unions.

The experience of literacy workers on the ground indicated the need to produce guidelines for good adult literacy work. The development of the adult literacy movement from local responses meant that no overall planning had been done. However, literacy workers were aware that they were devising a practice which did not follow the traditional classroom approach. They also began to see that this significant departure from the traditional approach seemed to enable adults to pick up reading and writing

* IR£1 = approximately C$2.

skills they had not previously acquired. NALA responded to the need to share these experiences and use them as the basis of a policy document.

During 1984 and 1985 the Executive Committee of NALA, in close consultation with NALA members, produced a policy document aimed at providing guidelines on acceptable standards of organization and practice in literacy work in Ireland.

The policy document[4] was launched in 1985, the same year that NALA received a grant-in-aid from the Department of Education to hire two staff members and set up a national office. The emergence of the policy document, which coincided with the allocation of the Community Education and Adult Literacy Budget and the establishment of a national office with a development team, was an important step in enabling literacy schemes to make the first move towards establishing a permanent and consistent provision for adults with reading and writing difficulties.

The principles

In considering the following principles, a number of important points must be kept in mind. The principles of good literacy practice evolve as perspectives and knowledge change over the years. At present, the policy document is being reworked in order to incorporate developments which have taken place since the initial version was published five years ago. A statement of principles should be seen as initiating an ongoing debate on good literacy practice. In dealing with such a wide-ranging and complex issue as adult literacy, it is obvious that there will be varying opinions. However, what is important is that the following principles have emerged from effective literacy work at ground level. People involved in literacy provision generally agree with the broad sense of purpose and direction contained in the following:

1. The problem of illiteracy must be understood in terms of the social and economic circumstances which create a situation in which a certain percentage of the adult population experiences difficulties with reading and writing.

2. Adult literacy students bring their own knowledge, skills and experience as a central contribution to the learning situation in which they are engaged. They must be supported in assuming responsibility for choices about what and how they are to learn.

3. Students must have the opportunity to meet with other students, to share their experiences and discuss their learning.

4. Learning content and materials are developed according to the experiences and needs of the adult learners. The adult student is encouraged to write from the beginning. This is a means of drawing on the student's own experience, while creating appropriate and relevant adult learning material that can be used by the student and circulated among other adult learners where possible.

5. Individual and group tuition are regarded as complimentary ways of accommodating the students' development as they progress in their learning, although some students require individualized tuition for reasons of confidentiality or specific learning needs. Experience has shown that, when students are supported during the transition to a group setting, this form of tuition provides a means of:

— tackling the social isolation felt by many students;

— promoting the students' involvement in all aspects of literacy work;

— creating an attitude which acknowledges learning as the exploratory acquisition of knowledge rather than the passive absorption of information from an expert.

6. The publication of student writings is a means of giving permanent expression to the cultural contribution that students bring to their learning, while providing relevant material for other learners.

7. Assessment revolves around a discussion or any other means by which learners can be encouraged to take control of their learning. The process is seen as an opportunity to help students mark out their progress and direction for future work, while reflecting on the value of learning. It also enables tutors to assess, with their students, the ways in which they are most successfully helping them to learn.

8. Literacy work emerges from a coherent body of values and skills which promote the development of the whole person.

9. The content of tutor training courses should enable tutors to acquire the attitudes, skills and knowledge which promote adult learning. It is important that the selection and development of teaching methods address the literacy problem in its

broadest sense, e.g., building confidence and improving technical skills, planning the work, making materials and encouraging student autonomy.

10. Tutors should have access to initial training courses, as well as to regular in-service training where they can exchange information and discuss all aspects of their work with colleagues. This is important, if schemes are to draw on the collective experience of tutors and build it into their development.

In reflection, it can be seen that the policy document has made it possible to translate the collective experience of students and tutors into a coherent framework which provides guidelines for literacy provision. The document is also helpful as a means of dispelling the misunderstanding that, because this alternative approach is informal, it must be haphazard. In fact, the last 15 years of literacy provision in Ireland suggest that, despite the wide variety of local experiences, there is general agreement as to the principles which must be reflected in the structures created within literacy work.

AN ACTION-RESEARCH PROJECT IN COUNTY OFFALY

Research methodology most suitable to promoting good literacy work

During 1987-1988 NALA worked with the County Offaly literacy program on a research project[5] aimed principally at discovering what encouraged adults with reading and writing difficulties to look for help and what enabled them to stay with the tuition once they had started.

Adult literacy workers in rural areas had repeatedly emphasized the specific problems of organizing provision in their context. Many regarded the fear of embarrassment, and of stigmatization in particular, as a greater problem in rural areas and the issue raised most often at the time was the difficulty of encouraging people to look for tuition.

County Offaly was chosen as an example of a rural part of Ireland where the literacy project had developed a stable basis gradually over a number of years. By 1987 it had reached the stage where the people involved welcomed an in-depth study which would help them plan and initiate developments.

County Offaly is situated in the heart of the midlands of Ireland. It covers 2330 square kilometres of mainly farming and peat land and has a total population of 59 000 (1986). The principal town has a population of 9442 and lies 111 kilometres southwest of Dublin. Most of the adult literacy activity in the county is based in and around this town. The main features of employment are mixed farming and peat-based industries (briquette factories and electricity-generating stations). Of the total work force, 18 percent are unemployed, a figure which rises to 25 percent in the principal town. The county is gradually being urbanized and is consequently becoming more dependent on industry and service employment. Thirty-five percent of the county population now live in towns of over 1500, while 49 percent live in settlements rather than the open countryside.

The evolution of the adult literacy scheme in County Offaly has followed a pattern very similar to that of schemes in other counties in Ireland. Provision has existed in the county for about 12 years, although on a very small scale in the early years, when there were only a few students and organization was very haphazard. In 1980 the newly appointed Adult Education Organizer for the county decided to give priority to the adult literacy scheme. Since then there has been a gradual development of the program, particularly over the last five years. During the main period of the research project (September 1987 — March 1988), there were 42 students taking part in the literacy scheme, mainly individual students working in isolation with a volunteer tutor. There were also eight women taking part in a "Brush Up Your English" course and about 15 young people attending literacy tuition as part of a Youth Skills course for early school-leavers.

In planning and carrying out the research project, NALA was keen to relate the process as far as possible to the philosophy and principles underlying good adult literacy work. We hoped to involve the learners as much as possible, to avoid creating a situation in which people feel they are being investigated but have no say in what is happening. The emphasis was on qualitative research, which was to be participatory if possible. At first it was hoped that a local person would work on the project, so that students and tutors could become involved to a considerable extent. However, as the county organizers felt that students might be less willing to talk to a local person, it was decided that the NALA development workers should carry out the research.

Within this framework, the research was centred on the views and experiences of literacy students in the county. The main research method was an in-depth semistructured taped interview with certain students. The interviewers based these sessions on a planned questionnaire, hoping that the questions would lead to fairly wide-ranging discussion and comment — and this is in fact what happened in a number of interviews. The purpose of the interviews was to give students the opportunity to describe their background and their experience as adults with reading and writing difficulties, to discuss their experience of deciding to attend tuition and to give some assessment of the literacy provision.

The main literacy organizer in the county approached 37 students whom she felt might be willing to take part. She explained to them the aims of the project and the process involved in the interviews. Twenty-seven students agreed to be interviewed, which was considerably more than the organizer had expected. In the main, students were willing to be interviewed when assured of confidentiality and of the usefulness of the research results for other adults with reading and writing difficulties. This was the first of many indications arising from this project that, once adults are attending tuition, embarrassment and fear of stigmatization become less of an issue. Organizers and tutors had tended to hear what students say when they first make contact and had not realized how the situation changes fairly quickly once this major step has been taken.

The other research methods were a structured questionnaire completed by individual tutors and a group discussion with tutors. It was felt that a review of the scheme must include some research into the experience and attitudes of literacy tutors. There were also in-depth semistructured taped interviews with the Adult Education Organizer, who was also the main literacy organizer in the county, and an established tutor-trainer with the reading and writing program.

The principal research findings relate to the experiences described by the students. These covered family background, how reading and writing difficulties affected their lives, their views of the causes of these difficulties, the process of deciding to attend literacy tuition and experiences of provision.

The students' personal histories emphasize yet again the close link between poverty in childhood and reading and writing difficulties. In addition, the majority of those interviewed felt strongly that the way they had been treated in school had caused their problems with learning. A strong theme running through the interviews was the experience of being ignored in school. In adult life, reading and writing problems affected work opportunities, travel, leisure pursuits, personal and social relationships and, above all, self-esteem.

These past experiences all affected the process of making a decision to attend adult reading and writing tuition. In particular, low self-esteem and embarrassment in relation to the problem made it difficult to seek help. However, a more notable finding was the difficulty of getting information about adult literacy provision. Of the 27 students interviewed, 19 had had considerable difficulty finding the information they needed and considered this to be the greatest barrier in looking for help. This figure includes people who had been actively interested in seeking help but had experienced difficulty in finding out what might be available. One basic point to emerge was that many people do not know where to seek general information about the services available in a community.

So while literacy "providers" in rural areas are finding it hard to recruit, it must be emphasized that adults seeking tuition are experiencing much greater difficulty in finding the information they need to make contact. The county organizer had not realized how hard it was for students to make contact with the scheme. People running adult education programs often feel they have made every effort to ensure that provision is well publicized and accessible. This research shows gaps between the beliefs of providers and the experiences of participants. At the same time, however, as the scheme became established in the county, a fairly effective word-of-mouth information system developed and the scheme was certainly able to attract as many students as it could cope with. But these were the ones who managed to persist in their search for information and who found the support they needed. It was not an easy task. A general point revealed about publicity was that it must be widespread and continual. In addition, general efforts to change public attitudes to literacy problems are likely to make it easier for people to look for information and find the necessary help.

Most students interviewed also mentioned support as being an important element in enabling them to start tuition. This support came from various sources, mainly family but also friends, workmates and, sometimes, professionals or members of the public. Support meant active help in getting information and making contact. This indicates that publicity aimed at the general public is also important.

The other major aspect of the research findings focussed on the question of confidentiality and fear of stigmatization, and on how the move towards working in small groups has been very slow in rural areas due to the emphasis on confidentiality. Learners are more interested in meeting and working with other people with literacy problems than had been realized. During the project, several of the students met as a group for the first time. These developments were a surprise to the organizers and indicated that they had underestimated the students' interest in breaking down their isolation. Eighteen of those interviewed expressed interest in working in a small group, whereas all were currently in one-to-one tuition. Any concerns and fears expressed about working in a group were in connection, not with confidentiality, but with the attention students felt they needed and their worries about the pressure of "keeping up" with the other students.

Much of the difficulty in establishing groups in Offaly at this stage is in finding suitable tutors and premises, and in organizing travel. The research revealed the huge amount of time needed to support and train volunteer tutors, most of whom do not stay long with the project. With paid tutors, fewer in number but working longer hours and backed by volunteers, the program would be more effective and better able to develop.

These results demonstrate how research conducted by a national agency can contribute to development and progress at the local level. Through sensitivity to the words and experiences of the students interviewed, this research has made it possible to initiate and support local action. It has also enabled students to meet and has generated an interest in student writings. Finally, the research results were used to encourage the local education authority to support necessary changes in the literacy schemes.

SIGNIFICANT DEVELOPMENTS OBSERVED DURING AND AFTER THE RESEARCH PROJECT

For those of us involved in the County Offaly reading and writing scheme, the NALA research project started a process of review, reflection, valuation and vigorous action. Far-reaching results ensued for the reading and writing provision here and certain preconceived ideas about research were firmly turned on their heads.

When involved in a variety of adult education programs, as some literacy providers in Ireland are, it is often difficult to take time to reflect on a particular program or project. This is even more difficult if, as with us, action takes precedence over the useful but time-consuming task of writing up reports. It is very easy to neglect evaluation if relatively major progress and good practice are evident.

Prior to and during the development of the questionnaire, we viewed our house anew with a visitor's eye. We became uncomfortably aware of the cobwebs and cracks hidden in the background by the relatively good work already being carried out and by other urgent demands on time and on an increasingly diminishing budget. Now, we could no longer ignore that new steps had to be taken to consolidate developments and move ahead.

New goals were set. The recommendations and conclusions of the project ensured that these and other new directions took shape. Indeed some of the plans envisaged for future development were implemented during the research period, as some instant responses seemed imperative during certain stages of the process.

The following results were obtained during the survey process:

— **Greater student involvement:** during the individual interviews carried out by the NALA team, students were asked if they would be interested in meeting others. We, the organizers, were really surprised at the lack of anxiety caused by this proposal.

We had obviously underestimated the development in student confidence over relatively short tuition periods.

Subsequently, one-third of the interviewed students were able to meet, and competed strongly for the limited number of places available at a national writing weekend, attended later on in the term by those who were successful.

— **Greater tutor involvement**: another consequence was that tutors got together for a meeting which focussed on their involvement. We became aware that tutors, paid and unpaid, felt that they could contribute a lot more to the organization of the scheme through regular contact with other tutors.

— **Shared morale boost**: while we had to confront the sobering aspects of our literacy provision, the survey itself and the launch of the book, *Getting Help with Reading and Writing: Co. Offaly Research Survey*, provided a tremendous boost to morale during the project and especially on the day of the launch. The lesson is clear. Ongoing interaction between tutors, students and organizers — and above all recognition and acknowledgment of the work done and in progress is crucial to the success of the scheme. All these elements were facilitated by the survey process.

— **New resources**: nine months later, the Adult Education Board appointed two additional tutor-organizers. As a result of the survey findings, we forged links with local community health centres, while a new centre with an organizer has been established at the southern end of the county.

— **Group work**: we actively encourage students to join small groups of two or three right from the beginning. In addition, we highlight the development approach, encouraging students to meet those who have progressed to examination level. Publicity leaflets announce the scheme as one providing help at all levels, right up to examination level.

— **Publication of student writings**: students have attended a second writing weekend, where they met students from two neighbouring counties. An editorial committee of students and tutors is preparing the writings for publication.

— **Resource development**: we had always felt that, because the work was voluntary (unpaid), tutors should not be required to develop materials for sharing. However, it has become clear that they are very keen to do this. Plans for 1989-1990 therefore include sessions on the preparation of materials.

— **Publicity:** the survey particularly underscored the need for a multifaceted approach to publicity. Nine months later, we have finally evolved a system of ongoing and frequent publicity targeted at as many different organizations and individuals as possible. It is very easy to publicize at the beginning of the year and then forget this aspect for another 12 months.

A side result of publicity is that tutors receive a boost to morale and are keen to become involved in this critical aspect of the scheme. Once student fears were allayed, they too were keen to become involved in publicity if it could help the scheme or other learners in any way. Some were disappointed at not being able to attend the launch of the publication because of work or other obligations. Those who did come were quite aware of the inevitable local and national publicity in newspapers, and on radio and television. They confronted their reservations and came regardless. They spoke publicly about their experiences and all attended the student workshop in the afternoon of the launch. The obvious confidence and commitment of students and tutors, of the Vocational Education Committee, the Chief Executive Officer, the Adult Education Board members and the Minister of Education were inspiring. Newspaper personnel stayed on to the very end, long after the Minister had to leave, and this unexpected interest heightened the euphoria generated by the whole process.

QUESTIONS FOR THE FUTURE

The above examples of how the development of a semi-independent, noncentralized movement has affected the quality of literacy provision, raise several very interesting issues which we feel have relevance for all countries with "advanced" school systems.

— Can the solution to the adult literacy problem be found by readjusting or reforming the current education system or does it require more radical out-of-school initiatives?

— Can a centralized and more institutionalized program tackle the problem in a significant manner? It is the belief of many literacy workers in Ireland that such an approach would simply hide the school under a patina of adult education, while exposing many learners to a repetition of all the negative experiences of their school days.

— The controlling energy for many institutional forms of education tends to come from the centre or the top — "the professionals know what is good for you!" It is essential that, in the development of any adult literacy service, methods and procedures be devised to ensure that the controlling force comes from below. The learners and local workers must always be the deciding factor in determining the nature of the service.

While every means must be used to prevent the reemergence of the school apparatus, it must also be clearly accepted that adult literacy provision cannot be done at low cost. It requires significant State resources, which ultimately means a political commitment to dealing with both the causes and current demands of the adult literacy problem. Literacy becomes a living right only when there is meaningful action.

NOTES

1. Con Murphy (Chairman), *Adult Education in Ireland: Report of the Committee Appointed by the Minister for Education* (Dublin: Stationery Office, 1973).

2. Department of Education, *Discussion Document on Adult Literacy* (1986), pp. 18-27.

3. National Adult Literacy Agency, *NALA Survey Report* (1987), p. 6.

4. *Guidelines for Good Adult Literacy Provision* (1985), pp. 11-34.

5. National Adult Literacy Agency, *Getting Help with Reading and Writing: Co. Offaly Research Project* (1988), pp. 55-56. This project was funded by the Department of Education, Ireland.

RESEARCH BEHIND A LANGUAGE TEXTBOOK FOR ADULTS IN BASIC EDUCATION

Franca van Alebeek
Tineka Krol
University of Amsterdam

In 1977, after a year of preparation, the Adult Education Project (abbreviated as PVE in Dutch) got under way at the University of Amsterdam. Until 1989, the PVE operated within the Department of New Rhetoric at the Institute for Dutch Language and Literature. Recently, the project found a new place in the postdoctoral Institute for Teacher Training of the University of Amsterdam. Members of the PVE (including Fie van Dijk, another contributor to this edition of *Alpha*) are involved in research, tutor training, development of educational materials and consulting in the field of adult basic education (ABE).

This article will briefly review the history of the Open School (the first branch of adult education developed in the Netherlands). It will then explain the authors' activities as university researchers working in cooperation with tutors and students in ABE. The article will end with a brief description of the language textbook *Learning in a Group*. The central thesis of the authors' work is that traditional training in language skills cannot meet the needs of working class adults with very limited formal schooling. The aims of language training in which students learn to see themselves and act as speakers, writers and people capable of critical response, can be served only by participatory research done from a socio-rhetorical point of view.

THE OPEN SCHOOL: FROM THE EXPERIMENTAL AND INTRODUCTORY PHASES TO BASIC EDUCATION

The Open School was inaugurated in the Netherlands in 1977 under the official name of the Open School Experimental Projects. In 1981, the experimental projects were modified and extended into the Open School Introductory Projects. In 1987, a new government regulation again restructured the Open School, this time placing it along with adult literacy courses for native speakers and second-language speakers within yet another new framework, that of adult basic education. The following is a brief review of the work done by the Open School.

Official and unofficial experimental projects

The Open School was established in the Netherlands as a result of developments that took place at an international level, particularly in the late 1960s and early 1970s. UNESCO, the Council of Europe and the OECD (Organization for Economic Cooperation and Development) expressed concern about the results obtained by the very expensive educational systems of the United States and Western European countries. Because of rapid ongoing changes in the institutions and technologies of these countries "lifelong education" was advocated but, to achieve this, more provisions for the education of adults had to be organized than existed at that time. Like every other country, the Netherlands had to make choices and this raised two major questions, both political.

Who should have access to education? Behind the first question lay a conflict. On the one hand, industry wanted a qualified, flexible work force able to use state-of-the-art production techniques. On the other, the then leftist government and feminist groups associated education with emancipation and control in order to motivate people to participate in discussions affecting their daily lives. The Social Democratic Party, which dominated the Dutch government in the mid-1970s, decided that the following groups would have access to education:

— working adults (men and women) whose private lives or work were affected by insufficient or outdated training;

— young working adults (men and women) experiencing difficulties due to a lack of social skills and democratic possibilities;

— married women seeking greater integration or reintegration into public life and the labour market, but hindered by insufficient or outdated training (especially if outdated because of the role of women and changing patterns in family life).

Officially, people could register at the Open School if, as children, they attended primary school for at least four years and secondary school for at most two years. Fourteen pilot projects were set up throughout the country, nine for women only. But the demand for this new type of education outpaced the number of places available. One explanation for this interest was that the feminists and people involved in sociocultural work encouraged the groups they worked with to go to the Open School as they agreed with its aims and felt it would open up new opportunities. This is why numerous unofficial groups, inspired by the Open School approach, sprang up alongside the official pilot projects.

The aims of the Open School are found in the recommendations of the Open School Commission, which was set up by the Department of Education and the Department of Culture and Social Welfare. The Open School was designed for people who, "because of a lack of basic knowledge and skills, cannot function optimally as members of society."

The ministers of these departments further emphasized the importance of "learning to assert and to defend oneself," adding that "the aim is to motivate people to understand changes in society, to assess them critically and to be able to contribute to their realization." In interviews, they repeatedly stated that adult learning is a process of learning from experience, and that it begins with the aims and wishes of the students themselves. The school was "open" because there were no formal tests at the beginning or end of the learning period. Many tutors in the new school — mostly women with experience in other types of adult training and education programs or in the women's movement — adopted these aims and used them as guidelines for their work.

Who will determine curriculum and course content? In answering the second question, the government turned to a group of curriculum designers. This group borrowed a system of teaching and learning units from Westinghouse Learning Corporation and asked secondary school teachers to complete the units (abbreviated as OLEs in Dutch) with more or less regular content. The majority of the designers and teachers were not familiar with the people for whom the Open School was intended. They established two types of courses: "thematic" courses and "training courses," both of which were supported by preprepared educational materials.

Given the experimental nature of this venture, the curriculum staff also had to decide how the project would be evaluated. They opted for measuring the intelligence and attitudes of students entering the Open School and for evaluating the curriculum and educational materials. This meant that the tutors in all 14 official projects were obliged to use the OLEs, regardless of the specific characteristics of their student groups (all male, all female or mixed; located in rural areas or urban centres). Tutors working with OLE samples in preparation for their new task were disappointed with the material. The OLEs were childish in tone and left hardly any room for experimentation. The chosen tests were also inappropriate. How would unemployed students react when asked to put Yes or No after statements such as "I do not feel like going back to work" or "I am happy with my job"? One of the tutors asked Tineke Krol to analyze the tests and materials, and to determine whether or not the curriculum and research plan were in keeping with the experimental and open nature of the School.

Thus, shortly after the inauguration of the Open School, a group of tutors was formed to find an alternative to the top-down-designed curriculum and research plan. This group received support from the practical expert (adult education) of the curriculum staff and from some "outsiders" like Tineke Krol. Within each team, and at regional and national roundtables, the tutors discussed their work, their difficulties and the solutions they found in adapting their teaching to the characteristics and needs of their learning groups. They contested the findings of the national curriculum staff, which ultimately accepted many of their arguments and conclusions.

At the end of the experimental period, the team leaders (mostly women) of the 14 official projects published a report which proved important for the further development of the Open School. They wrote:

> *It is essential that students learn from experience.*
> This means that the experiences of the students must in themselves be seen as educational material. Most important are the experiences that others can recognize, those that stem from the students' social situation. When people want to change their social situation, they need others who share their experiences and also want change. This kind of learning can take place only in groups. The aim of learning is to acquire a critical understanding of reality. To attain such understanding, we must not only know but act upon reality: we must see it differently, more critically than before, and must try to change it with the help of others. From this point of view, centrally developed educational materials cannot be used. The curriculum must be open, so that the students' experiences in life and work can show to full advantage. To achieve this, the program must not be fully developed, but must be adapted locally. The Open School must provide a framework that tutors and students together can transform into their curriculum.

Open School introductory projects

The above report was a statement against plans which had been drawn up by the departments of Education, Culture and Social Welfare, and Social Affairs and Employment. These plans were based on the assumption that the moment had come to introduce the achievements of the Open School experiments into traditional educational and training institutions. Some of the team leaders' recommendations were incorporated into the final plans. Indeed, guidelines were published, in which the underlying educational principles were summarized as follows:

— self-determination with respect to learning content,

— integration of education and training,

— learning from experience,

— learning from and with others.

The publication of these guidelines did not prevent a difficult and complex transitional phase, primarily because institutions with different backgrounds and tutors who were not all familiar with the Open School experiments were forced to work together. Despite this, the work continued and developed. It should be noted that, at that time, the government did not contribute to the development of educational materials and educational publishers were not yet active in the field of adult education. In the meantime, the Open School projects used part of their budget to organize documentation centres and local educational resource centres. Numerous articles and books were published about literacy provision and about the work being done in the Open School. Most of these publications were written by tutors or with their cooperation.

Adult basic education

The late 1970s and early 1980s saw spectacular developments, not only in the Open School, but also in literacy work with native speakers and second-language speakers experiencing severe reading and writing problems. Each of these three fields had followed its own pattern of development. The guiding principles were very similar, but the target groups, organization, subsidization and support were all different and there had been very little cooperation.

In 1987 the government adopted a new regulation on adult basic education. It applied to the three fields just mentioned. All types of adult basic education were brought under the Department of Education and given four years to reorganize and professionalize their services in accordance with the same instructions. The objectives behind this reorganization and professionalization were partially sound and logical: with a more flexible organization and more intensive cooperation, it would be easier for students to transfer from one learning group to another (for example, from a literacy group to an Open School group or a prevocational class). However, the government has not increased ABE subsidies, so that many fear for the practical outcome of the new regulation and wonder if further development of literacy work is still possible — certainly, it is still necessary. Ten years are too few to experiment with the practical application of new ideas in adult education. Things are not yet entirely clear or ready, as the professionalization and tutor training programs seem to suggest.

Apart from this, constant evolution must be expected in work originating with the social experiences of students and aimed at enlarging their understanding of and influence on surrounding reality. In our view, and in the view of many tutors, one of the regrettable consequences of the institutionalization of ABE work is that tutors have lost the time and facilities necessary for research and for organizing team teaching. They have become mere performers within their learning groups and are no longer involved in the recruitment of new students or development of new educational materials.

THE ADULT EDUCATION PROJECT
OF THE UNIVERSITY OF AMSTERDAM

As mentioned above, PVE members participated in the design and practical development of the Open School language training program. How did we researchers working in the field of New Rhetoric become involved in this experiment with undereducated adults?

The answer to this question was not, and is not, self-evident within our discipline. New Rhetoric, or Speech Communication, came into existence because of serious concern about "the careless use of style, vague wording, limited vocabulary and glaring errors in spelling and sentence structure" found in the papers of university students who "within five to 10 years, because of their education, [could] be expected to fill leading positions in education, the Church, law, science, trade and industry, the press and politics." These words are quoted from the 1952 inaugural address of Professor G. Stuiveling (Amsterdam), the first professor of New Rhetoric in the Netherlands. Major developments in the discipline have always centred on the group of language users referred to by Professor Stuiveling, and most of our colleagues work in this tradition. Some have adopted a technological approach, by describing the best procedures for speech activities. Others have taken a theoretical (pragmatic) approach and have established a normative theory of argumentation.

Fie van Dijk and Tineke Krol, on the other hand, (both in New Rhetoric for more than 20 years now) have always worked from the principle that their discipline must help *all* language users to solve their problems and must investigate these problems with the language users before proposing solutions. They use a sociolinguistic framework and ethnographic methods. This is why, in the early 1970s, they could be found with their students visiting cultural centres for young working adults, or on an advisory committee that developed a semi-open curriculum for the lowest level of vocational training for 12- to 16-year-olds, or in a movement of teachers and tutors working on the renewal of Dutch-language instruction at every level of education, and in a working group that formulated objectives for reading instruction based on the reader's rather than the writer's goals. Through all these projects, it became increasingly clear that our attitude towards people and society influences the type of language training we become involved in. Van Dijk and Krol chose to work with people who, socially, have the least rights and schooling, and are therefore the least able to manage decisions and situations of great importance for their lives, needs and wishes. In making this choice and accepting the consequences, Krol and van Dijk were inspired by, among others, the Brazilian philosopher and educator Paulo Freire and the French primary school teacher Célestin Freinet.

Small wonder that, since 1976, when publicity for adult education programs increased in the Netherlands, Krol has devoted herself to promoting the development of adult education. With her university students, she began to examine the conflicting ideologies behind the concept and suggested practice of adult basic education. She then discovered that many of her students were involved in community activities in various districts of Amsterdam or in the women's liberation movement. The students were excited about this, their first opportunity to interconnect their practical voluntary work with their university studies. Together, professor and students drew up a plan enabling successive groups of students to participate in research on language training objectives and methods in the Open School and in literacy groups. Although their colleagues in the Department of Speech Communication were far from enthusiastic, Krol and van Dijk succeeded in getting permission for their long-term research project.

THE PVE AND OPEN SCHOOL LANGUAGE TRAINING

In the working group with her students, Krol undertook an overview of the history of the ideas surrounding adult education and an analysis of the very complicated background of the Open School. The working group then analyzed the principles underlying the curriculum and drew up a critical description of the experimental educational materials. One of their conclusions was that the key concept of "learning from experience" was used ambiguously. The term sometimes referred to a well-known teaching practice, which consists in linking new learning content to concepts the students already know. It also referred to a more fundamental principle of learning: that the expression of confusion and conflicting life experiences is an act of knowledge and the start of a process of questioning and thought which leads to decisions about what new information is needed and what skills will be used. The working group concluded that the educational materials available for language training (the OLEs, among others) were barely compatible with the first interpretation of "learning from experience" and not at all with the second.

Despite this, the concept of learning from experience can be used to advantage in language training. In their stories, students tell about being silenced when they meet authorities like doctors or civil servants. They say: "When I'm put off, I don't know how to defend myself" or "When I apply for a job and see them writing, I think that writing is a sneaky business." Is it not the aim of language training to increase the skills of language users so that, in situations requiring communication, they can play a role more in keeping with their own intentions and objectives?

There is yet another reason why learning from experience is suitable for language training. In groups that learn together, communication is of prime importance. Students share experiences and ask each other questions. They decide which things are important to learn and inform each other about what they already know. They explore their knowledge and formulate questions that they put to people outside the group. They learn to do this orally or on paper. They read and write to get answers to their questions. They evaluate the significance of the answers in relation to their own thoughts and behaviour, and discuss how best to express — to themselves and to others — what they have learned and discovered. In this process, listening and speaking, reading and writing become means to explore reality and bring about or contribute to change. It is clear that learning language and using it are inseparably interconnected. We were not surprised, for example, when a woman who had been studying at the Open School for two years declared: "I'm living more consciously now and I think a lot more about things than I ever did before. I've learned to open my mouth and take a stand. I no longer feel that things happen to me: I can intervene now and make my own decisions when I want to. I've also learned to do things that please me..."

Sources for language training

In the relationship between learning and language training, we can identify four sources on which the design of language training can be based.

1. Students speak and write about what they see, hear, feel and experience. It is very important that they be able to put these events into words. Tutors and other students in the learning group ask questions which help them formulate significant stories. Everyone is involved in the process of finding the right words to express personal knowledge and experience, verbally or on paper, and in exploring the social context of these experiences. As one female student once said: "At first, I told myself 'Keep your mouth shut because you don't know how to say things, you can't put what you want to say into words.' Then I noticed that we all had the same problem from time to time. When we talked about it, we discovered we were trying to tell each other things we'd never talked about before, although we did have thoughts and feelings about them. That discovery brought some relief. Now we just try to talk. You could say that we're making our own language to talk about what is important to us." In this process, students learn to reevaluate their knowledge and experience, and to use them as a way of exploring and

acting. This also enables them to decide in which direction they want to work to further develop their knowledge, aptitudes and self-confidence.

2. Students in learning groups examine the barriers they meet in their daily lives. To increase their command of language and their possibilities for action, we must identify both the situations which cause language problems and the reasons behind the problems. Only then is it possible to determine the questions and aims which will guide the learning process. And only then is it possible to find the means and exercises that will help the students break away from being silent or being silenced, towards speaking and writing with authority.

3. Students in learning groups question themselves about their objectives in new areas of knowledge and behaviour, and about new language activities. Listening, speaking, reading and writing have many functions and forms. As children, not all of us had the chance, either at home or at school, to become acquainted with all these functions and forms, or to find out if they could be useful to us in our lives. This is all the more important as, historically and sociologically, access to participation and instruction in certain language activities is unequally divided among groups of language users. One has only to think of women, excluded for centuries from public debate (politics and law, for example), or students in ABE who cannot imagine that they could ever publish a book or a newspaper or magazine article.

4. The last source is the use of language itself. The choice of words, the structure and style of spoken and written texts are the object of observation and discussion. Texts can be written or spoken by the students or by people from outside the learning group. Words and texts refer to reality. Our interpretations of reality, the relationships and conclusions that are represented in our mind, are all elements of language. Discussion about words and texts shows that not all language users perceive reality in the same way. Class and sex appear to play an important role in these differing perceptions. This is why discussing language use can lead people to a better grasp of reality. Students better understand how they see themselves and would like to see themselves, as well as how other people perceive them and react to their texts. Thus, thinking about language use provides the students with a basis for judging the relevance of other people's texts to their own questions and goals, and for making decisions in speaking and writing their own texts.

From this outline of the sources, it can be concluded that in language training a study of the context in which language is used and of the intentions of the language users is indispensable.

THE PVE AND EARLY DEVELOPMENT OF EDUCATIONAL MATERIALS

In the summer of 1977, the PVE completed a report about its preliminary research. It was already evident that the production of the OLEs was in disorder and that the materials already available were not suitable for the tutors and students of the Open School. At the same time, there was an obvious need for educational materials. The PVE therefore decided to try to develop materials for language training. PVE students who were not familiar with adult literacy practice undertook voluntary work with adult learning groups.

While working on the first version of our language textbook, *Learning in a Group*, we determined what we and ABE groups expect from educational materials.

1. Educational materials should be based on research that examines the problems and questions of the language users for whom the materials are being developed, and includes the points of view and conditions that determine the learning process.

2. Developers of educational materials must have practical experience in the area for which the materials are being prepared. They must not work in isolation, but must remain in contact with the people who requested the materials and will be working with the final product.

3. Developers of educational materials must explicitly state their values, i.e., their views on people, society, learning, language, and language training. They must also justify the research, experience and knowledge on which their work is based.

4. Thematic work and language training like that of the Open School cannot be adequately covered and supported by educational material that must be worked through from the first page to the last, and which thus dictates the entire learning process. Educational material should be open as to the question of content: the learning groups decide this for themselves. The material should be compiled into a book, so that students and tutors can select the parts which best support their current learning activities.

5. When based on careful research, a book of this sort will touch on the students' most frequent questions and problems, thereby helping to answer or solve them. But other material can also do this, so that the book should indicate helpful sources where additional material can be found or developed.

6. Material that will be used to help people develop must itself remain in a state of development. It must challenge the people who work with it, while allowing them to add new material, and to reevaluate and revise the book.

7. The last point is that material meant to help people develop must reflect progress and achievement. This means that developers cannot stay behind their desks, but must collect stories, ideas and examples from tutors and students.

Research-based educational material which meets the above requirements will further the development of the methods devised by tutors and students, while providing the learning group with the means to record them.

The provisional version of *Learning in a Group*

The first version of *Learning in a Group* was a stencilled textbook with a silk-screen cover. In the introduction, we explained who had made the book and why, on which concept and experiences of language learning it was based and how it could be used. The book had two parts. In the first, we described the different steps in the process of learning from experience and offered suggestions supporting this process, particularly suggestions concerning the required language activities. The second part contained four chapters dealing with speaking and listening, writing, spelling, and reading. These chapters focussed on language activities that, in our experience, generate questions that students find important in their daily lives. We suggested topics for group discussion and provided ideas and instructions for learning situations: how to participate in a meeting, how to make a phone call, how to write a diary or letter, how to solve 10 spelling problems, how to read a newspaper and how to look for information in a library.

The 200 copies of this first version sold out in a few months. We asked for comments, which we used to revise the first version and publish a second one. We then decided to launch a new research project to evaluate our material. The following is a description of this research project and of its outcome, the language textbook *Learning in a Group*.

RESEARCH TO EVALUATE *LEARNING IN A GROUP*

This research, carried out from 1981 until 1985, comprised three subprojects:

— research into language questions;

— a series of roundtables with tutors on the subject of language and educational materials (meetings held in various locations in the Netherlands);

— a series of interviews with seasoned Open School tutors who used *Learning in a Group* with their students.

The three subprojects can be described as follows:

Research into language questions

We asked a small group of recognized experts in the practical aspects of the Open School to discuss our research questions and methods. These people indicated a very clear priority. While they endorsed our theory that, in language training, the problems and questions of the students must constantly be linked to actual situations in which students encounter the problems or ask the questions, they felt that the first version of *Learning in a Group* offered little on which to base a practical application of this theory and suggested that we improve the next version by including concrete suggestions along these lines.

Hoping to meet this priority objective, we decided that we would work for one year in collaboration with four Open School learning groups, one official and three unofficial. The question directing our research was: *What do learning groups do to establish the relationship between language questions asked by the students and concrete situations in their daily lives?* Some of the tutors in the four learning groups were PVE students at the University, working as volunteers in ABE. There were two tutors per learning group and all but one took part in the research group, which met once every three weeks. The students in the learning groups were informed about the research project and agreed to cooperate. In the research group, we read and discussed the weekly reports of the work done in the learning groups.

What did we discover? Briefly, we can say that, in the work of the four groups, we did not find many instances of the relationship referred to in our research question. This was unexpected, as all the tutors involved had agreed on the importance of this relationship. This meant that we now had to study the question of why it is so difficult to establish the relationship between language questions asked by the students and concrete situations in their daily lives.

To begin with, we focussed our attention on the knowledge tutors must possess to be able to interpret the students' (and their own) behaviour, stories and remarks during thematic work in the learning group and to be able to make choices for language training based on this interpretation. What knowledge (historical, sociological or biographical) do tutors need to understand, for example, why students lose interest in a self-chosen theme, to respond to remarks expressing apparent prejudice, to understand women who have difficulty speaking in public or discussing political themes, to understand why many students do not see themselves as learners, or to extract major clues from group discussions about work, unemployment or day care? And what expert knowledge do tutors require to condense all that they know into relevant conclusions which can then be applied to language training?

Secondly, we realized that the tutors found it difficult to identify the real language questions of their students, or the "questions behind the questions." As both students and tutors have been in school before, their frame of reference for language training is the subject "Language," which, in primary and secondary schools, is structured into a closed curriculum with tests and exams, spelling, analysis, parsing, dictation, compositions on given subjects, lectures, reading aloud and answering questions on a given text. When asked what they want to learn, ABE students often use terms drawn from their knowledge of primary and secondary school Language courses. One of the reasons for this is that they do not yet know what ABE language training can be. This implies that tutors must ask more precise questions and must be alert to answers during Open School courses, if they hope to understand what their students really want or need to learn, and to identify the context surrounding their language questions. In other words, it is not enough to take stock of students' language questions: tutors really must trace the questions back to their origin and must explore their context with the students.

As a result of this subproject on language questions, we were able to pinpoint events and topics to which tutors must pay particular attention in identifying the real language questions of their students. They include situations in the students' private lives which cause uncertainty or unhappiness, as well as new situations in their public lives. Their behaviour in these new situations mirrors the thematic research they have done in the learning group or on their learning experiences at the Open School, but they are confronted with unfamiliar rules and norms of communication to which they either cannot or will not adapt. Tutors must also be attentive to the names of things, people and events, as well as to their meaning.

Identified language questions must be explored further before tutors can be sure of understanding what lies behind them and before they can decide on the correct response. A simple remark such as "I want to learn difficult words (or jargon)" or "I want to learn to put my thoughts and opinions into words" does not provide tutors with enough information to ensure that they are designing a suitable language program. For example, if a student says: "Teach me to spell right," the teacher usually replies: "I'll explain and you try to learn." Both parties think the question and answer are appropriate. Behind this question, however, are other social realities and problems: "Why should I learn to write? I know nothing that is worth reading. There is no one I can write to. No one is interested in what I have to say. If I learn to write, I'll be able to fill out cheques, but that will cause lots of trouble with my husband."

Teaching spelling without consideration for the context is a waste of time. It is starting at the wrong end. No matter how hard they practise, people forget how to spell correctly unless they are writing for their own everyday needs. Writing really starts with the words and thoughts in our own mind. A tutor once wrote down a very moving story told by a woman in her literacy course and then read it to her, saying, "These are your words. They are written now." With joyful surprise, the woman answered: "If this is writing, then I have many books in my head!" A spelling program makes sense only within a framework in which the meaning and function of writing are the subject of research and learning.

The exploration of language questions (What is their context? What is the real question or the real meaning of the question? What are the points of contact on which to base our selection of an approach?) requires that tutors be able to ask the right questions. Their questions must clarify the situations from which the language questions arise and which enlighten them on elements affecting the use of language in these concrete situations. This requires a socio-rhetorical approach. ("Socio-rhetoric" is the name Tineke Krol has given to the kind of research which, within the scientific discipline of New Rhetoric, offers support to tutors who want to learn to ask the right questions.)

Roundtables on language and educational materials

In cooperation with a national organization that supports the Open School, we organized a series of roundtables in various locations in the Netherlands. The topic was "Language and Educational Materials." We prepared a collection of discussion papers, including examples of learning materials for use in listening, speaking, reading and writing activities. These examples were taken from school textbooks, learning group reports, collections of texts written by students and tutors, newsletters published by the students and tutors in most Open School projects, and books not originally intended as educational material.

At the roundtables, we discussed with tutors which materials in their opinion could or could not be used with their groups. In other words, we discussed criteria for selecting educational materials, with attention to content, learning and language training theory, language use, layout, and so on. Of course, we also asked the tutors where they found suitable materials and asked them to bring samples to the roundtable. Some tutors quipped: "Look, we can't bring our learning groups to the meeting!" — a remark which led us to discuss material other than books and written texts and exercises. This other educational material includes:

— information provided by the students about their life and work (e.g., during the period for greetings and conversation in ABE);

— students' previous school experiences;

— tutors' own ideas about what language training may include;

— tutors' knowledge of obstacles the students may meet in listening, speaking, reading and writing activities, and of ways to overcome them;

— students' stories about difficulties in their daily lives or about situations that cause fear or uncertainty;

— the knowledge and skills of fellow tutors on the same team or in the same region.

Interviews with experienced tutors

We asked very experienced tutors who were working or had worked with *Learning in a Group* to help us revise the language book for use with students in ABE. We set up an interview with 10 of them and asked them to discuss *Learning in a Group* with their students, if possible, and to bring along their evaluation. The reply to this revealed that most tutors used the book only for themselves, to find new ideas and compare their teaching with the concept of language training that underlies our textbook.

We listed themes for the interviews:

— information about the tutors' groups;

— the language questions of students in these groups;

— aspects of listening, speaking, reading and writing that are covered in the language program provided to these students;

— aspects of listening, speaking, reading and writing that are involved in the thematic research done by these groups;

— tutors' ideas about language training;

— problems encountered in language training;

— aspects of the language program which students and tutors find very satisfying;

— educational materials used in the language program (what they offer tutors);

— sources of materials;

— use made of *Learning in a Group* in the language program;

— tutors' opinions about changes to *Learning in a Group*: content, tone, language use, organization or layout;

— tutors' opinions about whether the book should be used as a guide for students or for tutors.

It would take too much space to provide all the details of the interviews in this article. Suffice it to say that they did provide us with a lot of useful information for the revision of *Learning in a Group*. Opinion was divided as to whether or not the book should be used by students. We took all the arguments into consideration and, as for the initial version, decided that we wanted to develop a textbook for students. We also realized that we would have to be more explicit in explaining why we felt it was important to make materials accessible to students.

LEARNING IN A GROUP

We regret that we cannot offer English-speaking readers examples of the result of our research project. It would be futile to include sample pages of *Learning in a Group*, as it is printed in Dutch! We will, however, attempt to describe the book as best we can.

Throughout *Learning in a Group*, a distinction is made between the left- and right-hand pages. Pages on the right contain the introduction, explanations, questions and suggestions. Pages on the left contain a collection of all kinds of texts (complete with drawings and pictures) written by Open School groups and individual students. The content and form of the texts on the left correspond to the item that is dealt with on the right.

The book has three parts. Because thematic research is the very essence of the work done in the Open School, Part One deals with getting acquainted, sharing experiences, asking questions, using verbal and written skills to find and assess information, and so on. In short, it deals with various communication activities that are important for students learning together about themes they themselves have chosen for personal reasons.

Part Two deals with listening and speaking, and Part Three with reading and writing. All kinds of oral and written activities can be used in thematic research and language training. Parts two and three begin with questions that lead students to examine their image and to use listening and speaking skills (Part Two), then reading and writing skills (Part Three). When discussing writing skills, for example, we ask: "Who does the writing in your home? Do you think it is important to know how to write? Is it difficult to write? When is it difficult? Why is it difficult? What do you remember about learning to write in primary school?" After the questions, both general and specific verbal and written language activities are suggested. In Part Two, these include: telling stories, participating in a conversation, interviewing, dealing with experts and authorities, discussing, stating and defending one's opinion, and making a speech. Part Three deals with various reading and writing functions, including: writing to remember or record, to clarify feelings and thoughts, to inform other people, and to have fun or amuse others.

In choosing items from the vast domain of language and language activities, we were guided by the results of the practice-based research mentioned above. Chosen items had been identified as problematic or important, but were as yet unknown to many people who would be using our textbook. We of course included information and suggestions aimed at helping students to listen and speak, read and write more knowledgeably and with greater self-confidence.

Learning in a Group can be classified as semi-open material. The book explains and illustrates the principles on which the Open School language training program is based. It dictates neither the sequence nor the content of the learning process, as the students in each learning group must decide these things together, based on their own experiences, needs and wishes. But once students have chosen a theme, they can refer to the book, especially if they encounter difficulties in their language activities (whether the difficulties relate to their thematic research or not). The book also provides ideas about what language training can be and about language items that would be interesting to study because they create new possibilities and perspectives.

RECENT PVE RESEARCH

Learning in a Group was published at the end of 1986 and is now used in ABE groups throughout the country. Some tutors order the book only for themselves, but the publishing firm often receives orders for 20 copies or more. It seems apparent that all the students in many groups have access to the book. We are also involved in training ABE tutors, which means that we often get to hear the experiences of those who work with the book and have a chance to answer their questions.

Since completing this project, we have undertaken new research, on the language training of women in ABE. At the time of writing (October 1989), we were just finalizing the first stage of this new project. We interviewed 22 women who, having attended the Open School, found paid or unpaid work outside the home. In two intensive interviews with each of them, we asked about their work, the related language activities, and their successes and difficulties in this area. We asked about what they were currently learning through their work, their life history (with particular attention to education and work), and the changes they are hoping for. In the second series of interviews, we discussed the reasons for their successes or difficulties, as well as their ability to deal with the latter and, therefore, to learn through their practical experience. These interviews have been enriching, both for us, as researchers, and for the respondents. The project should contribute to the development of recommendations and materials that will be used in the language training program for women in ABE (especially for women who want to prepare for vocational training or new paid or unpaid work). This is an important issue in the Netherlands because there are new initiatives (sought by government and by women themselves) to increase and enhance the opportunities of undereducated women in the labour market.

CONCLUSION

We mention this new research project simply because it is another illustration of how we work towards the concrete realization of the major thesis of this article: *The development of learning materials must be based on research in which the researchers verify their hypotheses and seek the active participation of students and tutors.* We feel that this thesis is valid for all educational activities but is seldom put into practice. As explained in the first part of this article, everyone involved in the Open School was obliged to do so from the start. Working at the University, we were able to contribute to this development because our own choices had brought us into contact with tutors and students in the Open School program. Everyone concerned has helped to create a new tradition. Much expert knowledge and materials have already been generated and this will make it possible to work on further development of ABE and perhaps to set the example for other forms of education.

NOTES

We could have included numerous notes in this article but they all referred to Dutch publications. Anyone wishing to know more about our work may write or call:

Franca van Alebeek and Tineke Krol
PVE, Instituut voor de Lerarenopleiding
Universiteit van Amsterdam
Herengracht 256
1016 BV AMSTERDAM

Call 020-5254707 (or 020-232091 or 020-231765)

ILLITERATES AND LITERACY TRAINING: THE FEDERAL REPUBLIC OF GERMANY HAS ITS SHARE

Helga Rübsamen
Gertrud Kamper
Hochschule der Künste, Berlin

DEVELOPMENT OF LITERACY TRAINING IN THE FEDERAL REPUBLIC OF GERMANY

Public awareness and education policies

For a long time public opinion in the Federal Republic of Germany — and before that in the German Reich — held that there were no illiterates among the Germans: among the Polish and other immigrants perhaps, but not among the Germans. After all, universal compulsory school attendance had been implemented and enforced during a lengthy process which began with the Prussian general school regulations in 1763, advanced with the Prussian Civil Code of the following year and ended with Article 145 of the Weimar constitution in 1919. The literacy skills of German soldiers were last tested in 1912. Thereafter the question was considered superfluous.

In 1980 the first nationwide conference on "the right to read: illiteracy among German-speaking young people and adults" was held at the University of Bremen in Northern Germany, drawing some 200 participants. The conference became possible and necessary because, since 1975, an increasing number of people had become aware of a problem of illiteracy: initiatives had been taken and the first literacy training courses had been organized in adult education institutions. These efforts and discussions focussed specifically on reading and writing problems among native German speakers rather than language difficulties and educational problems among immigrant workers and refugees.

Since that time there has been a certain amount of public interest in the existence of this phenomenon. The fact that there are adults in the "land of poets and thinkers," the German *Kulturnation*, who can neither read nor write correctly was construed as scandalous and shameful. In 1982 public pressure prompted the German federal government to initiate a three-year project aimed at helping individual adult education institutions in cities and *Länder* (German states) to plan and implement measures for providing literacy training for adults and upgrading for instructors. The project was prolonged for a second three-year period with the somewhat different objective of extending training to include a wider range of skills, such as arithmetic. Simultaneously another key idea was developed by which learning difficulties were approached from a perspective of individual psychology (based on Alfred Adler) and treated with special therapy-like counselling. Negative aspects of the learner's self-image, along with his ingrained distress and concealment strategies, were seen as central to the problem of learning difficulties in literacy courses. The project ended in early 1989 and, with it, the support provided for many literacy training measures. The federal government argued that literacy training is now established, that no further support is needed (e.g., federally tested models) and that literacy should henceforth fall under the auspices of the *Länder*, which have jurisdiction over education. From 1986 to 1988 television campaigns were run periodically (and rerun in the northern and western states) to inform viewers of the problem and encourage those in need of literacy skills to enrol in training measures.

As a result of these and many other smaller-scale activities the number of participants in literacy training throughout the country reached 8300 in 1987 (the year of the last survey). In the spring of 1988, an estimated 10 000 people were enrolled in literacy courses offered by some 308 public and private adult education institutions and 44 detention centres, employing some 947 instructors overall.

Generally we agree with UNESCO that between 0.75 and 3 percent of the total population is illiterate. In a population of slightly over 60 million this means that between 750 000 and 1.8 million adults have serious reading and writing problems, although estimates are frequently also quoted at 5 percent or 3 million. The source of these estimates is not known and their accuracy is rarely questioned.

Almost all adults in the Federal Republic of Germany have completed eight to 10 years of school. This accounts for the low number of basic illiterates. Efforts to define who should be considered illiterate generally fall back on the UNESCO definition of functional illiteracy. But this definition has notorious shortcomings, so that various attempts are being made to broaden the definition to include social and subjective learning difficulties. There is little discussion about the definition itself, possibly because no attempts have yet been made to empirically assess the number of illiterates in the population and because, consequently, the definition criteria have never had to be determined.

Literacy training carries little political weight. One sometimes hears that, in this era of increasing demands for skilled labour, illiteracy must be fought and measures must be taken to reduce the number of functionally illiterate children or young people coming out of the schools each year. However such statements are rare and do not carry far. Discussions and concrete measures lack the stamp of a firm educational policy. On the contrary, when unexpected pressure is exerted on public coffers — as has been the case since late 1988, with the massive influx of

Germans from the Soviet Union and the German Democratic Republic — funding and infrastructures (teachers, etc.) are sapped from already scarce literacy resources.

There is little hope that International Literacy Year (1990) will change this situation significantly. Preparations are progressing very slowly, and it is not known whether public or other means are to be earmarked for the organization and implementation of any activities. Individual organizations and institutions providing literacy training are doing what they can with current resources to prepare activities and heighten public awareness of the problems and needs of the illiterate.

Institutions and structures

The initial impetus for organizing literacy measures came from individuals and the organizations they have established through joint efforts. Today most courses are offered at *Volkshochschulen*, institutions which have traditionally provided adult education programs and which usually classify literacy courses as "special target group" programs under their language or vocational training sections. *Volkshochschulen* vary greatly in size and organizational structure: some are relatively independent, while others depend entirely on their community; student populations range from 20 000 to 30 000, and instruction may be limited to a single literacy course or may comprise a progressive curriculum of up to 20 courses. The institutions within each state form associations, some of which offer upgrading for literacy instructors. They also come under an umbrella organization which operates a teaching institute and a media institute, both of which took part in the federal government's temporary projects. A limited number of independent groups (literacy organizations, foundations, etc.) are also involved. Church groups are not active in literacy training.

Because of their small numbers, independent groups no longer play a major role. It was these groups, however, who initiated the illiteracy debate in the Federal Republic of Germany and who played a decisive role in developing an overall plan for organizing literacy measures and getting courses under way. The only current periodical for instructors is published by an independent association. Independent groups are not subject to the same organizational and structural constraints as public institutions (e.g., they are not required to interrupt courses to coincide with school holidays).

Unlike many other countries the Federal Republic of Germany does not have volunteer literacy instructors: the vast majority of teachers (most of whom are women) have completed teacher training courses. In 1987, 69 percent were trained teachers, while the rest had degrees in education, psychology, etc. Generally instructors are paid on an hourly basis although a very limited number hold permanent positions. Over the past few years emphasis has been placed on one- or two-year contracts which are part of a job creation program for the unemployed and are therefore funded through unemployment insurance rather than through institutional budgeting. As basic training does not prepare teachers to provide reading and writing instruction adapted to the needs of illiterate adults or to deal with the broader literacy-related problems of this group, some *Länder* offer non-mandatory upgrading activities. Several larger institutions also organize upgrading for their own teachers. Conferences and upgrading workshops usually take place during a weekend or over several successive weekends. Compared to the traditional teaching profession (very well paid in the Federal Republic of Germany) literacy training is quite poorly remunerated, while working conditions are very difficult and the work is often qualified as unsatisfying. As a result instructor turnover is high, a factor which considerably reduces the potential effects of upgrading activities.

Two main forms of cooperation exist: first, information is exchanged quite regularly among the various levels of the institutions and their organizations; second, programs involving several instructors make it possible to work as a team and support one another's efforts to further develop literacy training and course content. For the duration of the federal government's project, participating instructors published a periodical entitled *Informationen*. Currently there is *Alfa-Rundbrief*, a literacy newletter which is published by an independent organization and focusses on teaching aids and information. There is little collaboration between universities and literacy training institutions. In rare cases university (teacher training) seminars have initiated literacy training courses, usually followed by collaboration with the local *Volkshochschulen* or the founding of a literacy group. In two instances literacy instructors became lecturers at a university, where they contribute to program development and teacher upgrading. One research project studying the process of learning to read gave at least incidental consideration to adult literacy, in addition to regular schools programs.

Funding

There is little consistency in funding for literacy training. Some *Volkshochschulen* reserve a portion of their language program budget for literacy training. Others require additional funds — usually awarded for temporary projects and paid through unemployment insurance — to implement literacy measures. It is not unusual for these projects to end or to change instructors when funds run out. These short-term resources are also available to independent groups, which otherwise obtain public funds through various procedures and programs. These funds are never awarded for more than one year, after which extensions must be applied for. *Volkshochschulen* and independent literacy groups are often threatened with cutbacks and must expend considerable time and energy in the fight to maintain their level of funding.

The situation for learners also lacks uniformity: most institutions strive to offer free literacy training, but some charge nominal fees (approximately DM 25* for a 12-week semester). In one city course fees are known to go as high as DM 100.

LITERACY TRAINING RESEARCH IN
THE FEDERAL REPUBLIC OF GERMANY

Research on adult illiteracy and literacy training in the Federal Republic of Germany is rare and small scale. Many authors do not consider their work research: students work as literacy instructors and then research some aspect of literacy in preparation for examination essays. Sometimes they conduct small-scale empirical surveys: frequently they question participants about their lives, and about the causes and effects of their illiteracy. Some case studies are conducted. The extent and structure of literacy measures are described and analyzed, either generally or with a focus on specific aspects such as instructor upgrading or the availability of reading material. These studies are not published.

Over six years the federal government project at the teaching institute of the *Volkshochschulen* umbrella organization conducted three surveys on the scope and structure of the literacy programs offered throughout the Federal Republic of Germany. In the context of this project research was also conducted on factors causing illiteracy. Twelve course participants were interviewed on subjectively significant life experiences and empirical knowledge related to their inability to read and write. The results confirmed the hypothesis that negative factors which influence self-image play a key role in causing and sustaining illiteracy. The project carried out by the media institute of the umbrella association studied the media habits (radio and television) of literacy students and found that they did not differ from those of other population groups. The impact of the television campaigns was also analyzed and described.

No research has ever been conducted on the number of illiterates in the population. In contrast numerous studies have been conducted on the literacy skills of graduates from special schools for the learning disabled. One such study showed that over 30 percent of these students had not gone as far as the fifth grade. Young adults taking vocational training have also been tested, and 0.6 to 0.8 percent declared functionally illiterate. This would suggest that special-school graduates have little chance of accessing regular vocational training. We can also presume that the two studies did not target the same population group.

---

* DM 1 = C$0.65.

No studies to date have focussed on the success of literacy measures. Teaching effectiveness and evaluation criteria are largely taboo issues.

One West Berlin university clinic conducted clinical psychological tests on several literacy students, revealing major biographical or family-related burdens, various shortcomings in perceptive and cognitive performance and personality structure disorders. The University of Frankfurt conducted one joint project with the University of Jerusalem, studying underprivileged young people participating in a combined vocational and literacy training program. In isolated cases literacy students or teachers are involved in pedagogical or linguistic research projects, most of which, however, focus on children. University researchers generally demonstrate little interest in literacy and have barely contributed to its further development.

To date only one research project has dealt specifically with learning difficulties and the improvement of instruction. The project and its results are described in this issue of *ALPHA*.

AUTHORS' ASSESSMENT

Overall, the literacy training in the Federal Republic of Germany lacks uniformity and coordination. This affects literacy practices, organization and funding, while making it difficult to ensure the ongoing presence of qualified, experienced instructors. Research is also affected: on the one hand, many aspects of literacy are left unexplored and, on the other, studies are almost invariably small scale, carried out by one individual in preparation for examinations and destined to remain unknown because unpublished.

We were somewhat dismayed by these findings. Is this sober, even pessimistic, assessment a true reflection of the current situation? We have been working intensively and almost exclusively at almost every level of adult literacy for many years, and have discovered that the situation really is as described, though we may tend to suppress the fact in our daily lives. In our view future prospects are contradictory. On the one hand there is mounting pressure on the illiterate population, particularly as regards employment: the continued rise of unemployment has led to a demand for higher basic qualifications for workers and it has reached the point where workers whose literacy and numeracy skills served them well just a few years ago are now made to feel that these same skills are inadequate. At the same time, under current educational policies, the literacy infrastructure that has been developed over the past decade within the framework of adult education is being handled as though it will never again be needed or as if a new one could be magically created at a moment's notice with the next policy decision.

BASIC SKILLS INVOLVED IN LEARNING TO READ AND WRITE, OR TWO LITERACY TEACHERS TAKE RESEARCH INTO THEIR OWN HANDS*

Gertrud Kamper
Helga Rübsamen

* Owing to a tight production schedule, this paper did not undergo the linguistic and terminological revision usually undertaken by the ministère de l'Éducation du Québec.

Needless to say, you, the reader, know how to read and write. Presumably you are reading this article because you are in some way interested in literacy problems among adults in industrialized countries. Do you think that anyone can learn to read and write? Or do you hesitate when you are told that this depends on intelligence, which is a hereditary, immutable factor, and that below a certain intelligence quotient there is no successful learning possible?

We have been working in the field of adult basic literacy for over 10 years. We see many difficulties and obstacles barring the way to progress and success. However, our teaching is based on a conceptual orientation that allows us to proceed from the idea of every man's learning capability and to explore the difficulties in detail. We do not need biologically based explanations about intelligence, aptitudes and capacities. We mediate to our learners tools — provide them with mental tools. Not surprisingly, mechanics handle pliers, screwdrivers and hammers more skilfully than most office workers. They have learned their trade and practise it constantly. Nobody finds it surprising that children who begin by playing in their father's workshop, then help out and make amateur constructions, know how to repair their own cars and houses when they grow up. They have learned how to use the tools at an early age. And it seems quite natural that people who did not have this opportunity are likely to be "all thumbs" as adults, having difficulty with such basic tasks as using a wrench for a minor do-it-yourself repair. Well, our field is mental tools, ranging from the simplest to such complex ones as written language. The skills for using these tools must also be learned, although this may not be seen as easily as learning to use a pair of pliers. We suppose that this viewpoint may seem somewhat unusual for you. However, as we describe our project, we would ask you to try to adopt this viewpoint for the duration of this article. Further, we would be pleased if you would share your experiences in this attempt with us and write us.

THE CONTEXT

From 1985 to 1986 we conducted a small-scale research project in West Berlin to explore one specific aspect of learning difficulties in literacy courses and to improve teaching. For two years "Berlin-Forschung" (Berlin research), a program designed to promote hands-on research by young scientists, provided funding to employ a part-time research assistant (Gertrud) and ensured a nominal expense budget. The program also enabled us to hold a conference allowing experts to discuss research results after completion of the project. The project was housed at the "Institut für allgemeine Pädagogik" (institute for general pedagogics) at the "Hochschule der Künste Berlin" (Berlin high school of fine arts, one of the three universities in West Berlin). The institute allowed us to use its computers, equipment and lecture halls, and one of its professors, Dr. Rückriem, acted as scientific adviser.

Two organizations were involved in the project's hands-on aspects. One was the "Arbeitskreis Orientierungs- und Bildungshilfe" (workshop for guidance and training assistance), an organization dedicated almost exclusively to teaching young and adult illiterates to read and write. This group was one of the Federal Republic of Germany's literacy training pioneers and is also involved in increasing public awareness, producing and publishing teaching material and developing conceptions of literacy work with adults. Helga has been working for this organization for more than 10 years as a teacher and member of the board.

The second organization was the "Berufsbildungswerk des Rot-Kreuz-Instituts" (Red Cross vocational training institute), which provides vocational training and vocational school instruction to disadvantaged young people. German upgrading courses, equivalent to regular literacy courses and involving about 10 learners averaging age 20, are also available for trainees with significant reading and writing difficulties.

Part of the research was conducted at a *Volkshochschule* (people's high school), a traditional public adult education institution.

THE PROJECT

Virtually all German citizens attend school throughout their childhood. Despite this education, which may cover eight to 10 years, some of them have either no literacy skills or such poor skills that they are functionally illiterate as adults. This paradox reveals logically what was shown empirically in learners' biographical accounts: already in their first years at school all had severe learning difficulties. Moreover, experienced literacy teachers know that, despite great efforts, some learners make little progress in reading and writing, while others who receive the same instruction succeed.

Reasons for past and present learning difficulties are mainly sought in and discussed with regard to social and sociopsychological factors. Questions are asked about experiences during childhood in family and in school; current behaviour is discussed; and conclusions are drawn about the negative aspects of an individual's self-image and ingrained strategies of learned helplessness. On the practical level conceptions are developed focussing on therapy-oriented counselling. This method considerably boosts a learner's personality development and social relationships. In spite of this there remains some discontent because — as relevant and indispensable as it may be — such development does not always and necessarily lead to learning reading and writing, at least, not under regular instructional conditions.

The research project addressed this problem by examining how underdeveloped basic abilities affect learning difficulties of adult illiterates. It was inspired largely by two concepts developed in the field of children's learning difficulties: the idea of *Teilleistungsschwächen oder - störungen* (literally: partial performance weaknesses or disturbances, similar to specific learning disabilities) (Graichen, Berger, Schuch-Friedler) and the approach of starting at the *verbo-sensomotorischen Voraussetzungen* (verbo-sensory-motor prerequisites) of learning to read and write (Breuer and Weuffen). Both concepts presuppose that psychic performances are complex systems which are formed and developed throughout an individual's lifetime. Learning to read and to write involves many varied perceptive and cognitive skills as important elements, some of which are already acquired well before school age. This long-term process can miscarry, fail to occur or be disturbed. Depending on their viewpoint, researchers attribute such disturbances to organic causes (minimal cerebral dysfunction, etc.) or to inadequate stimulation and upbringing. Studies on "partial performance weaknesses" focus primarily on children who experience manifest and severe problems (e.g., dyslexia) at school, while the "verbo-sensory-motor prerequisites" approach focuses mainly on children in their last preschool year. Underdeveloped perceptive skills which could engender future learning difficulties are discovered as early as possible, and special encouragement is provided for children with such problems in their last preschool year. This significantly reduces the number of learning difficulties at school. However, these ideas need qualification to be adapted. First, there are differences between children and adults in varied aspects. Second, these approaches are not entirely satisfactory from a theoretical standpoint. Although both are based on the psychology of activity theory, they fail to take into account the important role of acquisition of mental tools mentioned in section 3 (General Information on Activity Theory) and the key role of speech in raising the levels of psychic functions.

Our experiences with literacy work and impulses from research findings on learning difficulties in children led us to formulate the following hypothesis: at the moment they begin with learning to read and write all individuals (children and adult illiterates alike) have not only different personalities and social experiences. They differ as well in their already developed levels of varying perceptive and cognitive abilities which are relevant elements for acquiring literacy. In elementary schools and literacy courses, the first instruction for learning to read and write is often extraordinarily uniform. Even if different individual experiences and needs are taken into account, a uniform high level of elementary skills is set for all. That means: traditional instruction is adapted only to some learners, making overly high demands on others. *This discrepancy between the perceptive and cognitive skill development level prerequisite for traditional instruction and the (lower) levels which some learners have actually attained produces learning difficulties.* Teachers often fail to realize that the instruction and assistance for learning they offer presuppose certain abilities and on what level these presuppositions are made.

The project's chief aim was to develop starting points and procedures to help learners with obvious difficulties make headway. This meant: first task was to develop a diagnostic tool to measure individual cases whether the demands placed on the learner by traditional instruction are too high. And, second, there were to develop modified methods for instruction which allowed to start teaching at relatively low perceptive and cognitive skill development levels. Emphasis was placed on adapting literacy instruction to learners, not on adapting learners to a set unqualified type of instruction by therapy or training sessions.

We also were interested in broadening and supplementing information and ideas on the set of conditions which lead to illiteracy despite schooling. Our own experiences with learners coupled with various reports convinced us of social causes and of the fact that illiteracy is related to difficult conditions for living and learning. However, this explanation did not seem sufficient. First, not all children who grow up and attend school in difficult conditions become illiterates. If we do not want to suppose that social conditions are active factors or subjects themselves, a mediation must exist between difficult conditions and the success or failure of learning processes — which are activities of human subjects. Knowledge about this mediation would greatly benefit the search for methods of stemming the yearly flow of new functional illiterates from schools.

The potential theoretical outcome was to give concrete form to the model of acquisition of complex psychic functions and the role of social-historically developed mental tools for learning to read and write. To verify and further develop aspects of the underlying activity theory touched primarily the interests of Gertrud and the scientific adviser.

In practice, first, an instrument was to develop to find out whether traditional instruction was too demanding for learners and, if so, in what areas (a series of tests similar to that of a psychological test battery). Second task was to develop and to determine how traditional instruction must be modified to avoid such overburdening — and the associated learning difficulties — in literacy instruction. The test battery had also to differ from usual tests in various aspects to be adequate to the points mentioned in the theoretical excursus in section 3.

Testing involved one teacher (including Helga) and one class of learners from each participating organization (the "Arbeitskreis" and the "Berufsbildungswerk"). Several learners were also involved in modifying instructions. The diagnostic instrument was tested by two teachers and learners from two classes at the *Volkshochschule*. It was also administered to 10 learners registered in a German course on special problems of spelling and writing at the same institution. These learners comprised the so-called control group, although they differed from illiterate adults in many ways (social situation, school experiences, self-confidence, etc.). The learners participated voluntarily in taking the tests (total 44) and in developing and testing modified instructions (total 7). Those from the « Berufsbildungswerk" were allowed to participate during their working hours. As research assistant, Gertrud was responsible for developing the tests, carrying out some testing and evaluating the results. Theoretical problems were discussed with Professor Rückriem when necessary.

SOME GENERAL INFORMATION ON ACTIVITY THEORY (EXCURSUS)

Origins and dissemination

It is a very difficult task to present the activity theory and its relevance in a few pages. It is a theoretical connection based on the philosophical, historical and sociological assumptions of dialectical materialism. The psychology of activity theory was originated in the early years of the Soviet Union and has developed continuously since then. Today this theory and its founders are the basis of a large international scientific community spanning a wide range of fields in research and practice.

The works of Vygotsky, founder of the cultural-historical school of Soviet psychology, have been known in Western countries for many years, especially among linguists. The works of Luria are renowned in medicine, especially among neurologists, psychiatrists and neuropsychologists. With the renewed interest shown by Western intellectuals in Marxist theory — one of the consequences of the student movements of the late 1960s and early 1970s — scientists and students in psychology and pedagogics also began to take an interest in the ideas of Leontiev, who conducted psychological research in a pedagogical institute for many years. In addition to the standard works of these authors (the "classics") there are numerous individual research studies of them and by their collaborators, students and successors.

The works of these three scientists — called the "troika," Russian term for a three-horse carriage — have been translated on many occasions into English, especially in the United States. Michael Cole and James Wertsch deserve well of publication and reception in English-speaking countries. In Canada Charles Tolman of the University of Victoria (British Columbia) participates actively in the international network which has developed over the past years around the activity theory. A number of works have also been published in French, although they are less numerous than those available in English or German. In many Western European countries activity theory is adopted, implemented and developed, especially in the Federal Republic of Germany and the Scandinavian countries. Volume 4.2, "Forschungsübersichten/State of the Art," of the proceedings of the First International Conference on Activity Theory, held in Berlin in 1986, provides an overview of the international situation. The second conference is scheduled for May 1990 in Helsinki.

Main concepts

I am uncertain whether it is possible in a few pages to paint a general yet accurate picture of the main concepts and relevance of the activity theory. I will begin by outlining the concept of Man underlying the whole theory and its various singular statements and then describe the role played by individual acquisition of human abilities, that is, learning. Finally, I will examine in greater detail those aspects which were most important for our literacy work. The limitations of this brief introduction preclude any discussion of methodology, especially dialectical materialism, which is a very effective cognitive tool.

Everything starts with taking men as living beings which are totally an integral part of nature and, however, *as its part* stand opposite to the "rest" of nature in that they are active subjects. Like all other living beings, they act upon nature, upon their environment to survive. However, different from animals, they do so cooperatively, that is, socially, and using tools which they produce themselves. These both developments are conditions for the emergence of consciousness.

In the course of its phylogeny, sociability and the production and use of tools led mankind to develop *language as a means of communication* and thinking as mental anticipation, that is, to imagine practical acts. The connection of language and thought gave rise, first, to *verbal thinking* which, together with other developments in mankind's long history, was prerequisite for abstract thinking. Second, this connection of language and thought enabled language to be used not only as a communication tool but also as a *means of representing* phenomena of reality (how human beings see and experience it, how they imagine the invisible, and how they recognize and explain all of this) and also what real phenomena and their interrelationships mean for men. Language (like other sign systems) *embodies entire systems of human meaning*. Third, language concepts (together with other sign systems such as mathematics) function as *tools for mental processes*.

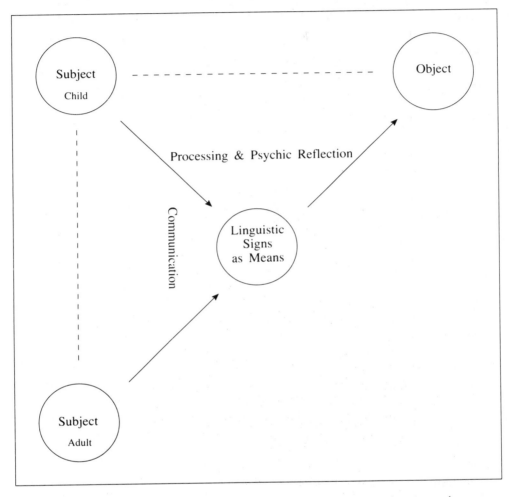

Figure 1 Linguistic signs as mediators of (1) human communication (e.g., between a child and an adult) and (2) the processing and psychic reflection of the Actions' Objects (e.g., by this child)

Tools may be considered as a kind of extended organs of the body which enable men to chop and cut, kill from a distance, carry heavy loads, see far-away objects, recall the distant past and much more. Like all other living beings too, men must transmit the characteristics of their species from one generation to the next one. While animals inherit their characteristics almost exclusively through chromosomes, that is, biologically, a substantial part of human characteristics, that is, most of the typical human abilities, are not genetically determined. Human skills are *materialized* in the tools. For example, the ability to dissect raw materials is materialized in tools like knives, saws and axes, thereby fixed outside the human body. At birth, every human individual does numerous of its species' characteristics not carry inside its body but stands opposite them as an external world of tools, sign systems, institutions, etc. Every single person is born with the need and the ability to *acquire* these concrete human abilites which stand opposite in materialized form. The learning person has to act with and upon the objects, the tools, and these actions must be adequate to the abilities materialized in the objects in question. In this way each individual subject must reconstruct these abilities within himself or herself. Science has already gained a fairly concrete picture of the associated processes on the neuropsychological, neurophysiological and morphological levels. I will not attempt to describe them here, having insufficient specialized knowledge in these fields.

One other aspect bears mentioning: the fact that essential characteristics of the species are developed and transmitted from one generation to the next externally was evidently very instrumental regarding speed and diversification of mankind's development. Whether we consider such progress still desirable in the current context of developing military technology and worldwide environmental destruction is another matter. The separation between the human body and characteristics specific to the species, which forces each individual to actively acquire his or her species' essential characteristics, implies that the acquisition may be not carried through, e.g., it can be attempted and fail. This is the central issue in all discussions and research on *learning difficulties*. In some cases it may happen that not even such an attempt takes place: for example, when for a human individual the objects upon which he or she must act, that is, upon which the new abilities must be carried out, are simply not available to him or her. History abounds with examples of entire groups that were denied or refused the possibility of acquiring certain skills due to sex, skin colour, social class, etc. However, this is a political not a psychological question. As all human beings belong to one and the same species, also all abilities developed by men in the course of their history fall to their shares: as a real potentiality. They themselves must transform this potential into reality by their own activity. Keep human abilities strangely standing opposite them is this part of the meaning of the concept of "alienation."

Human sociability is a characteristic of the species: it is true for every individual up from the beginning. Connected with cooperation, which is mediated by tools and language, the concrete ways in which men live and work together are also fixed outside their biological organs: that is, in institutions as clans, families, states, in rituals such as harvest celebrations or marriage ceremonies or elections, but also in laws. Consequently individuals must learn these forms of cohabitation. Like the tools, the concrete manifestations of human sociability were developed throughout history, giving rise also to societies based on the repression and exploitation of one group by another, that is, domination and subordination. And a special type of society evolved in which the common relationship between people is created and mediated in such a way that individuals experience themselves as single, private beings whose sociability must subsequently be established artificially: the bourgeois society with its capitalist means and form of production and the appearance of the isolated, private individual. In this context individuals and sometimes entire groups may fail in the constantly needed realization of their sociability, for example, when craftsmen misjudge the market and cannot sell their products or when workers cannot sell their labour due to unemployment. Many individuals experience society, which operates "behind their backs" (Marx) through their own activities, as foreign and opposite to them. This is another part of the meaning of "alienation."

Within every society the various groups or classes into which human communities have divided in the course of history interact. On the other hand — when the society is one of domination and subordination — these groups or classes have definitely different and partially even conflicting interests. On the psychological level, the result is that the "objective" meanings of objects or situations within the frame of a general social system of meanings do not longer coincide for all people with the "subjective" meaning (the personal sense) of these objects or situations they experience in their own lives. Analyzing lack of coincidence and *contradictions between learned social meanings and experienced personal sense* in important areas of life provides a better understanding of the relationship between social conditions and inner mechanisms in many psychic problems. It also sheds light on the way in which contradictions within personality structures, within motives, are *socially determined*, without losing sight of the *psychological aspect*.

For my work in literacy teaching knowledge was primarily relevant about *how* men acquire mental abilities and what role teachers play who try to provide instruction. Below a short summary of the points I consider most relevant:

1. The *learners* are the subjects in the learning process. That they *want* to learn, that they have a motive for acquiring a certain ability, is the first precondition at all for learning. And they can learn only if *they themselves* orient themselves in the task and perform the necessary acts upon the object. For more complex abilities, teachers must formulate tasks so that they are adequate as well to the abilities to be acquired as to the developmental level already reached by learners. If, through their teaching they hinder learners from becoming active themselves, they hinder their learning processes, *handicap* the learners.

2. The process of acquiring a new ability consists of three phases: (a) the orientation in the task (What is to do? Why is it

necessary or sensible to do exactly this? what is already known? Which operations are at hands for processing? In what order should they be performed?); (b) the actual "work" action itself (performing the operations on the object in the correct order, connecting them to a new action); and (c) checking (i.e., comparing the results with the model. If they do not correspond, the "work" action must be repeated with a modified orientation. The model may be external or already an internalized image. The individual steps of an action can also be checked against a detailed plan of the entire process.) In class often too little attention is devoted to learners' needs to *orient themselves* in the task. After a brief explanation by the teacher they are often left to their own devices. However such explanations are acts of the *teacher* only and not of the *learners* — they therefore do not learn by this. The second phase, that is, the actual "work" action itself, is virtually always performed by the learners, whereas the last phase (checking) is almost always seen as the teacher's responsibility. In this case learners do not learn that they *can* and *must* check their own work, nor *how* to do so.

3. The formation of mental abilities means — like of any other ability too — acquiring tools already socially developed. Mental tools are most often in the form of concepts. The task is to re-perform (but not reinvent) the processes that lead to the concept. (In German, the term "concept" is derived from the verb "to grasp," i.e., the movement of grasping or seizing something.) Hence there is nothing mysterious or incomprehensible of which one person has more and another less according to his or her fate or race, etc. as postulated by the construction of measurable "intelligence" whose quotient is said to remain the same throughout lifetime. It is merely a question of using tools — a skill that can be learned. With every new acquired tool or ability, he or she becomes "more intelligent."

4. The formation of mental abilities takes place in a movement "from the outside in." This means that the individual steps of a new action will initially be performed externally, involving the displacement of material objects (e.g., models, inside drawings, etc.). These steps are then by stages performed increasingly internally (in the imagination only) until they become entirely "mental." This process of "interiorization" can also be reversed: a virtually mental action can be performed with external objects (exteriorization).

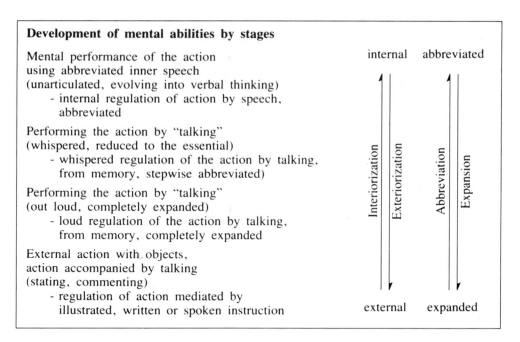

Figure 2 Simplified overview of the stages involved in developing mental abilities

5. Speech plays an important role in this process of interiorization. Speech regulates actions. This pragmatic function of speech arises first through the communication between adults and the child. The child acquires this function already at preschool age and uses his or her own speech to regulate his or her activities when not yet able to regulate them purely internally. (Piaget calls this "egocentric speech.") Children who do not do this later experience more extensive and fundamental learning difficulties than their peers. This regulative speech (first aloud, then whispered, finally internal) can also be used deliberately to foster acquisition of mental abilities.

6. The actions which form the basis for future mental operations are initially not only external but also fully expanded. In other words every partial step in the "chain" is carried out fully. As the new action is mastered, this chain is "shortened" or "abbreviated." This leads the performing of the process to become "automatic" and entails two advantages: first, the action can be performed much more rapidly than before and second, it no longer requires consciousness, that is, the individual needs no longer to think about each step. (This is often illustrated by the example of the difference between a student driver and an experienced one.) In the same way that interiorized actions can be exteriozed, abbreviated activities can be expanded. Both

possibilities are pedagogically interesting because only external and expanded actions are visible. Learners and teachers can talk about them and modify them if the actions do not correspond to the object, i.e., if they are not adequate to the order of necessary steps.

7. Learning to read and write does not merely mean transforming speech into writing by developing psychic processes analogous to that of speaking and hearing. The entire system of language must be restructured when acquiring literacy. The figure below gives a short overview of these relations.

Level	Relationship language / reality	Relationship with Other Means of Communication	Sentence Construction and Vocabulary	Language Awareness	Relationship prerequisite / Repercussion
Literacy	Writing about - facts - practice	Graphic appearance of texts (paragraphs, etc.)	Exhaustive and discriminative	Indispensable	Repercussion on
Speech - dialogue - monologue	Speaking about - facts - practice	Gestures, mimicry, intonation, etc.			
Practical doing	Speaking during action	Ingrained in the practical action	Minimal	Not essential	Prerequisite for

Figure 3 Simplified overview of the characteristics of the various forms of language

As I gained experience in literacy training I discovered that other findings of the activity theory too enabled me to define and understand problems more clearly. Two of these findings bear mention:

1. Psychic functions are organized hierarchically, that is, they can be seen as systems whose components are themselves other systems of a lower order. If an action is performed unsuccessfully in the learning process, this approach allows to look for the individual components or elements of the new system that is to acquire so that the learning process may be initiated at this point. This has an eminent advantage over helpless repeating again and again of an invariably unsuccessful action. (Supportive teaching at school unfortunately often adopts this form.)

2. Humans do not act upon isolated motives; their activities are determined by complex structures of converging or diverging motives. Any action (for example learning to read and write) can have contradictory personal sense for an individual if realizing one motive (for example, developing greater self-confidence in public, on the job or in front of the children's

teachers, etc.) threatens the achieving of another (for example, a relationship with someone who helps the individual by taking care of anything that requires writing). Structures of motives are dynamic as well as complex, that is, they change with age and experience. This includes what learners experience in literacy courses — and this part of their experience depends partly on us, the teachers. Gerald S. Coles in the United States emphasizes exactly this point in describing the relevance of centring literacy work on the activity theory.

RESEARCH AND RESULTS

The test battery on the elementary abilities involved in acquiring literacy was developed in several stages. These tasks, which were similar to those in various psychological assessments, were modified at key points. The final version of the test battery comprises tasks in seven categories or fields:

— moving/kinesthetic elements,

— looking/visual elements,

— hearing or listening language/phonetic-auditory elements,

— spatial orientation/integration of kinesthetic, visual and vestibular elements,

— rhythm/integration of auditory and kinesthetic elements, serial,

— comprehending sentences/grammar, syntax,

— deducting (syllogisms).

Moving, looking and hearing or listening language are each divided into two subcategories comprising discriminative perception and reproduction of an "isolated" object (modal level) and perception and exact reproduction of a series of objects (serial level):

— discriminative perception of movement (modal-kinesthetic),

— discriminative perception of series of movements (serial-kinesthetic),

— discriminative perception of graphic figures (modal-visual),

— discriminative perception of series of graphic figures (serial-visual),

— discriminative perception of phonemes (modal-phonematic-auditory),

— discriminative perception of series of words (serial-auditory).

Discriminative perception of spatial relationships includes four subcategories:

— orientation to the left and right sides of the body (turning),

— mobility within an imagined internal space (counting backwards),

— visual reception of spatial relationships on a plane (connecting the dots),

— mastering spatial prepositions within a line.

Tasks within a given category or subcategory are progressively more difficult. Wherever possible they are designed both with and without demands on memorization.

Classification of the abilities needed to perform a task in a given category (e.g., the modal-visual category) indicates only emphasis and does not mean exclusivity. This is fully adequate to guide educational practice. Cooperation of the various modalities in developing systematically structured abilities was partially taken into account in selecting tasks and categories of tasks. And imagination of the mutual influence of the various categories is important in result interpretation and subsequent hypothesis formation. Above all, the interacting of the various modalities is to be considered in outlining the instruction based on these hypotheses.

Tasks aimed at identifying individual phonemes within the spoken word were purposely omitted from the test battery. Sounding out words — that is, breaking down a spoken word into its phonemes and pinpoint their succession — is an indispensable subaction for learning a literacy that is based on phoneme-grapheme-correspondence. However, no reasonable instruction of literacy makes this skill a prerequisite for beginners. All studies on the "psychological reality of phonemes" in children or adults have concluded that this skill is a result of learning to read and write (cf. Morais et al. 1979 and 1987, Sendlmeier 1987). It therefore seemed unnecessary to identify discrepancies in this category between skills which are usually demanded in traditional instructions and those which learners have already developed.

Figure 4 gives a simplified overview of the categories targeted by the test battery and of general imaginations of the interaction between them.

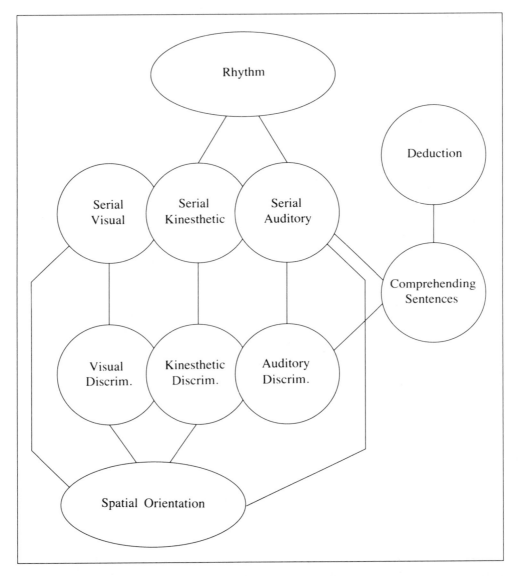

Figure 4 Overview of the categories targeted by the test battery for literacy-related elementary abilities

Experience with adult learners showed that for outlining an individually adequate instruction it is not enough to know which tasks of which degree of difficulty a learner masters. For this aim it is also important to know whether he or she employs linguistic or conceptual mediational means (spontaneously or voluntarily) in working on a task. Also, information is necessary if the learner when performing an action or an operation carries out the final phase (checking), too. Finally, it is important to know whether the actions by which a task was completed successfully are already firmly consolidated so that they can be used for developing other action systems, or whether they must be reinforced and stabilized further. The adult course in which this experience was gained was based on the activity theory's findings on the stages and phases of acquiring mental operations (Galperin) and on the role of regulative or mediating speech in attaining higher levels and, therefore, a greater capacity for psychic functions (Vygotsky, Luria).

These demands led to the need to combine and elaborate the diagnostic tools developed for children in the light of our own experience, and to modify them in a certain way:

— In all appropriate tasks it is important to observe whether the learner discovers errors himself or herself by comparing the results with the model.

— It is important to note whether the learner uses linguistic aids or other mediational means in completing tasks, that is, whether he or she regulates, accompanies or supports his or her actions with speech. For tasks linked directly with language, for example, those that involve memorizing and repeating word series, it is important to note whether other means, such as counting on fingers, are used. To get information as to whether external mediators are used, one of the word series tasks offers picture cards to facilitate memorization, while the others allow use of internal mediators only.

— It is important to note whether the learner in working on the task performs the necessary actions slowly or rapidly, self-assuredly or hesitantly.

— Upon completion of a task, the learner is to ask to judge its degree of difficulty subjectively.

For illustration, a copy of a page from the test battery is shown below. For example, to test an individual's capacity for visual discrimination, we used the figures developed by Breuer and Weuffen. We extended their original application somewhat by introducing a first attempt asking the learner to draw the figure from memory and by asking him or her to check the results himself. Besides the results of the above-mentioned observations and questions are recorded.

2.1 Discriminative Visual Perception (modal/visual) — Page 2

A. Products

	1. Trial (from memory)	Error Discovered by learner	2. Trial (using the model)
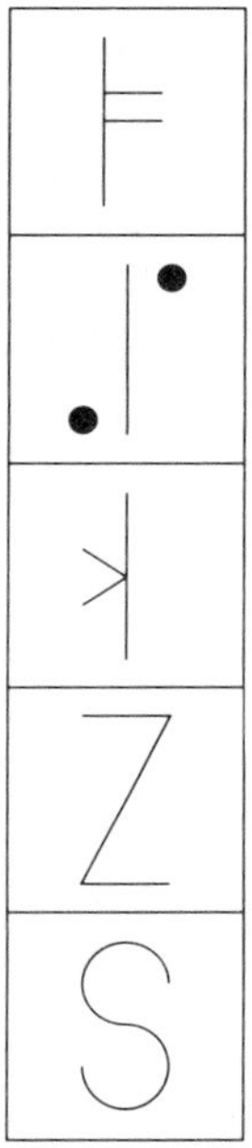	☐ ☐ ☐ ☐ ☐	☐ ☐ ☐ ☐ ☐	☐ ☐ ☐ ☐ ☐

B. Processes

Rapid ☐
Slow ☐

Self-assured ☐
Unassured ☐

C. Regulative Speech

Observable ☐
Not Observable ☐

D. Subjective Assessment

Very Easy ☐
Easy ☐
Somewhat Difficult ☐
Difficult ☐
Very Difficult ☐

Figure 5 Page 2 of the test battery

The results of working on the tasks (correct or incorrect) are to correlate to the results of observing the problem-solving process and the subjective degree of difficulty assigned. Only through such correlation they can be interpreted in a way that hypotheses can be formulated about the developmental level of the targeted abilities — hypotheses that allow the adaptation of an individually adequate instruction.

The analyzing and synthesizing components of perceptive operations must be developed throughout an individual's lifetime through active tackling the objects. Increase of the ability of discrimination in perceiving can be achieved through conscious, well-directed observation of the differentiating characteristics. And consciousness needs the use of mediators (images, concepts, signs, etc.) which are given in society and must be individually acquired. Voluntary memorization, too, requires conscious awareness — mediation. Use of such mediators (tools, aids) follows the general way of developing psychic operations, passing from external to internal and from expanded to automatic forms (cf. Leontiev 1973).

Therefore, the use or nonuse of speech (whether clearly audible or observable through lip movement only) must be correlated to the result of the activity, to the way the task is solved, in order to be able to interpret it.

— Completing the task successfully (at all required levels of difficulty) without use of visible external mediators indicates the use of mediators on internal level.

— Performing the task with errors (perhaps with the correct solution being found at the lowest levels of difficulty) but without the use of visible external aids indicates that no mediational means was used. However, this can also indicate a mediated, internalized action which is not properly suited to the object.

— Performing the task correctly with observable use of mediational means indicates that the mediators or the mediated action has not yet been internalized (interiorized), that is, it is not fully automatic.

— If the task was performed with errors and the use of mediational means was observed, it is important to determine whether the mediators and the way they are employed are appropriate for the objects or task. Moreover, it is important to verify whether the task completion process — which has not yet become automatic and stabilized when still external mediators are used — was disturbed by other external factors such as distraction.

The speed and assurance with which the task was performed together with the subjective judgment of the degree of difficulty must also be correlated to the success of the task performance to allow interpretation.

— Achieving a correct result through a continuous, rapid, self-assured action indicates a largely abbreviated or automatized action with internalized cognitive components — operations or steps of the action being appropriate for the object and well integrated. This assessment of the developmental level of the ability is confirmed if the learner subjectively judged the task to be easy. In this case the ability can be already considered a skill. On the other hand, if the task was judged difficult, this let one assume that the ability has not yet become completely automatic or interiorized. If the learner demonstrates self-assurance and finds the correct solution, one can assume that he or she carried through the checking part of the action.

— Slow performance when achieving a correct solution indicates that the entire action has not yet become automatic, that is, its various steps have not yet been firmly integrated. Observed lack of self-assurance may indicate lack of experience with the adequacy or with the succession of the individual steps. This may also indicate that the learner has difficulty checking his own doing without assistance.

— An incorrect solution indicates first of all that the learner did not perform the appropriate action, appropriate to the object or task. If he or she discovers his or her own error (in tasks in which a model is provided for comparison), this is an indicator that he or she can perform a controlling action, at least when asked to do so. The greater the speed and self-assurance with which the action was incorrectly carried out, the greater the indication that the learner did not perform the control step of the action. This is even likelier if the learner judged the task easy. The more slowly and less assuredly the incorrect solution was found, the greater the indication that the learner checked his or her actions and/or is aware that he or she does not master the skills needed to complete the task. This assessment is confirmed if the learner found the task difficult.

Combination of observations and indications from all tasks or categories of tasks and eventually possible generalizations about several categories allows to formulate hypotheses about and for the individual learners:

— For example, failure to profit from the instruction given does not depend on the developmental level of relevant perceptive and cognitive abilities.

— Or, for example, traditional instruction may be too demanding for the learner regarding one or the other of his or her perceptive and/or cognitive categories (visual, auditory, spatial, etc.). For most categories it is also possible to determine whether overburdening begins at the modal, serial or integration level.

— For example, the learner generally does not use his or her own speech to regulate and support, that is, mediate his or her own actions.

— For example, the learner consistently does not check his or her own actions, at least not when tasks are more mental or language-related or are given under conditions similar to those of school.

Combining the test results of several participants can reveal whether problems encountered are single phenomena or are frequent or even regular within the tested population. Combining results in this way unavoidably ignores details and variety in the information about individual levels of development of elementary abilities, which are indispensable for orienting individually adequate instruction. It does, however, reveal whether and to what extent there are discrepancies between individual development level of adult learners and teaching demands on perceptive and cognitive categories relevant to literacy. To combine the test results of the several participants, participants were divided into three groups:

— those who had no difficulties,

— those who had minor difficulties,

— those who had severe difficulties.

Of the 44 learners from literacy courses, *all* 44 had difficulties working on the tasks in at least one ability category tested. Two of the 44 learners experienced minor difficulties, while 42 experienced severe difficulties in one or more categories.

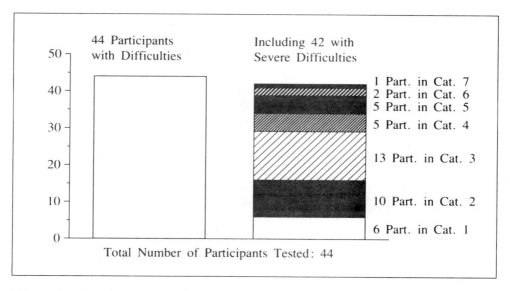

Figure 6 Overview of the frequency with which difficulties were encountered by literacy learners in performing test tasks, including the number of learners who had severe difficulties and the number of categories in which these difficulties were encountered

Of the 10 participants comprising the control group, six experienced difficulties in one category, with two having minor difficulties and four having severe difficulties.

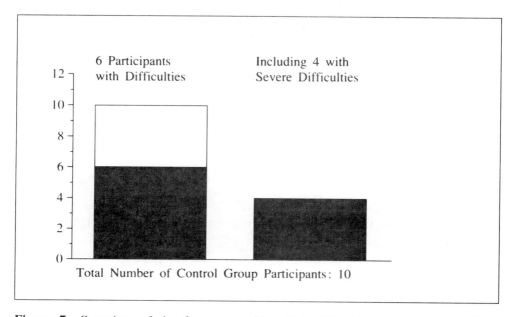

Figure 7 Overview of the frequency with which difficulties were encountered by control group participants in performing test tasks, including the number of participants who had severe difficulties and the number of categories in which these difficulties were encountered

The result that all 44 learners tested had difficulties completing the tasks in one or even all seven categories indicates that the usual demands of teaching methods generally do not start from the development level of the learners' perceptive and cognitive abilities. The fact that six of the 10 control group participants also had difficulties — although in only one to three categories — limits the significance of this indication for the present. However, as 42 of the 44 participants experienced *severe* difficulties in one or as many as all seven categories this limitation is cancelled out. With one exception: four of the six control group participants who had difficulties experienced severe difficulties in the same category, that is, the visual-serial one. This result will be discussed in the interpretation of the different frequencies of difficulties encountered in the various test categories.

Evidence that the usual demands upon development levels of perceptive and cognitive abilities in literacy courses are generally not adapted to these learners is strengthened when we look at the frequency with which the various participants experienced severe difficulties in several categories.

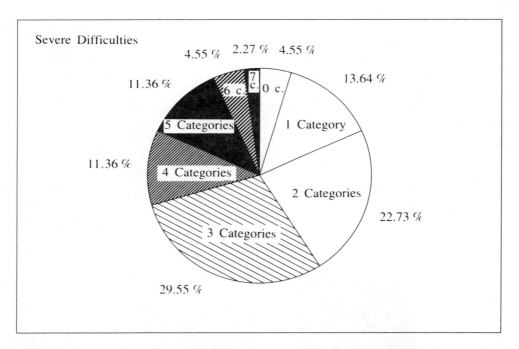

Figure 8 Frequency with which learners experienced severe difficulties in several areas (e.g., over 11 % of the 42 participants who had severe difficulties encountered them in 4 test categories)

We can assume that learners who encountered severe difficulties in only one or two categories would also benefit from instruction adapted to their development level. However, given the lack of criteria for defining learning success or difficulties in adult literacy courses, it is impossible to determine whether the inadequacy of traditional instruction in one or two literacy-related perceptive and cognitive ability categories causes manifest learning difficulties.

On the other hand there must be suspected danger that for most participants who experienced severe difficulties in three to seven categories — after all over half of the total 44 participants — the lack of adequacy to these categories in instruction seriously hinders their processes of learning to read and write. To prove this, criteria for defining learning success and learning difficulties in adult literacy work would be necessary. However, experience gained from developing more adequately adapted instruction provides some indication, though no actual proof.

If it is assumed that the 44 learners in the basic reading and writing courses who participated in the tests did not differ significantly or fundamentally from adult learners in other literacy courses at other institutions, the results provide a new perspective on the question of criteria for learning success and learning difficulty.

Should not the instruction given in literacy courses be adapted to the development level of learners' perceptive and cognitive abilities before discussing and attempting to determine the potential learning success level and especially the potential learning speed of adults taking literacy courses? Difficulties — especially severe difficulties in several categories at once — occurred so often that we must ask whether any of these learners has a hope to achieve really his or her potential success with the help of the traditional instruction?

The actual success and the time required to achieve it will finally be taken as measure of what can be considered feasible average goals. Hence actual progress will play an important and fairly direct role for the criteria yet to be worked out for learning success and difficulties in adult literacy training. If the overly high demands placed by instruction on the literacy-related elementary abilities are not taken into consideration or are considered normal, then, in our opinion, (1) the level of reading and writing progress that can be achieved by adult illiterates will be set too low, and (2) the teachers will not be sufficiently challenged regarding the quality of their pedagogical capabilities. [1]

The frequency of severe and minor difficulties in task performance varied according to the elementary abilities categories tested. The following diagrams show this frequency variation by category for: all 44 participants tested (fig. 9); the subcategories of the spatial orientation category (fig. 10); and the control group (fig. 11). In certain categories not all 44 learners completed the test tasks. The "deduction" category (syllogisms), the "word series repetition using picture cards" (serial-auditory with pictures) subcategory of the serial-auditory category and the "counting backwards" subcategory of the "spatial orientation" category were added to the test battery in the course of the project. By this time, several classes had already finished their testing. In categories involving perception and performance of movements, a few learners omitted the tasks because of a physical handicap (wheelchair confinement, spastic paralysis, amputated fingers). In one case, a learner refused to work on a series of tasks without giving a reason.

The shading in figures 9 to 14 indicates the number of participants with no difficulties (white), minor difficulties (grey) and severe difficulties (black).

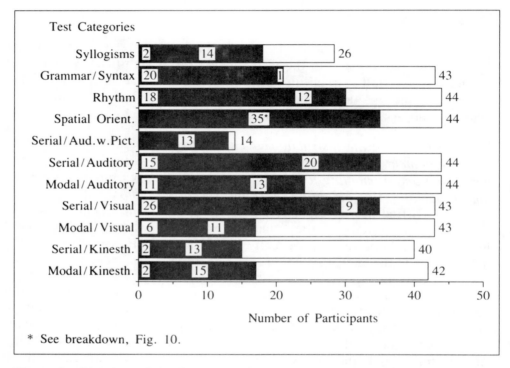

Figure 9 Overview of the frequency of severe and minor difficulties in the various categories tested encountered by literacy learners

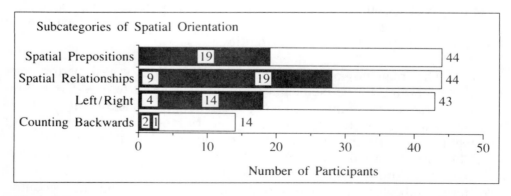

Figure 10 Overview of the frequency of severe and minor difficulties in spatial subcategories encountered by literacy learners

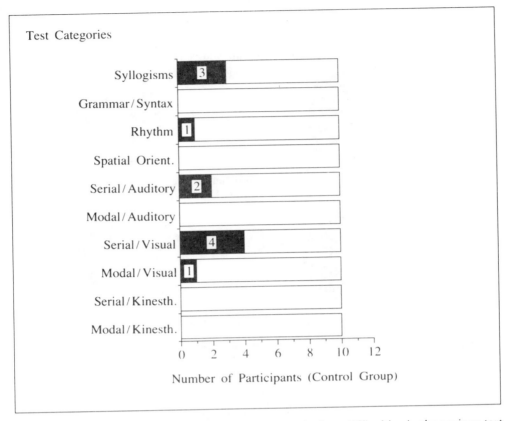

Figure 11   Overview of the frequency of severe and minor difficulties in the various test categories encountered by the control group participants

Information on the categories in which difficulties — especially severe ones — occur is above all necessary for adapting instruction to an individual learner's already achieved development levels. An overview of the overall and of the severe difficulties in the various test categories reveals that they are not evenly distributed. It would therefore be possible to adapt instruction common for the entire group relating to those categories in which the majority of learners in a group encountered difficulties. The practical advantages are immediately obvious as complete individualization of instruction for each participant in a course group — which would be necessary if all learners were assumed to be utterly dissimilar — would require a virtually impossible investment of energy on the teachers' part.

The frequency of difficulties in all tasks directly related to language, to discriminative language perception, articulation and language comprehension confirm the findings of other observations and studies stating that as well adult illiterates as school-age children with dyslexia have not attained the language skill development level required by traditional teaching methods, that is, the so-called average level.

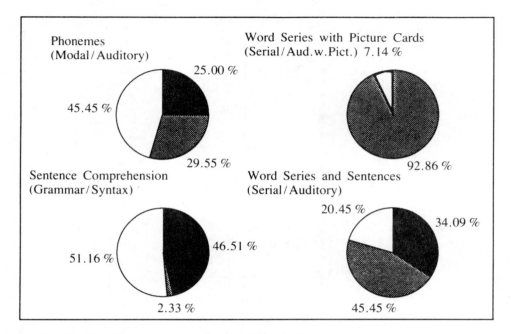

Figure 12 The frequency of severe and minor difficulties during performance of tasks directly related to language

With all due reserve, these results raise the question as to whether it is really sufficient when the preferred literacy teaching methods in adult literacy are based in the categories of vocabulary and sentence construction on the learners' prior knowledge, that is, comprehension skills already developed. In our opinion it should at least be explored what progress in learning literacy can be made when instruction for *further* development in the various categories — from distinctive discrimination between phonemes to conscious memorization of sentence fragments and sentences and to comprehension of utterances with somewhat more complicated structures — is as a general principle adopted and integrated into adult literacy training methods. [2]

Severe and minor difficulties were also encountered with varying frequency in categories situated lower down the hierarchy of elementary abilities tested (for example, perception and production of individual movements and series of movements and discriminative perception of individual graphic figures) and in categories — themselves involving integration of more than one category — which are vital for developing further perceptive and cognitive abilities (for example, perception and reproduction of simple rhythms and spatial orientation subcategories).

Considering how essential these elementary abilities are for building up the more complex actions in acquiring literacy, it is feasible to assume that severe difficulties in these categories — especially when

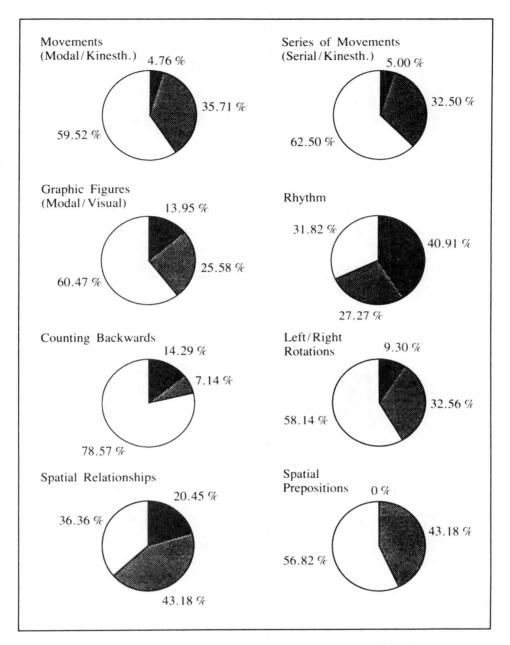

Figure 13 The frequency of severe and minor difficulties in tasks not directly related to language

occurring in several categories — are linked to the specific and manifest learning difficulties in literacy courses mentioned at the beginning. However, this hypothesis can only be developed further when criteria for intersubjectively determining the success or difficulties in literacy learning of adults is worked out. Another conclusion can, however, already be drawn from these results: in all literacy courses it is important to take care if learners have difficulties in these fundamental categories with the implicit requirements of the applied instruction. This appears all the more important the poorer the existent literacy skills despite former schooling.

In the category of perceiving and reproducing series of graphic figures (serial-visual), it strikes that four of the 10 control group participants encountered severe difficulties in completing the task. This presumably means that the degree of difficulty involved in memorizing a series of three semantically void figures was too high, that is, that this skill does not need to be developed to such an extent for learning to read and write under usual methods.

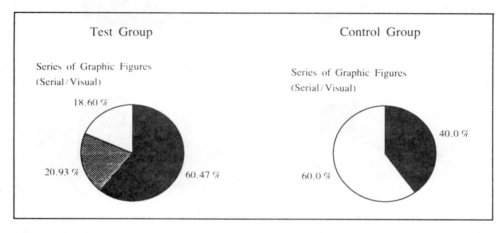

Figure 14 The frequency of severe and minor difficulties in completing tasks with series of graphic figures encountered by literacy learners and control group participants

Discriminative perception and memorization of letter sequences in written words and morphemes therefore does not seem to be absolutely necessary for ultimately learning to read and write German. (Many methods used in our schools focus strongly, if not exclusively, on the phonematic beakdown of spoken words and rules for converting phonemes into letters, thereby neither demanding nor developing this serial-visual ability.) However, there can be no doubt that *discriminative* perception and memorization of the written form is extremely useful, especially in learning to write. (Discriminative perception requires analytical examination of the written form, of the script, which is not often called upon or strengthened by global or whole-word methods.) Given that the quality of instruction for learning literacy must be optimal rather than minimal, information is of great interest if learners can spontaneously analyze and memorize sequences of graphic figures or symbols.

MODIFYING INSTRUCTION

Conducting the test battery has practical value only if instruction can be modified based on its findings. It was therefore our interest and question what form literacy training instruction could take when taking into account a fairly low perceptive and cognitive skill development level. The aim was to modify teaching methods to reduce the discrepancies between ability levels demanded by instruction and actual elementary ability development levels already attained by learners. This explicity means *not* forcing learners to conform to unchanged instruction through remedial or training programs or even therapy, but rather adapting instruction to learners' needs.

Up to this time literacy instruction responding to relatively low elementary ability development levels did not exist. Therefore they had to be elaborated and developed, a task that required cooperation with the learners. A "special course" was set up for a few of the learners involved in the tests, providing instruction based on our theoretical instructions and on test results and modified according to successes or difficulties encountered.

Instruction modification centred around the following basic premises:

— Through acquisition of the socially developed concepts for the different actions or operations speech-oriented and hence conscious mediation (intellectualization) of the actions is to achieve.

— If new skills are to be acquired, tasks must be adapted to the stages of development from external actions (preferably involving motor actions and material aids) to internalized (mental) operations.

— The learner must consciously complete *all three phases* of task performance: (1) orienting himself in the task, (2) carrying out the working action itself, and (3) checking.

— Insofar as possible, tasks must be related to oral and written language material. They must be regarded as part of the overall literacy learning process rather than isolated development of elementary abilities.

— Abilities and skills can be acquired only through the *learner's* actions, *not* through the teacher's actions.

— To ensure that the abilities and skills to be acquired may be generalized, learners must perform both the *analytical* and the *synthesizing* parts of the actions themselves.

Below are some examples of how these premises can be translated into practice.

1. Examples related to accurate perception of letters

To improve visual discrimination skills learners practise discriminating and accurately reproducing letters (letter shapes). This involves exploring and breaking down (analyzing) the components of individual letters. These components are drawn and orally described (designated).

For example, a lower-case "b" (printed) can be broken down into a *long stroke* from up to down (vertical) and a *small arc* to the right at the bottom. As learners are encouraged to describe the components in their own terms as much as possible, there is no fixed terminology. The letter "ingredients" are then reassembled (synthesizing stage). It is important that the *learners* perform both the analytical and the synthesizing stages of the entire action *themselves*. Initially they must carry through the actions with material aids and produce concrete results, such as drawings of an analyzed letter's components.

By comparing with other letters learners can judge which components are identical, which are different, and where they are positioned in relationship to the line and to each other to identify similarities and differences. For example, the letter "d" is often confused with the letter "b": a small "d" (printed) can be broken down into a *small circle* "sitting" on the line (basic line) and a *long stroke* from the upper line to the basic line. That means, taking into account the direction of writing, "d" and "b" can be described as composed of partly dissimilar elements (circle, arc) and sharing an identical "long stroke," which comes second in the "d" and first in the "b."

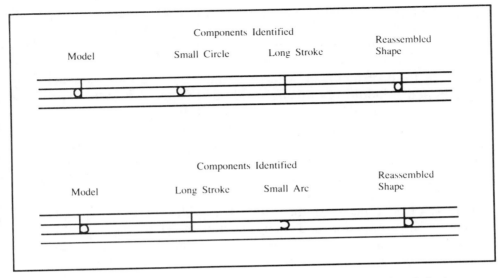

Figure 15 Example of breaking down and reassembling letters so that their shapes can be consciously analyzed

It is vital to determine whether a given error is due to a visual discrimination problem (i.e., the letter shapes) or a phonemic-auditory problem (i.e., confusion of the corresponding phonemes).

In the initial phase describing components out loud (arc/stroke, up/down, vertical/horizontal, large/small, etc.) regulates discriminative perception and written reproduction. Through this intellectualization (with the help of corresponding instruction) both actions (perceiving and producing) become conscious, systematic actions for methodically working on a letter's essential components. Teachers can also provoke regulative speech by noting components on the blackboard exactly as learners dictate them. Any "errors" thus made by the teacher will force learners to ensure that all essential components are included in their spoken description or regulation.

At the same time grasping the corresponding concepts and how to use them can reinforce or stabilize the *visual memory*. Here too language is used as a mediator to consciously memorize and recall comparatively minor differences between highly abstract letter shapes. Developing "internal letters" from the conceptually defined components can be reinforced by appropriate tasks. As an additional step in the next exercises, after the breaking down and reassembling of the letter, learners are asked to recite the components of the letter from memory in the order in which they occur in writing before writing them. This means that memorizing the components and their sequence is a task of its own — memorizing and recalling the composed letter shape thus become conscious actions aimed at memorization/remembering.

Drawing the letter components involves *kinesthetic perception* (perception of movements) of the writing hand and arm. Depending on their development level, learners can draw letters in various sizes on the blackboard with chalk, in the air using arm motions, on the back of the person in front of them, or with their fingers in the palms of their hands prior to and in addition to using pencil and paper. Kinesthetic perception of eye movements also contributes to visual discrimination. If learners are not focussing attentively, they may be assigned the added subtask of "fasten" their eyes at the tip of the finger on the hand that is writing or drawing and following motion with their eyes. Determining the sequence and direction of the various letter components involves *spatial orientation* skills — or problems. (For example, is the arc above or below the line? A small "f" has a hook to the right, but which side is the right? etc.) Accurate discrimination and memorization of letter shapes is part of the *actual process of learning letters*, that is, correlating phonemes and shapes so that letters also subjectively become *signs* for phonemes.

2. Examples related to accurate phoneme identification

To promote auditive phoneme discrimination ability, that is, to reduce confusion of similar phonemes in hearing, the features of (German) phonemes are made consciously aware through pointing, feeling, drawing and naming (for example, place of articulation, voicing, etc.). For example, place of articulation can be shown, felt, drawn; continuants or plosives can be shown and felt; and voicing can be felt. Features must be named as they are shown, drawn and felt to achieve conscious awareness of them. Sometimes drawing and naming are needed to develop a sensitivity for feeling (e.g., the place of articulation).

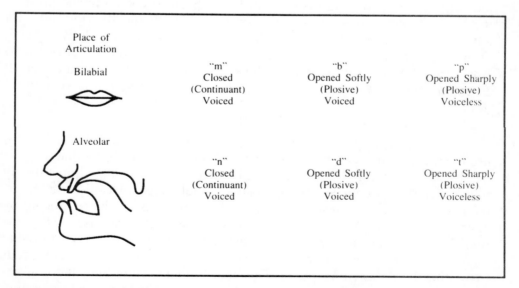

Figure 16   Example of an illustration showing that phonemes which are easily confused are often distinguished by only one feature (voicing, *or* place of articulation, *or* continuant vs. plosive)

Here it is vital to remember that this relates to discrimination of *phonemes* (generalized *speech sounds*), which are pronounced and heard, rather than *written letters*, which are written and seen. This is why the use of letter names to designate phonemes (in German, /bê/ for "b," /ka/ for "k," /es/ for "s," etc.) not only causes confusion, but is simply incorrect, even though many beginners may bring with them this identification of phonemes and letters from their earlier schooling.

To highlight this difference the ensemble of *phoneme* features can be labelled with a symbol for speaking or hearing (e.g., a mouth and an ear). The specific features of a phoneme, accompanied by a sketch of its place of articulation, can be contrasted with the *letter* (or various letters) which can represent that phoneme in written words. For example, in German, the phoneme /f/ can be written "f," "ph" or "v," and the combination /ts/ by the letters "ts," "ds," "z" or "tz." Written letters are to label with a symbol for writing and seeing (e.g., a pencil and an eye).

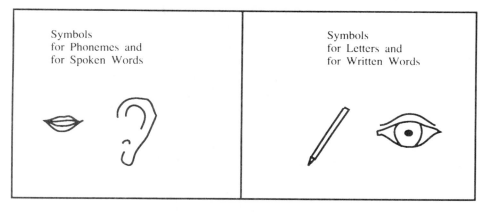

Figure 17   Example of very simple sketches that can be used as symbols for indicating whether an element being processed is related to spoken or to written language

Phonemes that are confused are often distinguished by only one of their essential features. For example, /m/ and /n/ are both voiced continuants, but /m/ is produced at the "front" with the lips, while /n/ is produced with the tip of the tongue pressing against the upper incisors or the alveolar ridge (we hope this is the correct English name for what we mean: the front edge of the palate). /d/ and /t/ are both produced at the same place of articulation as /n/ and both are stops, but /d/ is voiced, while /t/ is voiceless, that is, in speaking, little air is expelled for /d/ and a lot for /t/. The same procedure can be applied to learners who generally hear and discriminate phonemes correctly but have difficulties with one or the other specific pair of phonemes. In this case, however, it is usually sufficient to analyze only the features of the phonemes likely to be confused (e.g., in German, /d/ and /g/). Both are voiced stops. However, for /d/, the tongue is pressed from the back against the upper incisors, while for /g/ the back of the tongue is pressed against the palate.

Here speaking is used as a motor link for developing hearing. Learners acquire the ability to hear and determine phonemes consciously and voluntarily by becoming aware of kinesthetic perception in speaking sounds (sensations in the speech organs). This is mediated by intellectualizing this kinesthetic perception through the acquisition of corresponding concepts. Looking at and into the mouth and sketching the place of articulation (based on diagrams of the back of the mouth and throat as often seen in mouthwash advertisements) also involves visual perception. Applying such diagrams requires a certain level of abstract thinking, therefore it can be necessary to build it up in stages.

3. Examples related to series division in hearing and writing

German orthography is based on the principle that the *sequence of letters* in a written word follows the *sequence of sounds (phonemes)* in the spoken word. However, the correlation of sounds to letters is not so unequivocal that correct spelling could simply be derived from the spoken word. Therefore sounding out words (recognizing or reproducing the phonemes in a word in their sequence) and subsequently determining the parts of the word which are not spelled the way they are spoken ("commentated" sounding out) are important subskills of writing.

Use of hand movements and looking helps reinforce active handling with series of phonemes and their individual components. This means spatially doubling the temporal sequence of the spoken word. A neutral sign (small card or token or similar thing) is placed on the table for each phoneme already identified. If necessary the signs can also represent specific features, e.g., black for consonants and red for vowels. These neutral signs are better than letters for sounding out words in that they do not encourage the fallacy — popular in German — that words are spelled the way they sound. Moreover, they allow to develop analyzing and synthesizing spoken words before letters have been fully mastered. Given that concrete symbols remain after a word has been pronounced — unlike spoken sounds, which dissipate — actions with these cards can support the actions of breaking down and reassembling spoken words. By the way, this also helps focus on the true problem underlying "letter blending," that is, sounds blending.

Perceiving positions in a series involves the use of concepts such as before-between-after, beginning-end, first-next, etc. This means that making consciously aware the *temporal succession* of phonemes in the word is extensively mediated by concepts of *spatial orientation*. The initial use of neutral, tangible, visible signs for the phonemes facilitates this connection. For example, the formation of sounding out words can look like this: first the meaning of the word to be broken down is fixed with a picture (e.g., *Brot*, in English: bread), which also serves as a mnemonic. Then learners determine the first phoneme in the word; they determine if it is a consonant or a vowel, represented either with a black or a red dot. They place a small card with a black dot on the table to represent /b/ and draw a small square enclosing a black dot in their notebooks; they repeat for which phoneme they had placed the card (for /b/).

Guided by my questions the learners then identify the phoneme pronounced and heard directly after the /b/ (/r/ in the example); they determine whether it is a consonant or a vowel (a somewhat difficult task with /r/ in German, with several regional variants) and which colour to use; they place the card to the right of the first (direction of writing!); they repeat the present results of breaking down (here, /b/ and /r/) and put them back together (/br/). The same procedure applies for the next phoneme (/o/ — red dot); again the learners repeat the present results of breaking down the word separately (/b/, /r/ and /o/) and blended (/bro/). The same is done with the last phoneme (/r/).

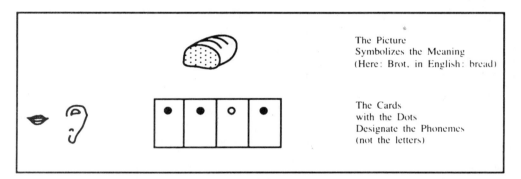

The Picture
Symbolizes the Meaning
(Here: Brot, in English: bread)

The Cards
with the Dots
Designate the Phonemes
(not the letters)

Figure 18   Example of how a broken-down word can be represented with material aids

The learners then try to repeat the word (divided and reassembled) without touching or moving the cards. In the next stage they attempt to perform the task without looking at the cards ("from memory" or "by heart"). Further stages on the way to mental operation are: leaving out the cards, using only the drawn dots, and then breaking words down out loud without material aids. The row of cards can also be disassembled again from end to beginning, whereby the word is once again broken down and the remaining letters pronounced each time. Closely linking the breakdown and reassembly actions (analyzing and synthesizing) prevents the tiresome problem that learners know the sounds of isolated letters but are unable to "blend" sounds.

Once sounding out words is introduced and the learners can do so using the cards, formation of the next partial or subaction can begin:

determining which parts of the word are not spelled the way they are pronounced. To do this the spoken and the written form of the word must be compared and the parts where the letters do not correspond unequivocally to the phonemes (for whatever reason) must be marked.

First, as a result of sounding the word out, the individual phonemes in their sequence are present. The spelling must be shown (on the blackboard, on a work sheet or later, in a dictionary), as it cannot (at least not in German) be deduced from the sequence of phonemes! The teacher then writes each letter in its own square beneath the squares containing the dots which represent the phonemes (here, for example, *wohnen* — in English: to live, to reside). Then learners with the help of the teacher compare: "*Wohnen*, we pronounce /w/ and write 'w' — correspond (in German, of course); we pronounce /o/ and write 'oh' — correspond not exactly, two letters ('o' and silent 'h') for one phoneme; we pronounce /ə/ and write 'e' — correspond, as the short and unaccented /ə/ in German counts like the long and more closed /e/ for writing purposes; we pronounce /n/ and write 'n' — correspond; therefore, *wohnen* — except for the pronounced /o/, for which we spell 'oh' — there is no important difference between pronouncing and writing." This commentary is accompanied by pointing to the dots and letters and drawing lines linking the squares. Two lines must be drawn from the dot representing the /o/ — one to the letter "o" and one to the "h." That the letters "o" and "h" belong together can be indicated with an arc drawn beneath the squares. And a drawn warning sign marks their irregularity. The learners write the entire word adjacently to coordinate also the normal written form.

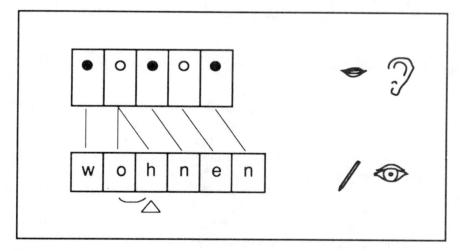

Figure 19 Example illustrating how the deviation from phoneme-grapheme-correspondence which is orthographically so important can be worked out by comparing the spoken word's phoneme sequence with the written word's letter sequence

The spoken word to be broken down can be repeated at any time to help learners determine each subsequent sound. Therefore sounding out a word does not make any particular demand on the memory for aural series. By contrast repeating a spoken sentence — that is, a series of words arranged following meaning, syntax and grammar — requires not only meaning comprehension but also development of voluntary recall for such spoken or heard sentences. Correct repetition requires precise, conscious perception and memorization of the individual words and their sequence. To develop these functions it is important here, once again, to introduce initially the use of external mediators. That may be neutral white cards, matchboxes, the initial letters of the words (less neutral), or one's own fingers. Objects which can be placed on the table have the advantage to facilitate establishing the connection between temporally progressing series and spatial orientation. Sentences can be pronounced to the learner, read by the learner or read out to him or her, or be formulated by the learner himself or herself. To improve serial-auditory recall it is important to give the task to repeat the sentence identically after first pronounciation, that is, to repeat the same words in the same order. Grasping the components (here: the words) in their sequence must be a conscious goal. Without this goal sentence construction and comprehension are other tasks.

While saying the sentence learners must put down cards (or other external aids) side by side for each word uttered. As they repeat the sentence the learners have to "work off" these cards — first by touching them or pointing with the finger, then by following them with their eyes. If this is successful the task can be broadened with the attempt to repeat the sentence from memory without looking at the cards. Once this, too, has turned out well, the action of laying out cards is to "internalize" step by step into imagination. It is entirely possible in the course of this process that the mediators change. For example, a learner with some knowledge of writing can use cards as external aids and the imaginary images of the written words as internal aids.

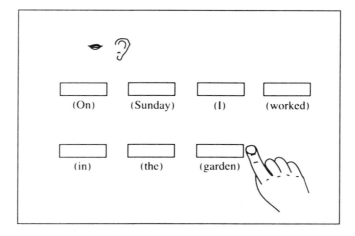

Figure 20 Example of how cards can be used as mediators to memorize words and their sequence before writing a sentence down

Another stage in the transition from actions to operations no longer requiring conscious thought is the incorporation of spoken sentence repetition as a secondary task into problem-solving procedures for more complex tasks. For example, in tasks requiring precise retention of word order — writing dictations or own text — it is important to repeat the sentence out loud between hearing or constructing it and writing it. Memorizing a spoken word sequence is mediated by laying out and looking at cards — as signs for "one word" — that is, by kinesthetic and visual perception and related actions. Beating out the rhythm of syllables, that is, calling rhythmic perception into play can be very useful as well. In breaking down a spoken sentence, external aids (one per word) help make word divisions visible which are usually inaudible in normal speech (e.g., "theseapples-pause-areripe").

Modified instructions which succeeded in significantly reducing the discrepancies between the elementary ability development levels required by instruction and those already attained by learners, could be expected to produce successes in learning to read and write. Moreover, any progress made must be considered all the more valuable given the difficult conditions imposed by the project context. For example:

— The more adequate instruction could not simply be implemented. It had to be developed progressively throughout the teaching process.

— The instructions developed were used almost exclusively in the project's "special courses," while the usual, unmodified methods continued to be used in the parallel "regular" teaching.

Modifying the complete literacy instruction for learners with relatively poorly developed elementary abilities should therefore have an even greater success rate than project conditions allowed.

Since there are, as yet, no tools for systematically evaluating the success of literacy training, in order to judge the success in learning to read and write attained with the modified instruction we used the possibility to ask the participants, their teachers in the "regular" courses and instructors in the "Berufsbildungswerk" (vocational training institute) for their subjective assessments. When performing the learning tasks under modified instruction, relatively elementary actions (e.g., perception-related) are carried through. In this process the learner develops gradually the analogous elementary skills internalizing the corresponding mediators. It cannot be assumed that these actions can be performed in fully condensed and internalized form (i.e., transformed into operations) after such a relatively short period, especially under the difficult project conditions mentioned above. That is, the related abilities are not sufficiently stabilized in the new scope and on the new level to be called skills.

This means not only that learners must continue in practising the newly acquired abilities, initially still consciously applying the newly acquired mediators in order for successful acquisition. It means, too, that in areas in which no instruction is provided (for example, test task completion), results depend upon whether or not participants apply their new abilities spontaneously. To get information as to whether these premises were valid, we repeated the test battery for elementary literacy-related abilities on four participants at the end of the project.

Overall seven learners including two women and five men initially participated in the "special courses." This supportive teaching, as a rule, was given in two weekly, one-hour sessions for slightly under one academic year. As the modified instruction first had to be developed, the "special courses" were given mainly in the form of individual lessons.

The modified instruction can be said to have helped three of the participants make substantial progress in learning to write. In the following we do not describe whether the course of the individual learning processes nor the sometimes protracted stepwise developing of appropriate instruction, rather limit ourselves to the main features of the cases.

One young man aged 20 initially wrote (whether copying or composing freely) so that individual letters were definitely recognizable but no one — not even the young man himself — could guess what the words and sentences meant. With the help of learning tasks which required him to carry out conscious, directed actions on spoken and written words at a relatively low hierarchical level and to consciously practise recalling written forms of words and word sequences, and which mediated him a strategy how to check his own writing, he made considerable progress within a few weeks. When copying (e.g., from the blackboard during his subject courses) he made considerably fewer errors. When composing freely he used a strategy of writing words as they sound, gradually improving his spelling of words he had exercised more often so that the results, though not faultless, were legible and intelligible. Simultaneously his self-confidence and need to express himself (in writing as well) grew. His teacher in the regular course described his progress as a "break-through." To place this success in perspective it should be noted that in the regular course he was made offers to write freely rather than those directed to "technical" principles. He nonetheless made this progress despite repeated absences from the special lessons due to occupational illness.

One young woman in her twenties initially wrote her own texts "without point or comma," that is, no visible separation between sentences. Despite misspellings the meaning of individual words could usually be discerned, but the meaning the sentences was sometimes unclear as some words and half phrases were missing and word order or the entire formulation had been altered in writing. She also made errors in copying, only few of which she was able to detect afterwards. In addition to conscious breakdown and reassembly of spoken and written words, she benefited particularly from tasks requiring her to break down the process from formulating a thought to writing a sentence into several steps, thereby focussing consciously on memorization of sentence word order. This learner, too, had yet to acquire a strategy for checking words and sentences. Exercises directed on spatial orientation revealed that she was not used to paying attention to such criteria as distance, location, direction, etc. Initially she was unable to deal with more than one such criterion at a time when analyzing a given pattern. It is probable that her difficulty in using external aids (fingers, cards, first letters of words) in remembering sentence word order were due to her relatively low spatial orientation development. She did not speak about her progress in reading and writing. Her instructor, however, found her progress so remarkable that she transferred her from the German upgrading course to the mathematics upgrading course at the end of the school year.

Another young man in his early twenties began taking "special lessons" four months after his colleagues, therefore participating for only five and a half months. In writing his workshop reports (which comprised elliptical phrases describing activities and objects rather than full sentences or even texts), he invariably followed the same painstaking procedure: he wrote a draft report, had it corrected by someone, recopied it, had it corrected again, copied it yet again, and so on before finally copying it into his apprentices' record book and making yet other errors. He was very cooperative in developing instruction adapted to his problems, accepted suggestions and reported, when asked, how he got on with them or how he modified them in practice. He benefited greatly from learning to check errors by comparing with a model. When writing he had a particular tendency to abbreviate long words of whose spelling he was unsure to a few letters. Aids and methods of analyzing and memorizing spellings and memorizing sentences were important. However, his greatest success was achieved with exercises aimed at rhythmic division of speech and coordination of rhythmic speech with (hand) movements. Once he began to master this coordination, we began to connect it with the external aids for memorizing sentence word order (cards or first letters). After twelve lessons already, the learner himself reported that he was applying the aids outside the "special course," found them useful, and had improved greatly. His regular teacher reported that he applied the aids and procedures learned in the "special course" (especially the cards and the rhythmic division) in her course. Not only had his reading and writing improved substantially, but his articulation had become clearer. Even his instructor, known for his reservedness, was favourably impressed by this participant's astonishing progress.

Little can be said about the potential progress of the next learner. The young man experienced twice that teachers changed in his regular course, this made the connection between the regular course and the "special course" much more difficult and made the lack of reports on successes and learning difficulties in the regular course taking more effects than in other cases. Because of personal and occupational pressure, he asked to take only one "special course" session per week, lowering his total attendance including normal absences to about half that of the other participants. One of his teachers initially reported that he applied various aids and procedures during the course himself and was aware that they immediately improved his performance. In this case it was particularly evident that he expected not only learning to make him progress rapidly but also the process of writing (e.g., a sentence) to take little time. He therefore sometimes refused to apply promising procedures such as those comprising several steps or those with preliminary stages with external actions. This invariably led to conversations about learning processes, action development and modification during learning, etc. During these conversations I developed sketches of a few lines to illustrate the relationships. Although this seemed to help him understand the relationships and necessities, he could accept them to guide his actions for very short periods only, repeatedly falling back on his tendency to perform tasks hastily. More coordination with the regular course would have been greatly needed here, and the conversations focussing exclusively on the learning process would have had to be integrated into counselling on his personality and its development as a whole.

The progress of the "special course" or supportive teaching with three other participants in various ways confirms the hypothesis that learning at the elementary ability level, too, depends largely on how meaningful it is for the learners, that is, what its personal sense is.

One woman in her thirties had a life history of many problems and difficulties related to her material well-being, interpersonal relationships and self-image. She also had an extensive history of various types of professional help. In the regular course she repeatedly quarrelled with other participants and finally abandoned the group classes entirely. The teacher who had initially counselled her and then devoted several hours to psychotherapeutic-like guidance felt that she urgently needed psychotherapy, a form of help the participant refused. Although the woman's illiteracy may have exacerbated her problems, it did definitly not determine them primarily. Therefore learning to read and write was not the route to solving her problems, and it had little subjective meaning, that is, personal sense for her. After several weeks she stopped attending the regular course, attended the "special course" sessions irregularly, and finally abandoned this attempt at learning to read and write altogether. The counsellor and teacher agreed that the crux of this problem did not lie in the (considerable) gap between her elementary ability development level and the traditional instruction. In our opinion the problem lay not in her significant literacy problems but rather in her difficult life interacting with her equally problematic personality.

One young man aged 20 took a course for young unemployed dropouts to improve his career prospects, where he allowed himself to be persuaded to take a literacy course. He often missed sessions in both the regular and the "special" courses. After a few weeks he said that this was "too much school" for him, ceased attending the "special course" and was absent from his regular course for extended periods. In his case it was clear up from the initial counselling that he was not attending the courses of his own initiative and that he was not totally convinced of the need to thoroughly improve his reading and writing skills.

Another young man aged 20 was undergoing vocational training. In the framework of this training he had to write workshop reports, read and write in vocational school courses and read and write final and mid-term exams. He voluntarily took the German upgrading course offered by the teacher at the training institution (in practice comparable to a literacy course) and the additional "special course" sessions I offered him. He actually felt a need to improve his literacy skills. At the same time, however, he suffered great anxiety that he might be incapable of learning due to psychological problems, and that he was becoming progressively weaker regarding his intellectual potential. I was unable to judge whether his anxiety alone hindered him from devoting himself intensively to learning. The true obstacle may well have been conflicts in his motivational or personality structure. What I could observe was that he was sometimes cooperative and sometimes reluctant, was able to work according to the instruction given and made considerable improvement in writing tasks when he did follow the instructions. Often, however, he consciously or even purposely did not apply the procedures learned. Above all he gave many excuses why being unable to apply them outside the "special course." His case clearly demonstrated that consciously taking into account the hierarchically lower actions in instruction can lead to improved literacy learning. However, realization of this potential depends upon personality factors such as readiness to learn and self-confidence.

Four of the five learners who participated at the "special course" in developing and testing modified instruction repeated the elementary abilities test battery at the end of the school year. (The fifth could not be contacted after he abandoned his training for health reasons.) The results in the various categories were slightly higher than they had been during the first tests, although they still fell largely within the range of "those with difficulties." Data analysis revealed that, as before, there was a discrepancy between learners' development levels and the demands of traditional literacy instruction in various areas of literacy-related perceptive and cognitive abilities. This confirms the hypothesis that the newly developed abilities had not yet become sufficiently stabilized skills to be spontaneously applied in task completion.

The assessment that learners would *not* have made the progress they did *without* this specific instruction is derived from the fact that throughout their schooling — over ten years in some cases — they did not succeed in learning to read and write. It cannot be derived from comparison with a control group which completed a literacy course with unmodified instruction under identical initial conditions. Perhaps, with much effort (subject to considerable practical difficulties), it would be possible to gather a group of learners with similar initial literacy skills and similar elementary abilities development levels in the same areas. However, human beings, especially adults — even adults who share significant reading and writing problems — lead such different lives, have such different personalities and motivational structures and undergo different changes in their personal lives during a project's time, that the idea of parallelling all of these "variables" which affect learning for the participants of a control group is fundamentally unrealistic and a methodological fiction.

The number of learners who participated in developing modified instruction was very low: seven began the "special course," while five continued with some degree of regularity. Every bit of progress made with the help of a modified instruction confirms that individuals who did not learn or learned very slowly given traditional instruction can learn successfully when instructed in a carefully directed way to acquire means adequate to the object and to their elementary abilities development level. Given the limited number of participants, however, it is impossible to predict the number of participants in other courses whose learning difficulties were in the foreground due to insufficient elementary abilities development, or to say for how many of them other conditions detrimental to learning play an essential role such as negative aspects of their self-image or lack of or ambivalent subjective meaning of learning.

Considering the conditions under which the progress described above was made — the fact that instruction was modified during the teaching process and that the "special courses" were relatively isolated from the regular courses — it seems justifiable to conclude that this modified instruction was a successful step towards adapting teaching methods to the prerequisites and needs of learners previously described as "being learning disabled" or "having severe learning difficulties." This is not altered by cases in which motivational conflicts or lack of subjective meaning of learning hindered progress. Such cases allow to integrate the specific question of elementary abilities into the general issue of learning difficulties in literacy courses and, consequently, to clearly demonstrate that all human actions depend on their personal sense for the individual, that is, their relationships to motives.

It can be assumed that those participants, too, who made progress in learning to read and write had to live with negative aspects in their self-images and had to deal with conflicting motives — like all human beings. Presumably, however, these problems were not serious enough to pose an effective obstacle on these learners. Some generalizations about my experiences in working with these participants are given below.

In all cases it was very clear that participants could improve considerably in task completion when they used speech to mediate or regulate their actions. None of them did so on their own initiative. In all cases the procedures had to be suggested and, in certain cases, demonstrated. Similar experiences were reported by Helga who began to introduce regulative speech as a mediational means in courses where learners had not undergone elementary abilities testing. She found that some learners were inhibited to accept this technique, whereas the progress made when it was applied was immediately visible. This regulative speech should not be confused with talking about subject matter, its subjective significance, experiences, moods, etc., which are heavily emphasized in all literacy courses. Even participants who professed to be very eloquent usually had to learn how to use their speech as a mediational means to regulate their actions.

As regards learners checking their own written products (sentences, words) — ultimately controlling their own writing and learning actions — none of the participants knew how to check their work. In other words they were not only not used to checking their own output, they also did not know that it is a matter of comparing (e.g., spelling) first against an external model and later against the internal "knowledge" of correct spelling. At best they had a vague idea of "reading-through." All had to acquire by steps the various criteria involved in checking writing (i.e., Are all the words in the sentence in the correct order? Inside the words, are there the correct letters in their correct order? etc.) before condensing the expanded action. Some participants first had to work out the technique of comparing (e.g., comparing a word letter by letter with a model). The direct results of taking checking into own responsibility by learners — that is, that they detect and correct their errors themselves — were proportional to the time learners took or were given outside the "special course" to complete the various steps of checking, and the models they were given for comparison in case of doubt. The indirect results of regular checking (increased attention already during the actual writing process, fewer "slips of the pen" when copying or writing familiar words) began to become apparent only at the end of the "special course." In both aspects fully integrating the "special course" modifications into the "regular" courses would have stabilized and accelerated the results. The meanings learners saw in learning and carrying through the task of checking ranged from: "At last, I no longer need to rely on the teacher for this!" to "Actually, this is the teacher's job, not mine!"

If we were planning concrete instruction today, we would, in light of our experiences with rhythmic speech division and spatial orientation exercises, include these techniques from the outset. Rhythmic speech division plays quite a significant role in memorization, helping overcome problems with discriminative perception and memorization of series (sentences as word series). Either it is already sufficiently developed, so it can be employed well-directed as subaction in memorization processes, or it must be developed through working on related tasks. The spatial orientation development level influences how easily external mediators for memorization (e.g., a card laid on the table for each word) and especially imaginary mediators can be applied. These experiences and considerations coincide with various findings from research on children with learning difficulties. For example, Breuer and Weuffen (1986) found that delayed development in discriminative perception of simplest rhythms presages always severe, prolonged learning difficulties. And several attempts to combine so-called "syllabic curves" with broad gestures have often had positive results. Finally, Schuch and Friedler (1982) focus on spatial orientation disorders in their work on "partial performance disorders" in children, as they affect a wide range of performance areas in school and daily life.

In all cases it was evident that results depended a great deal on learners' perception or images of the procedures to be acquired, of their relevance, and of the learning process. These perceptions or images determined learners' openness to accept the tasks and procedures I suggested. These images determined whether the learners — once they had learned the steps involved and their order — actually applied the procedures in question, and whether they applied them fully, or whether they modified them without comment at key points when applying them. They also determined whether learners applied the knowledge acquired in the "special courses," thereby turning protential into real progress. Participants' images of learning in general and, specifically, of the various steps of learning literacy were debatable. When asked how, or rather, why they did a certain thing in a given way or what they had thought while doing it, they were able to formulate and express their thoughts. And these discussions allowed to present other models (for example, of learning, of the regularity and principles of literacy) and to offer them as explanations. Needless to say that learners did not always and not immediately accept such modifications of own ideas. However, the conversations about learning — which were effectively illustrated or mediated with sketches — influenced learners' willingness to seriously try the procedures proposed. It would appear that the phase "to orient oneself in the task" involves not only an image of what, how and by what means something is to be done, but also an image of the "why and wherefore" of this "what and how." If learners are to encourage in feeling responsible for their own learning process, they must also be allowed to inform themselves about their learning. Only such a feeling of responsibility can counteract the feelings of helplessness, subjection and, consequently, passivity in the learning process.

In theoretical terms: the *way* in which (sub)actions, the later operations, are to carry through is related to the system of meanings which reflects the object and the actions contained in or related to it. If the procedure suggested in an instruction does not correspond to the system of meanings already acquired for the objet in question, the (sub)actions the suggested procedure requires seems to fail leading to the targeted goal, therefore having no positive relationship to the underlying motive. That is they seem to be subjectively meaningless, without personal sense. For example, in every literacy course there are learners who are firmly convinced that correct German is spelled the way it sounds, an idea most often imparted to them by their former teachers of German. They do not accept tasks designed to determine differences between word articulation and spelling and to memorize possible discrepancies. Logically they act consistently when they avoid applying such procedures acquired through several learning tasks outside those tasks, for instance, when writing independently. It must not be underestimated that what appears on the surface to be only acquiring a new operation actually requires modification of a preestablished system of meanings, often on a broader level than the object per se. In the example given modifying the system of meanings related to the role of phonetic spelling in German orthography can call into question the judgment and values of former teachers. For example, most learners initially do not have a system of meanings which matches with a perception of the learning process as performing actions in initially external, expanded forms. If the principles of human learning are not discussed it can happen that learners immediately fall back on their former inadequate practices whenever they are called upon to independently apply a step-by-step procedure learned through learning tasks. Presumably willingness to try new procedures, that is, to expose existing systems of meanings to potential modification, is also influenced by relationships of personal sense incorporated in the systems of meanings in question. For example, departure from a system of meanings in which learning is considered to depend on talents which one does or does not have can be closely related to major changes in a learner's self-image as being untalented by nature or heredity and therefore incapable of learning.

In all but one category the objects of the learning tasks were spoken or written language (sentences, words, phonemes, letters). Consequently the abilities acquired were directly related to working with language and resulted in immediate improvements in learning to read and write. The only exception was the spatial orientation category, for which we were unable, in the time available, to develop tasks directly related to language or literacy. The fact that the elementary abilities assessed in the test battery improved only marginally, whereas learning to read and write improved considerably, confirms our hypothesis that abilities to be acquired are determined by the objects of the related actions and must be generalized through extended practice and/or well-directed, relevant efforts. If therefore seems justifiable to adapt literacy instruction to elementary abilities levels — thereby allowing reading and writing to be learned — rather than to develop elementary abilities for their own sake through objects unrelated to literacy.

This view is adequate as long as the sole or preponderant goal is learning literacy. Otherwise, for example, spatial orientations skills are considered to play an important role in problem-solving (cf. Velickovskij 1988). And Feuerstein and his co-workers (1980) attained with their approach to instruct disadvantaged young people with learning difficulties to thoroughly and completely develop their perceptive and cognitive skills resounding success. These results raise the question as to whether adult literacy movement and work should not consider the scope of its tasks more comprehensive than actually doing.

The strategy observed in recent years of broadening literacy training to include "basic skills," already defines the educational needs of illiterates more widely than before. However, this strategy is thinking "forward" rather than "in-depth" in that it offers a broader range of courses, from "basic arithmetic" to preparatory driver training and transitional courses for *Volkshochschule* programs, without, however, paying any attention to elementary perceptive and cognitive abilities, which are prerequisites for all learning and for all intellectual activities. The more independently people have to learn, and the more multiply actions are mediated, and the less vivid and concrete the objects are, the less dispensable are these elementary abilities (think of the demands on skills required for computer work).

The results of elementary abilities testing after the "special course" confirm the assumption that long practice and much repetition are required to form new, stable skills. This means that instruction for literacy acquisition must be modified fundamentally and adapted to the initial development level at which learners enrol in the course. There should be no question of developing elementary abilities on an isolated, short-term basis through "therapy," hoping for a "transfer effect," without changing the quality of instruction. This supports the numerous criticisms voiced throughout the 1970s' dyslexia debate that specific perception training, etc. did not lead to any demonstrable improvement in learning to read and write. Unlike these authors, however, we do not regard this as proof that learning literacy is *not* related to relatively low perceptive skill development. We directly advocate that teaching methods for learning to read and write must be modified correspondingly.

Overall, the results support the argument that adapting literacy training instruction to the elementary abilities development levels already acquired by learners allows learners to make progress which was not made during school attendance or under traditional literacy training instruction. This is true on the condition, however, that the process of learning to read and write is experienced as personally meaningful for the learner on all levels — down to and including acquisition of individual operations — and that progress is not hindered by serious motivational conflicts or self-confidence problems. Results also show that two factors must be taken into account in addition to the levels of elementary abilities: (1) conscious utilization of pragmatic, regulative speech, that is, conscious acquisition of language or concepts as mediational means for performing actions; and (2) conscious completion *by the learner* of all three phases constituting acquisition of a new ability — that is, to orient oneself in the task, to complete the actual work action, and checking — rather than a kind of labour division whereby the learner's only task is to complete the action while the teacher is responsible for the other phases.

With all due reserve our results can be interpreted as follows: in cases where motivational conflicts, etc. are not in the foreground of learning difficulties, the discrepancy between the demands made on elementary abilities levels by traditional instruction and learners' already developed levels plays an essential role in learning difficulties, failure to progress, etc. The negative consequences of this discrepancy are intensified by the fact that usual instruction ignores vital learning factors such as self-regulative speech, that is, acquisition of language means of mediation, and the first and third phases of acquisition (orientation and checking). We conclude from this that a new quality of instruction must not only show interest for the development level already attained by learners — and that as far "down" as to the elementary abilities — but also direct at conscious learning activity, that is, "learning to learn." In this way learners for whom traditional instruction *created* difficulties, who "have learning difficulties," who are labelled as being "learning handicapped or disabled" and have been rejected with these arguments far too often, will be given a fair chance.

DISCUSSION OF RESULTS AND PROBLEMS

The project results are relevant to practical literacy training on several levels. First, the project provided a new model for approaching learning difficulties. This model is particularly valuable not only because it overcomes the exclusive consideration of psychosocial factors, but also because at the same time it avoids debates about limited capabilities, intelligence quotients, etc. by highlighting the role played by acquisition of mental tools. Although the developed test battery is directed exclusively at elementary perceptive and cognitive abilities, the quality of the theoretical basis allows to grasp the relationship between social conditions and relations, motivational structures, self-image and skill development. This can avoid futile debate about whether psychosocial factors *or* ignorance about the learners' development level contribute to the appearance of learning difficulties. *Both factors are involved and interact.*

On the practical level there is a distinction to be made between the test battery and the suggestions for modified instruction. The test battery can be administered independently by teachers after a relatively short introduction. Working at it definitely increases teachers' sensibility for the question whether the instruction they provide is too demanding for their learners. We have little information to what extent the test battery is actually administered in literacy courses throughout the Federal Republic of Germany. Helga's experience in her own courses and with her colleagues reveals that working at the test battery promotes awareness of the problem whether possibly too high demands are made regarding learners' elementary abilities level. Once this process has been set in motion, teachers focus more on possible modification of instruction and not longer on identification of individual discrepancies. Many teachers find the suggestions and examples for modifying instruction attractive, generally focussing on particular categories rather than on all categories. For many the challenge lies in pinpointing *minute* steps within what they already considered to be *minor* methodical steps when looking at elementary abilities.

A productive result of this project we see in the fact that it provokes self-examination among the teaching profession and provides food for thought on how the demands of individual teachers are manifested in literacy training. It is generally agreed in the field of adult literacy work that learners are subjects and must not be treated as objects of instruction. In practice, however, realization of this approach is limited to optional participation in courses, to gearing text content to learners' interests, and to adaptation of reading and writing to the learners' spoken language following the language experience approach. However, human beings learn only insofar as they *perform new tasks themselves*, and they perform such tasks only as far as they *understand* those tasks and *find them meaningful*. To take the learners' subjectivity seriously requires to put this knowledge into practice during even the most minute methodical steps. Not only that most teaching methods lack of appropriate aids for this. Moreover, the approach is a challenge to the professional self-image of teachers not to act for the learners but to enable them to act *themselves*.

On the theoretical level through working out the elementary abilities relevant to learning literacy the project results provided important concrete evidence and confirmation of the general statements that mental operations are structured hierarchically and are developed through acquisition of tools. They also provide important arguments against the biological reduction of the altercation of talent and intelligence.

We see certain problems in the limitation of the study's contents to perceptive and cognitive abilities. Such limitation was determined partly by the project's limited practical possibilities and financial means. On the other hand there is a lack of research and studies on the aspects of personality development related to illiteracy for instance learning literacy by adults till today. Although practical accounts from courses touching this aspect and learners' biographical statements were available, there was nothing that could be used as a theoretical or methodological basis. Moreover, the concrete relationships between the different aspects of human development (motivational structures, social relationships, motor and mental abilities, etc.) generally have not yet been sufficiently studied and understood.

In *interpreting* the test results and, particularly, in analyzing the results of *modified instruction*, special attention was paid to the interlacing of the development of abilities with various other factors of the processes important for the development of personality (e.g., social relationships, fears, self-judgment, etc.). However, for the reasons outlined above, the *tests* were limited to elementary abilities in several perceptive and cognitive categories. Therefore it is important to stress that the testing of elementary abilities deals with only one of many aspects which contribute to the appearance of learning difficulties. *At the same time we are convinced that this aspect — which is so closely related to the quality of our teaching — must absolutely be taken into account.* Identifying the various other factors and the concrete relationships between them is a task which remains to be completed.

Stemming from project's design and organization there were two interrelated shortcomings: the teachers who gave the "regular" literacy courses in the participating institutions did not have their normal workload lightened in any way to compensate for cooperating with the project. Therefore, despite their great interest, they did not have time to keep currently informed about the development of the modified instruction. Occasional conversations about progress and difficulties in this project phase were insufficient for fully adopting the modifications judged effective in the "special course" for the running teaching in their regular or upgrading courses. We are aware today that our inexperience in organizing and conducting research projects led us to overlook the time factor involved for teachers — rather than for learners only — from the project design stage. We also attribute to lack of experience the fact that in cases of unexpected events and problems arising in the institutions (an unavoidable reality) we postponed the project's interests more than might objectively have been necessary. We have now gained this experience, and time will tell whether we will have the opportunity to benefit from it.

The project's results aroused considerable interest among adult literacy training organizers and teachers. However, on several levels, we see certain limitations to rapid, widespread dissemination of the modified instruction. First, limited financial and staff resources make teacher training and, consequently, acquisition and discussion of the new approach difficult. Moreover, most institutions have little or no funds for providing counselling (in which diagnosis of elementary abilities has to be integrated) and individual learner support.

Another aspect of possible difficulties, modified instruction resulting from the project is limited to fundamental orientations and some concrete examples. We offer no generally applicable work sheets or "ready-to-use" programs. Therefore teachers themselves have to make the modifications concrete, that is, to put the suggested principles into practice based on their learners' needs. This requires considerable independence and flexibility in pedagogical tasks, willingness to develop and try something new and enjoyment from such work. Here we speak about features of teachers' personalities. However, considering that many literacy teachers in the Federal Republic of Germany are trained as teachers and that developing such traits and attitudes is not exactly the focal point of teacher training, we can see potential limitations and difficulties, for which teachers themselves cannot necessarily be held responsible.

On a third level it is apparent that the close relationship between ability development, personality structure and sociopsychological conditions does not apply to literacy learners alone. Although we did not conduct systematic research on this aspect Helga's experience in particular (from supervision and with a teaching staff) revealed that teachers are also subject to these general psychological rules. In other words the possibility for accepting learners in practice as subjects — in even the most minute methodical details — depends closely on the teacher's personality. Teachers who question their own ability to act as subjects, make changes and decisions, etc. also cannot really concede the learners to be subjects and show confidence in learners' activities in teaching.

The difficulties and limitations of this project are clear. However, we do not feel that they are insurmountable or that they must simply be accepted in the long term. Limitations of contents to perceptive and cognitive areas in testing were already overcome in practice and evaluation. In a future project the relationship between the various factors related to learning difficulties could be subject to empirical research, too. Models for ensuring teacher involvement in the development tasks could be created, once there is evidence that also such collaboration must be institutionalized. How far financial and staff resources for training and for the literacy courses themselves can be increased will depend upon comprehensive political decisions. Such decisions, in turn, are influenced (though not exclusively) by our actions. Those aspects, too, which are related to teachers' learning, teachers' attitudes, personality development, etc., we do not consider ultimately limited. It is necessary to change teacher training and upgrading and structures of work in institutions in a way that teachers can experience and consider themselves acting as subjects to be able to accept learners in this capacity as well. We cannot say here how such changes could be brought about. That will require the same step-by-step development combining practical experience and theoretically guided research like literacy training at all.

Finally, two points should be mentioned regarding the outlook for the future. First, the project's findings almost inevitably raise the question as to how learning difficulties — to which "illiteracy despite schooling" is almost always related — can be prevented altogether. This means focussing on children. In fall 1989 Gertrud will start with a corresponding project in a kindergarten. Second, in the literacy scheme in which Helga works, a need has arisen in teachers to broaden their own expertise and capacities for examining various aspects of their own work through research rather than dealing with constantly arising questions and problems on a pragmatic level only.

NOTES

1. Note that I mean specifically the demands on the *quality* of pedagogical capabilities. As far as investment of time and energy is concerned, many adult literacy teachers are currently overworked, driving themselves at a literally ruinous pace. In our opinion, improving quality, that is, better adaptation to learners' needs and prerequisites might even reduce this output of time and energy.

2. Giese severely criticizes the language experience approach in which the learners' language plays the leading role: "Hyperbolically speaking: Illiterate people cannot speak correctly. They have only an insufficient command of their mother tongue, and it would be completely false to presume that their deficiency consists in being unable to put 'their language' into written form." (Giese 1988: 128, originally in German). Giese's premise is that, nowadays, the oral and written form of realizing the language system "are closely interwoven (129).

REFERENCES

Berger, Ernst (Hrsg.). *Teilleistungsschwächen bei Kindern*. Bern/Stuttg./Wien: Huber, 1977.

_____. Stichwort "Teilleistungsschwächen." In Spiel, W. (Hrsg.), *Konsequenzen für die Pädagogik 2, Entwicklungsstörungen u. therapeutische Modelle*. (= Die Psychologie des 20. Jahrhunderts Bd. XII). Zürich: Kindler, 1980, 223-54.

Berk, Laura E. and Ruth A. Garvin. "Development of Private Speech Among Low-Income Appalachian Children." In *Developmental Psychology*. 2 (20), 1984, 271-86.

Braun, Charles. "The Status of the Soviet Cultural-Historical School of Psychology and of Leontiev's Activity Theory: a Canadian Survey." In *Proceedings of the 1st International Congress on Activity Theory* (1/1986, Berlin/West). Eds. M. Hildebrand-Nilshon and G. Rückriem. Berlin: System Druck, 1988. Vol. 4.2, 149-57.

Breuer, Helmut and Maria Weuffen. *Gut vorbereitet auf das Lesen- und Schreibenlernen? Möglichkeiten zur Früherkennung und Frühförderung sprachlicher Grundlagen*. Berlin (DDR): Dt. Verl. d. Wiss., 6. neugefaßte Aufl., 1986.

Breuer, Helmut. "Neue Forschungsergebnisse zur Früherfassung verbosensomotorischer Voraussetzungen für den Laut- und Schriftspracherwerb." In *Legasthenie. Bericht über den Fachkongreß 1988*. Hanover: Bundesverband Legasthenie e. V., 1989, 154-64.

Brügelmann, Hans. "Legasthenie — ein Denk-Problem? Naive Vorstellungen von Schrift und ihre Bedeutung für Schwierigkeiten beim Lesen- und Schreibenlernen." In *Legasthenie. Bericht über den Fachkongreß 1984*. Hanover: Bundesverband Legasthenie e. V., 1989, 208-21.

Cole, Michael. "Introduction: The Historical Context" and "Epilogue: A Portrait of Luria." In Luria, A. R., *The Making of Mind*. Cambridge, Mass., and London: Harvard University Press, 1979, 1-14 and 189-225.

Cole, Michael and James V. Wertsch. "Preliminary Remarks on the Soviet Socio-Cultural Approach to Mind and Psychological Research in the United States of America." In *Proceedings of the 1st International Congress on Activity Theory* (1/1986, Berlin/West). Eds. M. Hildebrand-Nilshon and G. Rückriem. Berlin: System Druck, 1988. Vol. 4.2, 135-46.

Coles, Gerald S. "Adult Illiteracy and Learning Theory: A Study of Cognition and Activity." In *Science & Society*. Vol. 47, 1984, 451-82.

Drecoll, Frank. "Freie Schreibversuche und Fehleranalyse. Hifen zur Beobachtung der Rechtschreibentwicklung." In *Alfa-Rundbrief*. Vol. 8, Summer 1988, 15-18.

Feuerstein, R., Y. Rand, M. B. Hoffman and R. Miller. *Instrumental Enrichment: An Intervention Program for Cognitive Modifiability*. Baltimore: University Park Press, 1980.

Friedler, Eva and Bibiana Schuch. *Teilleistungsschwächen. Diagnose und Therapie von Raumorientierungsstörungen*. Wien/München: Jugend u. Volk, 1982.

Frith, Uta. "Psychologische Aspekte des orthographischen Wissens: Entwicklung und Entwicklungsstörung." In Augst, G. (Hrsg.), *New Trends in Graphemics and Orthography*. Berlin/New York: de Gruyter, 1986, 218-33.

Galperin, Pjotr J. "Die geistige Handlung als Grundlage für die Bildung von Gedanken und Vorstellungen." In Gal'perin P. J. and A. N. Leonev. *Probleme der Lerntheorie.* Berlin (DDR): Volk u. Wissen, 1974, 33-49.

_____. "Zum Problem der Aufmerksamkeit." In Lompscher, J. (Hrsg.), *Sowjetische Beiträge zur Lerntheorie.* Köln: Pahl-Rugenstein, 1973, 15-23.

Giese, Heinz W. "(Sprach) Wissenschaftliche Aspekte der Kursleiterfortbildung im Alphabetisierungsbereich." In Harting, U. (Hrsg.), *Schift-Los. 10 Jahre Alphabetisierung.* Marl: Adolf-Grimme-Institut, 1988, 124-32.

Golden, C. J., T. A. Hammeke and A. D. Purisch. *The Luria-Nebraska Neuropsychological Battery.* Los Angeles: California Western Psychological Services, 1980.

Graichen, Johannes. "Faulheit — ein Symptom von Leistungsschwäche?" In *Supp. pädiat. prax., Beiträge zur Psychologie und Erziehung.* 18 (1977), 55-64.

_____. "Teilleistungsschwächen, dargestellt an Beispielen aus dem Bereich der Sprachbenützung." In *Z. f. Kinder- u. Jugendpsychiatrie.* 1 (1973) 2, 113-43.

Hamster, W., W. Langner and K. Mayer. *TÜLUC. Tübinger-Luria-Christensen Neuropsychologische Untersuchungsreihe.* Weinheim: Beltz 1980.

Kabylnitzkaja, S. L. "Die experimentelle Herausbildung der Aufmerksamkeit." In Lompscher, J. (Hrsg.), *Sowjetische Beiträge zur Lerntheorie.* Köln: Pahl-Rugenstein, 1973, 24-39.

Kamper, Gertrud. *Elementare Fähigkeiten in der Alphabetisierung. Band 1. Erkennen und Fördern unzureichend ausgebildeter elementarer Fähigkeiten bei Lernschwierigkeiten im Schriftsspracherwerb.* Berlin (West): Systemdruck, 1987 (1987a).

_____. (Hrsg.). *Elementare Fähigkeiten in der Alphabetisierung. Band 2. Beiträge der Expertenkonferenz am 24./25. Januar 1987 in der Hochschule der Künste Berlin.* Berlin (West): Systemdruck 1987 (1987b).

Leontiev, Alexej N. *Questions scientifiques.* Paris, 1955.

_____. *Le conditionnement et l'apprentissage.* Paris, 1958.

_____. "L'individu et les œuvres humaines." In *Les études philosophiques.* No. 3, 1957.

_____. *Probleme der Entwicklung des Psychischen.* Frankfurt/M.: Athena um Fischer TB, 1973.

_____. "Die Entwicklung höherer Formen des Gedächtnisses." In Leontiev, A. N., *Probleme der Entwicklung des Psychischen.* Frankfurt/M.: Athenäum Fischer TB, 1973, 313-76.

_____. *Tätigkeit-Bewußtsein-Persönlichkeit.* Köln: Pahl-Rugenstein, 1982.

Luria, Alexander R. *The Role of Speech in the Regulation of Normal and Abnormal Behaviour.* New York: Irvington, 1961.

_____. *Higher Cortical Functions in Man.* New York: Basic Books, 1966.

_____. *The Neuropsychology of Memory.* Washington: Winston, 1976.

—————. *The Making of Mind: A Personal Account of Soviet Psychology.* Michael Cole and Sheila Cole, eds. Cambridge, Mass., and London: Harvard University Press, 1979.

—————. *Sprache und Bewußtsein.* Köln: Pahl-Rugenstein, 1982. (= Studien zur Kritischen Psychologie. 31).

Morais, Jose, Luz Cary, Jesus Alegria and Paul Bertelson. "Literacy Training and Speech Segmentation. Special Issue: The Onset of Literacy." In *Cognition.* 24 (1-2) 1986, 45-64.

Morais, Jose, Luz Cary and Regine Kolinsky. "Awareness of Words as Phonological Entities: The Role of Literacy." In *Applied Psychology.* 8 (3) 1987, 223-32.

Piaget, Jean and Bärbel Inhelder. *La psychologie de l'enfant.* Paris: Presses Univ. de France, 1966.

Radigk, Werner. "Forschungsergebnisse zur Genese des Analphabetismus." In *Legasthenie. Bericht über den Fachkongreß 1984.* Hanover: Bundesverband Legasthenie e. V., 1989, 160-73.

—————. "Zum Aufbau funktioneller Systeme des Lesens bei unterschiedlichen Voraussetzungen und Bedingungen — Dazu: Diskussion zum Verständnis des Lesens als eines funktionellen Systems." In Kamper, G. (Hrsg.), *Elementare Fähigkeiten in der Alphabetisierung. Band 2. Beiträge der Expertenkonferenz am 24./25. Januar 1987 in der Hochschule der Künste Berlin,* 98-113 and 114-16.

Scribner, Sylvia and Michael Cole. *The Psychological Consequences of Literacy.* Cambridge, Mass.: Harvard Univ. Press, 1981.

Sendlmeier, Walter F. "Die psychologische Realität von Einzellauten bei Analphabeten." In *Sprache u. Kognition.* 6 (2) 1987, 64-71.

Velickovskij, Boris M. *Wissen und Handeln. Kognitive Psychologie aus tätigkeitstheoretischer Sicht.* Weinheim: VCH, 1988.

Vygotsky, Lew S. "The Problem of the Cultural Development of the Child." In *Journal of Genetic Psychology.* 36 (1929), 415-34.

—————. *Thought and Language.* Cambridge, Mass.: MIT Press, 1962.

—————. *Mind in Society.* Eds., M. Cole, V. John-Steiner, S. Scribner and E. Souberman. Cambridge, Mass.: Harvard Univ. Press, 1978.

Wertsch, James V. *Vygotsky and the Social Formation of Mind.* Cambridge, Mass.: Harvard Univ. Press, 1985.

—————. (ed.). *Culture, Communication and Cognition: Vygotskian Perspectives.* New York: Cambridge Univ. Press, 1985.

SOCIAL INTERACTIONS
AND THE TEACHING OF READING AND
WRITING IN UNDERPRIVILEGED AREAS
Action-Research Report

Jacques Fijalkow
Université de Toulouse — Le Mirail

On the basis of the principle that all children, regardless of their sociocultural background, can learn to read and write during their early school years, we have conducted several action-research projects over the past 10 years in order to gather supporting information and broaden our knowledge of the processes involved.

EMPIRICAL DATA

The first experiment was carried out in Israel in 1977-1978 and involved two grade 1 classes (Downing and Fijalkow 1984). The teaching strategy implemented at that time is still being used today in 120 to 130 first- and second-grade classes in underprivileged areas. The target population was identified within each institution, using criteria similar to those used in priority education areas (PEA). In the test classes the percentage of underprivileged Israeli children who had not attained the required reading proficiency by the end of grade 2 decreased from approximately 40 percent (official 1977 data) to approximately 10 percent (1985 estimate).

In 1983-1984 we conducted an action-research project in rural Québec. It was based on the same principles and involved two grade 1 and grade 2 classes. Two more studies were carried out in France with underprivileged grade 1 students. One study took place in 1982-1983; the other is ongoing in a working class district of Toulouse and involves two grade 1 classes, one of which is composed of a majority of Gypsy children, a minority of French nationals and a few children of North African descent.

The following information is based primarily on the Israeli project which, in light of the number of classes concerned, the length of time involved and the institutional recognition enjoyed, has provided the best empirical data.

THEORETICAL FOUNDATIONS

The teaching strategy implemented during these action-research projects is based on a number of factors relating to academic failure, the school, learning, language, etc. We will deal here only with the social interactions that come into play when a child is trying to master the written word.

Debates on teaching reading most commonly focus on "the method." This implies more or less implicitly that a child's reading difficulties can be attributed to the inadequacies of the method used. This technical approach to the problem is in our view extremely reductionistic. Attributing a child's difficulties only to the nature of the input (more or less phonetic or semantic) and/or to the way in which this is presented (more or less arbitrary or functional) does not account for the overriding fact that the greatest number of children with reading and writing difficulties come from underprivileged homes.

How can a reading method have socially selective repercussions? The conjectures are endless. In fact, the problem is seldom considered along these lines. The two notions of method and socially defined failure are mutually exclusive in this context. Pedagogues debate methods, while administrators, practitioners and social science researchers deal head-on with the social environment of children experiencing difficulties at school. This technical division of labour leads to bitter debates about the "illness," with no thought given to who the "patient" is and to why this *particular* patient has this *particular* illness.

While there is no overall theory to explain why some people find it difficult to learn to read (Fijalkow 1986), we can at the very least question whether the method is really the problem in the case of underprivileged children. In our opinion, it is not. No explanatory mechanism establishes a relationship between the method and socially selective factors. The reading method as such is therefore not the issue here. Our position is that the problem stems from what underprivileged children experience inside and outside the classroom while they are learning to read.

More specifically, given the fact that reading difficulties are a social problem, we feel that explanations and solutions should also be social, rather than technical. Reading brings into play a number of factors whose roots are sociological and which warrant special consideration at the outset. In other words, it is imperative that we extend our thinking about reading methods to include the students' social backgrounds; above all, we must reverse the order of our priorities, to concentrate primarily on the child's environment rather than on the reading method.

From this, it naturally follows that this action-research will focus on the social dimensions of what we perceive to be primarily a social problem. To a social problem, we therefore propose a social solution.

It is possible that learning to read at school may cause conflict between the child's social identity as it has evolved within his family and social setting and the social role he must play at school. A theoretical framework like this justifies the use of teaching strategies that accord high priority to the social interactions which take place during learning and which further the process.

Because this is essentially a pedagogical paper, we will deal with a few of these strategies, although we are unable at the moment to provide any specific theoretical justification for each of them or to assess their overall effectiveness.

VARIOUS TYPES OF SOCIAL INTERACTIONS

Teacher-parent

A considerable number of parents are illiterate and accordingly take a great deal of interest in their children's education. A parent-teacher meeting early in the school year enables the teacher to establish a first direct contact with the parents. The researcher is also present. This meeting is extremely important as it allows the parents to become familiar and comfortable with a teaching approach that differs from what they are used to.

Parents' concerns at the beginning of grade 1 normally revolve around their child's adaptation to the school environment and his success in learning how to read. These concerns multiply when they discover that their child is involved in an educational experiment. They have a genuine fear that the child will be used as a "guinea pig" and must be reassured with clear explanations.

The teacher, apprehensive about working in unfamiliar conditions and about dealing with parent reactions, needs the researcher's input at this first meeting. The parents must not only be given the explanations they request but, more importantly, must be involved in the teaching process. They may be anxious about not knowing how to help their child or about impeding the work done in class.

In some cases, a mini-school for parents may be set up: the teacher meets with interested parents, who take the place of their children and, with the teacher, act out real classroom activities. Such meetings take place early in the year, after school hours, approximately once a week. They provide parents with a surrogate experience of school life which allows them to feel that they are maintaining some control over their children's schooling.

Teachers who have been using the teaching strategy proposed here for some years no longer need the researcher's help; they turn instead to parents whose children have successfully learned to read in this way — a more effective approach with new parents.

Purchasing children's books to replace the regular reader and setting up library facilities are also ways to bring teachers and parents together.

Parent-child

Each child's birthday is usually celebrated in class and the child's parents can be invited to attend. Parents can also be asked to participate in school celebrations of certain holidays. Throughout the year, the results of various classroom writing activities can be sent to parents. These include:

— a request for school supplies, the first theme that the class works on together;

— a note from the class thanking a parent for providing a birthday cake;

— notices about class outings (circus, nature trip, etc.);

— a request for pizza ingredients, as determined by the various groups of students, who will then prepare the pizza in class;

— birthday cards or invitations to celebrations at the school.

Parents may also send written messages to the class and teacher. This occurs less often but nonetheless provides valuable opportunities for functional reading. These messages could include:

— recipes,

— information on television programs,

— children's books,

— replies to letters.

Unlike other researchers (Chauveau, Rogovas-Chauveau and Gazal 1984), we did not research the parents' contribution in the home, so that this remains an unknown factor.

Teacher-student

The goal is to move as soon as possible from the standard classroom organization that exists at the beginning of the school year — with most interactions occurring between the teacher and the students she calls on — to a decentralized setting.

Students able to work independently gradually move away from the initial class group to form their own work group, leaving the teacher free to work with the remaining students. Each group contains four or five children and, once all the children have been integrated into a group, a system of work centres is set up. The groups rotate among the work centres, which are equipped for the various activities that will be carried out (reading, writing, worksheets, reading games, etc.).

Rather than supervising all the groups, offering assistance as requested by the children and running from table to table like a waitress, the teacher is assigned to a specific work centre. The essence of the teacher-student relationship stems from this all-important condition. Once the students have understood the rule that they must not call on the teacher while she is working with another group, she can concentrate on the small group of students and can develop her interactions with them to the fullest.

At the teacher's work centre, reading and writing strategies are taught, while, through her interactions with the children, the teacher makes a day-to-day assessment of learning.

Teachers who have used this strategy agree that spending 15 minutes every day or every other day with the same four or five children enabled them to develop a more accurate profile of each child than would have been possible in the conventional classroom. Because the teacher deals with only a small number of students at a time, her attention is more evenly divided among the children in the class.

In the traditional classroom, working class students are doubly handicapped during the reading lesson. A well-known CRESAS study (Pardo, Duchein and Breton 1974) has shown that these students have less interaction with the teacher than children from more advantaged homes.

Must we interpret this as meaning that underprivileged children are the ill-loved of the education system? A study (Zimmerman 1978) which assessed the attraction-repulsion factor in teachers' relationships with underprivileged children suggests that this may be the case. More recent studies conducted at Toulouse (Albert 1985a, b) considered the problem from a different angle. These studies focussed on the manner in which teachers interact with students experiencing difficulty in reading a particular word out loud. The nature of the teacher's assistance depended on the child's performance (good student vs. weak student).

Given these findings, there is reason to fear that underprivileged grade 1 children are not only ill-loved but ill-helped.

Child-child

While one group is working with the teacher, the others are engaged in a number of unsupervised activities for approximately one hour and forty-five minutes of the daily two-hour schedule.

Tasks are most often performed on an individual basis (reading a book, writing a text, completing a worksheet) and occasionally on a group basis (reading game, etc.). Two singular characteristics prevail:

— **Complete freedom of choice**: a basket placed at each centre contains all the necessary material for carrying out the activity. The elements are as varied as possible in content, presentation, colour and degree of difficulty; there is only one sample of each.

— **Complete freedom of action**: the children are free to do an activity for as long as they wish, to set it aside and choose another, to choose a difficult or a simple one, etc.

— This freedom is made possible through the total absence of teacher control for the duration of the activity. The children are not required to show the teacher work done at the centres.

Obviously, the children are free to talk among themselves — and do so frequently, judging by the noise level in the classroom. The noise, however, is reminiscent of a beehive rather than a schoolyard: it is the sound of people working together.

The interactions which occur among the children are spontaneous, as most of the activities are carried out individually. Without systematic observation, it is difficult to describe the types of interactions that take place. Those that we observed most frequently included:

— sharing pleasure: showing an object, a picture in a book, completed work, etc.;

— asking for and giving help: as the teacher may not be disturbed, a child unable to solve a difficulty will call on a classmate for assistance, and a form of tutoring may subsequently evolve;

— pairing or grouping to read a book, complete a worksheet, etc.

Quick observation suggests that interactions occur most often between two children: a child tends to turn to his neighbour rather than to several children. It also appears that, while spontaneous interactions are frequent and harmonious, forced ones are not. When a group of children is assigned a task involving writing, for example, the work-sharing process creates problems. Conflicts frequently arise, at least at the outset or during the first attempts at group work. Again, detailed observations are required. We are currently attempting to set up work groups based on the results of a sociometric test that is administered periodically.

The importance of spontaneous interaction among children in the classroom has long been recognized. We know, for example, that in a multigrade class, the younger students often absorb information that is being taught to the older children. This explains why very young school children can learn a great deal about reading by observing older students. Spontaneous interaction of this sort undoubtedly accounts for the advantage enjoyed by weaker students when they belong to a heterogeneous group and, conversely, for the stagnation or regression that results when they are placed in a homogeneous group.

Copying and whispering are well-known forms of spontaneous interaction, and are discouraged among school children in the traditional classroom setting. This behaviour obviously does not occur in the classroom setting described in this paper, simply because the necessary conditions do not exist. In general, it would appear that the bonds of competition are replaced by tentative, but nonetheless real, bonds of cooperation.

This is doubtless largely attributable to the fact that the teacher does not mark or even see the work that is done in the work centres — itself a subtle form of control. The children therefore do not work to achieve good marks or to satisfy the teacher, but to please themselves. This alters their relationships with the other students considerably. As there are no situations where the children must compare their own performance with that of their classmates, no one is made to feel superior or inferior. Other students are perceived as peers rather than as rivals with greater or lesser ability.

Child-text

A special form of interaction takes place when a person learns to read, i.e., the interaction that develops progressively between the written text and the reader: the text challenges the reader and provides him with answers. The written text is after all a message produced by one person for another, so that reading, as a deferred form of communication, constitutes a unique form of interaction.

Consequently, it is essential that children's reading material be real and that they be required to do real reading. To promote the greatest possible variety of interactions between reader and text, the greatest possible variety of texts should be used. If the teacher were the sole author of the class's reading material (other than books), the children would be deprived of much enrichment. To ensure that a diversity of texts was used in the test classes, the teachers were asked to identify any texts that they had personally drafted.

In the traditional classroom, the teacher is perceived in a totally different way, as the "keeper of the text":

— She selects the text that must be read, the student who must read it and the moment when this will occur.

— She supplies corrections, which are either imposed (reading out loud) or sought (silent reading).

— She also makes a value judgment once a child has finished reading.

As a result, teacher-child interactions outnumber child-text interactions in the traditional classroom setting. It is to be feared that, in circumstances such as these, the development of a genuine rapport between the child and the text will be problematic. The child may come to see the act of reading, not as the reception of a linguistic message, but as an arbitrary gesture passively executed in accordance with the requirements of an omnipotent adult.

The adult's interventions may therefore create a barrier to the child's cognitive development, by creating misrepresentations of the act of reading. The child who is constantly interrupted and deprived of the opportunity to search and discover at his own pace may never learn to read properly. Perhaps some of the disparities between reading and mathematics, like those between social backgrounds, take root under conditions such as these.

During activities done at the work centres in our studies, interactions between the child and the written word were neither dominated nor systematically mediatized by teacher-child interactions. The children were therefore given the chance to develop a genuine interaction with the written text. We see this as being a factor that contributes to success in learning to read.

The researcher

The researcher is initially a participant in the interactive network. He works with the teacher (one meeting per week throughout the year), with parents (during the first parent-teacher meeting) and with the children (by acting as a teacher's aide during classroom activities once a week throughout the year).

CONCLUSION

The teaching strategy that we implemented generated new social relationships among participants in the network and subsequently fostered new types of interactions.

The teacher takes on a new role, becoming a technician who provides access to the written text (by teaching reading strategies) and an initiator who introduces the children to the pleasures of reading (by reading stories or having them read in class). She no longer intervenes systematically during reading activities, and does not have to control and judge students during the reading lesson.

Relationships between the children are no longer marked by raw competitiveness and individualism, as in the traditional classroom. A spirit of cooperation begins to emerge.

Child-text interactions finally supersede child-teacher interactions during reading.

Learning to read, perceived up to now — from the perspective of an individualistic approach to psychology — as a strictly individualistic process, can now, in the light of reflection, be seen as a social process.

Learning to read is not a laboratory procedure taught in a vacuum, or a technical problem involving only cognitive abilities such as language use, perception or memory. It is a social process. The child does not learn alone or by chance, but in the company of other children and flanked by adults, both parents and teacher.

The social dimension of learning to read can no longer be ignored. It is present in the traditional teaching approach, but not necessarily to everyone's benefit. By focussing on this dimension of learning to read and by striving to achieve a maximum number of interactions, we feel that it is possible to reduce the cultural conflicts that some children experience when learning to read. We hope, as a result, to move a little closer to our objectives of better understanding how children learn to read at school and of ensuring every child's success in this endeavour.

REFERENCES

Albert, J. "Analyse des comportements pédagogiques pendant la leçon de lecture au Cours Préparatoire." In *Les Dossiers de l'Education*, 1985 a, 8, 67-87.

_____. "Une approche psychopédagogique de l'enseignement de la lecture au Cours Préparatoire." Doctoral thesis. Université de Toulouse — Le Mirail, 1985 b.

Chauveau, G., E. Rogovas-Chauveau and M. Gazal. "Lire en famille: des familles immigrées et l'apprentissage de la lecture." In *Ouvertures: l'école, la crèche, les familles*. L'Harmattan-INRP, 1985.

Downing, J. and J. Fijalkow. *Lire et Raisonner*. Toulouse: Privat, 1984.

Fijalkow, J. *Mauvais lecteurs, pourquoi?* Paris: PUF, 1986.

Pardo, A.M., C. Duchein and J. Breton. "Performances en lecture au Cours Préparatoire; Participation à la classe et milieu d'origine des élèves." In *Recherches Pédagogiques*, 1974, 68, 49-81.

Zimmerman, D. "Un langage non-verbal de classe: les processus d'attraction — répulsion des enseignants à l'égard des élèves en fonction de l'origine familiale de ces derniers." In *Revue Française de Pédagogie*, 1978, 44, 46-70.

THE ROLE OF HOMEWORK SCHOOLS IN THE PREVENTION OF ILLITERACY

Véronique Marissal
Homework School Coordinating
Committee, Brussels

"Homework schools" were first established in Belgium in the early 1970s. Despite their name these institutions are independent of the school system and operate outside normal school hours. Located in working class districts they help children with their schoolwork and provide them with group activities and creative workshops.

BACKGROUND

In the late 1960s Belgium (along with other European countries) began to reexamine its school system and to look for new ways of dealing with social, cultural and educational issues. Teachers involved in new teaching programs, social workers and community leaders started to examine the "problem" of school and to look for alternatives.

At that time the government's policy of reuniting migrant workers with their families resulted in a massive influx of foreign children into Belgian schools. This underlined the schools' difficulties in addressing the specific cultural and linguistic needs of these children. Confronted with the problems involved in the education of immigrant students, community leaders, youth homes, and cultural, political and union organizations, often in response to parents' requests for help, were prompted to look for alternatives and "solutions." It is within this context that the development and diversity of homework schools (abbreviated as EDDs in French) should be examined.

Dopa scuola, alternative schools set up in Italy in the 1960s by Father Don Lorenzo Milani, were designed to use the sociocultural experiences of working class children as a basis for helping them with their education. These Italian schools can be considered the predecessors of Belgium's homework schools.

In Belgium these institutions are run either publicly or privately and are designed for children and young people between 3 and 18 years of age. Homework schools were first established in the early 1970s, with the objective of providing children with academic help, outside the regular educational system, in order to prevent academic failure and the resulting phenomenon of social exclusion. There are now approximately 200 such institutions in the francophone regions of the country. A third are located in rural areas; the others are concentrated in cities, particularly in Brussels, which has 73 in all (1989 survey).

In the 1980s the EDDs formed regional coordinating committees and a federation of francophone homework schools, hoping to attain a stronger voice in dealing with institutions and to participate in discussion regarding educational policies. The EDDs wanted to become partners in the search for major changes in school practices.

The increase in the number of EDDs is one of the indications that schools are finding it increasingly difficult to deal with academic failure, which affects large numbers of children, even as early as the lower grades, and has proven to be selective, hitting hardest among students in disadvantaged communities.

HOMEWORK SCHOOLS IN BRUSSELS

A study conducted by the homework school coordinating committee of Brussels, in collaboration with *Lire et Écrire Bruxelles*, a regional literacy organization, will serve as a basis in helping us to arrive at a better understanding of EDDs (where they are located; who they serve; their goals, activities, partners; etc.).[1]

EDDs are either nonprofit organizations, government agencies or volunteer associations. Some of them are devoted exclusively to helping students with their homework, while others are integrated into creative centres, continuing education associations, community centres, children's homes, self-help centres, cultural centres, libraries, (pre)vocational training centres, union centres, social centres, medical centres, and so on.

Most EDDs in Brussels are concentrated in the industrial areas (usually in older, run-down districts) where the population, for the most part, consists of people with very low incomes and very few options in terms of affordable housing (immigrants, seniors on fixed incomes, etc.). Most literacy programs are also concentrated in these areas. Eighty-five percent of literacy centres are thus located within the areas chosen by the Fondation Roi Baudouin[2] for its study of disadvantaged districts in metropolitan Brussels.

In very general terms, depending obviously on the income of the residents of the districts concerned, the location of EDDs is closely related to the percentage of labourers and foreigners living in a given district. (Approximately one-third of the labourers within metropolitan Brussels are immigrants, and they are generally the least qualified and lowest paid members of the blue-collar group, which itself tends to be very much affected by the problems of illiteracy and undereducation.)

WHO IS SERVED BY EDDs?

EDDs located in districts such as those described above thus serve children who come primarily from working class homes. A large percentage of these children are from immigrant families (Moroccans, Turks, Spaniards, Italians, etc.), some of whom are refugees (Armenians, Aramaeans, Kurds, Latin Americans, Vietnamese, etc.).

The 45 EDDs surveyed as part of the study serve approximately 1650 children (which, by extrapolation, means that EDDs serve over 6000 children in the city's francophone districts). Some EDDs open their doors to children as young as 3. The desire to combat academic failure has led these EDDs to give priority to projects designed for very young children.

One of the first requests encountered when meeting with children (and parents) for the first time is for help with schoolwork (or homework). Homework is an everyday reality for children; for EDDs it serves to establish a first "point of contact" with the public and the school environment.

Children who attend EDDs tend to lag considerably behind other children in their speaking and writing skills. The diversity of the children's cultural backgrounds and the fact that they come from various schools in the district[3] make EDDs an interesting environment for exchanges and comparisons among different cultures, institutions and teaching approaches.

Academic support activities play a very important role in EDD programs but are by no means the only activities offered. Of the 45 EDDs studied in Brussels 76 percent have been organized within associations offering other activities, such as after-hours social programs, legal and medical clinics, literacy courses, language courses, social skills courses, sewing courses, etc.

EDD STAFF MEMBERS

Children are supervised by staff members who for the most part are volunteers (over 50 percent) or temporary workers (30 percent). Most staff members are Belgian (70 percent). Recently, however, young people from immigrant families have started to work in EDDs. These people have a better understanding of the situation of immigrant children, having experienced it themselves, and may be able to help Belgian staff in dealing with the difficulties faced by these children. Having people on staff who can talk to parents in their own language can also be a real asset.

Paid staff members are usually trained in the social sciences (social workers), while volunteers are usually teachers. There are also a large number of students (future social workers, educators and teachers) who complete a practicum by working in EDDs. This type of practical experience allows students to come into contact with the daily realities of children in working class districts.

Since most people work on a volunteer or temporary basis staff instability is one of the most acute problems faced by EDDs. The great diversity in staff qualifications, on the other hand, may actually be quite positive, as the work is also very diverse in nature.

ACTIVITIES

EDDs are open from two to six days a week and offer after-school activities (usually for two hours a day, except on Wednesday afternoons and Saturdays, when they are open longer, as children are not in school). Children usually come to do their homework directly from school.

Schoolwork and remedial education

Homework is a feature of all schools, and children quite often spend two hours each day on this activity. EDDs provide children with a place to work, materials (dictionaries, grammar books, reference books, paper) and people to help them (one staff member for every five children, on average).

Because the children are not necessarily from the same school (and schools do not all use the same methods) or in the same grade, EDD staff members must be able to switch from one reading method to another, from subtraction to parsing, from the difference between "their" and "they're" to a problem with the metric system. In short they must be mental gymnasts!

Often a request for help is more psychological than anything else: children who are able to do their homework without help will not start until a staff member is there, and time is too short to make sure that everyone gets started! This sort of situation leads us directly to the heart of the problem of academic failure and reveals why many children fail in the first place.

In addition to children who are almost able to sort things out for themselves, there are others who come to EDDs simply to get their homework done, regardless of whether or not they understand, what answers they put down or how they obtain those answers (e.g., through copying, asking staff members or older children for answers). For these children homework is nothing more than an ordeal they cannot escape and they will not listen to any explanations from staff members.

Other children have such serious problems that they are not able to cope at all. In many cases staff members must consider organizing individual remedial sessions with these students, to review basic concepts (teaching games, supplementary exercises, speech therapy, etc.).

Finally there are children who are no longer interested in doing their homework and who often do not come or stop coming to the EDD. In some cases the EDD must refuse such children, as their presence is too disruptive for others who want to do their homework.

Thus EDDs try to help children with their education by helping them "produce" in accordance with school requirements and by restoring children's confidence in themselves. (After all, the essential task of EDDs is surely to show children that they are entitled to express their opinions, and that despite their problems, school is not just something they must submit to resignedly.)

Homework, and the time spent on it, has led us to ask ourselves some questions about our role in relation to the school, whose practices we would like to see changed. Are we not becoming a second school, a super study room? Is this our role? Should it not be the school's?

We may ask ourselves what role homework plays in the overall process of academic failure. We have no control over homework content, which is imposed by the school — often without regard for the child's background — nor over the evaluation. Actually children who are failing spend more time on their homework than others. In addition, after school they must complete work they were not able to finish in class (because they were too slow or did not understand), and must correct work that was poorly done (they are obviously the ones with the most mistakes) or complete an extra assignment as a punishment for not being "good" or for not doing their homework.

Our objective of providing remedial education often cannot be achieved, given the severe difficulties of some children.

Creative workshops and other activities

Staff members quickly realized their limitations in helping children with their homework. How can they accomplish in two hours what the teacher was not able to accomplish in a day? They have come to realize that this method is clearly not enough to help children integrate into the regular school system.

For this reason other activities are offered, including creative workshops which allow children to structure their world, rediscover their potential, express themselves and reestablish themselves within a noncomparative environment. The workshops involve various activities, from handicrafts (model making, sculpture, masks, puppets) to painting; from producing a play or a video (which can be put on at school!) to an exhibition of the children's work (with invitations for parents, teachers, members of the community) or the creation of a newspaper. They may also include reading workshops (storytelling, reading, imagining stories, acting them out) and writing workshops.

Not all EDDs organize all these activities, but there are not many that limit themselves to providing academic support through help with homework. Some EDDs are more teaching-oriented, while others are more social or cultural. What they all have in common is that, although they do deal with homework, they want to be more than just a drop-off point for children and their satchels.

EDDs do not see their role as being that of providing school activities or dealing with the shortcomings of educational institutions; nor do they seek to replace the parents. They do want to analyze the various processes involved in academic failure and find solutions to academic problems. It is for this reason that, in addition to the activities offered (and within their capabilities, with the limited resources at their disposal!), EDDs work in cooperation with other partners. This is important because, if we deal only with academic failure, we are attacking the symptoms and not the cause of the problem.

PARENTS

School plays a very important role in children's education, but a child's family environment is the first frame of reference in which he develops. It is in this environment that children have their first experiences. For youngsters from working class families, more than for others, starting school represents a break with the attitudes, lifestyle, rules and values they have learned from their families. EDDs thus act as intermediaries, not only between children and the school to which they must adapt, but also between children and their families.

For this reason EDDs should not become another place of acculturation for children (by acculturation, we mean the process by which individuals must assimilate the cultural values of another group and lose those of their own group, notably through the devaluation of their social, ethnological and linguistic points of reference by the other group). By meeting with parents, becoming aware of a child's home environment, enhancing through these exchanges the self-esteem of the child and family, and helping families to recognize their role as educators and to deal with the school, EDDs actually help decrease the distance between parents and schools.

EDD staff members, while assuming the role of auxiliary teachers for children, must never under any circumstances take the place of a child's parents. Their first task is to create an environment of confidence (room for discussion) in order to encourage parents to come to the EDD whenever they want. Their second task is to make it possible for parents to follow their child's progress in school, through an agenda (which details work to be accomplished at home and contains information from the school) or through the report card (which, we must admit is often written in jargon difficult to understand). This allows parents to ask questions about school, the EDD and their respective roles. Within this consultation process the family situation must not be forgotten (unstable financial situation, unemployment, level of education, culture, etc.) This should be taken into account when setting objectives to be achieved with parents as certain learning and development processes will be more productive than others, depending on the context.

In this type of work we are also called upon to deal with problems of a noneducational nature, such as health, housing and unemployment. Staff members must therefore set limits to what they will do and must direct parents towards other agencies which are in a better position to help them. Where, in fact, does the role of the EDD end? What are we capable of handling?

In reality contact with parents is often difficult. Many staff members feel that it is a long-term process, slow to produce results. Because of this contacts are usually infrequent and take place on a one-to-one basis.

In most cases it is parents who must register their children in the EDD. This gives staff members an opportunity to meet them, to explain the work that will be done with their child throughout the year, to discuss what is expected of the parents and to open the door for future visits (gaining parents' confidence during this first meeting is thus indispensable). This meeting is often followed up with a home visit some time during the year and with a final "evaluation" meeting at the end of the year. Other opportunities to meet with parents may develop during the year: helping parents prepare for a meeting with the school; accompanying them at such meetings, etc.

On a more general level parents are contacted when staff members discover that a child has particular academic needs or difficulties (failure, behaviour problems, etc.). In such instances staff members first try to make children feel that they have their parents' support.

Activities organized with groups of parents are more rare. These might include an invitation to a party (which often gives parents the opportunity to discover what their children have accomplished) or a chance for parents to attend a theatrical performance, visit an exhibition of children's drawings or view a film produced during the year.

Sometimes parents are asked to participate more actively. Fathers may help clear a space for a playground while mothers help make costumes for the neighbourhood party parade or bake cakes for the occasion. Parents are sometimes invited to attend information meetings on a particular subject (education, health, school, etc.), although staff members have noted that they rarely come to this type of meeting.

Although the objectives are achieved in some cases, staff members are often disappointed and discouraged by the lack of results. Apart from material difficulties (change of staff, lack of time and resources) staff members cite problems related to the parents themselves. These problems are :

— illiteracy or undereducation ;

— a lack of understanding as to how our society and education system function, and of their rights and the opportunities they have to act in these areas ;

— a feeling of rejection on the part of parents, who are often withdrawn ;

— parents' indifference to school or their feeling of powerlessness, resulting from a lack of understanding as to what causes academic failure ;

— cultural differences.

These problems are discussed regularly by staff members, particularly within the Brussels homework school coordinating committee. In its policy statement (drawn up by a group of staff members from various EDDs) the coordinating committee insists that the staff of each EDD give serious consideration to the following matters before contacting parents :

— the objectives they hope to achieve ;

— the role they want parents to play in the EDD ;

— the image they have of the parents ;

— the image the parents have of them ;

— the limits of the parents' responsibilities, the school's and the EDD's.

We should also stress the importance of having a good understanding of the public with whom we work: its financial and social situation, cultural characteristics, and particularly its methods of expression and communication.

We have noted that, for parents, regular meetings with the same staff member help to establish a climate of trust, that a person acting as an intermediary can help facilitate dialogue (an interpreter, for example), that a literacy course organized in the same building can help in encouraging this type of meeting and that parents find it easier to open up during an after-hours social program.

We have also noted that, in spite of stated intentions to look at parents more favourably, they are often seen in terms of their deficiencies. Too often we hear only that children find no stimulation at home (they are sent to play in the street or put in front of the television; they have no books), that no good examples are set for them at home, that parents are not interested in school. For this reason meetings with parents are often centred around "this problem we must solve," and amount in some cases to a monologue on the part of the staff member ("You should...").

Moreover, although EDD staff members often criticize the school because of the gap between what it expects of parents and what parents are actually capable of doing, we are tempted to throw the ball into their court and ask whether it is not much the same thing, expecting parents to "take an active interest" in their children's academic progress. (Parents may have communication problems because of the language, while their relationship with their children and their fear of being misunderstood may not be conducive to showing an active interest.)

Although most parents rarely attend meetings (if at all) or come only to make another request, we believe it would be hasty to conclude that they consider school problems to be secondary. On the contrary they may even be overly preoccupied with these problems. They often have a great desire to succeed through their children. School is the key to this success, ensuring that their children's lives will be better than their own. It constitutes an emotionally charged investment, so that failure is even more keenly felt. Registering their children in an EDD is tangible proof that these parents are interested, rather than an abdication of responsibility as staff members seem to feel.

THE SCHOOL

To bring families and schools closer together EDDs must also establish contact with the schools themselves: not only with teachers, but with all the partners in the school system (instructors, principals, school inspectors, school authorities and psychological/medical/social centres). Cooperation must take place at both the individual level (i.e., that of the children, their parents and school) and the institutional level (studying problems and formulating proposals for change with other partners in the school system).

The EDDs must maintain an objective point of view in working with schools. This means using prudence in dealing with what appears to be a contradiction. Ideally EDD staff should be reasonably familiar with the workings of the school system and able to explain the specific aspects of their own work to the other partners.

According to the study, EDD staff have been able to progress step by step from "hardline opposition" (there's no use in working with a school we don't agree with) to constructive cooperation (if we want to change the school, we have to cooperate with it). Nowadays alongside EDDs which refuse to have any dealings with schools (these are increasingly rare), there are EDDs which work in close cooperation with schools. These opposing attitudes reflect the different relationships that have developed between EDDs and schools over time.

EDDs call for significant changes in the practices of schools which produce failure. They want to make schools more receptive to the realities of the community, parents and children. They want schools to reevaluate their opinions, both of children and of parents.

Generally meetings are held between EDD staff and the teachers of each child (particularly children experiencing difficulties). The EDD staff familiarize themselves with the teaching methods being used and with the problems the child is experiencing in class. These meetings give each side an idea of how the other side works. They can lead to negotiations regarding the type of homework children are asked to do or the themes used for compositions and can even involve "contracts" (a child might be excused from homework on condition that he attend an EDD to improve his reading skills).

In addition to these meetings EDD staff, depending on their objectives, also participate in professional development sessions with teachers and inspectors. An EDD might train teachers in the use of creative workshop techniques. Others might offer workshops within the school: newspaper, reading, theatre. EDDs can thus become places of experimentation and innovation in teaching.

This sort of cooperation is not without difficulties. In addition to the material problems mentioned earlier the EDDs do not have an official status granting them access to schools, so that, as already stated, they have formed regional coordinating committees to increase their weight at the institutional level.

Within the framework of this cooperative process the Brussels EDD coordinating committee has developed a number of projects. For example, for a number of years, it has been organizing practica for students from teachers' training colleges. These allow future teachers to work in EDDs, where they become aware of how widespread the problem of academic failure is and of the realities faced by children in working class districts.

The coordinating committee also offers training programs (in reading methods and learning how to learn) and information sessions on themes such as: "Creative Workshops and Practical Teaching Methods," "EDDs and the School: Cooperation?" "EDDs and Children in Special Education," "School: Curriculum, Standards and Functioning." EDD staff form subgroups to work on projects such as the extensive survey on homework that is currently being prepared.

Numerous meetings and exchanges within the framework of the coordinating committee have also made us aware that there are other partners, in addition to parents and schools, who can cooperate in a broad range of activities designed to combat academic failure and social exclusion.

OTHER PARTNERS

Helping children experiencing difficulties and academic failure goes far beyond the jurisdiction of the EDDs. There are a large number of organizations which, within the same district, work in cooperation with or alongside the EDDs. These include social and legal aid centres, medical clinics, sociocultural associations for immigrants, sports associations, literacy centres, libraries, etc.

Local issues and ideas put forward by the Brussels EDD coordinating committee have been examined in the light of suggestions made by DEFIS[4] in connection with the school dropout problem. In Brussels this process has produced four experimental community partnership programs ("community" in the sense of an entity with a social and cultural life); these are inspired by the French example of priority educational areas (ZEPs).

The four districts involved in this program were chosen because they met the economic, sociological and geographical criteria that apply to disadvantaged urban areas. They also possessed significant social and human potential, and many of their inhabitants were already aware of the problem of school dropouts. These four community partnerships are described below.

The Saint-Gilles community partnership

Created in 1985, this partnership is made up of two primary schools, a psychological/medical/social centre, immigrants' associations, (pre)vocational training centres and EDDs.

In 1987-1988 the partnership's principal objectives were to improve communication between parents and schools (through meetings with mothers and fathers, inviting mothers to look in on kindergartens, literacy programs for mothers) and to develop innovative teaching programs through cooperation between teachers and partners outside the school system (in intercultural music workshops, health education, libraries and interschool newspapers).

The Anderlecht community partnership

Created in 1985, this partnership is made up of one primary school, one secondary school, a part-time vocational centre, psychological-/medical/social centres, youth groups, EDDs, literacy centres and social centres, and also includes local doctors and parents' associations.

Working subgroups share the tasks of developing areas for recreation and sports, projects designed to improve communication between the various members of the educational community, literacy projects, a library project and the organization of a neighbourhood party.

The Forest community partnership

Created in 1987, this partnership is made up of two primary schools, continuing education associations, EDDs, social agencies, a literacy centre and a baby clinic of the Office de la naissance et de l'enfance.

These organizations ensure follow-up on projects such as liaison between baby clinics and kindergartens, and the establishment of a reading centre.

The Schaerbeek community partnership

Created in 1987, this partnership is made up of one primary school, continuing education associations, EDDs, social agencies and psychological/medical/social centres.

For the moment the experiment is limited to one school and one grade level. Activities are divided between the school (a self-expression workshop) and the various associations (library sessions, an academic resource centre, help with homework, theatre).

The basic principles of France's ZEPs are affirmative action (more resources for those with the greatest need), individualized teaching methods and increased receptiveness of the school to the community and vice versa. Given the knowledge EDDs have of the children, parents and the community itself, they would seem to be indispensable partners in this process.

Within the framework of the experiments we have just described two EDDs have participated with two schools and the district of Anderlecht in the development of recreational areas (making proposals, setting up models with children). In Saint-Gilles one EDD (which does not deal with homework any more!) is organizing an "interschool newspaper" workshop, which will integrate children into social and cultural life and develop oral and written expression by creating a tool with which young people in the district can express themselves. In Forest another EDD is participating in the establishment of a reading centre.

Beyond these experiments we have found this sort of vitality in other districts as well. Our study, which was carried out in cooperation with Lire et Écrire Bruxelles and served as a partial basis for our description of the EDDs, must be seen from this perspective.

HOMEWORK SCHOOLS AND LITERACY

In our opinion there is room for cooperation between the EDDs and adult literacy centres both in terms of preventing illiteracy and of providing literacy training to the illiterate or undereducated population. Currently such cooperation is rare. This is incomprehensible as both groups are working to combat illiteracy and, though they deal with different levels, both are working in the same districts!

It is clear that EDDs, through some of their activities, play an undeniable role in preventing illiteracy. An example of this is the newspaper workshop organized by an association in Saint-Gilles, within the framework of a community partnership. [5]

This workshop is really a teaching workshop, which students attend during school hours. The groups of students are made up of volunteers and some children chosen by their teacher because of their difficulties in oral and written French. Students work on the newspaper in school and at the association, and carry out "exploratory work" in other locations.

The children work like journalists, choosing topics they wish to talk about, asking questions and making proposals. They then do research, using books, magazines, newspapers and information provided by resource people (a doctor, the cultural office of an embassy, a police commissioner, an alderman, journalists, etc). During this research process the students use both oral and written skills according to their own needs and capabilities; for some, writing may not come until much later. They select the information they want and integrate it into their reports. An introduction to word processing, illustrations and page layout rounds out the workshop, before the newspaper is printed.

The budding journalists also have the opportunity to make radio broadcasts and to contribute to televised news programs. Some of their articles have been published in larger newspapers.

The workshop deals with all styles, difficulties and rules of language. Children discover their own geographic, social and cultural environment. They work both with skills they have acquired in school and their own personal skills. They express themselves using the limited skills they have mastered, but are also encouraged to acquire new ones. A real process of interaction (with schoolmates not participating in the workshop, and with their teachers) and stimulation is created. The children also learn to demystify the media; they learn that the media are accessible and can be used, and that they are tools for learning.

This pilot project, begun four years ago, is beginning to show results. It is reaching other schools and other children. The newspaper is starting to earn a name for itself. According to the teachers the children are much more interested in current events, and have become more curious and better able to express themselves. They are better able to put sentences together. These children may have become real readers.

The newspaper workshop is not the only activity developed by EDDs. Other EDDs offer activities to foster a love of reading amongst children. To this end they provide a reading centre (shelves, books, cushions) where children can read on their own, or where different reading activities can be organized. Staff members read out loud from books, tell stories, or ask children to tell stories they know or that their parents have told them. Children visit libraries to choose books or sit in on "story hour." Staff members can see children gradually being attracted to a book, borrowing it, and returning it after they have taken it home and shared it with their sisters or brothers.

The last few years have also seen the increased development of writing activities in EDDs. Children read as a way of learning, as an activity, as a way of developing their imagination, as a form of amusement. They write as a means of communication. Although schools and libraries have become important partners in this regard, there still remains much to be accomplished with parents.

In a few cases EDDs and adult literacy programs have been set up in the same centre. While the parents of children attending the EDD may only rarely take part in the literacy courses, it is worth noting that meetings between parents and the schools have been most successful at these centres.

The EDDs should therefore be encouraged since they provide an opportunity for meetings between staff members, children and parents who are illiterate or who have poor French literacy skills. Moreover, given the type of work they do, literacy instructors are perhaps better equipped to involve parents in discussions concerning the school.

NOTES

1. Coordination des écoles de devoirs et Lire et Écrire de Bruxelles. *Des parallèles qui se rejoignent... écoles de devoirs — groupes d'alphabétisation: quelles collaborations?* Brussels, 1989.

2. Fondation roi Baudouin, rue de Brederode 21, 1070 Brussels: *Approche cartographique des quartiers défavorisés de l'agglomération bruxelloise.* (This foundation supports projects that focus on various aspects of the quality of life, such as the environment and social exclusion.)

3. There are three school networks in Belgium: the central State, municipal and private school networks (the latter generally Catholic).

4. DEFIS: Association pour le developpement, l'emploi, la formation et l'insertion sociale; av. Clémenceau 10, 1070 Brussels. Created in 1982, this is an umbrella organization of local organizations, university centres, union organizations and the continuing education section of the social integration service of Brussels.

    In particular, DEFIS includes a literacy section, youth training projects, publications designed to circulate information and/or respond to teaching needs (*Défipresse*, a monthly magazine, etc.); and training/retraining programs.

5. Formation-Insertion-Jeunes, 12 rue de Rome, 1060 Brussels. "En Savoir Plus."

A METHODOLOGICAL MODEL FOR A LITERACY PROGRAM INVOLVING ADULTS AND PRESCHOOL CHILDREN

Anna Lorenzetto
University of Rome

A METHODOLOGICAL MODEL

A pilot project which will eventually serve as a model for a number of other projects must be "reproducible." A "reproducible" project is one that, inasmuch as possible, can be set up within existing structures, since the time and costs involved in creating superstructures for a given project are generally so prohibitive that reproducing the project on a large scale becomes unfeasible.

An education project, by its very nature, must use an innovative approach and aim to achieve creative results.

A project that is both innovative and reproducible must also be flexible in order to adapt to social, cultural and economic variables and thereby ensure that it can be tailored to the needs of students from various backgrounds. In short, a pilot project must be a methodological rather than a normative model.

With respect to structures, the literacy project for adults and preschool children, implemented in Sicily within the framework of Council of Europe Project No. 9, is geared to two types of educational services which come under the jurisdiction of the Ministry of Education: preschool education and adult literacy programs.

With respect to methodology, the originality of this project lies in the establishment of regular and harmonious relations between two levels of instruction that are significantly removed from one another. It was found that such relations lend themselves well to the modular and creative approach generally used in adult education programs.

The methodology of the project is innovative in that it focusses on "centres of interest" common to both adults and children. The teaching/learning strategies used must therefore be "bipolar," i.e., must address the needs of children and adults at their respective levels and take into account the different cultural makeup of the child and of the adult.

Using the same themes with both age groups not only encouraged the children and the adults to learn to relate to each other in new ways but also created a desire to learn. As well, the teachers became aware of the need to develop methods and strategies based not on the traditional breakdown of learning into subject areas but rather on a global problem-solving approach that would better meet the complex cultural needs of the adult learners.

Clearly, the main difficulty of such an undertaking lay in developing an appropriate methodology and in finding creative solutions to meet varied literacy needs. However, the challenge inherent to the undertaking also ensured the project's success not only in helping children and adults acquire reading skills, but also, on a larger scale, in encouraging the involvement of the neighbourhood, the community and the local administration.

Finally, with respect to flexibility, the Sicilian project, when considered as a nonnormative model, capitalizes on the similarity between preschool and adult education. Both use a wide range of methods, instruments and strategies that centre on the learner's relationship with the immediate environment and exploit his or her social and cultural background, work situation and dealings with administration or government bodies. The reason for capitalizing on these similarities is not to pool resources and materials but to maximize their effectiveness, in order to promote development, participation and experimentation.

As a result, the project takes on a much broader scope and comes to play an important role in the neighbourhood, in events affecting the community, in efforts to improve the quality of life and in local government decisions. Once it truly becomes part of the community, it may serve as a springboard for other adult education initiatives.

WHERE DO THE CHILDREN FIT IN?

The Ispica case study, which was conducted between 1975 and 1980 and served as the basis for the Sicilian project, started as a program aimed at ensuring the early deconditioning of preschool children living in a culturally underdeveloped area by offering parent education programs. In light of the various hypotheses and theories on the effectiveness of parent education programs as a compensatory measure for underprivileged children, especially those put forward by English and American researchers, the results of the Ispica case study may be considered positive. However, the study also demonstrated that the children's influence and cultural interests had a "deconditioning" effect on their parents as well, in a broader sense, i.e., socially, culturally and emotionally and with respect to their participation in the program.

In the Sicilian pilot project presented to the Council of Europe with the aim of establishing literacy centres in Avola, Floridia, Pozzallo, Scicli and Siracuse, we proposed to reverse the epistemological approach used in the Ispica case study and decondition parents through their children, while attempting to determine whether the bipolarity of this relationship could be extended to create other "multipolar" relationships by encouraging greater community participation.

The children's gradual discovery of the world and of the ways in which they interact with the people in their environment led adults to rediscover themselves and potential or long-lost relationships. In some cases, the parents relived happy moments of their childhood, unearthed their dreams and experienced anew the vivid emotions stirred by nature and the senses.

This was especially true for the women, who, in the Italian tradition, stay at home and have almost no outside contact. The program provided them, on the one hand, with a good reason to get out of the house — i.e., their children's education — and, on the other, with an opportunity to experience freedom and develop friendships and a feeling of solidarity with other women. In a survey conducted at a later stage in the program, these women said they wanted to enrol in vocational education programs in order to learn, make themselves useful and earn money.

Coming to the literacy centre also gives parents an opportunity to see their children evolve in a different context where the focus is on developing interests and acquiring new knowledge and skills. As the parents participate in discussions with the children and answer the children's questions, they become more attuned to establishing a timeless dialogue that bridges the generation gap to unite both young and old in a loving relationship.

Through this relationship with the children (who are not yet old enough to attend elementary school), the parents (who have little or no education) often rediscover their oral traditions, not only as an effective and valuable means of communication, or as a way of sharing their heritage and their difficulties in sketches and plays, but also as a valid approach to writing, knowledge, values and literature.

This project for children and adults, which encompasses a wide range of teaching/learning strategies, allows participants to piece together the fragmented time and space of life in the modern world in order to see the different stages of life — childhood, youth, adulthood and old age — as a single continuum, arousing in them the ageless desire to learn, the need to know, participate and decide, and the spontaneous urge to play and invent.

The importance of "play" in the learning process is confirmed by Schiller, who defined it as an expression of the aesthetic instinct through reciprocal stimulation of thought and emotion: "The animal works if its activity is motivated by the lack of something, and plays if it is motivated by the abundance of strength, that is, if the very exuberance of life stimulates it to action."

Unification of space: As the adults gradually come to feel at ease in the environment where classes are held as well as experiments, presentations, sketches, plays, games, meetings and discussions concerning health problems, problems at home, in the workplace, or in the community, they develop a sense of ownership and responsibility with respect to their own environment.

This is why we did not attempt to set specific learning goals at the beginning of the program, but rather chose to let the participants — children, adults and teachers — express their needs and expectations freely and find their own answers, according to their imagination and creativity.

Although known to specialists, the methods and strategies developed during the first year were unique in that they were for the most part improvised by the participants and inspired by the needs and situations they were experiencing and by local tradition and culture. Some were even the result of spontaneous creative insights.

As well, during the first year, in-service training was provided through a series of seminars, courses, meetings, visits and discussions, in order to provide teachers with better resources and to support their efforts, in which we were all involved. During the second year of the project, a pattern had already started to emerge: in the five literacy centres established in Sicily, discussions and activities focussed, albeit in different ways, on the participants' immediate environment, on the problems affecting their region and their community.

Local organizations and groups cannot remain indifferent to an initiative that is geared to a large segment of the adult population, that encourages participants not only to become more involved as individuals and as members of their community, but also to take interest in the events that affect their country and their quality of life. Indeed, the renewed will of citizens to play an active role in their government contributes to establishing the kind of healthy cooperation that is fundamental to a democratic way of life.

METHODOLOGY FOR SOCIOCULTURAL ANIMATION IN SPAIN'S UNDERPRIVILEGED RURAL AREAS

Thomas Diaz Gonzalez
University of Valladolid

Florentino Sanz Fernandez
National University
of Distance Education

This report presents conclusions drawn from 15 years (1970-1985) of research on popular education in rural Spain. Of all the popular education experiments conducted in Spain's underprivileged rural areas during this period of political transition, the "peasant farmers' school" is the most significant.

During the 1960s Spain's rural areas suffered from the loss of millions of individuals who emigrated to the cities (Sanchez Jimenez 1982), leaving behind pockets of rural poverty (Fernandez 1982). The same phenomenon occurred in all OECD countries and was interpreted as the effect of unbalanced development, i.e., of economic benefits having been allowed to take precedence over the interests of individuals (Alonso Hinojal 1980). In this context Avila's "peasant farmers' schools" are particularly relevant, and have been studied by the OECD and the Ministry of Education and Science (1980). This experiment reflects the general situation in rural areas of EEC and OECD countries.*

The popular education experiment conducted in Spain contributed to the implementation of political democracy (1978) in poor rural areas. For this reason the schools proved to be a concrete universal experience that can be used as a model for other experiences.

We would like to give an overview of the situation in the underprivileged rural areas of Spain and several other European countries. While poverty affects the economy, culture, and social fabric, we want to show that these rural areas can be enriched through cultural resources: culture is the means whereby rural areas can recover their identity and build a future.

Education provides true functional literacy training when the latter is defined as the "ability to read, write and calculate so that a person may engage in community activities where literacy is required for effective functioning. Personal growth and community development become an outgrowth of this functional literacy training" (Titmus 1979: 47).

---

*OECD: Organization for Economic Cooperation and Development
EEC: European Economic Community

This functioning is what interests us, although we will focus on sociocultural animation, which, as "used in the field of education, social work and community development,...is the stimulation of people to awareness of their own needs as a group, so that they define the nature of the needs, determine the means to satisfy these needs and act to do so...[It is] the body of social, recreational, cultural and educational activities, organized outside the formal school system for people of all ages, intended to improve the quality of life of a community" (Titmus: 36 and 39).

We have therefore applied the term "animation" to all those activities which consist in stimulating areas that are socially "dying." We will describe the concept as well as the stages in its implementation: starting point, methodology and outcome.

THE RURAL ENVIRONMENT

Using EEC classifications we will situate Spain's underprivileged rural areas within a larger context. Once we have determined the boundaries of these underprivileged areas we will describe the profile of the peasant farmers who live there, as this is what makes it possible to implement projects adapted to their needs and situation. The average peasant farmer does not live alone: he works on a farm or family work unit which must be defined and quantified so that we may understand its human and economic impact on Spanish society.

This rural Spanish environment must also be viewed in terms of the common agricultural policy (CAP); for this reason our discussion of underprivileged areas will focus on the mountain farming (MF) programs of Spain and Europe, programs which are slowly disappearing.

Small farms

The rural environment can be seen from one of three perspectives: by considering it merely in terms of agricultural production, by contrasting it with cities or by situating it within a global framework. We have chosen the latter view, which was described as follows by the EEC Rural Commission: "The term 'rural environment' implies more than mere geographic demarcation; it refers to an entire economic and social fabric encompassing a wide range of activities: farming, crafts production, small businesses, industries, trade and services. As a buffer zone and regeneration area the rural environment is indispensable to the ecological balance and is increasingly becoming an ideal place for recreation and relaxation" (EEC Rural Commission 1988: 28), [Free translation].

This global perspective of the rural environment applies well to the rural communities which are the focus of our study. The EEC Rural Commission distinguishes three types of farming for the future:

— The first type, resulting from the "**pressure of modern development**," is found in rural regions that fringe large cities. In Spain this type of farming is represented by the large-scale farming operations in the central and southern regions of the country; these are companies which quickly replaced their labour force with machines and which produce large quantities of goods.

— The second type consists of **intensive family businesses**, which have been converted to adapt to market demands.

— The third type comprises **small family farms**, which are economically insignificant in Spain despite the large number of individuals involved.

In this study we will examine the type of education needed to animate the people who work on small farms. To draw up an appropriate training plan we must describe the target population from a sociological standpoint. According to Sevilla Guzman "the peasant farmer belongs to the social sector made up of family production and consumption units; this sector is a sociological observation unit in which various groups and communities coexist. The characteristics of the social relationship structure constitute a basic criterion for delimiting the observation units in which peasant farmers live. The peasant culture, a product of these types of social relationships, is basically the most characteristic feature of the peasant farmer" (1979: 25-26), [Free translation].

The types of relationships that exist between members of rural communities, i.e., the way in which their culture deals with the world, are an important key to understanding those who work on small farms. In this respect Regidor (1977) accurately described the situation of small farmers and part-time agricultural workers.

According to Spain's 1982 census farm ownership can be broken down as follows:

— 40.8 percent of inhabitants own less than 2 hectares,

— 22.1 percent own between 2 and 5 hectares,

— 24.6 percent own between 5 and 10 hectares,

— 9.5 percent own between 10 and 20 hectares,

— 1.3 percent own over 20 hectares.

In short 87.5 percent of the farming population operate small family farms and own a mere 18.2 percent of Spain's farmland, while 12.4 percent of the farming population own big estates and 81.8 percent of the farmland (Aganzo 1988: 6).

Although small family farms do not carry much weight in the rural economy they do represent a considerable social strength, particularly among the people who have suffered most from the consequences of unbalanced development.

The Mountain Farming Act

The Spanish government began to turn its attention to underprivileged areas in 1970: various laws and ministerial orders deal with poverty-stricken areas. In 1982 the government passed Bill 25/1982 on mountain farming (BOE 10-7-82), which took preliminary steps towards adapting agrarian structures in anticipation of the EEC membership treaty to be signed in Madrid in 1985. The Mountain Farming Act gives a legal voice to the rural region which has been marginalized for many years.

Since 1960 internal migrations to Madrid, Barcelona and the Basque Provinces have detrimentally affected 19 provinces. The immigrants are peasant farmers primarily from Andalusia, Extremadura, Galicia and both Castiles. As a result of these migrations Spain can now be divided into two parts: the rich Spain, which receives immigrants, and the poor, which is losing its population.

The average national population density was approximately 67 inhabitants/km^2 in 1970. Of Spain's provinces,

— 20 have a population density higher than the national average;

— 30 do not have a population density equal to the national average; of these provinces, 19 show signs of total desertion.

The "death" of the rural environment

Based on many years of day-to-day observation we have been able to identify a series of causes which underlie the aging of small villages and the emigration of their young people:

— Peasant farmers who inhabit small villages with a traditional mentality were overwhelmed by historical changes for which they were not prepared.

— Emigration in recent years is the highest in the history of Spain.

— Economic development in OECD countries has benefited large privileged areas at the expense of other areas and has left huge pockets of poverty.

— The ultimate aims and meaning of the development process have been lost (Baron 1971, Sender 1977 and Delibes 1987).

These general interpretations are supported by tangible proof in the small villages. For example:

— Traditional industries do not produce competitive goods and cannot compete with other types of industries which produce less expensive goods of higher quality (Gorosquieta 1973).

— Schools are closed in small villages, resulting in social rupture and a loss of identity for the inhabitants (Carmena and Regidor 1984, Grande and Rodriguez 1981).

— Family relationships have changed.

An explanation for the general poverty can be found in this society's simple outlook, which did not equip it to cope with major changes. A simple outlook is one which, subjected to reality, does not perceive causes or the links between causes and consequences, and therefore sees reality as static (Ecumenical Institute for the Development of Peoples 1978: 41), [Free translation]. It is this outlook or mentality which must serve as the starting point for change in the rural environment.

Mountain farming areas in the EEC

Agriculture in Spain today can be discussed only within the context of the common agrarian policy. The following data help situate Spain within this larger context and indicate that Spain has the largest mountain farming program:

COUNTRIES	Agricultural area in use (AAU) (1000 ha)		Country's total AAU in mountain areas (%)	Weight of country's mountain farming areas (%)	Weight of country's AAU (%)
	Classified as mountain areas	Country's total			
Germany	351.5	12 196	2.9	1.6	12.2
France	4 341.9	31 069	14.0	20.1	31.2
Italy	5 164.2	16 537	31.2	23.9	16.6
Greece	4 978.8	9 251	53.8	23.0	9.3
Spain	5 937.2	27 304	21.7	27.4	24.4
Portugal	854.6	3 234	26.4	4.0	3.3
Total	21 628.2	99 591	21.7	100.0	100.0

Source: Varios 1987.

In short, underprivileged rural areas inhabited by a large number of people have become a recognized focus of attention in Europe. During International Literacy Year, initiated for the new illiterates who have been forgotten by history, the rural environment in wealthy countries constitutes a subject for study.

CULTURE AS A DEVELOPMENT TOOL

Because of massive emigration and desertion the underprivileged areas discussed in this paper are showing signs of dying. Recovery and development must take root in and spring from culture, which has not waned in these areas despite the poverty. Our analysis of the types of culture that exist in rural societies may be outlined as follows:

Culture as the acquisition of knowledge (educated culture)	Culture as a lifestyle (cultural culture)	Culture as the creation of a personal and collective destiny (constructive culture)
Focus on knowledge Enlightened learning	Focus on the past Unconscious adaptation	Formulation of future plans Conscious anticipation

Each of these models contains a seed for cultural renewal (Ander Egg 1987: 19-22).

Culture as the acquisition of knowledge (educated culture)

Despite their problems underprivileged rural areas have a great heritage which can be described as follows:

— An **economic heritage**: crafts are made using skills handed down from generation to generation (Sanchez de la Fuente 1987).

— A **corporate heritage**: collective organizations have supported community work (e.g., irrigation community); small cooperatives have a definite status and a long history (A. Nieto 1964).

— A **heritage of beliefs**: religion and beliefs are the only means of interpreting life (Moreno Navarro 1972).

— An **ecological heritage**: although lacking technology and modern organizations the rural region does boast areas of great natural wealth such as rivers, mountains and abandoned trails; the rural tourist industry is beginning to develop this heritage, which is increasingly appreciated (V. Bote Gomez 1988).

— A **heritage of history and festivals**: the past continues to live in the rural memory; peasant farmers keep the memory of saints and "heros" alive by means of festivals; these memories help them to interpret history (Caro Baroja 1975).

Underprivileged rural areas contain amazing wealth that humanity cannot afford to lose. This so-called "traditional" culture stems from roots on which the development of these socially poor but culturally wealthy areas must be based. To attain true cultural development and not merely preserve cultural artifacts we should adopt the principles of cultural democracy which Ander Egg (1987: 51), corroborating the work of the Council of Europe, describes as follows:

— Animation activities must foster the most extensive cultural participation processes possible.

— The organizer acts as a catalyst, helping to establish a cultural revitalization process.

— Peasant farmers who live in underprivileged areas are not passive recipients; they are active players and participants.

The cultural models outlined above may be widely applied in underprivileged areas where, once the process of cultural revitalization is under way, it will be possible to formulate plans for the future.

Culture as a lifestyle (cultural culture)

This cultural model, whose origins can be found primarily in Anglo-Saxon anthropology, consists of "a group of traits which characterize the various forms of life through a series of objects and ways of thinking which are created and transmitted by men as a result of mutual relationships and working relations" (Ander Egg 1987: 22), [Free translation]. In this model, culture is used to interpret changes in society and thereby serves as a means to assimilate such changes.

To interpret life and history societies must be able to maintain a creative process whereby they are constantly renewed. This is the definition of "cultural identity" given by the Mexico City conference on cultural policies (Ander Egg 1987: 39). The significant traits of this cultural identity are historical memory, a sense of belonging and the freedom to plan the future of the group.

These traits are not widely apparent in underprivileged rural areas; major changes have not been analyzed and the exodus of human and economic resources has left the land deserted. Underprivileged rural areas lack a strong cultural identity; peasant farmers, living in an outmoded traditional environment, are solicited by a world which for them does not yet exist. Inhabitants of these poverty-stricken areas live in despair. Oscar Lewis' idea of a "culture of poverty" (1961) is very helpful in trying to understand the situation of people in these areas.

Culture as the creation of a personal and collective destiny (constructive culture)

Culture does not merely have a role in terms of the past (preservation of historical roots) or the present (interpretation of events); it must also play a role in the definition of outlooks for the future. This view of constructive culture is typical of living and dynamic cultures. "A living culture is one which, without losing its sense of the past, transposes its living traditions to the present and is capable of changing and moving forward. A culture's vitality expresses itself in the capacity to incorporate new outlooks and new demands using collective traditions shaped by the national and folk culture" (Ander Egg 1981: 21), [Free translation].

This cultural model is essential in our era. Several authors, including Lorente Medina (1974) and Marin Ibanez (1980), have described the criteria for social creativity as follows: sensitivity to the problems of others; receptiveness to new ideas; mobility or the capacity to adapt. The capacity to adopt new forms relies on the following aspects of culture:

— Culture as the creation of a personal destiny: this involves formulating personal goals, or creating ideals which incorporate material drawn from history and society; this is especially important for people who must develop and organize collective activities.

— Culture as the creation of a group destiny: there have been many books written on the birth of groups. A group is a living entity distinct from the individuals who represent its various parts (Ramirez 1983, Limbos 1979).

— Culture as a tool for regional development: Switzerland studied this aspect of culture during its regional planning (Guller 1981), and the Council of Europe incorporated the results of these studies into its cultural dynamics and regional development program (Bassand 1982). Endogenous regional development is defined by Bassand as the "process by which the inhabitants of a region refuse to systematically imitate outside models ill-suited to their problems and aspirations, and take their adaptation to the world and their future development into their own hands, by devising a plan that reflects their own characteristics and culture" [Free translation].

Culture appears to be a major springboard for the implementation of an endogenous development model suited to each community in underprivileged areas and calling for the use of local resources and the participation of local inhabitants. This is the most appropriate model for Spain's underprivileged rural areas.

SOCIOCULTURAL ANIMATION AS A REVITALIZATION METHOD

The dying and poverty-stricken rural environment has been dubbed "underdeveloped," which means that this zone has not developed as required to maintain a standard of life equal to that of inhabitants in other regions. The goal for this environment is to attain a certain level of endogenous integrated development. Culture is the chief means by which to encourage citizens to participate in the process of transforming poverty into a new and enriching life. The nature of this action is described below.

Sociocultural animation

Sociocultural animation (SCA) is the process of revitalizing culture in a society whose cultural models resemble those presented above. SCA is a dynamic action that stimulates institutions and social organizations, while eliciting the involvement of all the elements that make up the social fabric. In short we see sociocultural animation as the process of reinfusing a culture with life.

The cultural animation of underprivileged rural areas consists in recovering the cultural resources (economic, social, religious and natural) specified above under the educated culture model. These resources are the cornerstones on which future plans can be built. The key to a new life is to formulate plans in which the inhabitants feel involved and will participate. They must be brought to understand that a better life is possible, that such a life depends on them and that they must devote their efforts to achieving it (constructive culture). The formulation of plans for the future requires that the community discover its identity and create a network of relationships which will provide it with the strength to carry the plans through.

This dynamic vision of animation comprises three phases:

— A starting point — becoming familiar with the situation and planning measures which answer the question: Where are we going?

— Educational activities which will make it possible to arrive at the targeted goal — setting forth various means and methods which facilitate cultural development in underprivileged areas. The question for this phase is: will the means we have chosen lead to the desired end?

— Cultural development — the end product of this whole process. This phase will see an answer to the question: How will we know if the animation has been effective?

Cultural development has a place within the larger context of social, educational and community development. To reinforce the cultural fabric such development requires the cooperation of the various cultural networks which unify experiences, while respecting the autonomy of the culture. An integrated sociocultural movement must be initiated, as this will create a climate of hope in these underprivileged areas.

The starting point

The implementation of an animation project in underprivileged rural areas involves a whole series of activities.

1. **Planning**: Since all activities must be planned to ensure greater effectiveness in the search for alternatives in rural areas without hope, the overall development project must be studied down to the tiniest detail. (Ander Egg 1983, UNESCO 1979, Kaufman 1973 and Marcello 1973 have all discussed this.)

2. **Using local resources**: Development in areas that lack human and financial resources but boast a whole range of other resources requires a detailed study of the latter:

   — Certain areas have unused or underdeveloped resources; more efficient management of production and marketing could generate wealth.

   — Social needs must be satisfied.

   — The population has assets of which people have always been aware and which can be used to improve the quality of life and mobilize major sectors (Goezt Le Compte 1988).

3. **Qualified leaders**: Qualified and motivated leaders are needed to mobilize the resources in poverty-stricken areas. They may be categorized as follows:

   — volunteers who are already working in these areas for political, social or religious reasons;

   — teachers working on specific projects and who become involved in community development experiments;

   — coordinators who form the link between the various community experiments and other governmental institutions (Lopez Ceballos and Salas Larrazabal 1987).

4. **Content**: The content of an animation project must address areas of interest identified through research and must meet the expressed needs of the population. Development can be qualified as integrated when it incorporates all economic, social, political, religious and environmental considerations.

5. **Objectives**: To be successful an animation project in poverty-stricken areas must have utopic objectives which contrast sharply with the poverty of the area. To counter great poverty and lack of vitality (apathy, powerlessness) motivation tactics must be effective enough to mobilize a hesitant population (Monclus Estella 1987). The utopic vision must be clearly described and future plans must be formulated on the individual, group and regional levels.

   In the case of peasant farmers' schools these objectives are summarized by the expression: "To be a peasant farmer is one day to attain happiness on this land" (Diaz Gonzalez 1983), [Free translation].

6. **Creativity**: Creativity is the key objective of sociocultural animation. If apathy is a sign of death, then activity and creativity are signs of life. Creativity means making it easier for people to participate in experiences which will improve their lives. These group work experiences, whose underlying goal is to raise consciousness, consist in transforming the participants' simple outlook into critical awareness (Ecumenical Institute for the Development of Peoples 1987).

These aspects of the animation project constitute informal educational activities adapted to community development purposes.

Educational action

Sociocultural animation is held to be the means by which a community can be motivated and its members brought from a state of apathy and incohesiveness to the point where they will work together towards a common goal. The implementation of animation activities requires special methodologies.

1. **Human relationships in the educational process**: It is a very lengthy process to help the inhabitants shift from their traditional attitude of indifference and noncommitment to one of receptiveness to new values and involvement in public affairs. It means changing the deep-seated attitudes of an aging population which does not have a long life expectancy and does not willingly become involved in actions requiring great effort.

   Given this situation organizers must devise a plan that will motivate the inhabitants and must establish emotional ties and lines of communication that will shore up structural deficiencies within the rural community. This population is traditionally mistrustful, full of successive disappointments and unfulfilled dreams. A large number of inhabitants believe they are condemned to live and die without hope and desire only that their children will have a better life by finding a job in the city, far from their place of origin.

   When peasant farmers are presented with a revitalization project and told that "to be a peasant farmer is one day to attain happiness on this land," they turn their back on the whole idea. One by one, however, they gradually begin to believe that perhaps one day this will come true.

2. **Projects based on farmers' concerns**: Peasant farmers can be interested in projects that are based on what they know and compensate for their negative experiences. They need to prove to themselves and to their neighbours that what they do contributes to their immediate happiness. By carrying out small projects it is possible to build a program adapted to the activities of small rural communities.

   The participatory teaching method is highly useful with respect to education in these rural areas (Planchard 1987).

3. **Methodological alternatives**: Methodology should alternate between the inductive or ascending approach and the deductive or descending. The inductive approach should preferably comprise the following phases:

— Presentation of a concrete case: a real situation, drawn from daily life, is studied by the group, which must be able to identify with this situation.

— Universalization: the concrete case is stripped of details, leaving only the essential values.

— Analysis: the causes and consequences of the situation are examined and the inherent values and action models are identified. An attempt is made to transform the community's simple outlook into critical awareness (Freire) by viewing the situation in a larger context with respect to the economic, social, political, religious and environmental implications.

— Development of theory application models to solve the problem: if effective, sociocultural animation in "problem" areas should lead to the solution of the problems. The incidence of change in living conditions is a measure of the validity of the teaching method used with the peasant farmers.

— Information: for this analysis, the peasant farmers will need certain information which must be obtained through the deductive or descending approach.

— Creation of organizational frameworks: the process ends with the creation of organizational frameworks which will support the community in solving the problems studied.

All of these activities, which are found in the informal education models used in community development, are compatible with the programs of the Council of Europe (Council of Europe 1987), with OECD programs such as the education and local development program (Alonso Hinojal and Fuente Salvador 1980) and with UNESCO programs (UNESCO 1980).

Development: the ultimate objective

Development is the ultimate aim of sociocultural animation. In a general way, and more specifically in relation to human beings, development may be defined as "an action which focusses on and satisfies basic human needs with a view to ensuring self-sufficiency and an organic interaction between human beings, nature and technology, between global processes and local organizations, between personal relationships and community relationships, between planning and self-direction, between community life and the state. Human needs, self-sufficiency and organic relationships are the underpinnings of development on a human scale" (Hormrell and Nord Berg 1986: 4), [Free translation].

1. **Cultural development** (Ander Egg 1987) is a condition for achieving integrated development. A sign of this development is the search for cultural identity. This development is not the province of the state, but is open to all public and private initiatives and institutions. Cultural development and continuing education have been the two key pillars of the Council of Europe (Junoy 1979).

2. Cultural development is part of an **integrated development framework** (Valcarcel 1987) and is characterized by several distinctive features:

   — It involves endogenous development, i.e., development which draws on local resources while also accepting outside assistance.

   — The local community is actively involved in its own social transformation (Vazquez Barquero 1988). The OECD (1984) has established local job initiatives.

   — It resembles community development, which is viewed as the result of the process or as the process itself. The goal is to enhance the life of the entire community through the active participation of its members (Garcia Linaza 1982).

3. The organization of cultural development requires the **ordering of society through networks**. The organizational formula for establishing networks within the framework of adult education experiments under community development projects has been used within the Council of Europe since the implementation of Program No. 9 (1982-1986) (Fernandez 1985).

   Some features of the network set up by the Spanish Ministry of Education foster dynamic cultural development. They include:

   — the large number of participating institutions;

   — the wide-ranging topics of investigation;

   — the variety of professionals involved: staff includes civil servants from the ministries of education and labour, as well as volunteers.

4. The ultimate purpose of cultural development is to implement an **integrated cultural movement**. Social movements are collective efforts to bring about change in social institutions and to create a totally new order (R. Heberle 1979).

All movements rest on two pillars: the masses and the minorities. The masses are an essential factor in a movement for structural change, but all movements are supported by elite groups who are familiar with the "mystique" and are able to apply it to specific contexts.

Development, as an expression and sign of revitalization in areas which have been radically disadvantaged as a result of unbalanced development, attempts to carve out a role for the inhabitants within the context of a new society.

CONCLUSION

On the occasion of International Literacy Year we wanted to draw attention to underprivileged rural areas, a field which we feel warrants further study. Our paper can be summarized as follows:

There are poverty-stricken rural areas in Spain and in the wealthy countries of the Northern Hemisphere which are the product of development which focusses uniquely on economic benefits while ignoring the situation of the people who have traditionally farmed these lands.

These areas are socially poor, yet boast great cultural wealth. Modern society cannot lose these ecological assets and traditional products without losing values which are necessary to restoring an integrated quality of life.

Traditional culture cannot be recovered unless we facilitate the lives of those who have been the guardians of this culture and still maintain its values.

Many of the people who have remained in these areas are functionally illiterate. In this context education must take the form of sociocultural animation which revitalizes the peasant culture by interpreting it and according it an active role in history.

The description of this methodological process may serve as a guide for projects in other marginalized areas of poverty.

REFERENCES

Aganzo, A. *Lo rural en nuestro pais: Una aproximación.* Madrid: Cáritas, 1988.

Alonso Hinojal and Fuente Salvador. *Seminario de Barco de Avila sobre educación no formal de adultos para el desarrollo rural.* Paris: OCDE, Madrid: MEC, 1980.

Alonso, Ponga. *Teatro Popular.* Valladolid: Diputación de Valladolid, 1986.

Ander Egg, E. *Introducción a la Planificación.* Buenos Aires: Humanitas, 1983.

Ander Egg, E. *Léxico de Animación Sociocultural.* Buenos Aires: Humanitas, 1987.

Baron, E. *El final del campesinado.* Madrid: Zyx, 1971.

Barrenechea, E. "Las dos Españas" in *Informaciones* (2-3-74). Madrid, 1974.

Bassand, P. *Le développement régional endogène — Idées, ambiguïtés, espoirs.* IREC Lausanne, 1982.

B.O.E. *Ley 25/1982 sobre Agricultura de Montaña,* Madrid, 10-7-1982.

Bote Gomez, V. *Turismo en españa rural* (Rehabilitación del patrimonio sociocultural y de la economía local). Madrid: Popular, 1988.

Carmena and Regidor. *La escuela en el medio rural.* Madrid, MEC, 1984.

Caro Baroja. "Santos y Campesinos" in *Cuadernos para el dialogo.* Madrid, March 1975.

Commission rurale (CEE). *L'avenir du monde rural.* Com. (88) 501 Final, Brissels-CEE, 1988.

Council of Europe. *Conférence "Education des adultes et développement communautaire."* (Rapport) Strasbourg: Council of Europe, 1987.

Delibes, M. *Un mundo que agoniza.* Barcelona: Plaza y Janés, 1987.

Diaz, J. *Guía de Romances.* Valladolid: Diputación de Valladolid, 1987.

Diaz Gonzalez, T. "La cultura como instrumento de recuperación de la identidad perdida" in *Laicado,* No. 62 (1983), Madrid.

Fernandez Fernandez. *Bolsas rurales de pobreza.* Madrid: Cares, 1982.

Fernandez Fernandez. *Hipótesis de una Red Española de Iniciativas Locales de Educación de Adultos y Desarrollo Comunitario.* Madrid: MEC, 1985.

Furter, P. *Educación y reflexión.* Montevideo: Nueva Visión, 1983.

Fustier, *Pratique de la créativité.* 4th edition. Paris: E.S.F., 1985.

Garcia Linaza. *Crisis, política económica y participación.* Malaga: Universidad, 1982.

Goetz Le Compte. *Etnografía y diseño cualitativo de la investigación educativa.* Madrid: Morata, 1988.

Gorosquieta, J. *El campo español en crisis.* Bilbao: Mensajero, 1973.

Gorosquieta, J. *Economía de la explotacíon agropecuaria.* Bilbao: Mensajero, 1975.

Grande Rodriguez. *Escuela Rural*. Granada: Popular, 1981.

Gulher, Ed. *La Suisse et le pari regional*. Lugano-Porza: Verlai, 1981.

Harmurell and Nord Berg. *Desarrollo a escala humana (Una opción para el futuro)*. Uppsala, Sweden: CEPAUR, 1986.

Herbele, R. "Movimientos sociales" in *Enciclopedia Internacional de Ciencias Sociales*. Madrid: Aguilar, 1979.

Hoyos Sainz, (Coord.) *Manual de folklore (La vida tradicional en España)*. Madrid: Istuo, 1985.

Inodep. *Experiencias de concientización*. Madrid: Marsiega, 1978.

Jundy. *La cooperación intergubernamental, cultural y educativa en el marco del Consejo de Europa (1949-1978)*. Madrid: MEC, 1979.

Kaufman. *Planificación de sistenas educativos*. Mexico: Trillas, 1973.

Lewis, O. *Antropología de la pobreza*. Mexico: Fondo de Cultura Económica, 1961.

Limbos, *Como animar un grupo*. Madrid: Marsiega, 1979.

Lorente Medina. *Directrices actuales de la educación*. Madrid: Universidad Politécnica, 1974.

Lopez Ceballos and Salas Larrazabal. *Formación de animadores y dinámicas de formación*. Madrid: Popular, 1987.

Marin Ibarez. *La creatividao*. Barcelona: CEAC, 1980.

Merelo. *Perspectiva, teoría y práctica*. Buenos Aires: Guadalupe, 1983.

Monclus Estella. *Didáctica y planificación de la educación, Utopía y praxis*. Barcelona: Humanitas, 1987.

Moreno Navarro, J. *Propiedad, clases sociales y hermandades en la baia Andalucía. La estructura social de un pueblo del Aljarafe*. Madrid: Siglo XXI, 1972.

Nieto, A. *Bienes comunales*. Madrid: Revista de Derecho Privado, 1964.

O.C.D.E. *Iniciativas locales para la creación de empleo*. Madrid: Ministerio de Trabajo y Seguridad social, 1984.

Planchard, E. *Pedagogía contemporánea*. 7th edition. Madrid: Rialp, 1987.

Ramirez, Mª S. *Dinámica de grupo y animación sociocultural*. Madrid: Marsiega, 1983.

Regidor, J.C. *¿Qué es la reforma agraria?* Barcelona: Gaya Ciencia, 1977.

Rids Rodicio. *La agricultura Castellano-Leonesa ante la integración en la Comunidad Económica Europea*. Valladolid: Simancas, 1983.

Sanchez Jimenez. *Del campo a la ciudad*. Madrid: Salvat, 1982.

Sanchez de la Fuente. *Estudio de la judía de Barco de Avila*. Salamanca: Centro de Edafología y Biología Aplicada, 1987.

Sender, R.J. *Requien por un campesino español*. Barcelona: Destino, 1977.

Sevilla Guzman. *Evolución del campesinado.* Barcelona: Península, 1979.

Suarez Inclan. *El patrimonio histórico artístico en Castilla-León.* Burgos: Consejo de Castilla-León, 1982.

Titmus, Ed. *Terminología de la educación de adultos.* Paris: UNESCO, 1989.

UNESCO, *Métodos y objetivos de la planificación cultural.* Madrid: Ministerio de Cultura, 1979.

Vazquez Barquero. *Desarrollo local.* Madrid: Pirámide, 1988.

Varios. *Política socioestructural en zonas de Agricultura de Montaña en España y en la CEE.* Madrid: MAPA, 1987.

COMPUTERS AND LITERACY:
THE LABO PROJECT

Jean-Louis Berterreix
LABO, Bayonne

> Although the electronic media as a whole may make
> some people illiterate, they can be important tools
> for making others literate. [1]

This paper describes a five-year project conducted on the Basque coast of France by a team of professionals and volunteers working with groups of youths and adults in need of basic literacy and numeracy training.

This project is currently supported by an association which, to ensure lasting work, opened the LABO training centre (Laboratoire d'apprentissage de base par ordinateur*). The association also makes every effort to establish or promote satellite projects under various social assistance programs.

Seven employees and 30 volunteers work full time for the association, whose originality lies partly in the use of microcomputers for teaching basic skills, with the aim of enabling participants to develop self-teaching strategies.

This paper describes LABO's computer-assisted teaching program. We will see how LABO was created, outline the underlying theory and discuss the advantages and limitations of computer-assisted teaching, along with its implications for both the instructor and the learner.

A PROJECT IS BORN

From 1985 until September 1987 microcomputers were used to teach 106 undereducated adults living in a shelter in Bayonne. The four-storey 90-bed shelter houses adult males who meet the criteria given below. The length of stay is six months, renewable if the social reintegration process, which is the aim of this type of institution, is under way. Accommodation is paid by the ministère des Affaires sociales.

The men in the shelter find it difficult to maintain a self-sufficient mode of existence, a problem which manifests itself in their lack of a fixed

---

* Computerized basic skills laboratory

address or adequate means of support. Their reasons for seeking shelter are many and varied (family breakdown, former wards of the State, long-standing unemployment, delinquency, job failure, alcohol, drug addiction, etc.); despite their backgrounds, most have not become vagabonds.

The pattern of these men's lives is as intricate as the countless interwoven threads of a spider web, with painful experiences glimpsed in the gaps and tears of a pattern damaged in the struggle to stay alive. For the luckier residents, finding a steady job and establishing a happy relationship with a new girlfriend — a factor essential to putting down roots — may lead to renting an apartment and gradually reintegrating into the local social fabric.

These men have suffered too much from the negative aspects of society, have too often been victims of the selective marginalization it produces, have too often felt they were failures — the dregs of humanity — to accept all the restrictions imposed by a "normal" social life. Their loneliness is no doubt too deep to be cured by a paycheque, a woman, an apartment or a ballot paper. They need a presence, communicative warmth and a socially accepted, valid reason for living. But, like a butterfly burnt by the flame, they are no longer able to experience ties and love without instinctively suspecting they are being manipulated or subjugated.

Unemployment and illiteracy

When these men did work, they often took temporary jobs or short-term contracts for which no official qualifications were required. Beginning around 1975 these were the first workers to find themselves in the street as a result of the growing unemployment caused by industrial and technological change. It was then, when they found themselves forced to cope with joblessness (their new social status) and obliged to report to various agencies, that another cause of their dependency emerged: their failure to master basic communication skills made it difficult for them to understand coded administrative messages, express themselves orally, write correctly or understand the social system.

An internal survey showed that 40 percent of these shelter residents fell within the usual French definition of "functional illiterate," i.e., they did not have a basic practical mastery of reading, writing or arithmetic, although they had attended school.

Ignorant and uneducated?

I would like to state clearly that this lack of basic skills is not synonymous with "uneducated" or "ignorant." When we interviewed these men in 1979[2] we found that they were able to make subtle distinctions between education and knowledge, learning and experience, curiosity, encyclopedic knowledge and culture:

Being educated, intelligent...the ability to assimilate, to relate to the history of your people, the arts,
music, the value of work. I think that, for me, that's
all culture; it doesn't mean you have to have diplomas. Jean Marc (p. 150)

Social conditions and culture are clearly related.
You usually find more cultured people among the
higher classes. Philippe (p. 183)

Oral culture:

Culture is what I am learning, what I want to learn.
Some guys at the shelter have helped me learn things
I didn't know. Culture also comes from contact with
others. Jean Michel (p. 178)

Contrary to what a lot of people think, a bar isn't
only a place to go and get drunk. Why? Because the
bar is the poor man's club. You meet your friends
from the neighbourhood, you exchange ideas, discuss things, the news, this and that. It keeps you up-
to-date. It's the neighbourhood paper. It's a place
where all kinds of things are exchanged, even culture. (p. 130)

Education and culture:

It's true that education is the basis of culture, but
there are other things like intelligence and savoir
vivre that are very important, almost more important. Raoul (p. 182)

Culture is a combination of general and personal
knowledge that has very little to do with education.
Jean Marc (p. 143)

If you don't have a diploma, forget it! Everybody
thinks you're a fool, and nearly every door gets
slammed in your face. Albert (p. 150)

Maybe our society judges a man's worth by his
diplomas. Jean Michel (p. 179)

The problem with society is that the most important
requirement is education. People are trained, and it

all has to be made official by stupid exams. Personally I find it ridiculous. You'd be just as well off to
learn the encyclopedia by heart. Frédéric (p. 148)

Experience, adjustment and culture:

If you learn about life, you learn about culture. But
you can't learn about culture until you have learned
about life. It's impossible. And today it's just the
opposite, because parents and the government tell
you to do it that way. René (p. 121)

I tell myself I'm not necessarily inferior to others
because I didn't enjoy school or get a good education. Maturity comes with age. Jean Michel (p. 179)

Culture is each person's way of adjusting to all kinds
of situations. Philippe (p. 179)

Towards a solution

The initial experiment in computer-assisted training was conducted
at the shelter at the request of and with the collaboration of the residents.
Many of them had failed psychological and technical screening tests and
were not eligible for diploma programs run by the ministère du Travail et
de l'Emploi.

This first computerized training project, which is described in detail
in a separate report, [3] was implemented by a small team made up of one
social worker, one resident (an inspired computer buff) and two volunteer
teachers. Eight months after the first configuration was purchased, the first
module had six computers.

For a nine-month period beginning in October 1987 this teaching
method was used intensively with 26 youths aged 18 to 25 enrolled in a
job preparation program and an individualized teaching workshop. These
unemployed youths, of whom three-quarters were from Bayonne and other
cities in the area, were paid to take this training.

In May 1988, with the support of the GPLI (Groupe interministériel
permanent de lutte contre l'illettrisme), a new association was formed in
response to requests from local and regional partners. Its stated aim is to
"promote the use of microcomputers by youths and adults in difficulty,
with a view to facilitating their social and occupational integration."

Since November 1988, 105 learners between the ages of 16 and 42 have attended LABO, the association's new training centre. The characteristics of these learners are described in greater detail below.

WHY COMPUTERS?

Our decision to use the microcomputer as a teaching tool was based on observation of this population group and the identification of certain behavioural tendencies:

— Their incomplete sentences, confusion when speaking, confusion about time, constant use of narration, memory gaps, inability to do abstract reasoning and reduction of thought to binary expression were possible indications of incoherence and instrumental deficiencies in the reasoning process.

Our teaching method would have to entail individual reflection and a restructuring of these modes of expression, without being merely therapeutic.

— Psychological needs are usually a dominant feature in relationships with these youths and adults.

We had to ensure that this would not disrupt the learner's ability to concentrate and assimilate, or the teacher's ability to transmit knowledge.

— The cultural identity of these men, based on fragmentary knowledge, a multiplicity of initiatory experiences, moral values built on resourcefulness or avoidance, the burying of failures and the development of a derisory self-image was such that they in fact formed a subculture characterized by individuality, isolation and the absence of meaningful identification with any specific social group.

What then should be the content of our program?

— The men in our learning group were allergic to, bored by or antagonistic towards anything resembling a sheet of paper or a book. Their school careers were marked by memories of the school's refusal and rejection of nonacademic aptitudes or abilities, and of the use of reading and writing for the sole purpose of controlling knowledge acquisition. They had failed to discover that reading and writing are merely tools, aids or techniques used for communication and cultural enrichment.

It seemed evident that our program could not be based on traditional teaching methods.

In fact three teaching experiments, all involving traditional methods, had been conducted at this shelter with this type of group. The following excerpts from reports on these attempts confirm what we have said above:

> The relationship was based solely on instruction. Instruction is necessary and should therefore be considered useful. In the workshops, however, it was virtually nonexistent. Teaching was difficult. To create a favourable atmosphere the instructor's efforts would have to be supported by a socioeducational team. (Volunteer, philosophy teacher, 1980)

> Inconsistent effort and difficulty working alone. Need for 90-minute periods of individual instruction because of the differences in level and problems in learner relationships. Strong negative rivalry in the group, increasingly difficult to manage. (Teacher, 1983)

OUR WORKING HYPOTHESES

In 1984 we suggested setting up a computerized training program. Our initial hypotheses were as follows:

An intermediary in the teaching relationship

By introducing the microcomputer as the chief teaching aid and by placing these youths and adults on their own, face-to-face with the screen and the keyboard, we hoped to offer a strategy that would help them overcome the shame of their failures or personal limitations.

In using computers, an emotionally neutral activity which is nonetheless amusing and bolsters the ego, we hoped to avoid the learners' rejection of everything that reminded them of school, while circumscribing their need for affection from the instructor.

A meaningful learning experience

We also felt that it was essential to create a situation in which each individual would feel obliged to "learn how to learn" with the means placed at his disposal, a situation in which mistakes would no longer earn either approval or ridicule, but would actually fuel the learning process.

It seemed to us that the computer would allow each person to progress at his own speed, rather than being forced to keep pace with the group or pitch his abilities against those of other students in trying to understand, remember or assimilate the subject matter.

Computerized file handling offered the flexibility that was indispensable to the use and development of the learners' personal histories, knowledge and experience-based vocabulary. The computer would provide each student with a self-teaching strategy based on the use of his own language and thought processes.

Self-directed training

We wondered if the computer's passivity and the evaluation of work through printouts would not help the participants overcome the attitude of blaming their failure on others. If a learner sat with folded arms in front of the computer it would make no difference to the work done by others or to the instructor's mood. Recognizing the choice between switching off his mind and using it to check his work gives the individual independent control over the training process.

Choice of a tutor

It was felt that each person who became involved in the training process should be able to choose a tutor. This "tutor-coach" would become a confidant, providing psychological support and a social base, and using his or her volunteer position to help weave a new social fabric for the learner and to seek support from various sources.

Reducing cultural gaps

By providing this group with access to the computer, it might be possible to stop the widening of the cultural and technological gap that separated them from other groups in their society. This training would reintegrate them, at least symbolically, into the work and social environments in which the use of computers is growing steadily.

Enabling these learners to work at a computer terminal for the duration of their training was a way of introducing them to the business world and preparing them to occupy a work station. In fact using the microcomputer as a teaching tool can develop specific skills and aptitudes which are directly transferable to the job market.

Skills:

- use and understanding of a computer configuration,

- computerized data entry and working with files,

- word processing and production of a finished product (printout),

- computer-assisted design.

Aptitudes:

- the ability to adjust to a complex system,

- meticulous and independent work at a terminal,

- situation analysis and task breakdown prior to decision-making,

- self-control and moderation of impulsiveness.

CREATION OF LABO

At its June 1988 annual meeting the association undertook to promote measures aimed at fighting illiteracy:

— operating a laboratory responsible for the development of software and computerized training modules;

— conducting a training project using the microcomputer as a teaching tool;

— training instructors.

The training activities were to be provided both within the laboratory and in conjunction with social agencies and structures (shelters, neighbourhood agencies) that serve a population for whom literacy measures are a necessary aspect of integration.

Premises

LABO is located in a villa along a road between Bayonne and Biarritz. The premises are on the second floor and include seven rooms with a total floor space of 140 m^2. Two five-room annexes, one of them rented, the other loaned by the Office municipal des habitats à loyers modérés, make it possible to meet the growing demand for training. The premises include:

— two computer rooms, one equipped with 12 Thomsons, the other with 10 Olivetti PCls,

— three meeting rooms,

— one classroom/workshop for manual writing activities, equipped with a library,

— one lounge (smoking permitted),

— three offices.

Staff and volunteers

As of 31 December 1989 LABO's staff consisted of eight employees and 20 volunteers (see Table).

TABLE — SALARIED AND VOLUNTEER STAFF

Salaried staff

Position	Duties
2 instructor-teachers	individualized computer-assisted teaching of basic skills; writing workshop
2 psychologist-advisors	input during project development
2 psychologists	input for preparation of RMI project
: occupational	occupational counselling (part-time)
: clinical	rehabilitation (part-time)
1 secretary	general office work, bookkeeping and learner records
1 director-coordinator	pedagogical research, setting up satellites training instructors and volunteers guidance and leadership
2 clerks	data entry and training support
1 volunteer, computer training	PC software adaptation (2 days/week)
1 computer science student	research on voice synthesis (3-month training session)

Volunteers

Position	Duties
5 administrators (meeting once every two weeks)	implementation and monitoring of LABO policy; public relations
2 administrators	software packaging and shipping; advertising
2 administrators	library relations
6 teachers, 1 technician 2 instrutors, 1 nurse 1 student, 1 speech therapist (meeting every Wednesday)	pedagogical research, computer programming, technical assistance and advice
1 teacher	regular input into RMI sessions
1 artist-sculptor (3 times/month)	
7 tutors	involved in satellite projects

LABO ACTIVITIES

Pedagogical research

Ten of the association's 35 volunteers work within the pedagogical research team; some design and test programs, others work on programming or on copying software designed for the Thomson TO8-9 to PC compatibles. (Dissolution of the Thomson computer department has made this transfer necessary.)

Software produced by the team:

— INITIATION CLAVIER (introduction to the computer and keyboard) with audible prompt

— LESMO II (reading software) with audible prompt

— CREAFRA and PROGFRA (designer software and user program for learning the rules of written French and 21 disks containing progressive thematic exercises)

— TIC-TAC (software for learning time)

— 4 OPERATIONS

— MONNAIE (introduction to making change in a bar)

— VOCABULAIRE

— FIGGEO (recognizing geometric figures)

— BUDGET FAMILIAL (introduction to budget management using MULTIPLAN)

With the cooperation of the computer science department of the Institut universitaire de technologie de Bayonne we are currently developing a pedagogical application for voice synthesis. With this we hope to detect and treat certain learning disabilities (dyslexia, spelling and speech problems) and to overcome the literacy problems of foreign-born learners.

Books:

In cooperation with the public library we have been able to build up a selection of books suited to our learners.

Action-research:

Since October 1989 LABO has been taking part in an action-research project sponsored by the GPLI (ministère de la Formation professionnelle) with the cooperation of 12 psychologists and speech therapists. The project works with the teams of instructors in nine training centres for the illiterate.

Local satellites:

Two satellites are currently in operation. In each volunteer tutors provide coaching and support to other adults who are experiencing difficulties.

One satellite has been operating in a subsidized housing development since 15 February 1989. ATD Quart-Monde was responsible for fitting it up and helps run it. The second satellite is set up in the community centre of a large town some 30 kilometres from Bayonne and is run by the Association des chômeurs "BIZI-NAHI." It opened in mid-April 1989. Five additional satellites are planned, with one expected to open in 1990 at a shelter in Pau.

Volunteer tutors:

For the two existing satellites seven volunteer tutors took a six-month training course at LABO. The program, involving three hours of classes per week, includes tutor training per se and an introduction to the use of computers and software.

Illiteracy screening sessions:

Fifteen instructors, technical advisors and social service managers took part in two days of training on illiteracy screening. The session, run by LABO's coordinator, was sponsored by the local mission and financed by the Délégation régionale à la formation professionnelle.

Training

The training given at LABO ranges from letter recognition to the CAP-BEP level of vocational training (CAP — certificate of vocational competence and BEP — certificate of vocational studies). LABO also assesses learners' knowledge for career counselling purposes.

Since July 1989, under an agreement with the department prefecture and its general council, we have a mandate to rehabilitate RMI recipients (Revenu minimum d'insertion, a program providing a subsistence income to the unemployed) and to work individually with them to draw up a personal and/or job plan, and keep them up-to-date on the local job situation. These sessions last six weeks.

On 15 December 1989 a second agreement signed with the regional vocational training commission gave us a four-month mandate for a similar project involving 40 youths between the ages of 16 and 25. On completing the project participants will move on to recognized vocational programs leading to certification. These young men are paid by the government.

Between November 1988 and November 1989, 125 persons trained at LABO, including 22 who trained as instructors. These activities may be broken down as follows:

Individual program: 41 participants (100 to 700 hours)

Qualification course: 16 participants (700 hours)

Extra tutoring for school children: 5 pupils (470 hours)

Appraisal — TUC assessment: 12 participants (40 hours)
(Travaux d'utilité collective, a
program providing work to
unemployed young people)

Preparation of RMI plans: 29 participants (180 hours)

Instructor and tutor training: 22 participants

Depending on the type of training computer time ranges from three to five half-days per week, with each session lasting from two to four hours.

Twenty-two learners work independently in the satellite programs. Some were encouraged to participate by a social worker, educator or local literacy worker, while others heard about the program through the press, radio or word-of-mouth.

TABLE — CHARACTERISTICS OF LABO LEARNERS

(November 1988-November 1989)

Sex and origin

Men	53.3 %	French citizens	86.4 %
Women	46.6 %	Immigrants	13.6 %

Place of Residence

Urban	84.5 %	Rural	15.5 %

Age

13-15	4.8 %	26-35	26.1 %
16-17	18.4 %	37-50	15.5 %
18-25	34.9 %	Average age	27

Marital Status

Married	12.7 %	Single	69.6 %
Divorced	5.8 %	Common law	5.8 %
Single mothers	5.8 %		

Education

Literacy + Foreign	8.1 %	SES	15.1 %
IRP-IMP	8.1 %	CAP, 1st or 2nd yr.	15.1 %
Primary	2.3 %	BEP, 4th or 3rd	18.6 %
6th or 5th	8.1 %	Second cycle	8.1 %
CPPN-CPA	9.3 %	Postsecondary	6.9 %

METHODOLOGY: ESSENTIAL COROLLARY TO OUR HYPOTHESES

The aim of our methodology is to promote advancement at both the technical and personal levels, with the latter considered to be a prerequisite to knowledge acquisition (see Table).

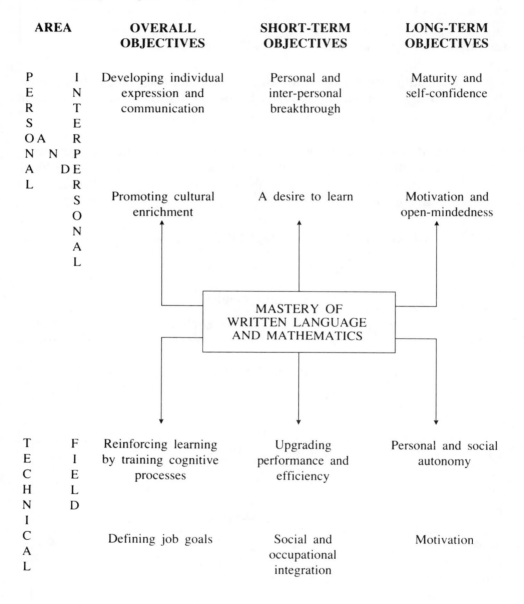

AREA		OVERALL OBJECTIVES	SHORT-TERM OBJECTIVES	LONG-TERM OBJECTIVES
P E R S O A N N A L	I N T E R P N E R D S E O R N A L	Developing individual expression and communication	Personal and inter-personal breakthrough	Maturity and self-confidence
		Promoting cultural enrichment	A desire to learn	Motivation and open-mindedness

MASTERY OF WRITTEN LANGUAGE AND MATHEMATICS

AREA		OVERALL OBJECTIVES	SHORT-TERM OBJECTIVES	LONG-TERM OBJECTIVES
T E C H N I C A L	F I E L D	Reinforcing learning by training cognitive processes	Upgrading performance and efficiency	Personal and social autonomy
		Defining job goals	Social and occupational integration	Motivation

Two approaches are used in attaining these objectives: individual work and group work. The two most usual scenarios are part-time individual work and a full-time training session. The differences in participant status have already been mentioned. (It is hoped that tion of the training credit[5] will compensate for some of the inconsistencies in classification.)

We mentioned above that, in one year, 41 participants took individual programs lasting from 100 to 700 hours. These young people and adults basically work at a computer terminal, with the assistance of an instructor. Session frequency varies from three to five half-days per week. Although there are no fees, the participant is not paid unless referred to us by another training organization for reinforcement of basic skills. There is no group work, although some participants benefit from the support of a tutor.

Full-time training usually involves a class of 15 paid participants for a period ranging from 600 to 800 hours. The teaching method combines individual and group instruction. Participants spend 50 % of their time working at a computer terminal.

INDIVIDUAL	develops personal work methods and habits

Method
interaction

GROUP OR WITH A TUTOR	structures the group and helps participants develop social skills

Individual Work

Initial assessment:

At the first session each participant (regardless of education level) is invited to sit down at a computer terminal and learn how to use it. There are no explanations from the instructor; the learner is assisted only by LABO's custom software package with audible prompt. The purpose of this immediate hands-on experience is to make the participant understand that most of his contact is to be with the computer.

Throughout this and every other session the instructor intervenes only on request or if a breakdown in participant/computer interaction risks turning the learning process into a failure. During the initial assessment phase the instructor observes and records the learner's existing knowledge and the gaps in his basic skills (spatialization, lateralization, adaptability to a system, memory skills, anxiety/emotionalism, structuring of logical thinking).

Later a number of custom software packages assess reading skills, text comprehension, writing skills, functional mechanisms, mental arithmetic, recognition of geometric figures and problem-solving. The results of these steps are automatically given through the printer.

Objective-based contract and work plan:

After one or two sessions the results of the tests described above are discussed in a personal interview. After joint discussion of strengths and weaknesses the instructor suggests a work plan which takes into account the participant's original request for training and his job goals, and is geared towards a step-by-step attainment of training objectives. At this point the various software training packages are described and included in the work plan. The participant chooses his own training strategy, i.e., is free to select the subject matter and corresponding software program for each session.

This individualized work with a computer has a threefold aim:

— developing mental processes,

— ensuring that specific skills are acquired,

— deferring affective needs.

Computer-assisted learning, with results automatically provided on printout, should enable the participant to:

— work independently,

— think at his own speed,

— use or not use the programmed assistance,

— immediately correct or obtain correction for his mistakes,

— assess his progress.

At the beginning and end of each computer session participant and instructor discuss the participant's work schedule and results. The learner describes his progress and his plans for the next session. Once a climate of trust has been established, he will also talk about his problems. Analysis and adjustment of work are an ongoing, daily activity that helps the participant to:

— become aware of his mistakes and weaknesses;

— eventually restructure nonstandard speech patterns and expressions;

— begin anew after each session.

After each discussion of results participants may record their progress on the computer (most of their problems are memory-related) by entering the following data on a personal progress sheet: date, subject, exercise title, results indicated by the printer and any comments. At the end of the first month of training the participants assess their progress, measuring how much they have learned and comparing it to the work plan prepared after the initial assessment.

Group Work

Logical reasoning:

During full-time training programs, in addition to individual work at the computer, group games and exercises involving logical reasoning are used to develop the participant's autonomy and sense of success. These exercises promote rapid development of the basic skills that underpin all learning, i.e., attention, concentration and comprehension, and thus enable participants to upgrade the efficiency and speed of their thought process (see Chart).

DEVELOPING SUCCESS AND AUTONOMY

COMPREHENSION
— exercises in understanding
  and following instructions
— attention
— concentration
— breakthrough:situation turnaround
          through one-on-one assistance

     ACHIEVEMENT
— using the various
  cognitive processes
— making the thought process
  clear, consistent and effective

         SUCCESS
         — "making success a habit"
         — positive reinforcement of material learned

Exercise content

— Knowing how to observe and select visual and verbal information; self-training in focussing attention.

— Knowing how to reproduce: realizing the importance of perception and the related element of interpretation.

— Knowing how to identify and compare (relationships of equivalence and nonequivalence).

— Knowing how to sort, reorganize, count in sets, classify, communicate effectively, argue.

Reading activities

The objectives are to help participants become aware of the positive aspects of self-imposed reading in any personal, social or occupational context; to allay their fears and bring them to the point where they no longer shun reading; and to promote rapid and selective comprehension of the written word.

Reading from the monitor:

Enhancement of perception skills, understanding written messages: working with a computer requires that the user understand the message before carrying it out.

At the beginning of the training period, no matter how weak the learner's reading skills, he is immediately placed in a situation where he must read from the monitor. If he can read only a little or not at all, he may use the audible prompt. Encouraged and independent, the participant proceeds at his own speed through a software package which introduces him to the components in front of him.

Using the computer makes him see that reading can be useful and valuable: he sees and hears the names of the components he is working on; he learns to find the keys he will use to move from one page to the next of the software. When he is familiar with the operation of the computer and recognizes simple words, he stops using the headphones and finds that, in all learning situations, he is reading effectively and painlessly.

At the outset neither the instructor nor the computer expects the learner to do "test" reading (out loud), as his understanding of meaning is translated into proper handling of the software. In addition a menu appears from which he may select an exercise by name and level; absorbed by the appeal or prompting of the machine he concentrates far better than if he were doing the same exercises on paper and progresses steadily at his own speed.

It is surprising to see people considered total failures spend many hours without apparent fatigue, happy to come back time and time again, and to progress in this "bookless" reading.

If a participant is at the decoding level (cannot understand a sentence) he uses the LESMO software package; we enter a file containing his own language, which is used as content for a broad range of exercises. The learner thus finds himself in front of a computerized text which transcribes his own language. When he sees his own words and sentences onscreen the reader is confronted with his own meaning and feels directly concerned by the writing before his eyes. This method makes it easier to remember how a word is spelt and allows for more flexible word discrimination and identification, constant movement between reading, writing and checking of results, greater independence from the instructor's reading strategies, and increased pleasure and motivation.

Even if he finds it difficult the participant begins to learn, understand, remember, copy and do original work. No participant has ever been heard to say that his work was useless, even if he did find it hard going. Working on a computer increases self-esteem and, when the learner is asked what he does at the training centre, he can reply, "I'm working with computers." Who will deny that, for a 28-year-old, this is much easier to say than "I'm learning to read and write"!

The participant is no longer faced with something he has always considered impossible. He discovers the written form of his own words; he discovers himself and develops links with himself (by reading his words) through a different communication medium. The task, although difficult, becomes feasible. He begins to understand, to achieve, to succeed. It is uphill work, but the process is under way.

In our opinion this initial phase of "reorganization" is over when the participant can express his own level of knowledge clearly, without undue difficulty. He has discovered that the relearning process includes this step, which he integrates into his work method.

The second phase is the step-by-step monitoring of his progress. Later his own word processed texts become the first pages he reads, out of which he can make a small book. Eventually the reader is given technical texts containing the terms most commonly used "on-the-job" so that he may familiarize himself with the vocabulary essential to his social and occupational integration.

As he reviews vocabulary and rules of grammar the participant learns first and foremost to use, on his own, the different types of reading presented by the computer: reading for a purpose, reading his own writing, reading on a particular topic, and technical and job-related reading.

Reading hard copy:

Work based on content level (adapted to individual expectations): note-taking, text analysis and summary, vocabulary enrichment and use, and etymological research.

Reading and the reader's social status:

Strategies for research-oriented reading were developed using dictionaries, directories, technical and documentary books, and other publications. A library set up at LABO using books from the Bayonne library enables participants to reestablish contact with books and use specific documents to determine or narrow down their job choice.

Discovering a place to read:

The public library cooperates with LABO throughout our training programs. We attempt to meet participants' needs by studying their reports on their reading experiences and by considering their expressed desires. The first step is to give them an opportunity to become accustomed to the library and feel at home there, for many participants are intimidated by shelves full of books. We try to awaken their curiosity about the shelves of books, then about a single book — many begin by simply taking a book from the nearest shelf. The next step is to develop their taste for contact with books by having them wander freely among the shelves and select one or more books of particular interest. After the third visit to the library participants seem to develop a taste for leafing through a book (an important step), usually an attractive one with pictures. Once a more difficult book has been selected they may want to borrow it and take it home (especially if it is a novel), although most books are read, examined or leafed through at the training centre.

Written expression

The objective is to have participants master the codes of written communication. Writing involves letting go, overcoming the "culture complex" and assimilating a new communication skill.

Writing with a computer:

When a participant is learning to read he works with software and thinks it is a game. When he is learning to write he works mainly with a word processing program and feels like a "secretary." Once he has understood the principal phonemes and recognizes the letters in a familiar word, he can start writing on the computer. Hitting the keys and seeing results displayed onscreen and printing them on a page become mediative acts in the process of learning to write. The same screen that replaces books for reading now replaces exercise books for writing.

The act of writing is less difficult: in being able to display his own words on the screen, as he pronounces them, without having to form the letters, without making smudges or mistakes — the learner takes his first step toward being able to write. Content before form! Ideas before style! The handwriting of some participants is so illegible (sometimes purposefully, to hide poor spelling) that they cannot read it themselves. Alone with the computer, however, fired by imagination or a pleasant memory, the learner writes, prints, reads his own work and corrects it with the instructor.

Our teaching method recognizes the value of mistakes. A mistake becomes a springboard to research, understanding and development, and we use the participant's mistakes to assess and assist his progress. The participant is surprised to see our interest in his mistakes and pleased that no one seems to disapprove. The act of writing is no longer a chore, but a wonderful means of self-expression, communication and self-awareness: at this stage long-buried memories of school resurface, shameful experiences which the learner is now willing to discuss in order to further his progress.

Once the learner perceives the rewards of writing mental blocks vanish and he is well on the way to mending the gaps in his basic knowledge. At the outset he is free to use only the computer, as much as he wishes and for the subject matter of his choosing. For assessment purposes he must produce a handwritten text at the beginning and end of the training program.

If the participant has difficulty forming letters he is given access to two software teaching packages, one for writing and one for drawing. Also at his disposal are books, dictionaries and even guides which we custom design in keeping with his needs. These include:

— more advanced work to be done at home,

— keyboard operation exercises (answers on reverse side),

— help with writing a report, if one is required.

Word processing enables the participant to build words and sentences; to delete, move, duplicate, organize and correct them. He can compose a text, paginate and print it. Subsequent to this "spontaneous writing" the participant learns to write his résumé, a letter, and a diary or an account of the day. This is how the "LABO memory book" was born. Every day, at first freely and later in turn, the participant summarizes his day in a logbook, adding a poem to be read by the others if he wishes. The aim is to encourage participants to share their writing with others.

While the participant is learning word processing he also uses programs on grammar, vocabulary, conjugation, history, poetry and other subjects; all include automatic correction functions. Onscreen display of correct answers encourages him to go on. Mistakes on the printout enable the instructor to follow the participant's progress and adjust the training plan accordingly.

Group writing project:

The transition to writing on paper comes naturally during group activities or extra work on an individual project. Some time in the second month the instructor suggests that the students write a text together. The aim of the exercise is to have everyone contribute to the same story by taking a collective journey through a series of fantastic themes; the journey activates each participant's imagination and enables him to step into a brand new world. The instructor intervenes only to give technical assistance, but never suggests ideas. The instructor is the first person to read the texts, which he does with the proper intonation and well-chosen breaks to correct imperfections in style. No one knows who the author is. Although this is not the aim of the technique the participants try to guess his name. Their guesses can be flattering to a participant who finds himself compared to the person considered tops by the group. The objective is to make the participant a little more comfortable with writing and to reduce his tendency to shun it.

Arithmetic

Using the same process as for reading and writing the participant follows instructions given by the computer and may progress to Level V Mathematics. At each session he may review the same programs to reinforce his knowledge, upgrade his performance, or learn more.

A software package for teaching time was designed for nonreading adults: the program requires them to match the numerals on a clock to their daily activities.

Designing a teaching package about "making change" was somewhat more of a challenge. A simulation involves a customer and a barman in a cafe: the barman must give the customer his change after calculating the price of the drinks ordered by the computer. It is astonishing to see the motivation of participants who "hate arithmetic" when they are working with this program!

Mental arithmetic packages are made up of exercises that progress in keeping with the accuracy of the learner's results. With this method answers become automatic and acquired knowledge is retained. Some of the mental arithmetic exercises take the form of tables or games (e.g., dominoes) and participants willingly play with numbers in this context. Exercise speed and complexity are controlled by a menu and the accuracy of answers.

Other software packages contain written exercises as a preparation for reasoning (relationships, means, classification). The learner, freed from the burden of written formulation, is guided in his questions and answers by simple signs: if his answer is wrong he can request immediate correction or go back to the beginning and redo the exercise step by step.

A teaching package on the four basic operations allows for constant review of acquired knowledge and includes a help function for learning the tables.

A program disk contains everything related to the concepts of "the whole," "parts," and "parts in relation to the whole" (extremely difficult concepts): fractions, proportions and percentage. Two geometry packages are designed for learning to identify plane figures and calculating perimeter and area.

Problem packages are meticulously selected to relate to the daily lives of participants. In order to train the participant in reasoning and doing a good job, problems are expressed in simple terms, questions are asked step by step, the beginning of each answer is given, units are used correctly and operations are accurately performed. In return the software requires attentiveness and care in formulating answers. Although a computer is infinitely patient and corrects systematically, it never accepts an approximation.

Working with tutors

When engaged in individual training (i.e., outside the framework of a full-time program) the participant works independently at the computer, and we maintain contact throughout the training period with a volunteer tutor who accompanies and supports the participant within the framework of a local project. For some learners in full-time programs an ongoing relationship of this kind may also be maintained either with the instructor, if the participant needs help in preparing his integration plan, or with a social worker, if he has a health or housing problem that could temporarily interfere with the learning process.

Occupational integration

Our training program never loses sight of the close links between the fight against illiteracy and job integration. At the beginning of the training program a personal and employment record is drawn up for each participant as a starting point for structuring training objectives in relation to job goals. The latter are put to the test during work experiences with actual companies. Each trial work period and its length are designed to match the abilities of the participant. The purpose is to either reinforce or invalidate the job goals.

At the end of the training program each participant is guided (with the assistance of those who have been working with him) toward the realization of his goals. For most this means embarking on a recognized training program leading to a certificate or diploma attesting to job skills. For others it means finding a job or beginning a training program geared to a specific type of industry.

As complete statistics are not yet available the following table illustrates the individual progress and current situation of the 17 most recent participants in the four-month program.

TABLE — INDIVIDUAL PROGRESS

Legend: dark — assessment at time of arrival
        light — progress

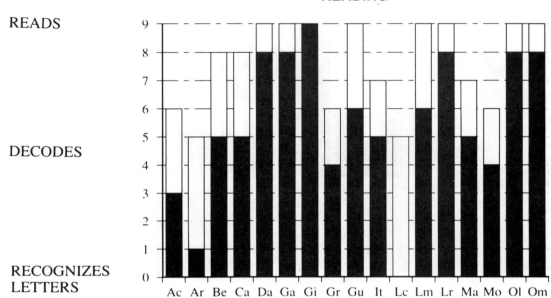

READING

READS

DECODES

RECOGNIZES
LETTERS

PARTICIPANTS

WRITING

WRITES
CORRECTLY

EDITS
OWN WRITING

WRITES
WITH MISTAKES

WRITES
PHONETICALLY

RECOGNIZES
LETTERS

PARTICIPANTS

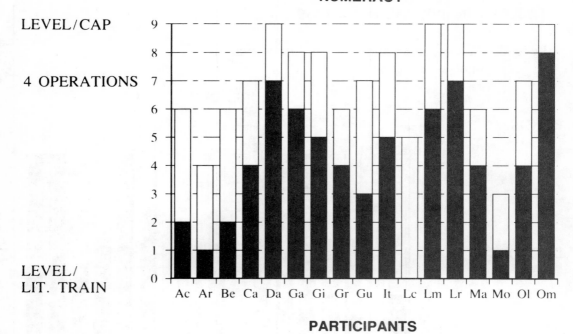

NUMERACY

LEVEL/CAP

4 OPERATIONS

LEVEL/
LIT. TRAIN

Participants: Ac Ar Be Ca Da Ga Gi Gr Gu It Lc Lm Lr Ma Mo Ol Om

PARTICIPANTS

Job situation one month after training:

Apprentice in a trade: 5 (5 different trades)

Training for qualifications: 4 (2 data processing, 2 business)

Employed: 2 (1 pastry cook, 1 salesperson)

Job training: 1 (gardener)

Waiting for a job: 1 (remote camera monitoring)

Other: 3 (move or marriage)

Return to school: 1

THE PARTICIPANTS' PSYCHOLOGICAL NEEDS

What are these needs?

Almost all participants have a negative self-image. At the same time they have a strong desire to be listened to, to receive attention and to be recognized as individuals. They want to be respected for what they know by that "guardian of knowledge," the instructor, who is perceived as being able to heal the wounds of previous failures in school. This creates a paradoxical situation. In the past it was teachers who gave these students a negative self-image, yet it is now through a teacher that they expect to recover their self-esteem. At the same time they are prepared to blame the teacher for any new failures, and are hypersensitive to being called illiterate or to having their knowledge questioned.

The computer: intermediary and mirror

At LABO we have abolished teacher-pupil confrontation. Participants "learn how to learn" or, more prosaically, learn to process data with an automatic recording system. The computer automates the teaching relationship. It frees knowledge from its usual emotional context, of which the transmission of knowledge in the school setting is the formalized model. What we do is to dissociate knowledge from knowledge transmission.

The monitor and printer become the participant's new mirror. At first he finds this threatening. Gone is the face of the "judge" on which he could read or interpret signs of encouragement, complicity or disapproval. Whether or not he needs affection the learner placed in this "teaching triangle" is on his own, locked into a chain of interaction that only he can break (unless the system crashes). Through his initial request for training he is also "the prisoner" of a plethora of software packages.

This experience changes the learner's image of the teacher. An imbalance sets in and will not be righted by the usual relationship of approval or disapproval. Two types of reaction occur. The independent person handles the situation very well and adjusts to this new work method. Dependent individuals constantly ask the instructor for help or sit stock-still in front of the computer. Asking for help and inhibition reflect needs that must be dealt with. In the first case the instructor will help the learner locate and analyze the procedure suggested by the software. In the second he will suggest that the learner ask for help and will lead him to describe what is going on behind the apparent inactivity. It should be remembered that, under LABO's teaching approach, the instructor may intervene during a training session only at the request of the learner, and then only to offer technical advice or additional information.

From dependence to self-sufficiency

Faced with a computer a passive learner can become an active one. If he does not hit the key as requested, nothing happens. This brightly coloured, new type of "monitor" is impassive and patient, but not dead: the constant flashing of the cursor indirectly attracts the user's attention. The teaching package elicits the learner's participation; without it nothing happens onscreen and there is no interaction. The learner may leave the room or change his program; he may not consult his neighbours or avoid the learning sequence by engaging in conversation. From the outset the participant finds himself either in an active and rewarding situation of success or in the situation of refusing all training of this type. This situation is especially helpful for participants who no longer see themselves as worthwhile creators or producers.

The computer: main source of esteem

Computer-assisted learning comprises another important difference: the teacher is no longer the person who approves work and is thus no longer open to all the learner's frustration and aggressiveness.

In the LABO situation there is no question of "winning the teacher over" or vice versa. Only the computer tells the participant that an answer is right or wrong, and sometimes rewards, advises or makes a joke. The printer records mistakes and lists successes. This feedback is essential: it reinforces the participant's motivation, encourages him to surpass prior results and leads him through the steps in the learning process.

A different instructor model

When the learner has completed a learning session the instructor invites him to discuss what he has done, encouraging him to analyze the procedure and evaluate the results; together they plan the next step. At this point the learner often expresses his reaction to what he has accomplished and relates it to previous experience. The work of restructuring the personality or thought patterns, required by the computer, is put into words — the first sign that the participant's new knowledge is being applied.

During the initial recollection of prior learning experiences, it is essential that the instructor listen closely, with the heart rather than the ear. In other words he must empathize, a situation in which he is truly a pedagogue (in our case more accurately an "andragogue") — a leader.

Deferred demand

When a learner wishes to modify his original training plan the instructor asks him to use word processing to draw up the request in writing: recognized and taken seriously, the request is nonetheless deferred.

The participant, unsure of his request, vague in his intent and blocked in his desire for an immediate response, transforms his quandary into writing, which is displayed on the screen and then printed. The necessity of writing it down obliges him to structure his request, to make it objective. Because his need is deferred the learner shifts from the emotional mode to the rational and sheds some of his anxiety in the process.

Reversed roles

A further reversal occurs with regard to his request: the instructor is no longer the person who urges the learner to work or pay attention. The computer plays these roles with the learner or the learner plays them with the instructor. This is crucial and totally reverses the relationship between the instructor and learner. The instructor is there only to authenticate and advise.

The participant is in a reactive environment where self-expression is not only permitted but constantly solicited — on condition that it be written or drawn! During learning sessions, emotional demands are thus deferred and the relationship with the instructor is no longer distorted by requests for the type of assistance that would be more properly sought from a social worker or therapist.

DOES THE COMPUTER REPLACE THE INSTRUCTOR?

A change in status

The preceding sections clearly show that, in LABO's computer-assisted training program, the instructor changes status but is not removed from the learning process. As mentioned above group work currently accounts for about 50 percent of the full-time program. This proportion will doubtless be reduced.

At LABO the instructor acquires a new tool and must use it in an automated teaching situation. No one worries about losing status or being replaced by the computer. What is important is that the instructor be able to teach in a computerized context. It is essential that he possess this skill in addition to knowledge of pedagogical theory and program content. If the computer is to fulfill its role as an intermediary the instructor must develop software adapted to the target population.

The instructor is responsible for the hoped-for objectives and for the items the participant must learn in order to reach them. This means that the instructor must supply software adaptable to the participant's observed needs. The tasks are reversed: the instructor becomes a creator and designer, while the computer becomes a transmitter. They do not replace one another, but each is of service to the other, with the computer subject to the instructor.

Responsibility

During the learning session the instructor is no longer in sole charge of formulating and disseminating knowledge. The learner is no longer obliged to pass through the instructor to acquire knowledge. Some software is even developed by people other than the instructor. His knowledge no longer gives him the power to intervene verbally, while the power derived from possessing knowledge the participant has yet to acquire is transferred to the software.

The computer obliges the instructor to formalize the subject matter thoroughly. Computer formulation leaves no room for imprecision, improvisation, rewording or lack of preparation. The complexities of processing and programming oblige the instructor to work with others. At LABO this means cooperating with a multidisciplinary teaching team composed largely of volunteers.

True the significant training activities are no longer guided by the instructor, but by the computer. On the other hand there is no work to correct, as the computer handles that simultaneously. The instructor becomes an observer and a technician, responsible for smooth system operation and for the participant's step-by-step progress toward targeted learning objectives.

A different kind of teacher

The instructor's time is organized in a different way. He is no longer in charge during training sessions. He has more time for individual assistance but, when answering participants' questions on specific content, must keep both previously learned content and subsequent content in mind. The instructor's new role is tiring because of the wide range of levels and skills that must be mastered. But there is none of the tedious repetition or student disinterest and hostility found in a regular single-grade classroom.

LEARNER REACTIONS TO THE COMPUTER EXPERIENCE

How effective is our teaching method?

The current dropout rate at LABO is very low (2 to 3 percent). Personal satisfaction is extremely high (over 95 percent), and participants are keenly interested in the computer. (For some this interest may even be reflected in their dress and appearance!) Once initial fears have been overcome, the atmosphere of concentration that reigns throughout the work sessions is striking. There is not a sound, since everyone is hard at work.

To evaluate progress we should normally take the following five parameters into consideration:

— commencement and completion levels (known),

— intellectual capacity (not measured),

— causes of the illiteracy (reported by participants, but not easily verifiable),

— course length (known),

— knowledge application and permanence, i.e., impact of training on participant's future (known on completion, difficult to measure over a long period).

Thus, until we have additional measuring instruments, we must remain modest when discussing progress in knowledge acquisition. Suffice it to say that some participants make spectacular progress and that others pass the general education examination.

And our initial hypotheses?

The following observations are drawn from the evaluation sheets completed at the end of a training program.

An intermediary in the teaching relationship:

The first things the learner discovers are his ability to concentrate ("It's easier on the brain!") and a loss of the sense of time. These formerly "hyperactive or disruptive" men can spend three hours in front of a computer. Three-quarters of them say it is easier to concentrate for "more than an hour, up to three." "It's not so boring with the computer."

> There's no one looking over my shoulder, always telling me what to do.

> The computer doesn't get my goat. It doesn't make me feel stupid.

> Self-correction is great. You find your mistakes yourself and there's no teacher marking you. You don't get discouraged like you do in school.

> Nobody makes fun of you.

Eighty percent of the participants find an hour in a regular classroom more tiring than an hour at the computer. We have also observed that the more problems a participant has (lower literacy skills) the more he will prefer working on a computer to being taught by an instructor.

Self-directed training:

The qualities that seem to appeal most to learners are tolerance, patience, strictness, precision and logic. They very quickly learn to enjoy the computer's flexibility and precision, the logic that structures thinking and the satisfying challenge of "constantly moving ahead." "The computer demands that you work well, that you outdo yourself," "learn properly" and "give exact answers."

Seventy percent of the participants need no explanation from the instructor to understand what they have to do. They all say that, with the computer, they can work more slowly without being bored and so learn better and more easily. "It seems to me that learning is easier."

When the participant plays an active part in his own training he learns to recognize his shortcomings and inability to give the right answer on the first try. He is able to admit that he does not understand and backtrack in his training schedule. He must look hard at himself and will sometimes go through a lull of more than a month before he fully accepts the need for training and stops using avoidance strategies or answering off the top of his head.

For participants the fact of working with a computer is in itself at least as interesting as the actual subject matter. Some even find that computer-assisted learning renews their interest in "subjects they used to hate." If they had to choose between the computer and the instructor, only 20 percent would choose the instructor.

A meaningful learning experience:

The possibilities offered by electronic writing eliminate the participant's fear of the blank page, along with related anxieties which take the form of hesitation, clumsiness, blots, erasures, fatigue and negative self-image. "It writes well in spite of our mistakes. Before I couldn't read my own writing!"

The right to make a mistake and correct it without going all the way back to the beginning liberates self-expression and promotes reflection and progress. "I really like doing these exercises on the computer, but not on paper." The legibility of the form reinforces the desire to write.

The learner sees what he writes onscreen and printed on paper. When he uses the keyboard his thoughts are projected and unfold before his very eyes; and the ability to change them without leaving a trace thrills him. He is not penalized for his mistakes, some of which are even corrected automatically.

The possibility of turning a written text inside out and upside down shakes the participant's previous learning experiences to their very foundations: word processing soon makes him understand that ideas are more important than form or style.

Greater isolation or communication?

Many people feel that placing learners with interpersonal difficulties in a computerized learning situation is at the very least incongruous, as their isolation will only be reinforced.

Our observations indicate that the exact opposite is true: the first phase in the learner/computer interface enables the learner to do "therapeutic" work on himself. He renews his links with the past. The breakdown of his tasks requires a restructuring of his thought processes and control mechanisms. As he identifies and defines his shortcomings he sheds the inhibitions generated by an overall feeling of failure.

At the outset the participant is possessive about the private world of his workstation and so hypersensitive about having others watch him that he may even stop working in their presence. When he has been using a microcomputer for about a month he is unaffected by others watching him work. He begins to discuss his work with the other participants and may even offer to help them.

All the participants believe that "it will soon be possible to learn everything with the help of a computer" and at least half of them approve of the idea.

CONCLUSION

"Computers, computers, computers! If they were really the answer we'd all have heard about it by now. Why don't we just sit these guys down in front of TV sets!" This reaction from a school inspector implies that using microcomputers for training specific groups is only a fad, shortcut or cop-out. In the past five years, however, 230 youths and adults ranging in age from 13 to 47 have operated our 24 computers with the secret hope of becoming more literate or with the simple wish of preparing for a job training course.

Some critics claim that teaching and computers are incompatible, others assume that the complexity of computers should limit their use to "professionals," and still others tout the risk that thought processes will be standardized...These arguments must not be allowed to kill experimentation.

When a tool has performed outstandingly well in any given field, and a solution to an urgent problem is being sought in another, it is only logical to examine the possibility of harnessing that performance through transfer or adaptation. It must not be assumed a priori that learner groups such as those at LABO are incapable of using computers — although it is equally important not to overestimate the value of computerized teaching. As for the question of conditioning and the risk of uniformity: does freedom not consist in choosing one's own form of conditioning from the selection available?

Problems noted during the training program

Pedagogical:

The time required for the development and adaptation of software by our computer experts and teachers slows down the response to some learners' needs.

Specially adapted commercial teaching software is difficult to find; most of what is available is application software.

It is also difficult to find instructors trained in the educational use of computers.

Financial:

The investment in terms of human and technical resources, and the cost of training illiterate participants are disproportionately high.

We are short of research funds and currently cannot afford a salaried computer expert on staff.

NOTES

1. Colloque de MARL (Ruhr, Federal Republic of Germany), quoted by Antoine Lion, "Illettrés," *L.I.R.* No. 29-30, FNARS, 1985.

2. Atherbéa, *Paroles d'exclus*, Collection FNARS, Éditions Le Relais Bois l'Abbé, 1979.

3. Jean-Louis Berterreix, *Illettrisme et apprentissages par ordinateur*, LABO (14, av. du Maréchal Soult, 64100 Bayonne, France), 1985.

4. These are the ATD Quart Monde Pays Basque, the ACEPB (Association de prévention contre la délinquance), the LEO LAGRANGE clubs (Association d'éducation populaire), the Maisons des jeunes et de la culture, BIZI NAHI (Association des chômeurs), the Mission avenir jeunes de Bayonne, district social workers, and the FNARS (Fédération aquitaine des associations d'accueil et de réadaptation sociale).

5. The individualized training credit is a second chance that is offered to the school dropout. The objective is that, this time, he will obtain a vocational training certificate, by taking ad hoc training at his own pace.

REFERENCES

Espérandieu, V., A. Lion and J.P. Bénichou. *Des illettrés en France*. Rapport au Premier Ministre. Paris: La Documentation française, 1984.

"Illettrés." *L.I.R.* No. 29-30. FNARS. 76, rue du Faubourg Saint-Denis 75010.

"L'illettrisme." *Informations sociales*. No. 8/1984. 23, rue Daniel, 75634.

Dossier noir de l'illettrisme. Éditions Avis de recherche, Paris, 1989.

Vélis, Jean-Pierre. *La France illettrée*. Éditions du Seuil, Paris, 1988.

Fijalkow, Jacques. *Mauvais lecteurs, pourquoi?* P.U.F., Paris, 1986.

Les actes de lecture. Association française pour la lecture, B.P. 13505 Paris, Cédex 05.

Gillardin B., and C. Tabet. *Retour à la lecture*. Éditions Retz, Paris, 1988.

Richeaudeau, François. *Linguistique pragmatique*. Éditions Retz, Paris, 1981.

Lefebvre, Jean-Michel. *Le guide pratique de l'E.A.O.* Cedic/Nathan, Paris, 1984.

Depover, Christian. *L'ordinateur média d'enseignement*. Éditions De Boeck-Wesmael, Brussels, 1987.

──────── . *Communication et langage*. No. 56.60.62, Editions Retz.

Bremond. *La révolution informatique*. Hatier, Paris.

Papert, Seymour. *Jaillissement de l'esprit*. Flammarion, Paris.

Bestougeff, H., and J.P. Fargette. *Enseignement et ordinateur*. Cedic/Nathan, Paris.

MULTIMEDIA OPEN INSTRUCTION FOR LOW-LEVEL TARGET GROUPS

Bernard Obled
CUEEP, Université de Lille

This study is the result of observations and experiments carried out at or under the direct supervision of CUEEP (Centre université-économie d'éducation permanente, l'Université de Lille, France).

The target group consists of adults who are designated as either illiterate, functionally illiterate, or low-level. It does not constitute a category per se, but rather a group of individuals who have comparable learning objectives with respect to basic skills and knowledge of a mainly academic nature.

This paper aims to give a snapshot of current trends and recent developments in the areas of open learning and the use of multimedia materials with this target group.

For the most part, we will confine our comments to instruction, access modes and the dynamics of training, without getting into what comes before and after training (a matter that doubtless warrants further consideration).

MULTIMEDIA INSTRUCTION AND OPEN LEARNING

One last look at the little piece of paper he had carefully taken out of his pocket: Resource Centre, 4 rue de l'Arrosoir. This was definitely the right address. Jean pushed open the glass door after first checking that the name of the Centre matched what was written on the piece of paper Marcel had given him. Marcel never had problems with papers — he was a real wizard. One look and he knew, unlike Jean, who had a lot of trouble. But as far as work was concerned, Jean was the one who could teach Marcel a thing or two when it came to adjusting the machine. Mind you, that was before they started installing those confounded numerical controls, which turned you into an "intellectual in work clothes." You hardly needed to talk to the boss anymore: he sent you papers and you sent them back. You hardly even needed to touch the machine, only a keyboard. It was enough to make you wonder whether it was still a blue-collar job!

"Good," thought Jean, "that woman looks like she works here. I'll ask her where I can find out how the Centre works."

"Excuse me, ma'am, I want to find out about French and math courses. Can you tell me where I should go?"

"I'm sorry, I can't help you. I don't work here."

"Oh! When I saw that pile of papers, I thought you were a teacher."

"No, I'm bringing these documents back to the resource centre. I've finished with these and I'll be working here this afternoon. For information, go to the reception desk on the second floor."

"Thanks. Good luck with all your... um... documents."

Jean was already a little worried.

"It must be like school here. There must be homework to do, and if you don't do it on time or if you get bad marks, they must throw you out."

A lot of bad memories came flooding back.

"RESOURCE CENTRE — RECEPTION"

Generally speaking, Jean was not any shier or any more "hung up" than the next guy. He was a good worker and everyone at work knew it. Here, however, things were a bit different. No one knew him and he had come to learn something that all children were supposed to know after a few years in school.

If the person at the reception desk looked down on him or said "You poor man, you can't read. What a shame," things would not go well and he would leave a lot faster than he came. Jean did not like being treated like a child or a mentally handicapped person. Besides, what did they know about him?

A man was seated behind a small desk. He invited Jean to come in. Next to him was a woman looking at something on a computer. Those machines really were everywhere!

"Hello, my name is Gérard and this is Cécile."

"Hello. My name is Jean Tronchu. I'd like some information on your courses."

"Well, I'll get out of your way," said Cécile as she left the office. "Have a good day."

"So, Mr. Tronchu, what can I do for you?"

"Well, I came to see whether I could sign up for courses in French, and a bit of math. But let me warn you, I have to start from scratch...I never really got the hang of school, if you know what I mean. I really want to learn, but I'm 41...and I've got a job and don't have much time for school..." (Jean could still see that woman with all her homework.)

Gérard could tell that Jean wasn't feeling very comfortable and could understand why. What could he do to show Jean that he didn't have to justify himself or prove a lot of things in order to sign up for a course when he didn't even know what it was all about or how it would be taught?

"Take it easy! You're going too fast! Let's try and look at one thing at a time. Since you've told me a bit about yourself, I'll do the same thing and try to tell you about the centre and how it operates. Afterwards, we'll see what we can do to help you reach your goals.

"This is called a learning resource centre because all sorts of equipment and people are pooled together here for one specific reason: learning."

"It's a kind of school, isn't it?"

"Yes, except it can be a different kind of school for everyone."

"What does that mean?"

"Well, for us, it means that one person does not necessarily want or need to do the same thing, at the same time, in the same way or in the same place as another person. As you said earlier, not everyone can study all the time, and people have their individual preferences as to how they use the time they have. And not everyone necessarily learns the same way either."

"Oh, so there's more than one way of learning something? I wonder if I learned reading and writing the right way because it never sank in. I've got to admit I wasn't very interested back then. What I really liked was manual stuff, making things, you know..."

"Sure. And that was easy, right?"

"Sure was! I'm pretty good when it comes to making and fixing things for myself or my friends. At the plant, it wasn't long before they put me on the machines, alongside people who have diplomas: I'm really good. But that might change now."

"Why? Don't you like your work any more?"

"Oh, sure I like it! Only, the job is changing, and I'm going to have trouble keeping up because it's getting more and more intellectual."

"What do you mean by intellectual? Are the machines more complicated or the things that you make?"

"Oh no. If that were the problem, I could find a way to manage. This isn't the first time I've had to change machines. No, what bothers me is that, more and more, I've got to work with my head and less with my hands."

"But working with a machine — adjusting it, checking your product — that's always involved working with your head, don't you think?"

"Yes. But it's different now. More and more they're asking us to read stuff and write everything down. The whole job has changed. We get sheets saying what has to be done and how. And once the work's been done, we have to fill out other sheets saying so. Not to mention the papers for when there's a breakdown or too many defects. Write, write, write. I've been asking a buddy to do it for me, but you can only do that so long."

"OK, so basically, you want to be able to do your own reading and writing at work and maybe for other reasons?"

"Yes. That's it: it's not only for work, it's for anytime I need to read or write something."

The two men continued talking in this vein for a while and identified Jean's needs, expectations and goals. Gérard took advantage of the opportunity to take notes on Jean's academic background, his attitude toward school, his reading and writing habits and his ideas on how people learn. After a while, Gérard had enough information to come to the conclusion that Jean needed basic skills training. Jean, on the other hand, did not know exactly what kind of training he wanted. It was Gérard's turn to explain.

"You see, what we can do is help you find the methods that meet your needs, to the best of 'our' knowledge. Your job is to decide what you are prepared to do and whether the methods we suggest suit you: the amount of time involved, where and when you'll study, how you'll go about it and with whom, the tools you'll use (sure, we work with tools too and sometimes with machines)."

Gérard went on to explain the centre's various activities. We will come back to these later.

At first glance, this account of an intake interview reveals one aspect of the philosophy underlying what we will call open multimedia instruction: an enquiry about a course in a specific area often prompts a reply that is expressed in terms of systems, available resources, work methods and contracts meant to provide a clear idea of what the resource centre has to offer and the adult student's status within this environment.

This leads us to reflect on certain basic considerations:

— the relationship between supply and demand;

— how the adult learner ranks real time available for structured learning in relation to other activities;

— the status of training itself with respect to the adult's project, and the role it plays in his or her strategy for social or professional change;

— the adult's status with respect to the training itself, in terms of the "rights and obligations" linked to the concept of a contract.

In "open multimedia instruction" (OMI), "open" refers to access and to the co-management of learning objectives and activities, "multimedia," to instructional tools and alternatives with respect to media and environment, and "instruction," to the instruction provided, which is part of a training program and involves learning.

Jean's case is not unusual. There is a growing concern among adult educators to find personalized solutions to adult learners' needs. In the following pages, we will see how OMI can effectively meet these needs in terms of systems and strategies. We will be paying special attention to the multimedia component of this approach.

Those whose need for basic skills training is the greatest are often those who are the least well equipped to direct their learning and find solutions adapted to their low level of autonomy with respect to various aspects of learning: formal means of communication, cognitive modifiability, sociocultural relation to the desired learning, knowledge and understanding of the learning objectives, learning tools and methods.

This argument is too often used to justify their being overlooked as far as program development and delivery is concerned and their being suspected of an "inability" to integrate certain systems that use highly individualized methods and tools and put learners in charge of major learning decisions.

However, regardless of the difficulties involved, it seems that these individuals are precisely those who should justify the greatest efforts in finding imaginative and innovative ways to remove the barriers to learning. With these learners, therefore, autonomy must be an objective and not an absolute prerequisite that would prevent their benefiting from innovative training approaches. It is the systems that must be adapted in order to help low-level adults become autonomous with respect to learning (help them learn to learn), more specifically, to help them extend their autonomy in order to become autonomous learners, as they may well be autonomous in other areas of their lives. They should not be characterized as having a negative attitude toward learning, when the problem is often our inability to understand exactly why they need training, how they learn, how they assimilate the various forms of knowledge and what they do with them.

We realize that nothing we have said so far is new, but a quick review from time to time can only help us keep it all straight in our minds.

The concept of OMI was not the product of sudden inspiration. Rather, it was developed as the result of the convergence of various trends. For purposes of clarity, we will outline only the three major ones here:

— changes in the demand for training on the part of government, business and individuals and subsequent efforts to adapt the systems on offer;

— the use of certain new technologies for instructional purposes and the rediscovery of certain media;

— the development of innovative instructional approaches based on individualization.

There is a strong link between these trends, which have developed dialectically over the past few years.

Changes in the demand and consequences

Greater productivity

For some time now, public sector demand with respect to adult basic education has put considerable pressure on both systems managers and instructors. Indeed, it seemed aimed at reconciling irreconcilable goals: to provide training to as many people as possible, in the shortest time possible, while individualizing (even personalizing) the training provided, in order to ensure efficiency and profitability. At the same time, the business sector wanted instruction to tie in more closely with its philosophy and constraints (productivity, quality, flexibility).

Whether public or private, the funds allocated for adult basic education were to be used toward a specific economic end: productivity. This trend developed as a result of the economic crisis and growing competition on the economic front. A number of management-related ideas (such as the measurement of effectiveness, cost, profitability or return on investment, and the law of supply and demand) therefore made their way into adult education.

Human resource development

Education and training systems are under strong pressure to increase the programs on offer, due to the urgent and now permanent need for a skilled work force. This need is created by a demand for greater productivity, but in a way that warrants closer consideration.

The demand is for programs that adapt workers' professional profiles rather than retrain workers. Among other things, this means that training programs on offer must not only keep up with technological changes, but also (and this is perhaps more fundamental) with changes in the workplace and a changing conception of the human activity called work. With the progress of technology and the consequent pressure on business and industry to remain competitive and resulting changes in the workplace, the job descriptions of "low-level" employees have started to include tasks such as quality control, minor maintenance and day-to-day production management. At the same time, autonomy, flexibility and accountability have all become bywords. Concrete signs of these changes are the streamlining of business organizations and the trend toward limited local self-management of production.

What impact have these trends had on the demand for training?

Impact on the demand

Business and industry

The demand on the part of business and industry has been marked by a certain urgency, and its short-term development has involved certain constraints:

— Training must be adapted to production rates and operations (limited time which must be used as cost-effectively as possible; "customization" of training objectives and programs to corporate projects; maximum flexibility of programs to avoid disrupting production, etc.).

— Training programs must meet standards set in terms of short- or medium-term productivity and profitability (return on investment).

Government

The demand on the part of the public sector is not significantly different. It is characterized by:

— the same feeling of urgency with respect to the socioeconomic context and particularly the integration of low-level adults, except that the demand has "vacillated" between integration into society and integration into the workplace;

— the development of stricter guidelines regarding the use of public funds allocated for adult basic education (which have increased considerably), coupled with a desire for greater efficiency;

— the will to provide greater access to training for adults outside of existing systems;

— the desire for better management of training time through the increased individualization of programs.

Individuals

Changes in the demand for training on the part of individuals have also been influenced by the concept of "renewed" continuing education. Specifically, these changes are related to the difficulties encountered by adults with specific training projects in finding programs that are adapted to their concerns, availability and rate of learning, when most training is delivered in the form of modules in a specific location, at a predetermined time and with a predetermined content. The latter type of system should not be altogether scrapped, as it still meets the needs of a considerable number of learners. In certain cases, however, it is too restrictive (e.g., workers wishing to make long-term career plans or adults whose training is affected by successive periods of employment and unemployment).

In addition to a demand for training that is tied to individual projects, there is the type of demand that is related to a particular set of circumstances or an uncertain situation, e.g., an individual attempting to organize his or her life at a given moment and struggling with as-yet unspecified projects and sometimes contradicting attitudes toward learning. It is important to keep in mind that learners are much more than mere consumers of training products: they have mapped out their own strategies regarding the time they are willing to invest in a training program. Of course, we can formulate hypotheses regarding their needs and interpret their requests, but a large part of why they want training and how it relates to their own life context remains personal. Let us not be so pretentious as to believe that the learning contract negotiated with an individual on the basis of his or her stated objectives and needs will reflect all aspects of his or her personal strategy. The individual may use the training he or she receives for purposes other than those intended by the organization delivering it and this is quite legitimate and respectable. We cannot reduce an individual's request for training to preconceived ideas about his or her economic and social situation or generalizations regarding the training needs of a category of learners.

Response in terms of systems

Changes in the training on offer became necessary as a result of these changes in the demand. These mainly took place along four lines:

— the adaptation of systems to provide training that is more flexible and varied, with a strong thrust toward modular training;

— reflection on "à la carte" training programs;

— the creation of new types of specialized training centres, such as learning resource centres, personalized workshops and, on a higher level, assessment-counselling centres;

— research for the development of new instructional tools.

The introduction of new educational technologies

Let us now put the matter of systems aside and turn our attention to that of training, although, as we have long known, the two are inseparable.

The introduction of new educational technologies into the field of adult basic education has met several types of needs and desires:

— the need for an institutional strategy that addresses the socioeconomic needs discussed above;

— the need for instructional innovation or rediscovery with respect to training tools;

— the desire to use socioculturally overvalued "technology" for adult basic education in the name of modernity.

New educational technologies and institutional strategies

Given the strong demand, a number of conclusions were drawn that were in some cases accepted as truths — for example, that innovation in the field of education could be accomplished only by the modernization of tools. This notion was based on the introduction of new technologies in business and industry: after all, there had to be a good reason to explain why businesspeople were investing so much money into technology.

Also, what better way to "rationalize" the methods of instructors, those gentle humanist dreamers, and to "quantify" the efficiency and profitability of training programs? Another argument that opened the way for the use of new educational technologies was that they were seen as providing exceptional instruments for the individualization of instruction.

The industrialization of instruction

For some time, attempts have been made to create a new market for "training products geared to the needs of industry" and based on the use of new technologies. Indeed, the phrase is often used in slogans, but this is the language of industrialists. What does it really mean?

The term was coined mainly for business and industry to designate personnel training (companies make for an attractive market, as they are solvent and have substantial buying power). The public sector could also be an interesting market but a less attractive one, given the difficulties involved in dealing with bureaucracy and government positions on the provision of training.

Whatever the case, multimedia instruction has become synonymous with independent learning using sophisticated tools, which are a sound investment if they can be used by several learners, according to an "initial investment/potential target group" ratio. Some, also thinking in terms of profitability, favour the idea of a catalogue of training products that could eventually be used to set up self-service outlets for ready-made training to be "consumed" at any time, anywhere, even by anyone. Others will carry the metaphor a bit further and go so far as to say we should no longer base training on learners' needs but copy the restaurant industry: offer a range of training products and create consumer habits and needs ("fast-food" training?). Provocative images presented by a service industry that wants recognition as such? No doubt, but the matter of the target groups remains to be considered.

The target groups

For target groups that are already consumers of training products and have developed structures with respect to knowledge and its transmission, totally independent learning in a multimedia environment certainly seems to be a valid solution (the trend toward greater individualization is even seen as "natural"). But what about the insolvent learners of yesterday and today? When we say "insolvent learners," it is in terms of the sacrosanct notion of profitability, in this case, the replacement of "x" hours of traditional instruction by a software program that can repeat its "y" hours of instruction *ad infinitum*. If its users do not read at a high enough level or have not developed the autonomy required to use it independently, then its profitability ratio drops sharply. The potential market (composed of these insolvent learners) loses its appeal. Who will invest in the less profitable deal? Social solidarity would have the public sector invest, but are those in power always fully aware of the educational reasons for this apparently low profitability?

One thing is certain, however: new educational technologies have stimulated extensive research on instruction and teaching/learning strategies. In that respect, they have already been very useful. Indeed, the introduction of new educational technologies created a dialogue between systems managers, who wanted to increase access to training and improve its effectiveness for economic reasons, and the developers/users of new educational technologies, who brought these issues back to the domain of education and training, whether they were "pro" or "con."

Those who held the purse strings believed that, even though computer equipment and software development (for example) might be costly investments, they were worthwhile if, in return, they yielded products and methods that could be used with a large number of individuals and provided quality training (see above).

Impact on instructors

The introduction of new educational technologies provided instructors with an opportunity to reflect on their teaching methods by calling into question certain ideas and, more particularly, by formalizing existing practices with a view to using them in conjunction with the new media or developing them further. This reflection has yielded concrete results and the new technologies have started to carve out a very special niche among training tools. At present (at least, at CUEEP), we have moved beyond discussions about the best media (some had apprehensions about any form of computer-assisted learning whatsoever) to an approach based on flexibility and complementarity.

In fact, our research on new educational technologies and their possible impact on training have revealed that some instructors tended to see their work as the neutral transmission of knowledge using more or less sophisticated media. We have had to remind them on several occasions that "how the learner learns" is a vital component of the instructional act and that the new media had to be considered from this perspective as well. Otherwise (as was the case with the first products), instructional considerations may be overshadowed by technical considerations relating to the logic particular to each medium.

Another aspect involved changes in the status of instructors. At first, there was an imbalance (or at least, the risk of an imbalance) between media specialists (for example, programmers or instructors familiar with instructional media) and other instructors. It was some time before we came to the conclusion that, in developing these kinds of tools, the most important design consideration had to be instruction and that everyone should participate. Far from requiring that instructors become computer or video specialists, we asked them to provide input at the design stage and learn to use the tools we developed by creating suitable environments. Of course, the instructors did have to learn the language used by specialists and become familiar with the basic technical procedures and operations involved in using various types of equipment (the most obvious examples being cameras, computers and VCRs).

For their part, our media specialists have had to become familiar with instructional considerations in order to be able to talk with the instructors involved. Not that the media specialists contributed only their technical knowledge to development projects — far from it. Some, at times, were more aware of instructional considerations than the instructors themselves.

Our instructors have also had to learn to deal with new problems related to media management, due to the single proliferation of the media and equipment available to them, which entailed new time and space constraints, new sources of documentation, and often new organizational modes. We will consider this matter in greater depth in our discussion of the instructor's role in the management and use of multimedia resources.

The focus on individualized instruction

Refocussing on the individual

Here again, we can observe parallel trends in education and business. The last few years have seen companies make efforts to improve human resource management practices. Changes in the corporate structure have required corresponding changes in production engineering and work organization. We are rapidly moving away from the Taylor system of management toward greater autonomy and responsibility, toward local self-management of production. This translates into consideration of workers as individuals and no longer as mere cogs in the wheel. The fact that certain companies motivate their personnel to aim for zero inventory, zero defects, zero breakdowns illustrates this shift toward individual accountability. Every employee is important.

At the same time, individualization has become (or once again become, when referring to programmed instruction) a byword among instructors and systems managers. Some consider that the goal of individualization is to improve the management of heterogeneous groups by taking into account each learner's projects, level, rate of learning and work methods. Others feel it is to respond to changes in the demand for training, as discussed earlier in this paper.

Other more specialized currents, such as learner-centred learning, which is based on educational psychology, contribute to the trend toward individualization. Examples of these are methods based on cognitive modifiability (instrumental enrichment, logical reasoning, etc.).

In this context, it followed that instructional media, which allow a high level of interactivity and individualization, would immediately draw instructors' attention. Isolation has perhaps too often been confused with individualization, and independent learning with learning alone.

Further analysis of this trend leads us to draw two conclusions:

— first, that individualization is both an organizational mode and a teaching strategy that can be adapted to any type of learning environment (group work, tutoring, independent learning in a learning resource centre or at home);

— second, that any medium can be used for individualized instruction, depending on the learning environment provided during the instructional sequence.

Certain media are more effective than others at certain moments in the instructional sequence and for certain types of activities, but the use of a particular aid or medium does not necessarily guarantee that instruction will be individualized. We should perhaps clarify this concept by explaining what we mean by "individualization of instruction," a term some prefer to "individualized instruction."

The individualization of instruction

CUEEP developed OMI in an effort to find a comprehensive solution. The objectives of OMI may be summarized as follows:

— to ensure programs will match possible learners' personal objectives as closely as possible;

— to ensure programs will optimize real time available for learning and take into account the constraints of learners' work and home environments;

— to help learners manage interruptions due to periods of unemployment;

— to make the most of the public funds allocated for adult basic education by optimizing the use of resources and increasing turnover through rolling intake;

— to make training more accessible to adults working in small- and medium-sized businesses and even large corporations by eliminating the problems caused by the fixed time and location of "traditional" training (for learners who work on shifts).

These objectives were used as the basis for a project called "Interactive Multimedia System for Individualized Instruction" (IMSII):

— INTERACTIVE because several types of interactivity are possible. Selective interactivity is the opportunity to choose what one wishes to work on, and how one wishes to work. Reflective interactivity refers to the ways in which the media used encourage dialogue and provide learners with feedback on their input, with opportunities to experiment, etc. Last but not least, collective interactivity refers to the mutual benefits stemming from contact with other people.

— MULTIMEDIA refers to the use of various media (described further on) for instructional purposes.

— SYSTEM refers to the development of a program based on objectives set in terms of training needs, certification to be obtained and skills to be developed. It also stands for coherence between reception, orientation, assessment, development of the training plan and evaluation. This in turn entails management based on guidance, self-evaluation and constant monitoring (comanagement). Lastly, it stands for well-defined criteria regarding the validation of training and certification of studies in the case of learners requiring recognition of the training they received.

— INDIVIDUALIZED refers to individualization. For the moment, we will focus on the individualization of courses, programs, methods and modes.

— INSTRUCTION refers to training which may be modular and referenced (i.e., objectives, content and conditions may either be predetermined or tailored to individual needs).

The advantages of this approach are that it is:

— "Multi-environment": In a group, with a tutor at the resource centre, at work or at home, or a combination of these types of environments, as is most often the case with low-level learners (However, are the latter not entitled to the status of students in this case?)

— "Multi-media": Print materials, audio and audiovisual aids, CAI (tutorials, courseware, applications), telecommunications (Who knows what the future will bring?)

— "Multi-objective": Personal development, professional development, project follow-up, studies toward a diploma, etc.

— "Multi-method": Individualized group instruction, assisted independent learning, individual work

— "Multi-partner": People at the learning centre, in the learner's work or social environment, etc., who can all be resource persons at one time or another

Programs geared to "students" whose achievement level is very low must consist of a harmonious combination of different methods and types of environments. This may entail working on developing the learner's autonomy before he or she can develop greater flexibility.

This approach to individualization requires extensive guidance: reception, assessment, follow-up and orientation must all be interwoven with the training itself through individual learning contracts. Such contracts can be divided into three sub-contracts:

— The first sub-contract is based on the adult's objectives, on his or her stated goals. It consists of a training plan established on the basis of an interview and an assessment. It concerns all aspects of the training to be delivered.

— The second sub-contract deals with the management of time, space, methods and resources: most appropriate learning context, pace, schedule, etc. It is drawn up with the various partners involved once the training plan has been established.

— The third sub-contract (or sub-contracts, as there may be more than one) is concluded between the instructor teaching in a given field (in the broad sense of the term) and the learner, for a specific length of time. The duration of the contract depends on the learner's level of autonomy. A typical contract would state: "With your current knowledge in this field, given your constraints, in 'x' time you should have attained this or that objective."

It is obvious such practices require developing learners' awareness that they are responsible for their own learning.

Of course, we have just described an ideal situation in an attempt to give a general idea of our aims and objectives, knowing that many adjustments are made on a day-to-day basis and that some types of training integrate only parts of this philosophy.

Individualization and learning

We must distinguish between two terms that are sometimes confused when speaking of individualization: independent learning and autonomy. For the moment we will not discuss the concept of independent learning that relates to self-instruction (learning alone, outside of any institution or curriculum).

We will discuss independent learning in relation to learning in general, as being what the learner must do to transform, in one way or another, what is transmitted by an instructor or some other source of information.

We will discuss autonomy in relation to training, i.e., in relation to a period of time allotted to training within which the learner must develop the tools, skills and habits that will enable him or her to achieve learning objectives, using available resources and in keeping with his or her personal strategy.

Independent learning

The first terms that come to mind when discussing training are "trainer" (or instructor) and "learner." We also use other terms to speak of learners, such as "trainees," "apprentices" and even "students." While it seems appropriate to call learners "students," each of these terms in fact corresponds to a specific reality.

To caricature, we might say that, a trainer is a person who provides training and who, if he or she does a good job, produces trainees! However, even excellent trainers do not always "produce" "good trainees" and sometimes trainers who are considered "not so great" manage to produce some "good trainees." This is doubtless because trainees play an active role in their training! We therefore have a trainer or instructor on the one hand and an adult who is training him or herself — a learner — on the other.

It is easy to accept that learners are to a large extent responsible for their own learning, but we can even take this idea a little further.

The instructional act consists in the transmission of knowledge in more or less educational forms by instructors and the reception and processing of the transmitted knowledge by learners. It must be recognized that learners process the transmitted knowledge using what they have already learned, the decoding systems they have developed and the interpretations and meanings they have worked out for themselves: in a word, they more or less do what they like with the transmitted knowledge to create their own vision of the world (the rascals!).

Hence, we can come to the conclusion that the instructor delivers the content in the most educational form possible in order to make it accessible and explains how that content may be processed, while learners receive the information, translate it, decide whether or not to follow the instructor's suggestions regarding processing it and interpret it in accordance with their own schemata and references. This explains why instructors find that the knowledge they transmit does not always produce the effect they wanted and expected and that very often learners learn something other than what was intended — or learn it in a different way.

This is the aspect of independent learning we call "learning strategy" when speaking of "how the learner learns," "achievement" when speaking of what is actually learned and "attitude toward learning" when speaking of the psychosociocultural background for the entire process.

This being said, it is obvious that a great deal of attention will be paid to the question of using multimedia materials for instructional purposes and that the concept of independent learning, as defined above, will become of vital importance.

Evaluation as a driving force behind individualized instruction

We are getting into an area that ties in very closely with interactivity in all its forms, as interactivity cannot exist without the constant input provided by evaluation and self-evaluation.

The role of evaluation

In this section, we will discuss the role of three well-known types of evaluation: predictive evaluation, formative evaluation and summative evaluation.

As a part of OMI, these types of evaluation are performed at different times during the training program, according to conditions and for purposes that remain to be established.

Predictive evaluation is carried out when setting the objectives to be included in the learning contract. It may also be performed before a series of activities on a given theme or before using a particular medium in order to set a mini-objective. In either case, its role is basically the same: to assess learning potential at a given moment in relation to the objectives to be attained within a certain period of time.

Summative evaluation will be performed to determine whether predictions were accurate and to measure the degree to which learning objectives were attained. It may also eventually serve as the basis for validation of training (granting of a diploma, for example). There is nothing really new in this respect, except that new instructional media may allow new, more effective ways of performing these evaluations. For example, various media can be used to simulate situations that provide an opportunity to assess the learner's knowledge, skills and work methods, and through procedures that can be more or less complex, gather data on the learner's performance.

Formative evaluation is characterized by its ongoing nature and by the role it can play in the learner's learning. Formative evaluation makes it possible to monitor learning and redirect strategies in a progressive manner.

The status of evaluation

If evaluation is to be perceived, understood and used as yet another tool to facilitate learning, all forms of evaluation must be transparent to learners, i.e., they must guide learners through the delicate transition from evaluation to self-evaluation. However, this transition may be complicated by the number of methods and media used for evaluation purposes and by the interplay between them.

The evaluation of the learning achieved using one medium cannot be used as a basis for hypotheses regarding the transfer of the achieved learning to another medium. Furthermore, as the terms and conditions of the evaluation vary according to the medium used, the results of such an evaluation can always be questioned: what specific role did the medium play and what role did the activity itself play? For example, some learners are convinced that on-computer activities helped them master certain writing skills only when they see that they are able to do the same thing with pen and paper.

There is also the question of the management, by learners and instructors, of the various sources of evaluation.

Self-evaluation is an important aspect of the work method to be developed by the learner in order to become autonomous. We should also not hesitate to formalize this work method and even implement it by designing materials and documents specifically for the management of evaluation (self-evaluation booklets, logbooks, printouts of results of on-computer sessions, use of work samples).

The conditions required for this type of evaluation are the transparence and comanagement of instructional media materials, which must be based on voluntary use and trust. Practice shows that when learners cannot understand the why and how of evaluation, they are no longer willing to cooperate and become mistrustful, even indifferent.

It is vital that learners perceive evaluation as the way to get the most out of their instruction time, and not as the obligation to account for what they have done.

Individualization and independence

Schematically, training is situated on a continuum between two extremes:

— a "classical" system, in which the instructor defines a teaching strategy for a target group which becomes a group of learners, with the instructor choosing tools and methods according to his or her own practice;

INSTRUCTOR	teaching strategy	1 instructor — 1 group 1 teaching strategy
TOOLS		1 location 1 pace instant feedback
LEARNERS	target	deferred feedback

— a learner-centred system, in which the learner defines an independent learning strategy (sometimes called self-instruction).

OTHER LEARNERS (1)			1 learner in a relationship with 1 instructor (1) learning resources
TARGET	LEARNER	learning strategy	several locations 1 learning strategy 1 plan
INSTRUCTOR		TOOLS	1 individual pace instant feedback (2) deferred feedback

(1) In the case of a group, the other learners are an integral part of the relationship.

(2) During tutorials or group work.

Between these two extremes lie as many types of systems as one can imagine.

It is interesting to compare systems and the investment they require from the learner. In the first system described above, the learning strategy moulds itself on the teaching strategy, that is, it conforms to the teaching strategy as much as possible in order to maximize its efficiency. Since the choice of tools, methods and progress is based on the teaching strategy, it becomes difficult to adapt them to various individual strategies.

The major advantage of such an approach is that it guarantees internal coherence, as it is based on a teaching strategy developed by an instructor to teach specific course content and objectives following a certain progression. The learner is not required to create this coherence from day to day but to adapt to it and try to adapt his or her own strategy accordingly. Presuming that the learner has not developed a strategy or is unable to develop one, this model is the only possible solution.

Presuming that the learner can develop his or her own strategy or that it is important that he or she develop one (and that it matches his or her needs and resources to the greatest extent possible), the best solution will be to find a teaching strategy that identifies the learner's personal learning strategies, suggests adapted activities and tools and encourages the learner to make his or her learning coherent with stated learning objectives.

The purpose is to make these strategies as transparent as possible.

A short theoretical digression seems appropriate at this point. What underlies opposition to either of the models described above is the debate over what is called experiential learning or problem solving or the experience-based approach. The classical model is based on mediation by the instructor, the learner-centred model, on direct exposure of the learner to a given environment (a problem) and the stimulation of his or her responses to that environment (the situation is experienced). The instructor therefore becomes a resource person with a personal approach to the situation. (There is a comparison of each person's experience of the situation.)

However, the shift toward allowing the learner to make certain choices and decisions is not without creating problems. (It would be too easy otherwise!)

Defining one's own learning strategy requires a certain level of autonomy. If the learner is not autonomous, he or she risks making incoherent decisions with respect to his or her learning. In the case of low-level adults (are they the only ones?), the fact that they have their own learning practices (they had some learning before they signed up for basic skills training) does not ensure that their learning strategy will be coherent and in keeping with the training objective they have set for themselves. A learning strategy acquires its true value only when it is sufficiently structured and conscious to be associated with stated objectives and methods. "How can I optimize my opportunities to learn..." must become a conscious and structured response, i.e., a learning objective in its own right.

This does not mean that learners are required to take a methodology course in order to learn to learn. We have already established that learning strategies were a function of both the learner and the learning objective. We should not hope for a "prerequisite standard training program" that will enable anyone to learn anything.

In fact, it appears that experience encourages us to compromise, i.e., use a teaching strategy that is as transparent and open as possible, so that learners gradually work out strategies that suit them and map out their own conscious strategies with the help of an instructor (an ongoing guarantee of coherence). The important role played by the instructor consists in helping learners develop autonomy in their learning and, more specifically, in directing their learning.

The notion that all we need to do is give learners learning resources and let them figure things out on their own is based on the presumption that the resources available are sufficiently sophisticated to transmit the content, the various learning strategies, the methodology required to manage and direct both content and strategies, the different criteria used for ongoing evaluation and ranking related to course management and finally, the inevitable adjustment of learning objectives to the learner's pace and to the needs that arise during the training program.

If someone has invented this automatic "training machine" but not put it on the market, that person is losing a fortune in royalties!

Let us not transform what should be a learning objective into a barrier. Let us not expect low-level adults to function "automatically and immediately." On the contrary, let us focus on helping learners discover and progressively understand how training works and understand the methods used in order to help them progress toward autonomy. We cannot want (or demand) that they understand everything from the start. The quality of the training process rests in the thoughtful, structured transition from one form of learning to another.

A system that lists autonomy as a prerequisite would be of no interest to us. The system exists to provide an environment; the instructional act remains largely based on the mediation between the person facilitating the learning, the learner and the learning objective.

THE MULTIMEDIA STRATEGY, OR "BEYOND TECHNOLOGY"

We use the term multimedia "strategy" to highlight our desire to look beyond the tools and techniques and reflect on teaching and learning from a pedagogical point of view. Furthermore, we wish to position this reflection within the broader framework of individualization as discussed in the first part of this paper.

The questions under consideration here are:

— What does the use of instructional media imply with respect to the transmission of knowledge?

— What new elements does the use of new instructional media bring to learning and how do they enhance the quality of learning?

— Does the use of these new media change the relationship between the learner and his or her learning?

The transmission of information and instructional media

Training, and broadly speaking, education, are based in large part on mediation designed to provide the learner with a reading of the world and what it contains by coming between the learner and the learning objective to facilitate the perception, comprehension and objectivity required for the structuring and active integration of the knowledge transmitted.

To simplify, we could say that there are mainly two aspects of knowledge acquisition that interest us:

— the role of instructional media and beyond that, of mediation,

— the role of learning as a factor of self-instruction by the learner.

In this context, mediation is not necessarily provided by an instructor but may be provided by any medium or method that helps the learner understand a situation, a reality, etc.

We will therefore first direct our attention to mediation by an instructor and then go on to the broader topic of the greater level of interactivity made possible by the use of media.

Instructional media

To the extent that we believe the transmission of information is a significant part of the instructional act, the quality of the transmission should be a concern.

Even if we think learning consists mainly in self-instruction, there must nonetheless be some type of input that must be received in some form or another. The media that allow the learner to absorb input are the stable elements of mediation. By media, we mean the instructor (obviously, the instructor plays many other roles, including that of a medium), handwritten or print documents, audiovisual aids, hands-on materials, simulation materials or any other materials or devices that can be used as a vehicle for information.

The "extended" instructor

The instructor, even when acting as the leader during an instructional sequence and not using any teaching aids, is already a highly interactive multimedia package. One could even say the most sophisticated and versatile package. To help learners achieve the training objective by providing different kinds of information, the instructor may use speech, gesture, movement or mime, in short, all the evocative means used by two individuals to communicate. The instructor can also receive the same kind of messages from learners and modify his or her transmission, as required, thus adapting his or her mediation. However, depending on the objective to be attained, the instructor's mediational methods are limited by:

— **Content** The instructor must make the message explicit, univocal (as required), legible and comprehensible. The difficulty of this task varies according to the subject matter, its nature, complexity and distance or remoteness from the receivers' field of knowledge. Examples of elements that increase the complexity of a message are the presence of multiple and simultaneous interrelations, the level of abstraction, logical or chronological sequences, etc.

— **Time** Since the message is limited to a specific lapse of time, at a specific moment (speech, gesture, sight), receiving it requires attention and memory (which are not developed or available to the same degree in each learner) as well as the ability to perceive and decode, which varies from one individual to another. The transmission is limited to "here and now."

— **Target** If there are many receivers, most likely, the extent to which they effectively receive the message will vary for the reasons mentioned above, and the methods used to provide "feedback" will also vary according to the adjustments required. Let us confine ourselves to these few points, which will suffice to help us understand why the instructor needs instructional media to mediate his or her messages more effectively and push back the limits we just described.

The media selected by the instructor to facilitate transmission, and we shall confine ourselves to these for the time being, must extend and improve his or her own means of communication. The media must, therefore, enhance his or her evocative powers, ensure greater independence with respect to time and space and allow him or her to formalize complex relationships, translate abstract ideas into decodable terms and allow this decoding to occur at a pace adapted to or even controlled by the receiver. This, however, cannot be achieved without creating new limitations or magnifying existing ones.

Limitations of instructional media

For the purposes of this section, we shall look at a number of factors separately. One should bear in mind that, in reality, all of these are interrelated.

Symbolization

Since language itself is a symbol-based form of communication, any medium that uses language involves a high level of symbolization which in turn requires a great deal of decoding. The same holds true for images that are "domesticated" or functionalized for instructional or communication purposes. There are rules for reading images just as there are rules for reading words. These rules enable the reader to decode images and give them meaning. In the same way, decoding is also involved in manipulating or observing physical objects that are man-made or dedicated to a specific function. Does one understand what a house is on seeing the materials used to build it?

Focus on one type of communication

As soon as information is stored on a stable, physical medium, processing it requires an understanding of the medium itself. The medium and the set of symbols it uses are interposed between the message and the learner and therefore require decoding. Decoding is also necessary to understand information transmitted by an instructor. However, the instructor is both a multimedia package (i.e., can vary the type or level of symbolization he or she uses) and an interactive package (i.e., can immediately adapt his or her evocative strategy by switching from one medium to another or by using one to reinforce another, for example, using gestures to reinforce words). As for instructional media, each medium uses its own signs and particular form of transmission. If the intended receiver masters the decoding of both the signs and form used, the medium then extends the instructor's mediation, which becomes more effective and less tied down to the context in which the media was developed. In fact, media materials are often the result of several instructors' efforts to pool and capitalize their knowledge.

The multimedia strategy seen from the transmission viewpoint

To solve the problems posed by this phenomenon of "specialized transmission" while taking advantage of the potential power and effectiveness of instructional media, the instructor must attempt to adapt the information to the learner by varying the forms of transmission used and the types of decoding required. This is not a new idea: consider, for example, the use of various media in advertising. Repetition and coherence are the key factors in using a number of media to transmit a message.

Repetition, because the same content must be vehicled so that the learner can grasp that the same message is presented in different forms.

Coherence, because the different forms in which the message is presented must lead to the same interpretation. In other words, there must be no contradiction in the basic meaning of the message, regardless of the various forms it may be given from one medium to another. This coherence is, of course, vital for the learner, who must put together the pieces of information provided by the various media in order to understand the whole message.

Occasionally, too large a variation in the form of a message (the way in which it is presented) can impede or prevent understanding, as the learner may not be able to see how the various pieces fit together. This leads us to examine how learners comes to understand the information presented to them.

Absorbing information and giving it meaning

In this section, we will try to see how and in what forms information is presented by multimedia materials and what conditions must exist to ensure the effective transmission of information.

The concept of transfer to the identical

The first concept involves transferring on a medium all or part of the transmission usually mediated by the instructor, attempting in the process to improve its effectiveness and thus "extend" the instructor, thanks to technology and the rigourous stability of form and content, which are fixed on the medium once and for all.

This idea of stability is also linked to the permanence and availability of the messages carried by media: they can be used when one wishes, for as long as one wishes and, in some cases, at one's own pace.

In addition, the formalization and stabilization of a mediation on a medium also make it possible to capitalize the practices of a number of instructors by combining them into a validated collective production.

What rules must be followed to ensure that the use of instructional media will improve mediation, if only by ensuring better transmission?

Instructors who venture to develop multimedia materials are often led to analyze their practices and knowledge:

— How do I usually transmit such a message?

— Which form is the best to get this message across?

— In which order should I present the various parts of the message? What links or connections should I make?

— Which type of language goes over best?

When the developer realizes that he or she will not necessarily be with the learner using the materials and immediately available when help is required, he or she tries to anticipate any possible way in which the form used may impede or prevent understanding. Also, the developer is designing materials for learners he or she does not necessarily know, apart from general characteristics and hypotheses based on other learners he or she has known. This stage in the development process is often quite complex, even when the developer is working with content he or she apparently had no difficulty getting across in face-to-face encounters with learners. The developer wonders how the message will be interpreted and attempts to minimize potential problems by seeking the form and content that guarantee univocal transmission. He or she tries to make instructions and comments as clear as possible, even if this entails giving them a symbolic form such as a colour, a pictogram or a particular sound, depending on the medium used. This process is necessarily analytical: trying to isolate units of meaning to the greatest extent possible and to present them in a standard form in order to maximize the predictability of the interpretation and comprehension of the information transmitted, in the order in which it is transmitted.

Of course, the advantage of the multimedia approach is that one can vary the form of transmission and is therefore not limited to a single analysis of the transmission/comprehension relationship. This is undoubtedly the key element: when considering each medium separately, it may seem that mediation is weakened because it is limited to a single form of transmission (and of interactivity, as we shall see later) that can never match the different types of decoding developed by various potential learners. The solution to this problem is in the use of complementary media and in self-directed programs.

Complementarity

Our quest for complementarity therefore brings us to try to put together an instructor from the various pieces that were transferred onto various media.

We could say that we are looking for "inter-understanding": an attempt to understand one form of transmission will either be reinforced or weakened by comparison with another form, and so on, until full understanding is achieved. A learner will sometimes achieve understanding as the result of a comparison with a form of mediation that is particularly suited to him or her or as the result of a combination of forms. It is often difficult to tell, given our previous comments on the importance of self-instruction in coming to a full understanding of the information transmitted: the instructor suggests, the learner chooses.

Interactivity and multimedia instruction

Let us now put the subject of transmission aside and turn our attention to multimedia instruction from the learner's point of view by examining the learner's contribution to the instructional process.

We shall differentiate between three types of interactivity: selective, reflective and collective.

Selective interactivity

This may be defined as the extent to which the learner can select the type of medium, activity or content he or she will use to achieve a training objective.

Selecting resources

Interactive learning resources are resources that can respond to the learner's choices by offering a range of options. Interactive resources must therefore be structured to allow for choices.

— Their content must be transparent.

— Their objectives must be transparent.

— They must be accessible.

— They must be available.

— The learner must have a general idea of all resources available to him or her.

— The learner must have the option of consulting an instructor if he or she hesitates or wants to make sure his or her choices are coherent with a given objective (we shall come back to this later).

Selective interactivity consists in allowing the learner to choose between:

— various themes,

— various activities based on the same theme,

— various levels of difficulty for the same activity,

— various combinations of activities,

— various modes (learning, evaluation, report, ranking),

— a combination of all or some of the above.

We can therefore speak of "deprogramming" content, forms and learning. What precautions must be taken and conditions met in order to allow this type of interactivity?

The right to make mistakes

Freedom of choice exists only to the extent that a choice is neither irreversible nor penalizing. The learner must be allowed to try different things, experiment with choices, in order to discover the solution that is the most appropriate at that point in time, with that content. He or she must have the option of going back to make new choices at all times. For example, in the case of educational software (computer-assisted learning), if the learner can choose between several modules in a menu (describing a content or type of activity), he or she must have the option of quitting when he or she realizes that the selected module is not suitable in terms of either content or method. The same holds true for the level of difficulty. Why not give the learner a way out of an exercise that is too easy or too difficult? Self-evaluation will allow the learner to find a suitable level of difficulty, provided that he or she can exit the software program and choose a new exercise.

The same is also true for the sequence in which the learner carries out activities: the learner must have the option of deciding the order in which he or she will carry out activities or whether he or she will carry them out at all.

Although this type of interactivity encourages learners to develop personal strategies, it is not without risks that only the instructor can minimize.

The instructor's role

The instructor is the guarantor of coherent learning, and this is especially true when the learner is allowed little control over his or her learning. When the level of selective interactivity is high, the instructor plays an even more important role. Let us think back to our discussion of teacher-centred versus learner-centred instruction. We must avoid falling into the trap of demagogy (or is it laziness?), which would consist in stating that leaving all of the choices and decisions up to the learner guarantees the development of the best and most coherent learning strategies. In reality, at the beginning of a training program, and indeed, often during a major part of it, the instructor plays an indispensable role in ensuring coherence:

— with respect to the objectives initially set out in the learning contract;

— with respect to the problems encountered and possible solutions or alternatives;

— with respect to the actual "return on investment" of certain choices (progress is not always possible if one always chooses the most pleasant or the most gratifying or the easiest alternative).

The instructor still plays an essential role as the reference and resource person who ensures the smooth running of the course and the attainment of learning objectives. The only difference is that choices are not made for the learner in advance: the learner is given the opportunity to find out what suits him or her, even if this is not always enough.

The instructor must monitor individual learners' progress and be able at any time to review, point out weaknesses or obstacles and suggest solutions. Anyone who sees selective interactivity as an opportunity to eliminate instructors and replace them by instructional media managers must realize that this is far from being the case. On the contrary, the approach requires even greater competence on the part of instructors.

From the learner's perspective, we have already seen that autonomy could only be developed progressively in a system that allows the learner to make choices and decisions, providing these are coherent.

Reflective interactivity

In general

Reflective interactivity refers to the establishment of a proposal/response/modified proposal system based on learner-media interaction. In this context, "reflective" has two meanings:

— as in mirroring, i.e., the responses provided to the learner are the direct consequences of his or her actions or proposals;

— as in thinking, i.e., the learner analyzes the consequences of an action and draws links between the action and the response provided by the medium in order to understand.

Examples of reflectively interactive media are self-correcting activity sheets and audio tapes that include a recorded correction key learners can listen to in order to compare their responses. Other examples include software programs, which may provide different types of feedback, and interactive videos with interfaces that allow learner input and provide feedback, etc. The "etc." covers other types of instructional media, such as simulation materials or devices.

A special case: CAL software

The reflective interactivity of a software program can often be measured by how it processes responses.

By response, we mean any action that allows the processing of a situation based either on a question or on a task to be performed. The reflective value of this processing will vary according to the analytical possibilities it offers with respect to action/effect relationship.

What we are proposing here is an initial typology based on CUEEP's field-testing of a mathematics software package entitled *M.A.C.6 (Mathématiques à la carte)*.

Binary feedback

The computer provides feedback of the YES/NO type with every imaginable variation, using words or other symbols (pictograms, coded colours, sounds).

This type of response does not give any indication as to the nature of the error or the difference between the learner's response and the expected response.

This type of processing is often appropriate for evaluation activities, which involve review more than actual learning, or for activities in which the goal is systematization rather than learning.

Indicative comment

In this case, the computer will respond with a comment (extremely simple, given the learner's low reading level) that will give some indication of the difference between the learner's response and the expected response.

As the learner's reading level rises, comments can become more structured, but this quickly leads to problems with respect to analyzing the response and providing an appropriate comment. Using currently available technology, the complexity of the comments provided as feedback is limited by the programming and processing involved in analyzing all possible interpretations of the learner's error.

Visual feedback

In this case, the learner's response will produce visual feedback which he or she can use to measure the validity of his or her input. There are a number of forms of visual feedback.

— The original image stays onscreen and the same image, modified by the learner's response, appears to one side of the screen. The learner compares both images and draws conclusions.

— The original image is modified. The learner must analyze it to see what has changed and whether this change corresponds to what he or she expected. This simulation does not necessarily involve graphics. Simulations may use text only, but graphics are often more evocative.

Software applications

Software applications are software programs that are used "to do something," versus drill or tutorial software.

The learner is placed in a situation similar to simulation as his or her only criterion for evaluation is whether he or she obtains the desired outcome. This is very close to experimentation. Applications can be used in a way that requires greater analysis and methodology on the part of the student, according to specific learning goals. Specialized business applications can also be "highjacked" and used for instructional purposes. However, the problem with these types of applications is that the amount of analysis and methodology required to use them cannot be adapted to the user's level. In the case of low-level adults, it is important that activities remain within their ability. They are likely to get discouraged if the software is so complex that they can no longer analyze their errors.

Audiovisual aids

We shall not launch into an in-depth analysis of audiovisual aids, which would require the help of a specialist. Instead, we shall explore possible uses of audiovisual aids for instructional purposes. Like other media, images designed for instructional purposes (by instructional developers) will be read by the learner to achieve specific objectives. The question is, which reading modes are involved and to what ends?

When an instructor designs an audiovisual aid for instructional purposes, his or her goal is to make it as evocative as possible and often also as univocal as possible, in order to be able to anticipate how it will be read.

These two objectives may perhaps be incompatible, as any image is polysemic (i.e., can be read and interpreted in many ways) and can be read at a number of different levels.

The only alternative left is to focus on one content or form in an attempt to control (shall we say tame?) the image and how it is read.

Guided reading

Given the evocative power of images, even when they are designed for instructional purposes, their use will most often require the creation of a reading scenario to guide decoding towards specific activities:

— **Selective reading** The learners look for a particular word, phrase or idea following given criteria or a reading grid. In short, the reader tries to narrow down possible interpretations by focussing on what is being sought and nothing else. The reading grid is therefore handed out before the image.

— **Semifree reading** The learners try to talk about a given subject based on a number of different images. A theme is established beforehand but does not influence the reading itself in any other way. The learners may or may not subsequently refer back to a reading grid.

— **Free reading** The learners try to establish a common vocabulary to speak about an image they have read. This activity may be followed by a collective attempt to make up a reading grid or by a discussion of individual interpretations.

Reading images to learn or learning to read images?

The instructor thinking in terms of basic skills training may at first be strongly tempted to use images as an aid in teaching to read text, for example. In this case, a large part of the work consists in progressing from reading an image to more or less formalizing its interpretation in writing. From a methodological point of view, this image-to-text translation is interesting, as it involves decoding, discriminating, formulating, organizing and structuring information, drawing links and finding relationships.

However, instructors are not as comfortable with the idea of using images strictly as images, undoubtedly because this involves teaching learners how to read them. Given the development of modern communications, being "image literate" is just as important to learners' personal development as is being able to read the world around them, whether conveyed through words, numbers or technology.

Collective interactivity

Interactivity between learners

What we call collective interactivity refers to any action or influence arising from an encounter between the learner and other participants, and for the purposes of this paper, in a multimedia environment. In our opinion, an instructional session during which multimedia materials will be used should combine independent learning, tutoring and group work, regardless of the usual organizational mode. At this time, we cannot conceive of a program for low-level adults that would eliminate any of these three types of modes. Programs may vary, however, as to the time allotted to each type of activity and as to the location of these activities.

Collective interactivity takes place at those moments during a program when other learners are present or, more rarely, when comparing a learner's work with that of distant learners.

What are the different forms of collective interactivity? The first could be called comparative: learners are led to compare the work they produced as the result of the same activity. In the process, they explain (try to formalize) and try to convince (explain how they see the problem). Discussion is based on the information provided by the media materials and any hypotheses can be verified by referring back to these materials with one or more learners.

Media materials designed for individual use can also be used for group activities by having learners discuss their responses and verify their hypotheses. The group (together physically or dispersed in various locations) can also be organized into workshops in which each individual is assigned a complementary task to be carried out on a specific medium. The use of media materials designed mainly for individualized instruction does not necessarily mean the learner will be systematically isolated and lose out on the learning opportunities afforded by group interaction. We have found, for example, that a work session in a computer lab is never silent nor static.

Interactivity between media

Interactivity between individuals is not the only type of interactivity. From the learner's point of view, there is also interactivity between the different types of media used, insofar as they can be combined for the purposes of a same activity.

"Inter-understanding," defined earlier in this paper, may occur when a learner is exposed to a number of different media simultaneously. Imagine instructional sequences in which the materials are media-based and involve systematically alternating between interrelated media. An example would be a computer activity that sets a goal and gradually brings the learner to do research, organize the information found in print and audiovisual documents and produce a handwritten or word-processed report. An experiment of this kind at CUEEP involved two groups, one at CUEEP and another group in another centre, each preparing information using a number of tools and sharing it via telecommunication links.

This innovative approach does not necessarily require the use of new technologies, but it is important to note that these technologies can be used in this context and that they can be used to diversify learning activities.

Transfer of training and multimedia instruction

Increasingly, the skills objectives of adult basic education programs incorporate the idea of transfer of training (to structure the action methodologically). Some prefer to speak of the development of reasoning abilities. Others yet refer to cognitive modifiability (the mastering and development of a series of mental operations with a view to learning to learn).

As the development of methods and conscious strategies are among the objectives of OMI, it can be said to encourage the development of transferrable skills, not as specific content, but rather on an ongoing basis. All learning of this type is, in this case, systematically finalized.

In addition, certain tools that require a strong potential for method and "applied" logic (e.g., any of the business or other specialized software applications that are sometimes used in French and math courses) provide opportunities to build cognitive strengths in an interdisciplinary manner.

Also, as each medium uses its own particular form of transmission or dialogue, learners must identify, understand and integrate each form and reconstruct its logic before they can actually use the medium. Here we mean not only the way in which resources are organized or the user interface, but the internal logic of the medium. For example, using an activity sheet involves being able to locate visual cues in a given space (the sheet) in order to find the information required to carry out the activity:

— Where are the instructions?

— Are there any questions and where are they?

— Where and how are answers to be recorded?

— Is there any reference to an answer sheet?

The same applies to the use of software. Additional questions will pertain to how the software operates and to its interactive nature:

— Why has the screen changed?

— How do we move on to the next screen?

— What does "it" want me to do now?

— Why isn't anything happening? Is there any help available?

Other examples could be cited to show how working with various media requires an ability to adapt to various types of logic. It is something the learner learns, from the first moment the instructor sits down with him or her to formalize the why and how of actions required to interact with the aid. People are often interested in finding out how the machine "thinks" and works and why it occasionally seems stupid and stubborn. A timely explanation can help the learner understand not only that he or she did not respect the only form of logic the machine understands but also that several types of reasonings can apply to the same action.

Motivation and multimedia instruction

We shall make only a few comments on this much-discussed topic. Indeed, it seems that working with multimedia materials motivates low-level adults. How is this motivation generally explained?

— Learners' self-esteem is boosted by the fact that they know how to use sophisticated tools.

— Learners use equipment considered to be the epitome of modern technology.

— When using the materials for individual work, the learner feels that instruction is centred on him or her, since he or she has the computer's full attention.

— The more timid find that this feeling of intimacy encourages them to take more initiatives, to try more things, without worrying that their errors will upset or bother the machine.

Beyond these general explanations are others that relate to learners' attitude toward learning and training:

— The "mirror" phenomenon (reflective interactivity) encourages some learners to try to push back their limits and invest more effort into multimedia activities. This may be explained as the development of demands on oneself with respect to knowledge.

— The form of transmission used by the media may help learners overcome blockages caused by past failures, which may have been consciously or unconsciously associated to a specific form (fear of speaking in public, the blank page syndrome, fear of the instructor).

— The fact that various types of activities focus on the same learning objective may help learners become more objective with respect to their learning. The realization that there are a number of ways to learn the same thing may help learners relativize past failures and fight against fatalism, in other words, "move on" if they fail and look for another way, another solution. This is a giant step toward autonomy.

CONCLUSION

Given the role learners are expected to play in the co-management of learning resources, evaluation and day-to-day activities using the various media, it can be hypothesized that as they play this role, they develop autonomy and gradually modify their attitude toward learning.

This is not only true for hyperindividualized types of training systems: it is also holds for systems in which learners work in groups but in which an attempt is made to introduce as many as possible of the individualization methods and approaches described earlier. In other words, in this context, the individualization of instruction (or individualized instruction) should not be confused with learning alone, in isolation, with no other interlocutor than a machine, however sophisticated it might be. This, however, brings up another question:

Is distance education an alternative for low-level adults?

Certain recommendations made earlier regarding individualization and work methods naturally lead to this question. What differences are there between individual work at a resource centre, at home or at work?

First, we must acknowledge the fact that some learners occasionally bring papers home with them to work on alone or with a friend or family member. Is not this "homework," whether done voluntarily or assigned by the instructor, the beginnings of distance education?

Objections to distance education as a viable alternative for low-level adult learners are that:

— as learners, they are not autonomous enough;

— they cannot work alone, without the support of a group and an environment to maintain their motivation and deal with discouragement;

— the home environment sometimes represents a double obstacle to learning: psychological (doubts about the validity of the decision to "go back to school") and material (no adequate workspace, no quiet place and time to work);

— the learning resources pose material problems: cost, or for example, competition between the learner and family members for time on the home computer.

Everything we have said up to this point suggests a partial solution to these problems, given that the solution provides for complementarity and freedom of choice.

In our opinion, it is possible to envisage low-level adults doing individual work at home or in other locations outside the centre, once they have learned to function according to the strategies described earlier in this paper, given the following:

— distance education is a free and revocable choice by the learner, who is the only one to know how he or she can function outside of the centre;

— the learner can come back to the centre and use its resources at all times, as required;

— the learner is part of a stable group with which he or she meets regularly to avoid isolation (instructors, other learners);

— ensuring access to the required learning materials does not pose insurmountable organizational or financial difficulties (a system to provide required materials such as the one in place for distance education at higher levels might be a solution to this problem). Imagine a highly polemic tone for this last phrase!

We could therefore develop programs that combine learning time both outside the centre (distance education) and at the centre.

Although it would be difficult to discuss this alternative without research to support our hypotheses, it should not be rejected too quickly, as it does provide solutions for adult learners for whom set times, dates and locations pose problems.

In the same series:

ALPHA 78 (out of print)   ALPHA 80 (out of print)
ALPHA 82 (out of print)   ALPHA 84
ALPHA 86   ALPHA 88

Other works published by the ministère de l'Éducation du Québec:

Hautecœur, Jean-Paul. *Analphabétisme et alphabétisation au Québec*. Québec City, 1978 (out of print).

Rive, Sant N-A. *Alphabétiser en créole*. Québec City, 1981 (out of print).

Pratiques d'alphabétisation. Edited by Jean-Paul Hautecœur. Québec City, 1982 (out of print).

Expérimentations du traitement de texte en alphabétisation. Edited by Jean-Paul Hautecœur. Québec City, 1989.

Works available from other publishers:

Hautecœur, Jean-Paul. *Anonymus Autoportraits*. Montréal: Éditions Saint Martin, 1984.

Introduction aux pratiques et politiques d'alphabétisation. Edited by Jean-Paul Hautecœur. Montréal: Édition André Dugas, Université du Québec à Montréal, 1987.

Stratégies d'alphabétisation. Edited by Jean-Paul Hautecœur. Montréal: Édition André Dugas, Université du Québec à Montréal, 1990.

(Copies of the last two titles may be obtained by writing to: André Dugas, UQAM, Département de Linguistique, C.P. 8888, succursale "A," Montréal, Québec, CANADA H3C 3P8)

Other titles in the *ALPHA* series are available free of charge from:

the MEQ's Direction régionale
in your region
(Québec residents)

Solange Cyr
Ministère de l'Éducation
Direction des communications
Centre de documentation
1035, rue De La Chevrotière
Québec, QC   G1R 5A5
(Nonresidents of Québec)

ALPHA 90 est également disponible en version française.